BENCHMARK SERIES

Microsoft®

ACCESS 2002

CORE CERTIFICATION

MICROSOFT OFFICE USER SPECIALIST

APPROVED COURSEWARE

Pierce College at Puyallup
Puyallup, Washington
NITA RUTKOSKY

EMCParadigm

Senior Developmental Editor	Sonja M. Brown
Developmental Editor	James Patterson
Special Projects Coordinator	Joan D'Onofrio
Senior Designer	Jennifer Wreisner
Editorial Assistant	Susan Capecchi
Tester	Desiree Faulkner
Copy Editor	Sharon O'Donnell
Indexer	Don Glassman

Publishing Team—George Provol, Publisher; Janice Johnson, Director of Product Development; Tony Galvin, Acquisitions Editor; Lori Landwer, Marketing Manager; Shelley Clubb, Electronic Design and Production Manager

Acknowledgments—The author and publisher wish to thank the following reviewers for their technical and academic assistance in testing exercises and assessing instruction:

- David Parker, St. Charles Community College, St. Charles, MO
- Daphne Press, Ozarks Technical Community College, Springfield, MO

Special thanks to Daphne Press for preparing Internet Projects and Job Study scenarios as part of the Unit Performance Assessment sections.

Library of Congress Cataloging-in-Publication Data
Rutkosky, Nita Hewitt.
Microsoft Access 2002: core certification / Nita Rutkosky.
p.cm. – (Benchmark series)
ISBN 0-7638-1437-7

Text: ISBN 0-7638-1437-7
Order Number: 05542

Published by **EMC**Paradigm
875 Montreal Way
St. Paul, MN 55102

(800) 535-6865
E-mail: educate@emcp.com
Web site: www.emcp.com

Printed in the United States of America
10 9 8 7 6 5 4 3 2 1

CONTENTS

WELCOME

You are about to begin working with a textbook that is part of the Benchmark Office XP Series. The word *Benchmark* in the title holds a special significance in terms of *what* you will learn and *how* you will learn. *Benchmark*, according to *Webster's Dictionary*, means "something that serves as a standard by which others may be measured or judged." In this text, you will learn the Microsoft Office User Specialist (MOUS) skills required for certification on the Core and/or Expert level of one or more major applications within the Office XP suite. These skills are benchmarks by which you will be evaluated, should you choose to take one or more certification exams.

The design and teaching approach of this textbook also serve as a benchmark for instructional materials on software programs. Features and commands are presented in a clear, straightforward way, and each short section of instruction is followed by an exercise that lets you practice using the new feature. Gradually, as you move through each chapter, you will build your skills to the point of mastery. At the end of a chapter, you are offered the opportunity to demonstrate your newly acquired competencies—to prove you have met the benchmarks for using the Office suite or an individual program. At the completion of the text, you are well on your way to becoming a successful computer user.

EMC/Paradigm's Office XP Benchmark Series includes textbooks on Office XP, Word 2002, Excel 2002, Access 2002, PowerPoint 2002, Publisher 2002, Outlook 2002, and FrontPage 2002. Note that the programs include the year 2002 in their name, while the suite itself is called Office XP (for "experience"). Each book includes a Student CD, which contains prekeyed documents and files required for completing the exercises. A CD icon and folder name displayed on the opening page of each chapter indicates that you need to copy a folder of files from the CD before beginning the chapter exercises. *(See the inside back cover for instructions on copying a folder.)*

Introducing Microsoft Office XP

Microsoft Office XP, released in May 2001, is a suite of programs designed to improve productivity and efficiency in workplace, school, and home settings. A suite is a group of programs that are sold as a package and are designed to be used together, making it possible to exchange files among the programs. The major applications included in Office are Word, a word processing program; Excel, a spreadsheet program; Access, a database management program; PowerPoint, a slide presentation program; and Outlook, a desktop information management program.

Using the Office suite offers significant advantages over working with individual programs developed by different software vendors. The programs in the Office suite use similar toolbars, buttons, icons, and menus, which means that once you learn the basic features of one program, you can use those same features in the other programs. This easy transfer of knowledge decreases the learning time and allows you to concentrate on the unique commands and options within each program. The compatibility of the programs creates seamless integration of data within and between programs and lets the operator use the program most appropriate for the required tasks.

The number of programs in the Office XP suite varies by the package, or edition. Four editions are available:

- **Standard:** Word, Excel, Outlook, PowerPoint
- **Professional:** Word, Excel, Outlook, PowerPoint, and Access
- **Professional Special Edition:** All Professional package programs plus FrontPage, Publisher, and SharePoint. This edition is available only for a limited time and only to current Office users.
- **Developer:** All Professional package programs (except SharePoint) plus Developer tools

New Features in Office XP

Users of previous editions of Office will find that the essential features that have made Office popular still form the heart of the suite. New enhancements focus on collaboration, or the ability for multiple users to work together on the same document from different locations over the Internet. Another highlight is the Smart Tag feature, which is an icon that when clicked offers a list of commands that are especially useful for the particular job being done. In Word, for example, a Smart Tag might offer the ability to turn off automatic capitalization or other types of automatic formatting. A more comprehensive kind of targeted assistance is offered in a new Task Pane, which is a narrow window that appears at the right of the screen to display commands relevant to the current task. Speech recognition technology is available with this edition, offering users the ability to dictate text into any Office program. This feature must be installed separately.

Structure of the Benchmark Textbooks

Users of the Core Certification texts and the complete application textbooks may begin their course with an overview of computer hardware and software, offered in the *Getting Started* section at the beginning of the book. Your instructor may also ask you to complete the *Windows 2000* and the *Internet Explorer* sections so you become familiar with the computer's operating system and the essential tools for using the Internet.

Instruction on the major programs within the Office suite is presented in units of four chapters each. Both the Core and Expert levels contain two units, which culminate with performance assessments to check your knowledge and skills. Each chapter contains the following sections:

- performance objectives that identify specifically what you are expected to learn
- instructional text that introduces and explains new concepts and features
- step-by-step, hands-on exercises following each section of instruction
- a chapter summary
- a knowledge self-check called Concepts Check
- skill assessment exercises called Skills Check

Exercises offered at the end of units provide writing and research opportunities that will strengthen your performance in other college courses as well as on the job. The final activities simulate interesting projects you could encounter in the workplace.

Benchmark Series Ancillaries

The Benchmark Series includes some important resources that will help you succeed in your computer applications courses:

Online Resource Center

Internet Resource Centers hosted by EMC/Paradigm provide additional material for students and teachers using the Benchmark books. Online you will find Web links, updates to textbooks, study tips, quizzes and assignments, and supplementary projects.

Class Connection

Available for both the WebCT and Blackboard e-learning platforms, EMC/Paradigm's Class Connection is a course management tool for traditional and distance learning. The Class Connection allows students to access the course syllabus and assignment schedule online, provides self-quizzes and study aids, and facilitates communication among students and instructors via e-mail and e-discussions.

APPROVED COURSEWARE

What Does This Logo Mean?

It means this courseware has been approved by the Microsoft® Office User Specialist Program to be among the finest available for learning Microsoft Access 2002. It also means that upon completion of this courseware, you may be prepared to become a Microsoft Office User Specialist.

What Is a Microsoft Office User Specialist?

A Microsoft Office User Specialist is an individual who has certified his or her skills in one or more of the Microsoft Office desktop applications of Microsoft Word, Microsoft Excel, Microsoft PowerPoint®, Microsoft Outlook® or Microsoft Access, or in Microsoft Project. The Microsoft Office User Specialist Program typically offers certification exams at the "Core" and "Expert" skill levels. * The Microsoft Office User Specialist Program is the only Microsoft approved program in the world for certifying proficiency in Microsoft Office desktop applications and Microsoft Project. This certification can be a valuable asset in any job search or career advancement.

More Information

- To learn more about becoming a Microsoft Office User Specialist, visit www.mous.net.
- To purchase a Microsoft Office User Specialist certification exam, visit www.DesktopIQ.com.
- To learn about other Microsoft Office User Specialist approved courseware from EMC/Paradigm, visit www.emcp.com/college_division/MOUS_ready.php.

EMC/Paradigm Publishing is independent from Microsoft Corporation and not affiliated with Microsoft in any manner. This publication may be used in assisting students to prepare for a Microsoft office User Specialist Exam. Neither Microsoft, its designated review company, nor EMC/Paradigm Publishing warrants that use of this publication will ensure passing the relevant exam.

* The availability of Microsoft Office User Specialist certification exams varies by application, application version and language. Visit www.mous.net for exam availability.

OFFICE XP

GETTING STARTED IN OFFICE XP

In this textbook, you will learn to operate several microcomputer application programs that combine to make an application "suite." This suite of programs is called Microsoft Office XP. The programs you will learn to operate are the *software*, which include instructions telling the computer what to do. Some of the software programs in the suite include a word processing program called *Word*, a spreadsheet program called *Excel*, a presentation program called *PowerPoint*, and a database program called *Access*.

Identifying Computer Hardware

The computer equipment you will use to operate the suite of programs is referred to as *hardware*. You will need access to a microcomputer system that should consist of the CPU, monitor, keyboard, printer, disk drives, and mouse. If you are not sure what equipment you will be operating, check with your instructor. The computer system displayed in figure G.1 consists of six components. Each component is discussed separately in the material that follows.

FIGURE G.1 ***Microcomputer System***

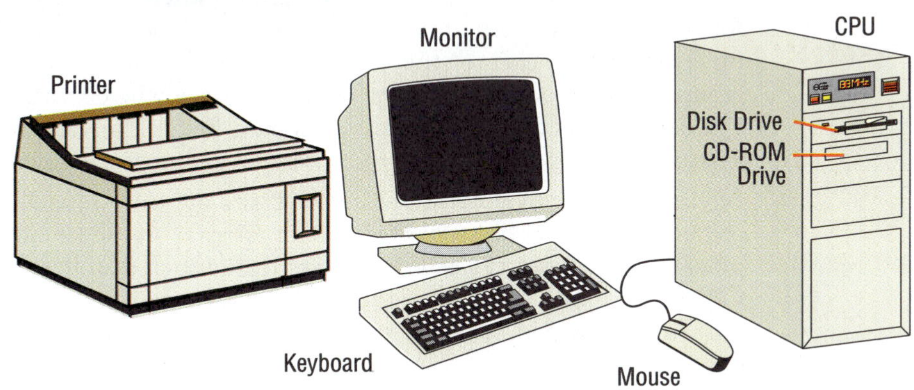

CPU

CPU stands for Central Processing Unit and is the intelligence of the computer. All the processing occurs in the CPU. Silicon chips, which contain miniaturized circuitry, are placed on boards that are plugged into slots within the CPU. Whenever an instruction is given to the computer, that instruction is processed through circuitry in the CPU.

Monitor

The monitor is a piece of equipment that looks like a television screen. It displays the information of a program and the text being input at the keyboard. The quality of display for monitors varies depending on the type of monitor and the type of resolution. Monitors can also vary in size—generally from 14-inch size up to 21-inch size or larger.

Keyboard

The keyboard is used to input information into the computer. Keyboards for microcomputers vary in the number and location of the keys. Microcomputers have the alphabetic and numeric keys in the same location as the keys on a typewriter. The symbol keys, however, may be placed in a variety of locations, depending on the manufacturer. In addition to letters, numbers, and symbols, most microcomputer keyboards contain function keys, arrow keys, and a numeric keypad. Figure G.2 shows an enhanced keyboard.

FIGURE G.2 ***Microcomputer Enhanced Keyboard***

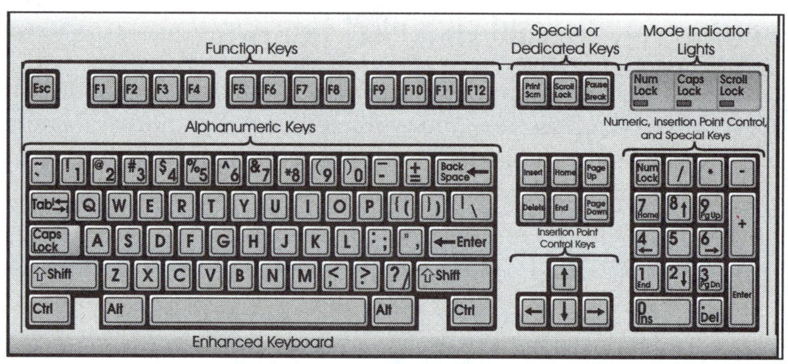

The 12 keys at the top of the enhanced keyboard, labeled with the letter F followed by a number, are called *function keys*. These keys can be used to perform functions within each of the suite programs. To the right of the regular keys is a group of *special* or *dedicated keys*. These keys are labeled with specific functions that will be performed when you press the key. Below the special keys are arrow keys. These keys are used to move the insertion point in the document screen.

In the upper right corner of the keyboard are three mode indicator lights. When certain modes have been selected, a light appears on the keyboard. For example, if you press the Caps Lock key, which disables the lowercase alphabet, a light appears next to Caps Lock. Similarly, pressing the Num Lock key will disable the special functions on the numeric keypad, which is located at the right side of the keyboard.

Disk Drives

Depending on the computer system you are using, Microsoft Office XP is installed on a hard drive or as part of a network system. Whether you are using

Office on a hard drive or network system, you will need to have available a CD drive and a floppy disk drive. You will insert the CD (Compact Disk) that accompanies this textbook in the CD drive and then copy folders from the CD to a disk in the floppy disk drive. You will also save documents you complete at the computer to folders on your disk in the floppy drive.

Printer

When you create a document in Word, it is considered *soft copy*. If you want a *hard copy* of a document, you need to print it. To print documents you will need to access a printer, which will probably be either a laser printer or an ink-jet printer. A laser printer uses a laser beam combined with heat and pressure to print documents while an ink-jet printer prints a document by spraying a fine mist of ink on the page.

Mouse

Many functions in the suite of programs are designed to operate more efficiently with a *mouse*. A mouse is an input device that sits on a flat surface next to the computer. A mouse can be operated with the left or the right hand. Moving the mouse on the flat surface causes a corresponding mouse pointer to move on the screen. Figure G.1 shows an illustration of a mouse.

Using the Mouse

The programs in the Microsoft Office suite can be operated using a keyboard or they can be operated with the keyboard and a mouse. The mouse may have two or three buttons on top, which are tapped to execute specific functions and commands. To use the mouse, rest it on a flat surface or a mouse pad. Put your hand over it with your palm resting on top of the mouse and your wrist resting on the table surface. As you move the mouse on the flat surface, a corresponding pointer moves on the screen.

When using the mouse, there are four terms you should understand—point, click, double-click, and drag. When operating the mouse, you may need to *point* to a specific command, button, or icon. Point means to position the mouse pointer on the desired item. With the mouse pointer positioned on the desired item, you may need to *click* a button on the mouse. Click means quickly tapping a button on the mouse once. To complete two steps at one time, such as choosing and then executing a function, *double-click* a mouse button. Double-click means to tap the left mouse button twice in quick succession. The term *drag* means to press and hold the left mouse button, move the mouse pointer to a specific location, and then release the button.

Using the Mouse Pointer

The mouse pointer will change appearance depending on the function being performed or where the pointer is positioned. The mouse pointer may appear as one of the following images:

The mouse pointer appears as an I-beam (called the *I-beam pointer*) in the document screen and can be used to move the insertion point or select text.

The mouse pointer appears as an arrow pointing up and to the left (called the *arrow pointer*) when it is moved to the Title bar, Menu bar, or one of the toolbars at the top of the screen or when a dialog box is displayed. For example, to open a

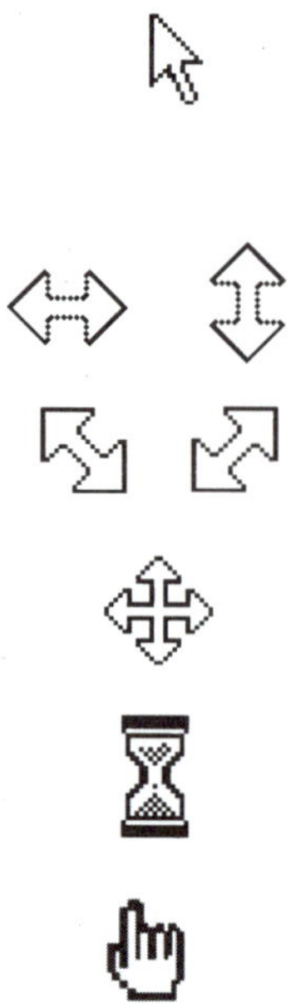

new document with the mouse, you would move the I-beam pointer to the File option on the Menu bar. When the I-beam pointer is moved to the Menu bar, it turns into an arrow pointer. To make a selection, position the tip of the arrow pointer on the File option, and then click the left mouse button. At the drop-down menu that displays, make selections by positioning the arrow pointer on the desired option, and then clicking the left mouse button.

The mouse pointer becomes a double-headed arrow (either pointing left and right, pointing up and down, or pointing diagonally) when performing certain functions such as changing the size of an object.

In certain situations, such as moving an object or image, the mouse pointer becomes a four-headed arrow. The four-headed arrow means that you can move the object left, right, up, or down.

When a request is being processed or when a program is being loaded, the mouse pointer may appear with an hourglass beside it. The hourglass image means "please wait." When the process is completed, the hourglass image is removed.

The mouse pointer displays as a hand with a pointing index finger in certain functions such as Help and indicates that more information is available about the item.

Choosing Commands

Once a program is open, several methods can be used in the program to choose commands. A command is an instruction that tells the program to do something. You can choose a command with one of the following methods:

- Click a toolbar button with the mouse
- Choose a command from a menu
- Use shortcut keys
- Use a shortcut menu

Choosing Commands on Toolbars

When a program such as Word or PowerPoint is open, several toolbars containing buttons for common tasks are available. In many of the suite programs, two toolbars are visible on the screen. One toolbar is called the Standard toolbar; the other is referred to as the Formatting toolbar. To choose a command from a toolbar, position the tip of the arrow pointer on a button, and then click the left mouse button. For example, to print the file currently displayed in the screen, position the tip of the arrow pointer on the Print button on the Standard toolbar, and then click the left mouse button.

Choosing Commands on the Menu Bar

Each of the suite programs contains a Menu bar that displays toward the top of the screen. This Menu bar contains a variety of options you can use to perform functions and commands on data. Functions are grouped logically into options, which display on the Menu bar. For example, features to work with files are grouped in the File option. Either the mouse or the keyboard can be used to make choices from the Menu bar or make a choice at a dialog box.

To use the mouse to make a choice from the Menu bar, move the I-beam pointer to the Menu bar. This causes the I-beam pointer to display as an arrow pointer. Position the tip of the arrow pointer on the desired option, and then click the left mouse button.

To use the keyboard, press the Alt key to make the Menu bar active. Options on the Menu bar display with an underline below one of the letters. To choose an option from the Menu bar, key the underlined letter of the desired option, or move the insertion point with the left or right arrow keys to the option desired, and then press Enter. This causes a drop-down menu to display.

For example, to display the File drop-down menu in Word as shown in figure G.3 using the mouse, position the arrow pointer on File on the Menu bar, and then click the left mouse button. To display the File drop-down menu with the keyboard, press the Alt key, and then key the letter F for File.

FIGURE G.3 ***Word File Drop-Down Menu***

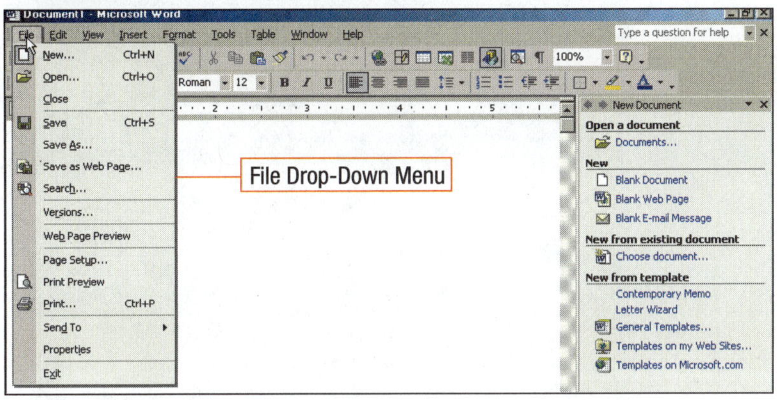

Choosing Commands from Drop-Down Menus

To choose a command from a drop-down menu with the mouse, position the arrow pointer on the desired option, and then click the left mouse button. At the drop-down menu that displays, move the arrow pointer down the menu to the desired option, and then click the left mouse button.

To make a selection from the drop-down menu with the keyboard, key the underlined letter of the desired option. Once the drop-down menu displays, you do not need to hold down the Alt key with the underlined letter. If you want to close a drop-down menu without making a choice, click in the screen outside the drop-down menu; or, press the Esc key twice.

If an option can be accessed by clicking a button on a toolbar, the button is displayed preceding the option in the drop-down menu. For example, buttons display before the New, Open Save, Save as Web Page, Search, Print Preview, and Print options at the File drop-down menu (see figure G.3).

Some menu options may be gray shaded (dimmed). When an option is dimmed, that option is currently not available. For example, if you choose the Table option on the Menu bar, the Table drop-down menu displays with dimmed options including Merge Cells, Split Cells, and Split Table.

Some menu options are preceded by a check mark. The check mark indicates that the option is currently active. To make an option inactive (turn it off) using the mouse, position the arrow pointer on the option, and then click the left mouse button. To make an option inactive (turn it off) with the keyboard, key the underlined letter of the option.

If an option from a drop-down menu displays followed by an ellipsis (...), a dialog box will display when that option is chosen. A dialog box provides a variety of options to let you specify how a command is to be carried out. For example, if you choose File and then Print from the PowerPoint Menu bar, the Print dialog box displays as shown in figure G.4.

FIGURE G.4 ***PowerPoint Print Dialog Box***

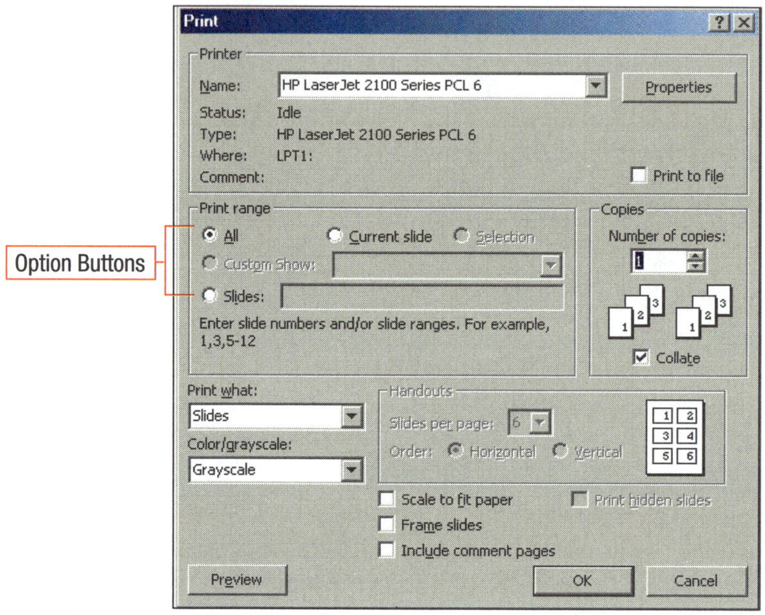

Or, if you choose Format and then Font from the Word Menu bar, the Font dialog box displays as shown in figure G.5.

FIGURE G.5 ***Word Font Dialog Box***

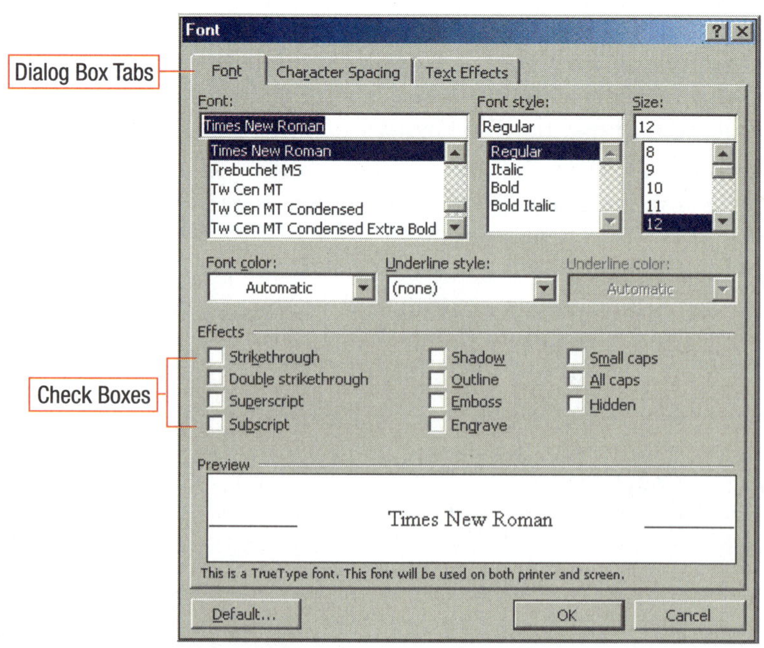

Some dialog boxes provide a set of options. These options are contained on separate tabs. For example, the Font dialog box shown in figure G.5 contains a tab at the top of the dialog box with the word Font on it. Two other tabs display to the right of the Font tab. The tab that displays in the front is the active tab. To make a tab active using the mouse, position the arrow pointer on the desired tab, and then click the left mouse button. If you are using the keyboard, press Ctrl + Tab or press Alt + the underlined letter on the desired tab. For example, to change the tab to Character Spacing in the Font dialog box, click Character Spacing, or press Ctrl + Tab, or press Alt + R.

To choose options from a dialog box with the mouse, position the arrow pointer on the desired option, and then click the left mouse button. If you are using the keyboard, press the Tab key to move the insertion point forward from option to option. Press Shift + Tab to move the insertion point backward from option to option. You can also hold down the Alt key and then press the underlined letter of the desired option. When an option is selected, it displays either in reverse video (white letters on a dark background) or surrounded by a dashed box called a *marquee*.

A dialog box contains one or more of the following elements: text boxes, list boxes, check boxes, option buttons, spin boxes, and command buttons.

Text Boxes

Some options in a dialog box require text to be entered. For example, the boxes below the Find what and Replace with options at the Excel Find and Replace dialog box shown in figure G.6 are text boxes. In a text box, you key text or edit existing text. Edit text in a text box in the same manner as normal text. Use the left and right arrow keys on the keyboard to move the insertion point without deleting text and use the Delete key or Backspace key to delete text.

FIGURE G.6 **Excel Find and Replace Dialog Box**

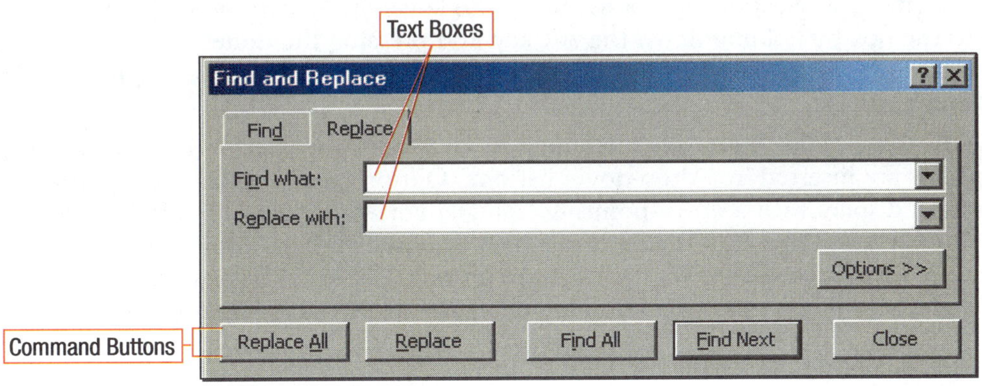

List Boxes

Some dialog boxes such as the Access Open dialog box shown in figure G.7 may contain a list box. The list of files below the Look in: option is contained in a list box. To make a selection from a list box with the mouse, move the arrow pointer to the desired option, and then click the left mouse button.

FIGURE

G.7 ***Access Open Dialog Box***

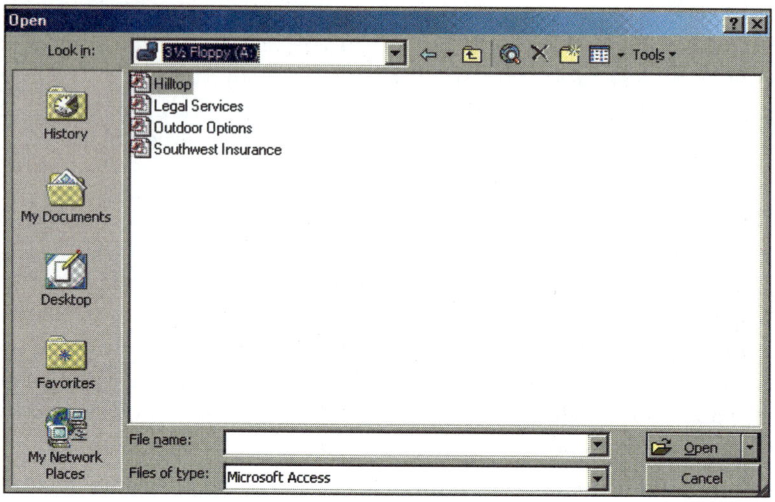

Some list boxes may contain a scroll bar. This scroll bar will display at the right side of the list box (a vertical scroll bar) or at the bottom of the list box (a horizontal scroll bar). Either a vertical scroll bar or a horizontal scroll bar can be used to move through the list if the list is longer than the box. To move down through a list on a vertical scroll bar, position the arrow pointer on the down scroll triangle and hold down the left mouse button. To scroll up through the list in a vertical scroll bar, position the arrow pointer on the up scroll triangle and hold down the left mouse button. You can also move the arrow pointer above the scroll box and click the left mouse button to scroll up the list or move the arrow pointer below the scroll box and click the left mouse button to move down the list. To move through a list with a horizontal scroll bar, click the left scroll triangle to scroll to the left of the list or click the right scroll triangle to scroll to the right of the list.

To make a selection from a list using the keyboard, move the insertion point into the box by holding down the Alt key and pressing the underlined letter of the desired option. Press the up and/or down arrow keys on the keyboard to move through the list.

In some dialog boxes where enough room is not available for a list box, lists of options are inserted in a drop-down list box. Options that contain a drop-down list box display with a down-pointing triangle. For example, the Underline style option at the Word Font dialog box shown in figure G.5 contains a drop-down list. To display the list, click the down-pointing triangle to the right of the Underline style option box. If you are using the keyboard, press Alt + U.

Check Boxes

Some dialog boxes contain options preceded by a box. A check mark may or may not appear in the box. The Word Font dialog box shown in figure G.5 displays a variety of check boxes within the Effects section. If a check mark appears in the box, the option is active (turned on). If there is no check mark in the check box, the option is inactive (turned off).

Any number of check boxes can be active. For example, in the Word Font dialog box, you can insert a check mark in any or all of the boxes in the Effects section and these options will be active.

To make a check box active or inactive with the mouse, position the tip of the arrow pointer in the check box, and then click the left mouse button. If you are using the keyboard, press Alt + the underlined letter of the desired option.

Option Buttons

In the PowerPoint Print dialog box shown in figure G.4, the options in the Print range section are preceded by option buttons. Only one option button can be selected at any time. When an option button is selected, a dark circle displays in the button.

To select an option button with the mouse, position the tip of the arrow pointer inside the option button, and then click the left mouse button. To make a selection with the keyboard, hold down the Alt key, and then press the underlined letter of the desired option.

Spin Boxes

Some options in a dialog box contain measurements or numbers that can be increased or decreased. These options are generally located in a spin box. For example, the Word Paragraph dialog box shown in figure G.8 contains spin boxes located after the Left, Right, Before, and After options. To increase a number in a spin box, position the tip of the arrow pointer on the up-pointing triangle to the right of the desired option, and then click the left mouse button. To decrease the number, click the down-pointing triangle. If you are using the keyboard, press Alt + the underlined letter of the desired option, and then press the up arrow key to increase the number or the down arrow key to decrease the number.

FIGURE G.8 **Word Paragraph Dialog Box**

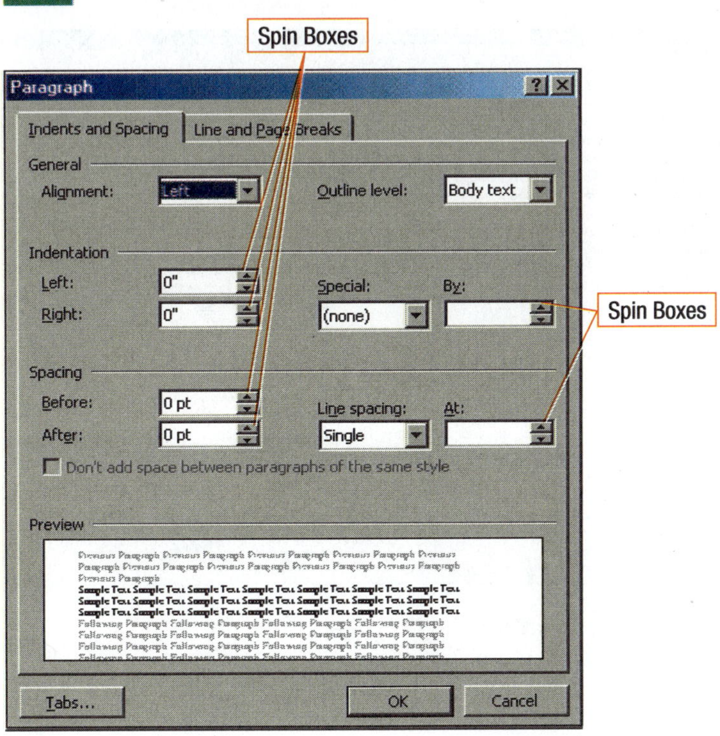

Command Buttons

In the Excel Find and Replace dialog box shown in figure G.6, the boxes along the bottom of the dialog box are called *command buttons*. A command button is used to execute or cancel a command. Some command buttons display with an ellipsis (...). A command button that displays with an ellipsis will open another dialog box. To choose a command button with the mouse, position the arrow pointer on the desired button, and then click the left mouse button. To choose a command button with the keyboard, press the Tab key until the desired command button contains the marquee, and then press the Enter key.

Choosing Commands with Shortcut Keys

At the left side of a drop-down menu is a list of options. At the right side, shortcut keys for specific options may display. For example, the shortcut keys to save a document are Ctrl + S and are displayed to the right of the Save option at the File drop-down menu shown in figure G.3. To use shortcut keys to choose a command, hold down the Ctrl key, key the letter for the command, and then release the Ctrl key.

Choosing Commands with Shortcut Menus

The software programs in the suite include menus that contain commands related to the item with which you are working. A shortcut menu appears right where you are working in the document. To display a shortcut menu, click the *right* mouse button or press Shift + F10.

For example, if the insertion point is positioned in a paragraph of text in a Word document, clicking the *right* mouse button or pressing Shift + F10 will cause the shortcut menu shown in figure G.9 to display in the document screen.

FIGURE G.9 **Word Shortcut Menu**

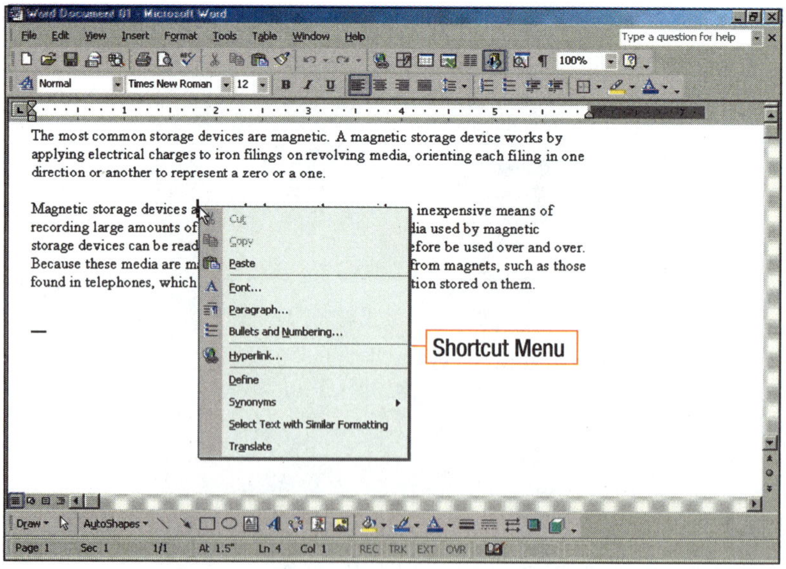

To select an option from a shortcut menu with the mouse, click the desired option. If you are using the keyboard, press the up or down arrow key until the desired option is selected, and then press the Enter key. To close a shortcut menu without choosing an option, click anywhere outside the shortcut menu or press the Esc key.

Working with Multiple Programs

As you learn the various programs in the Microsoft Office suite, you will notice how executing commands in each is very similar. For example, the steps to save, close, and print are virtually the same whether you are working in Word, Excel, or PowerPoint. This consistency between programs greatly enhances a user's ability to easily transfer knowledge learned in one program to another within the suite.

Another appeal of Microsoft Office is the ability to have more than one program open at the same time. For example, you can open Word, create a document, and then open Excel, create a spreadsheet, and copy the spreadsheet into Word.

When a program is open, the name of the program, followed by the file name, displays in a button on the Taskbar. When another program is opened, the program name and file name display in a button that is positioned to the right of the first program button. Figure G.10 shows the Taskbar with Word, Excel, and PowerPoint open. To move from one program to another, all you need to do is click the button on the Taskbar representing the desired program file.

FIGURE G.10 *Taskbar with Word, Excel, and PowerPoint Open*

Setting Clicking Options

You can set clicking options for the Windows environment and specify either a double-click or single-click to open a program or file. Steps in this textbook assume that you will double-click to open a file or program. To change from single-click to open (point to select) to double-click to open (single-click to select), complete these steps:

1. At the Windows desktop, click the My Computer icon.
2. At the My Computer window, click Tools on the Menu bar, and then click Folder Options at the drop-down menu.
3. At the Folder Options dialog box with the General tab selected, click the Double-click to open an item (single-click to select) option located in the Click items as follows section.
4. Click the Apply button and then click OK.

Completing Computer Exercises

Some computer exercises in this textbook require that you open an existing file. Exercise files are saved on the CD that accompanies this textbook. The files you need for each chapter are saved in individual folders. Before beginning a chapter, copy the necessary folder from the CD to a preformatted data disk. After completing exercises in a chapter, delete the chapter folder before copying the next chapter folder. (Check with your instructor before deleting a folder.)

Copying a Folder

The CD that accompanies this textbook contains numerous files you use to complete some exercises and assessments in chapters. As you begin working in a chapter, copy the chapter folder from the CD to your disk. (Not every chapter contains a folder on the CD. For example, when completing exercises in the Access chapters, you will copy database files from the Database folder rather than individual chapter folders. This is to ensure that there is adequate space on your disk for saving files.) Copy the chapter folder from the CD to your disk using Windows Explorer by completing the following steps:

1. Insert the CD that accompanies this textbook in the CD drive.
2. Insert a formatted 3.5-inch disk in the disk drive.
3. At the Windows desktop, open Windows Explorer by clicking the Start button, pointing to Programs, pointing to Accessories, and then clicking Windows Explorer.
4. Double-click My Computer in the Folders pane.
5. Double-click the CD drive in the Folders pane (probably displays as OFFICEXP_BENCH followed by the drive letter).
6. Double-click the desired program folder name in the Contents pane. (For example, if you are copying a folder for a core Word chapter, double-click the *Word 2002 Core* folder in the Contents pane.)
7. Click once on the desired chapter subfolder name to select it.
8. Click the Copy To button on the toolbar.
9. At the Browse For Folder dialog box, click *3½ Floppy (A:)* in the list box and then click OK. (If *3½ Floppy (A:)* is not visible, click the plus symbol preceding *My Computer.)*
10. After the folder is copied to your disk, close Windows Explorer by clicking the Close button (contains an X) located in the upper right corner of Windows Explorer.

Deleting a Folder

Before copying a chapter folder onto your disk, delete any previous chapter folders. Do this in Windows Explorer by completing the following steps:

1. Insert your disk in the disk drive.
2. At the Windows desktop, click the Start button on the Taskbar, point to Programs, point to Accessories, and then click Windows Explorer.
3. In Windows Explorer, click the down-pointing triangle at the right side of the Address list box.
4. At the drop-down list that displays, click the drive where your disk is located.
5. Click the chapter folder in the list box.
6. Click the Delete button on the Windows Explorer toolbar.
7. At the message asking if you want to remove the folder and all its contents, click the Yes button.
8. At the message asking if you want to delete a read-only file, click the Yes to All button.
9. Close Windows Explorer by clicking the Close button located in the upper right corner of Windows Explorer.

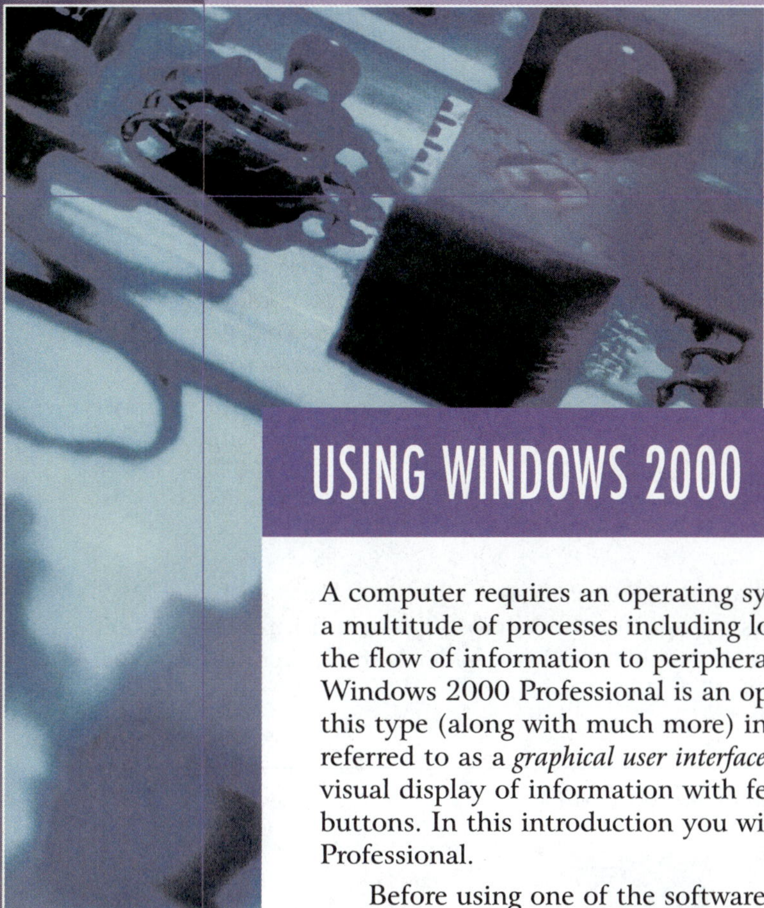

OFFICE XP

USING WINDOWS 2000

A computer requires an operating system to provide necessary instructions on a multitude of processes including loading programs, managing data, directing the flow of information to peripheral equipment, and displaying information. Windows 2000 Professional is an operating system that provides functions of this type (along with much more) in a graphical environment. Windows is referred to as a *graphical user interface* (GUI—pronounced *gooey*) that provides a visual display of information with features such as icons (pictures) and buttons. In this introduction you will learn basic features of Windows 2000 Professional.

Before using one of the software programs in the Microsoft Office suite, you will need to start the operating system. To do this, turn on the computer. Depending on your computer equipment configuration, you may also need to turn on the monitor and printer. When the computer is turned on, the Windows 2000 operating system is automatically started and, after a few moments, the desktop will display as shown in figure W.1. (Your desktop may vary from what you see in figure W.1.)

FIGURE W.1 ***Windows 2000 Desktop***

Exploring the Desktop

When Windows 2000 is loaded, the main portion of the screen is called the *desktop*. Think of the desktop in Windows as the top of a desk in an office. A business person places necessary tools—such as pencils, pens, paper, files, calculator—on his or her desktop to perform functions. Like the tools that are located on a desk, the desktop contains tools for operating the computer. These tools are logically grouped and placed in dialog boxes or panels that can be displayed using one of the icons at the left side of the desktop.

The desktop contains a variety of icons and features for using your computer and software programs installed on the computer. The features available on the desktop are described in the following text.

Using Icons

Icons are visual symbols that represent programs, files, or folders. In figure W.2, the figure on the left shows an icon for the Microsoft program Internet Explorer and the figure on the right shows the Windows folder icon. To open a folder or start a program, you double-click the icon.

FIGURE W.2 ***Internet Explorer Icon and Windows Folder***

Using the Taskbar

The bar that displays at the bottom of the desktop (see figure W.1) is called the Taskbar. The Taskbar, shown in figure W.3, is divided into four areas: the Start button, the Quick Launch toolbar, the program button area, and the System tray.

FIGURE W.3 ***Windows 2000 Taskbar***

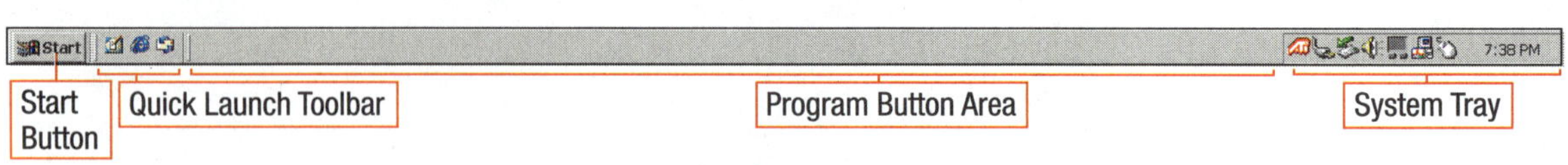

The Start button is located at the left side of the Taskbar. Use this button to start a program, use the Help feature, change settings, and open files. To display the options available with the Start button, position the arrow pointer on the Start button, and then click the left mouse button. This causes a pop-up menu to display, as shown in figure W.4.

FIGURE W.4 **Start Button Pop-up Menu**

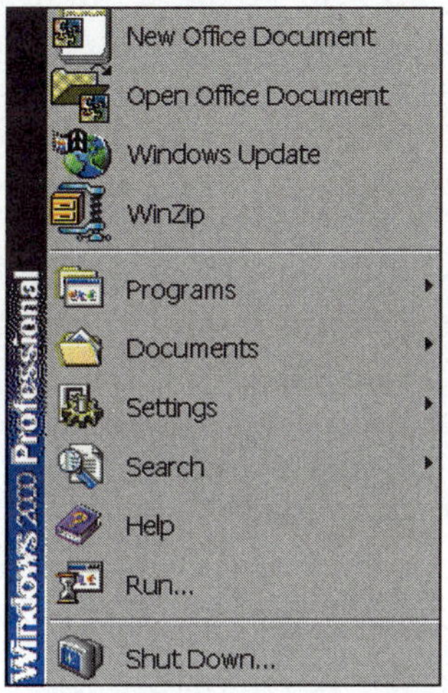

To choose an option from this pop-up menu, move the arrow pointer to the desired option (referred to as *pointing*), and then click the left mouse button. Pointing to options at the Start pop-up menu followed by a right-pointing triangle will cause a side menu to display with additional options.

When a program is open, a program button appears in the Taskbar. In the Taskbar shown in figure W.5, the Microsoft Word 2002 program is open. An icon representing Word displays in the program button area of the Taskbar.

FIGURE W.5 **Windows Taskbar with Microsoft Word Open**

Switching between Open Programs

To switch between open programs, click the program's button on the Taskbar. In figure W.6, three programs are open—Microsoft Word, Excel, and Publisher. Microsoft Excel is the active button. Clicking either the Microsoft Word or Microsoft Publisher button will activate that program.

FIGURE W.6 **Taskbar with the Microsoft Excel Program Active**

Almost every program you open will appear on the Taskbar. (A few specialized tools may not.) Each button on the Taskbar gets a little smaller each time you open a program.

exercise 1

OPENING PROGRAMS AND SWITCHING BETWEEN PROGRAMS

1. Open Windows 2000. (To do this, turn on the computer and, if necessary, turn on the monitor and/or printer. Check with your instructor to determine if you need to complete additional steps.)
2. When the desktop displays, open Microsoft Word by completing the following steps:
   a. Position the arrow pointer on the Start button on the Taskbar and then click the left mouse button.
   b. At the Start pop-up menu, point to *Programs*. (This causes a side menu to display.)
   c. Drag the arrow pointer to *Microsoft Word* in the side menu and then click the left mouse button.
   d. When the Microsoft Word program is opened, notice that a button representing Word displays in the program button area of the Taskbar.
3. Open Microsoft Excel by completing the following steps:
   a. Position the arrow pointer on the Start button on the Taskbar and then click the left mouse button.
   b. At the Start pop-up menu, point to *Programs*.
   c. Drag the arrow pointer to *Microsoft Excel* in the side menu and then click the left mouse button.
   d. When the Microsoft Excel program is opened, notice that a button representing Excel displays in the program button area of the Taskbar to the right of the button representing Word.
4. Switch to the Word program by clicking the button on the Taskbar representing Word.
5. Switch to the Excel program by clicking the button on the Taskbar representing Excel.
6. Exit Excel by clicking File on the Excel Menu bar and then clicking Exit at the drop-down menu.
7. Click the button on the Taskbar representing Word.
8. Exit Word by clicking File on the Word Menu bar and then clicking Exit at the drop-down menu.

Exploring the System Tray

The System tray is the recessed area on the far right side of the Taskbar. The System tray contains a digital clock and specialized programs that run in the background. Position the arrow pointer over the current time on the Taskbar and today's date displays in a small yellow box as shown in figure W.7. (Your date will vary.)

FIGURE W.7 ***Current Time and Date in System Tray***

Double-click the current time displayed on the Taskbar and the Date/Time Properties dialog box displays as shown in figure W.8.

FIGURE W.8 ***Date/Time Properties Dialog Box***

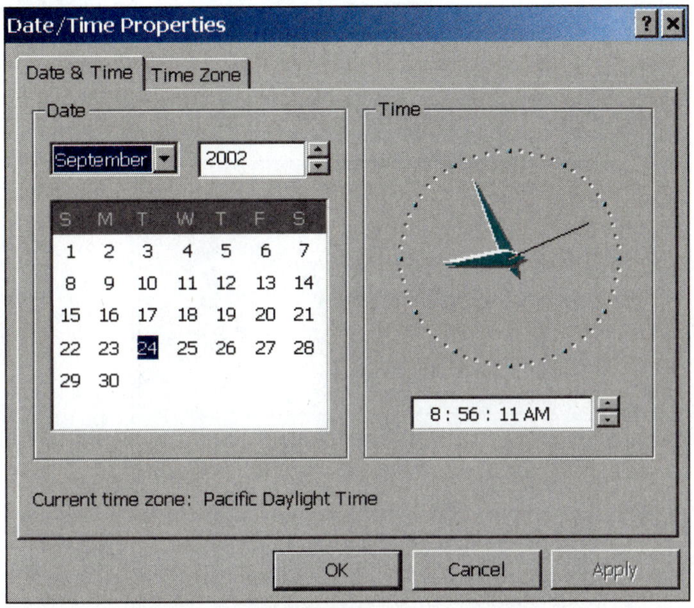

Change the date with options in the Date section of the dialog box. For example, to change the month, click the down-pointing triangle at the right side of the list box containing the current month, and then click the desired month at the drop-down list. Change the year by clicking the up- or down-pointing triangle at the right side of the list box containing the current year until the desired year displays. To change the day, click the desired day in the monthly calendar that displays in the dialog box. To change the time, double-click either the hour, minute, or seconds and use the up and down arrows to adjust the time.

Using the Quick Launch Toolbar

The Quick Launch toolbar is positioned between the Start button and the program button area on the Taskbar. It contains icons for programs that can be launched with a single click, such as Internet Explorer. The appearance of the Quick Launch toolbar can vary considerably depending on your installation of Windows 2000. A typical installation is shown in figure W.9.

FIGURE W.9 ***Windows 2000 Taskbar Quick Launch Toolbar***

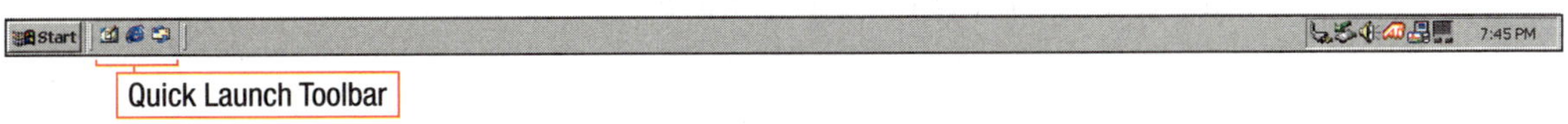

Setting Taskbar Properties

The default settings for the Taskbar display it at the bottom of the desktop with the time displayed. These default settings can be changed with options at the Taskbar and Start Menu Properties dialog box, shown in figure W.10. To display this dialog box, position the arrow pointer on any empty spot on the Taskbar, and then click the *right* mouse button. At the pop-up menu that displays, click *Properties*.

FIGURE W.10 **Taskbar and Start Menu Properties Dialog Box**

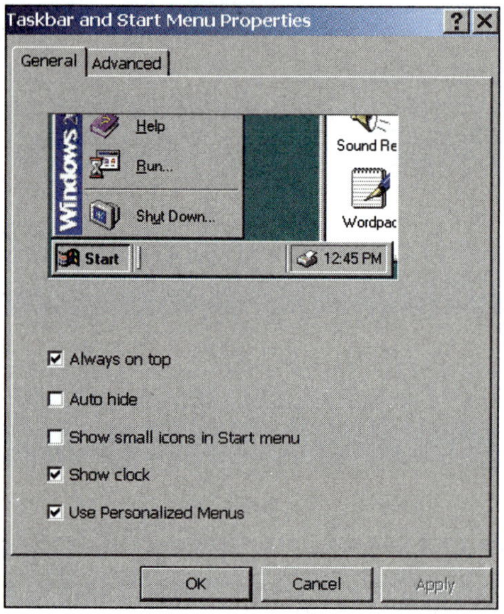

Each property is controlled by a check box. Property options containing a check mark are active. Click the option to remove the check mark and make the option inactive. If an option is inactive, clicking the option will insert a check mark in the check box and turn on the option (make it active). The Taskbar and Start Menu Properties dialog box contains these options:

Always on top: Keeps the Taskbar visible at all times. Check this if you want to see the Taskbar even when you are running programs.

Auto hide: Collapses the Taskbar into a thin line at the bottom of the screen. When you move the insertion point to the bottom of the screen, the Taskbar will display.

Show small icons in Start menu: Displays small icons in the Start menu. If unchecked, large icons are used (see figure W.11).

Show clock: Shows or hides the clock.

Use Personalized Menus: Keeps the Programs menu clean by hiding items you have not used recently. Access hidden programs by clicking the down-pointing triangle at the bottom of the Programs menu.

FIGURE

W.11 ***Start Menu Showing Large and Small Icons***

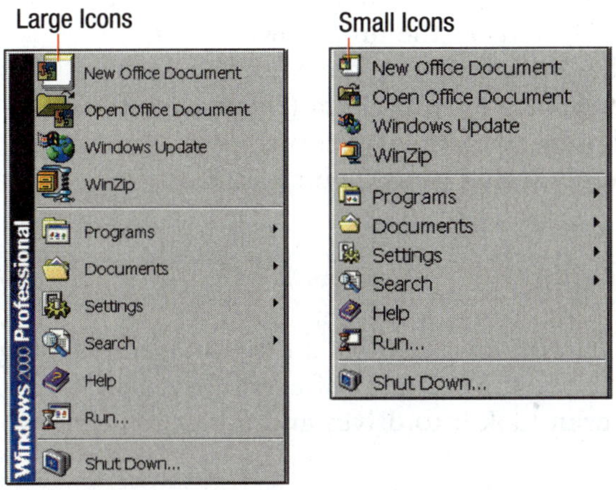

exercise 2

CHANGING TASKBAR PROPERTIES

1. Make sure Windows 2000 is open and the desktop is displayed.
2. Change the size of the icons in the Start pop-up menu and remove the display of the clock by completing the following steps:
   a. Position the arrow pointer on any empty area on the Taskbar and then click the *right* mouse button.
   b. At the pop-up menu that displays, click *Properties*.
   c. At the Taskbar and Start Menu Properties dialog box, click *Show small icons in Start menu*. (This inserts a check mark in the check box.)
   d. Click *Show clock*. (This removes the check mark from the check box.)
   e. Click the Apply button.
   f. Click OK to close the dialog box.
3. Notice that the time no longer displays at the right side of the Taskbar. Click the Start button at the left side of the Taskbar and notice that the icons in the pop-up menu are smaller. Click on any empty spot on the desktop to remove the pop-up menu.
4. Return to the default settings for the Taskbar by completing the following steps:
   a. Position the arrow pointer on any empty area on the Taskbar and then click the *right* mouse button.
   b. At the pop-up menu that displays, click *Properties*.
   c. At the Taskbar and Start Menu Properties dialog box, click *Show small icons in Start menu*. (This removes the check mark from the check box.)
   d. Click *Show clock*. (This inserts a check mark in the check box.)
   e. Click the Apply button.
   f. Click OK to close the dialog box.

Setting Clicking Options

You can set clicking options for the Windows environment and specify either a double-click or single-click to open a program or file. Steps in this textbook assume that you will double-click to open a file or program. To change from single-click to open (point to select) to double-click to open (single-click to select), complete these steps:

1. At the Windows desktop, click the My Computer icon.
2. At the My Computer window, click Tools on the Menu bar, and then click Folder Options at the drop-down menu.
3. At the Folder Options dialog box with the General tab selected, click the Double-click to open an item (single-click to select) option located in the Click items as follows section.
4. Click the Apply button and then click OK.

Using Windows Explorer

Windows Explorer in Windows 2000 is a file management program. Use Windows Explorer to see the contents of every drive and folder attached to your computer. You can even look into drives and folders on a network.

Looking at the Windows Explorer Window

To open Windows Explorer, click the Start button on the Taskbar, point to *Programs*, point to *Accessories*, and then click *Windows Explorer*. This displays the Windows Explorer window similar to the one shown in figure W.12. (Your Windows Explorer window will vary from what you see in figure W.12.)

FIGURE W.12 ***Windows Explorer Window***

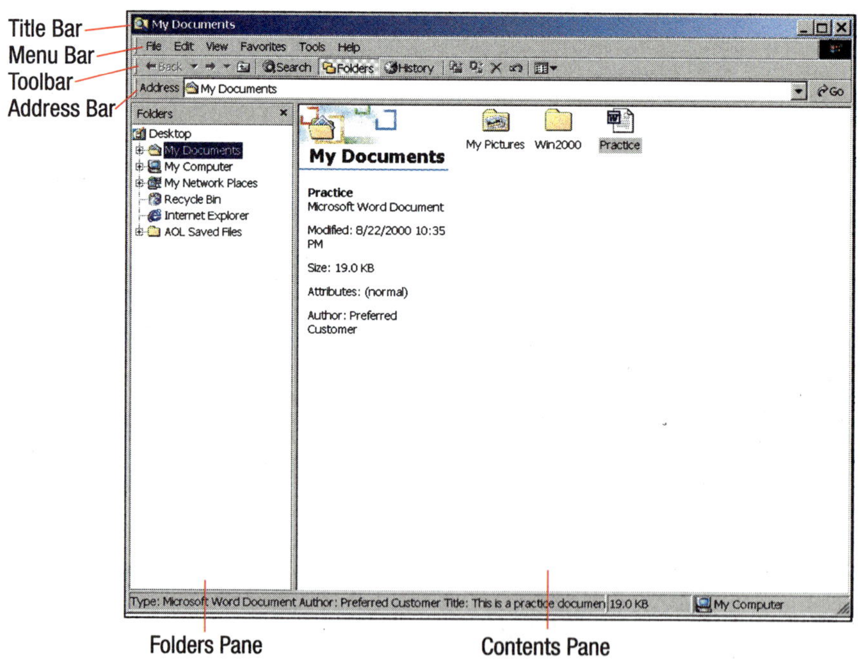

The left side of the Windows Explorer window is referred to as the Folders pane. (You can turn off the display of the Folders pane by clicking the Folders button on the toolbar.) The Folders pane shows special system folders and gives you a large view of your computer system. The right side of the Windows Explorer window is referred to as the Contents pane and displays the contents of the folder as well as related hyperlinks. (The related hyperlinks display as underlined blue text. Click a hyperlink and the hyperlinked folder displays in the Contents pane.)

Open Windows Explorer and the My Documents folder opens by default as shown in figure W.12. The Folders pane is based on a *hierarchy* with Desktop displayed at the top. As you can see from figure W.12, all the other icons are shown below the Desktop icon.

A folder may display preceded by a plus symbol. This plus symbol indicates that the folder contains additional folders (or drives). Double-click the folder name in the Folders pane and the contents of the folder display in the Folders pane as well as the Contents pane. You can also click the plus symbol and the contents of the folder display in the Folders pane but not the Contents pane. When the contents of a folder display, the plus symbol changes to a minus symbol. Click the minus symbol and the contents of the folder are hidden in the Folders pane. Double-click the My Computer folder name in the Folders pane and the Windows Explorer window displays as shown in figure W.13 (your window may vary slightly).

FIGURE W.13 ***Contents of My Computer***

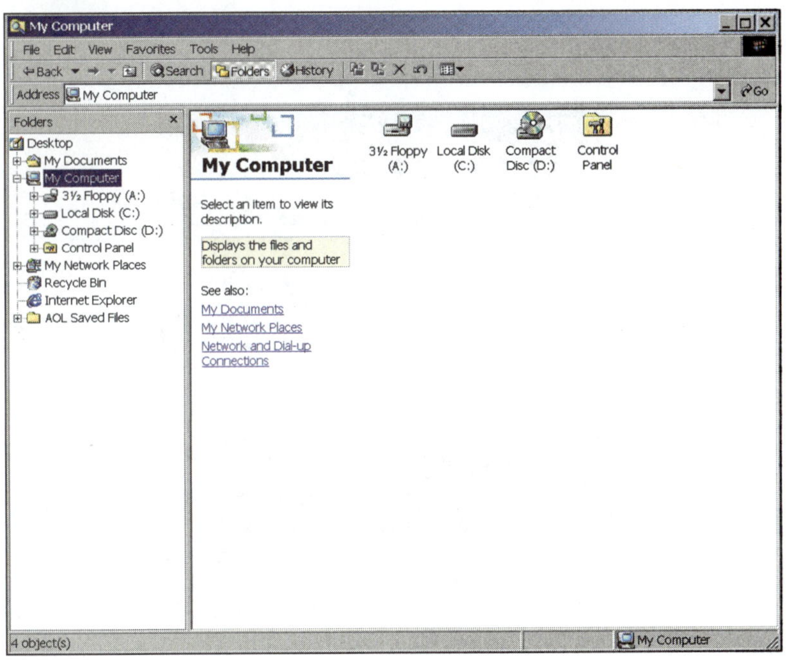

Clicking the *Up* button on the toolbar moves Windows Explorer up the hierarchy. You can also click the Back button on the toolbar to move back to the previously displayed folder or drive. Figure W.14 identifies the buttons on the Windows Explorer toolbar.

FIGURE W.14 ***Windows Explorer Toolbar Buttons***

Copying, Moving, and Deleting Files/Folders in Windows Explorer

File and folder management activities can be performed in Windows Explorer. These activities include copying and moving files or folders from a folder or drive to another or deleting files or folders. Windows Explorer offers a variety of methods for copy, moving, and deleting files/folders. You can use buttons on the toolbar, drop-down menu options, or shortcut menu options. This section will provide you with the steps for copying, moving, and deleting files/folders using buttons on the toolbar.

To copy a file/folder to another folder or drive, select the file or folder by clicking it in the Contents pane and then clicking the Copy To button on the toolbar. At the Browse For Folder dialog box shown in figure W.15, click the desired folder or drive (you may need to click a plus symbol to display hidden folders) and then click OK. To move a file or folder to another folder or drive, select the file or folder and then click the Move To button on the toolbar. At the Browse For Folder dialog box, specify the location, and then click OK. Copying a file or folder leaves the file or folder in the original location and saves a copy at the new location while moving removes the file or folder from the original location and moves it to the new location.

FIGURE W.15 ***Browse For Folder Dialog Box***

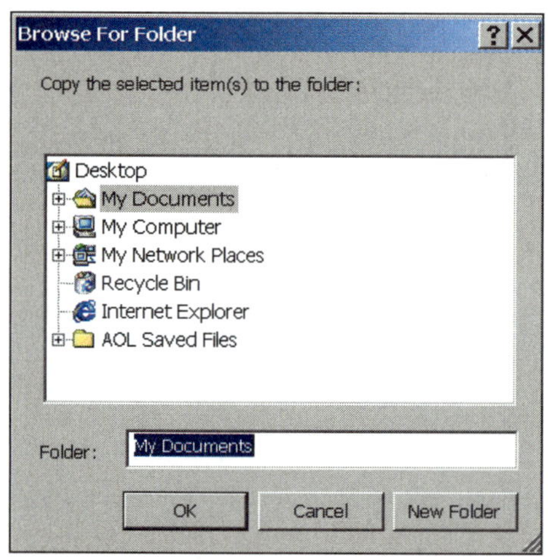

A file or folder can be easily removed (deleted) from Windows Explorer. To delete a file or folder, click the file or folder and then click the Delete button on the toolbar. At the dialog box asking you to confirm the deletion, click the Yes button. A deleted file or folder is sent to the Recycle Bin. You will learn more about the Recycle Bin in the next section.

exercise 3

COPYING A FILE AND FOLDER AND DELETING A FILE

1. At the Windows 2000 desktop, open Windows Explorer by completing the following steps:
   a. Click the Start button located at the left side of the Taskbar.
   b. At the pop-up menu that displays, point to *Programs*, point to *Accessories*, and then click *Windows Explorer*.
2. Copy a file from the CD that accompanies this textbook to a disk in drive A by completing the following steps:
   a. Insert the CD that accompanies this textbook into the CD drive.
   b. Insert a formatted 3.5-inch disk in drive A.
   c. Double-click the My Computer folder name in the Folders pane.
   d. Double-click the name of the drive containing the CD in the Folders pane (probably displays as OFFICEXP_BENCH followed by a drive letter). (Make sure you double-click because you want the contents of the CD to display in the Folders pane as well as the Contents pane.)
   e. Double-click the *Windows* folder in the Contents pane.
   f. Click *Word Document 01* in the Contents pane to select it.
   g. Click the Copy To button on the toolbar.
   h. At the Browse For Folder dialog box, display the drives and folders in My Computer by double-clicking My Computer in the dialog box list box. (Skip this step if the drives and folders are already displayed.)
   i. Click *3½ Floppy (A:)* in the dialog box list box.
   j. Click OK.
3. Delete *Word Document 01* from drive A by completing the following steps:
   a. Scroll up the display in the Folders pane until *3½ Floppy (A:)* is visible and then double-click *3½ Floppy (A:)*.
   b. Click *Word Document 01* (all of the document name may not be visible) in the Contents pane to select it.
   c. Click the Delete button on the toolbar.
   d. At the message asking you to confirm the deletion, click the Yes button.
4. Copy the *Windows* folder from the CD drive to the disk in drive A by completing the following steps:
   a. Scroll down the display in the Folders pane until the drive containing the CD displays (this will probably display as OFFICEXP_BENCH followed by the letter of the CD drive) and then double-click the drive.
   b. Click the *Windows* folder in the Contents pane to select it.
   c. Click the Copy To button on the toolbar.
   d. At the Browse For Folder dialog box, click *3½ Floppy (A:)* in the list box.
   e. Click OK.
5. Close Windows Explorer by clicking File on the Menu bar and then clicking Close at the drop-down menu. (You can also close Windows Explorer by clicking the Close button [contains an X] located in the upper right corner of Windows Explorer.)

Selecting Files/Folders

More than one file or folder can be moved, copied, or deleted at one time. Before moving, copying, or deleting files/folders, select the desired files or folders. Selecting files/folders in Windows Explorer is easier when the display of the Files pane is changed to List or Details. To change the display, open Windows Explorer and then click View on the Menu bar. At the drop-down menu, click the List option or the Details option.

To move adjacent files/folders, click the first file or folder and then hold down the Shift key and click the last file or folder. This selects and highlights all files/folders from the first file/folder you clicked to the last file/folder you clicked. With the adjacent files/folders selected, click the Move To button on the toolbar and then specify the desired location at the Browse For Folder dialog box. To select nonadjacent files/folders, click the first file/folder to select it, hold down the Ctrl key and then click any other files/folders to be moved or copied.

exercise 4

COPYING AND DELETING FILES

1. At the Windows 2000 desktop, open Windows Explorer by clicking the Start button, pointing to *Programs*, pointing to *Accessories*, and then clicking *Windows Explorer*.
2. Copy files from the CD that accompanies this textbook to a disk in drive A by completing the following steps:
   a. Insert the CD that accompanies this textbook into the CD drive.
   b. Insert your disk in drive A.
   c. Double-click My Computer in the Folders pane.
   d. Double-click the CD drive in the Folders pane (probably displays as OFFICEXP_BENCH followed by the drive letter).
   e. Double-click the *Windows* folder in the Contents pane.
   f. Change the display to Details by clicking View on the Menu bar and then clicking Details.
   g. Position the arrow pointer on *Word Document 01* in the Contents pane and then click the left mouse button.
   h. Hold down the Shift key, click *Word Document 05*, and then release the Shift key. (This selects *Word Document 01, Word Document 02, Word Document 03, Word Document 04,* and *Word Document 05*.)
   i. Click the Copy To button on the toolbar.
   j. At the Browse For Folder dialog box, click *3½ Floppy (A:)* in the list box and then click OK.
3. Double-click *3½ Floppy (A:)* in the Folders pane to display the files saved on the disk in drive A. (You may need to scroll up the Folders pane to display *3½ Floppy (A:)*.)
4. Delete the files from drive A that you just copied by completing the following steps:
   a. Change the view by clicking View on the Menu bar and then clicking List.
   b. Position the arrow pointer on *Word Document 01* in the Contents pane and then click the left mouse button.
   c. Hold down the Shift key, click *Word Document 05*, and then release the Shift key. (This selects *Word Document 01, Word Document 02, Word Document 03, Word Document 04,* and *Word Document 05*.)
   d. Click the Delete button on the toolbar.
   e. At the message asking you to confirm the deletion, click the Yes button.
   f. At the message telling you that the document is a read-only file and asking if you want to delete it, click the Yes to All button.
5. Close Windows Explorer by clicking File and then Close, or clicking the Close button (contains an X) located in the upper right corner of Windows Explorer.

Manipulating and Creating Folders in Windows Explorer

Organize and group files in folders. To help you organize files, you can create folders in Windows Explorer. To do this, double-click in the Folders pane the drive or folder in which you want to create the new folder. Click File on the Menu bar, point to New, and then click Folder. This inserts a folder icon in the Contents pane and names the folder *New Folder* as shown in figure W.16. Key the desired name for the new folder and then press Enter.

FIGURE W.16 ***New Folder Icon in Windows Explorer***

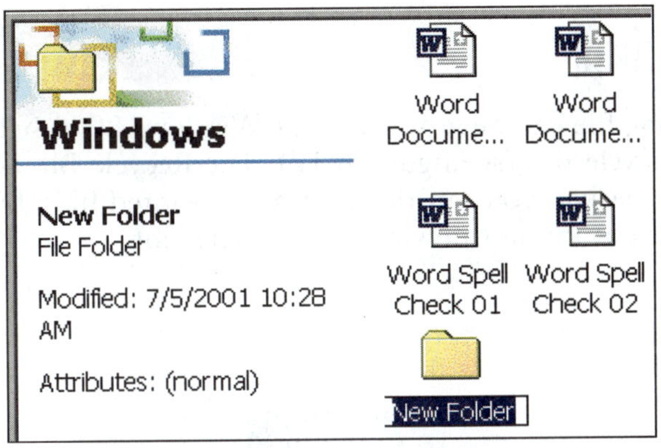

exercise 5 — CREATING A NEW FOLDER

1. At the Windows 2000 desktop, open Windows Explorer.
2. Create a new folder by completing the following steps:
   a. Insert your disk in drive A (this disk contains the *Windows* folder you copied in exercise 3).
   b. Double-click *3½ Floppy (A:)* in the Folders pane.
   c. Double-click the *Windows* folder in the Contents pane. (This opens the folder.)
   d. Click File on the Menu bar, point to New, and then click Folder.
   e. Key **Spell Check Files** and then press Enter. (This changes the name from *New Folder* to *Spell Check Files*.)
3. Copy *Word Spell Check 01, Word Spell Check 02, Word Spell Check 03,* and *Word Spell Check 04* into the Spell Check Files folder you just created by completing the following steps:
   a. Click View on the Menu bar and then click List.
   b. Click once on the file named *Word Spell Check 01* located in the Contents pane.
   c. Hold down the Shift key, click once on the file named *Word Spell Check 04*, and then release the Shift key. (This selects *Word Spell Check 01, Word Spell Check 02, Word Spell Check 03,* and *Word Spell Check 04*.)
   d. Click the Copy To button on the toolbar.
   e. At the Browse For Folder dialog box, double-click *3½ Floppy (A:)* in the list box.
   f. Double-click *Windows* (below *3½ Floppy (A:)*) in the list box.
   g. Click once on *Spell Check Files* in the list box (below *Windows*) and then click OK.
4. Display the files you just copied by double-clicking the Spell Check Files folder in the Contents pane.
5. Double-click *3½ Floppy (A:)* in the Folders pane. (This displays in the Contents pane the contents of the your disk.)

6. Delete the Spell Check Files folder and its contents by completing the following steps:
   a. Double-click the *Windows* folder in the Contents pane.
   b. Click the Spell Check Files folder in the Contents pane to select it.
   c. Click the Delete button on the toolbar.
   d. At the message asking you to confirm the deletion, click the Yes button.
   e. At the message telling you that the document is a read-only file and asking if you want to delete it, click the Yes to All button.
7. Close Windows Explorer by clicking File and then Close, or clicking the Close button (contains an X) located in the upper right corner of Windows Explorer.

Using the Recycle Bin

Deleting the wrong file can be a disaster but Windows 2000 helps protect your work with the Recycle Bin (see figure W.17). The Recycle Bin acts just like an office wastepaper basket; you can throw away unwanted files, but you can reach in and take paper out if you threw it away by accident.

FIGURE W.17 ***Recycle Bin Icon***

Deleting Files to the Recycle Bin

A file/folder or selected files/folders deleted from the hard drive are automatically sent to the Recycle Bin. Files/folders deleted from a disk are deleted permanently. (Recovery programs are available, however, that will help you recover deleted text. If you accidentally delete a file/folder from a disk, do not do anything more with the disk until you can run a recovery program.)

Another method for deleting a file is to drag the file to the Recycle Bin icon on the desktop. Drag a file icon to the Recycle Bin until the Recycle Bin icon is selected (displays with a blue background) and then release the mouse button. This drops the file you are dragging into the Recycle Bin.

Recovering Files from the Recycle Bin

If you accidentally delete a file to the Recycle Bin, it can be easily restored. To restore a file, double-click the Recycle Bin icon on the desktop. This opens the Recycle Bin window shown in figure W.18. (The contents of the Recycle Bin will vary.)

FIGURE

W.18 **Recycle Bin Window**

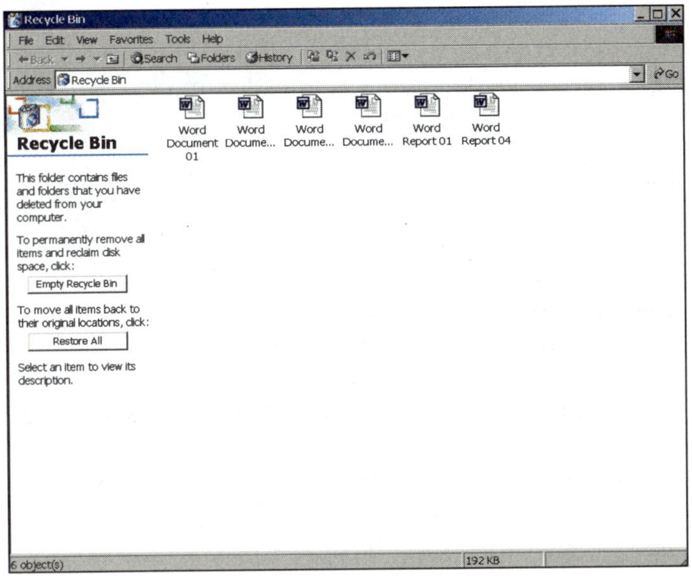

To restore a file, click the file you want restored, click File on the Menu bar, and then click Restore at the drop-down menu. The file is removed from the Recycle Bin and returned to its original location. You can also restore a file by positioning the arrow pointer on the file, clicking the *right* mouse button, and then clicking *Restore* at the pop-up menu.

exercise 6 — DELETING FILES TO AND RECOVERING FILES FROM THE RECYCLE BIN

(Before completing this exercise, check with your instructor to determine if you can copy files to the hard drive.)

1. At the Windows 2000 desktop, open Windows Explorer.
2. Copy files from your disk in drive A to the My Documents folder on your hard drive by completing the following steps:
   a. Insert your disk in drive A (this disk contains the *Windows* folder).
   b. Double-click My Computer in the Folders pane.
   c. Double-click *3½ Floppy (A:)* in the Folders pane.
   d. Double-click the *Windows* folder in the Contents pane.
   e. Position the arrow pointer on *Word Spell Check 01* and then click the left mouse button.
   f. Hold down the Shift key, click *Word Spell Check 04,* and then release the Shift key.
   g. Click the Copy To button on the toolbar.
   h. At the Browse For Folder dialog box, click *My Documents* in the list box.
   i. Click OK.
3. Double-click My Documents in the Folders pane to display the files located in the folder. (The files you copied, *Word Spell Check 01* through *Word Spell Check 04,* will display in the Contents pane in alphabetical order.)
4. Delete *Word Spell Check 01* through *Word Spell Check 04* from the My Documents folder and send them to the Recycle Bin by completing the following steps:

a. Select *Word Spell Check 01* through *Word Spell Check 04* in the Contents pane. (If these files are not visible, you will need to scroll down the list of files.)
b. Click the Delete button on the toolbar.
c. At the message asking you to confirm the deletion, click the Yes button.
d. At the message telling you that the document is a read-only file and asking if you want to delete it, click the Yes to All button.

5. Close Windows Explorer.
6. At the desktop, display the contents of the Recycle Bin by double-clicking the Recycle Bin icon.
7. At the Recycle Bin window, restore *Word Spell Check 01* through *Word Spell Check 04* to the My Documents folder by completing the following steps:
   a. Scroll to the end of the list of files.
   b. When *Word Spell Check 01* through *Word Spell Check 04* display in the list box, select all four files.
   c. With the files selected, click File on the Menu bar and then click Restore at the drop-down menu.
   d. At the message asking you to confirm that you want to move the read-only file, click the Yes to All button.
8. Close the Recycle Bin window by clicking File on the Menu bar and then clicking Close at the drop-down menu.
9. Open Windows Explorer.
10. Make sure the My Documents folder is selected. (If it is not, select it by double-clicking My Documents in the Folders pane.)
11. Delete the files you restored by completing the following steps:
    a. Select *Word Spell Check 01* through *Word Spell Check 04* in the Contents pane. (If these files are not visible, you will need to scroll down the list of files. These are the files you recovered from the Recycle Bin.)
    b. Click the Delete button on the toolbar.
    c. At the message asking you to confirm the deletion, click the Yes button.
    d. At the message telling you that the document is a read-only file and asking if you want to delete it, click the Yes to All button.
12. Close Windows Explorer.

Emptying the Recycle Bin

Just like a wastepaper basket, the Recycle Bin can get full. To empty the Recycle Bin, position the arrow pointer on the Recycle Bin icon on the desktop and then click the *right* mouse button. At the pop-up menu that displays, click *Empty Recycle Bin*. At the message asking you to confirm the deletion, click the Yes button. You can also empty the Recycle Bin by double-clicking the Recycle Bin icon. At the Recycle Bin window that displays, click the Empty Recycle Bin button that displays at the left side of the window. At the message asking you to confirm the deletion, click the Yes button. (You can also empty the Recycle Bin by clicking File on the Menu bar and then clicking Empty Recycle Bin at the drop-down menu.)

Emptying the Recycle Bin deletes all files/folders. You can delete a specific file/folder from the Recycle Bin (rather than all files/folders). To do this, double-click the Recycle Bin icon on the desktop. At the Recycle Bin window, select the file/folder or files/folders to be deleted, and then click the Delete button on the toolbar. At the message asking you to confirm the deletion, click the Yes button.

exercise 7

EMPTYING THE RECYCLE BIN

(Before completing this exercise, check with your instructor to determine if you can delete files/folders from the Recycle Bin.)

1. At the Windows 2000 desktop, double-click the Recycle Bin icon.
2. At the Recycle Bin window, empty the contents of the Recycle Bin by completing the following steps:
   a. Click the Empty Recycle Bin button that displays at the left side of the window.
   b. At the message asking you to confirm the deletion, click the Yes button.
3. Close the Recycle Bin window by clicking File and then Close.

When the Recycle Bin is emptied the files cannot be recovered by the Recycle Bin or by Windows 2000. If you have to recover a file, you will need to use a file recovery program such as Norton Utilities. These utilities are separate programs, but might be worth their cost if you ever need them.

Customizing the Recycle Bin

The Recycle Bin settings can be customized at the Recycle Bin Properties dialog box. To display this dialog box, position the arrow pointer on the Recycle Bin icon on the desktop and then click the *right* mouse button. At the pop-up menu that displays, click *Properties*.

Using My Computer

Use the My Computer folder to display the contents of the floppy disk and hard disk, CD-ROM drive, mapped network drives and to open the Control Panel. To display the My Computer window shown in figure W.19, double-click the My Computer icon on the desktop.

FIGURE W.19 ***My Computer Window***

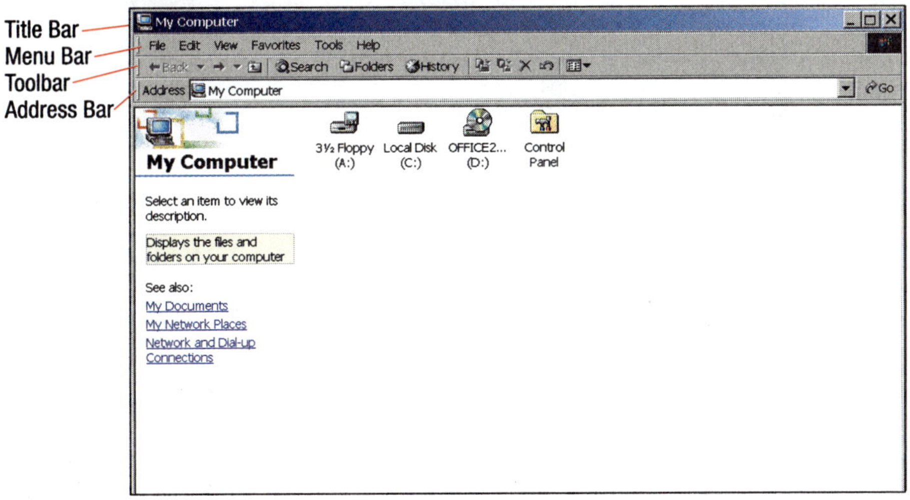

Using the My Computer window, you can navigate to the various drives and folders on your computer. You can also double-click on a file in the My Computer window and the program in which the file was created is opened (provided the program is located on your computer) as well as the file. You can copy, move, and delete folders and files in My Computer following the same steps you learned earlier in the *Using Windows Explorer* section. For example, to copy a file/folder, click the file or folder, and then click the Copy To button on the My Computer window toolbar. At the Browse For Folder dialog box, click the desired location in the list box, and then click OK.

Changing the My Computer Window Display

By default, the My Computer window displays objects in the window as large icons. With the Large Icons option selected at the View drop-down menu, the My Computer window should look something like the window shown in figure W.19.

Click the Small Icons option at the View drop-down menu and the icons in the My Computer window are reduced in size. Clicking the List option displays objects in the My Computer window in a list towards the left side of the window. Click the Details option at the View drop-down menu and a detailed view of each object displays in the My Computer window as shown in figure W.20.

FIGURE W.20 ***My Computer Window in Details View***

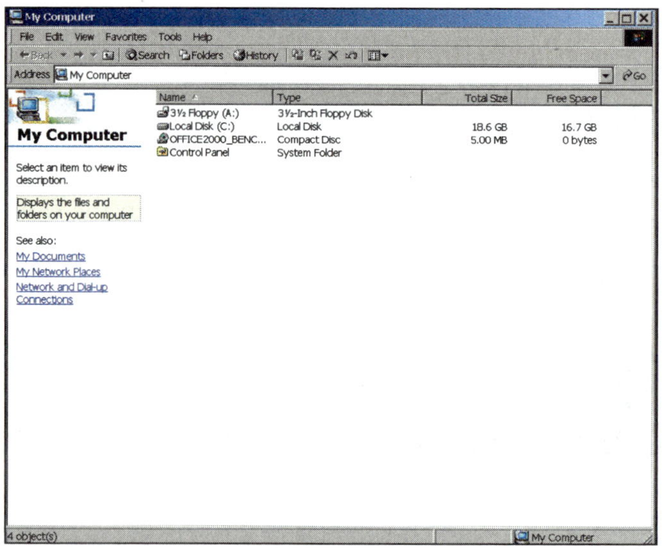

exercise 8

CHANGING THE DISPLAY AND COPYING AND DELETING A FILE IN MY COMPUTER

(Before completing this exercise, check with your instructor to determine if you can copy files to the My Documents folder on the hard drive.)

1. At the Windows 2000 desktop, double-click the My Computer icon.
2. At the My Computer window, display folders and files in a list (rather than large icons) by clicking View and then List.
3. Insert your disk in drive A.
4. Copy a document from the *Windows* folder on the disk in drive A to the My Documents folder on the hard drive by completing the following steps:
   a. Double-click *3½ Floppy (A:)* in the My Computer list box.
   b. Double-click the *Windows* folder (this displays the documents in the folder).
   c. Change the display of the files in the *Windows* folder by clicking View on the Menu bar and then clicking Details.
   d. Click once on the document named *Word Document 01*.
   e. Click the Copy To button on the toolbar.
   f. At the Browse For Folder dialog box, click My Documents in the list box.
   g. Click OK.
5. Delete *Word Document 01* from the My Documents folder by completing the following steps:
   a. Click the down-pointing triangle at the right side of the Address bar located towards the top of the My Computer window (just below the toolbar).
   b. At the drop-down list that displays, click *My Documents*.
   c. Click *Word Document 01* to select it.
   d. Click the Delete button on the toolbar.
   e. At the message asking you to confirm the deletion, click the Yes button.
6. Close the My Computer window by clicking File on the Menu bar and then clicking Close or by clicking the Close button (displays with an X) located at the right side of the My Computer Title bar.

Creating a Shortcut

Shortcuts are specialized icons. They are very small files that point the operating system to the actual item, whether it is a file, a folder, or an application. For example, in figure W.21, the *Shortcut to Practice Document* icon represents a path to a specific file in the Word 2002 program. The icon is not the actual file but a path to the file. Double-click the shortcut icon and Windows opens the Word 2002 program and also opens the file named Practice Document.

FIGURE W.21 ***Practice Document Shortcut Icon***

Shortcuts provide quick and easy access to files or programs used every day without having to remember where the file is stored. One method for creating a shortcut is to display the My Computer window and then display the drive or folder where the file is located. Position the arrow pointer on the file, hold down the *right* mouse button, drag the outline of the file to the desktop, and then release the mouse button. At the pop-up menu that displays, click *Create Shortcut(s) Here*. This creates a shortcut icon on the desktop like the one shown in figure W.21.

A shortcut icon can be easily deleted from the desktop by dragging the shortcut icon to the Recycle Bin icon. This deletes the shortcut icon but does not delete the file to which the shortcut pointed.

exercise 9

CREATING A SHORTCUT

1. At the Windows 2000 desktop, double-click the My Computer icon.
2. Insert your disk in drive A.
3. At the My Computer window, double-click *3½ Floppy (A:)*.
4. Double-click the *Windows* folder.
5. Change the display of files to a list by clicking View on the Menu bar and then clicking List at the drop-down menu.
6. Create a shortcut to the file named *Word Letter 01* by completing the following steps:
   a. Position the arrow pointer on *Word Letter 01*.
   b. Hold down the *right* mouse button, drag the outline of the file to the desktop window, and then release the mouse button.
   c. At the pop-up menu that displays, click *Create Shortcut(s) Here*.
7. Close the My Computer window by clicking the Close button located in the upper right corner of the window.
8. Open Word 2002 and the file named *Word Letter 01* by double-clicking the Word Letter 01 shortcut icon on the desktop.
9. After viewing the file in Word, exit Word by clicking File on the Menu bar and then clicking Exit at the drop-down menu.
10. Delete the Word Letter 01 shortcut icon by completing the following steps:
    a. At the desktop, position the arrow pointer on the Word Letter 01 shortcut icon.
    b. Hold down the left mouse button, drag the icon on top of the Recycle Bin icon, and then release the mouse button.

Customizing the Desktop

The Windows 2000 operating environment is very customizable. You can change background patterns and colors and set screen savers directly from the desktop. To change display properties, position the arrow pointer on any empty location on the desktop and then click the *right* mouse button. At the pop-up menu that displays, click *Properties*. This displays the Display Properties dialog box with the Background tab selected as shown in figure W.22.

FIGURE W.22 ***Display Properties Dialog Box with Background Tab Selected***

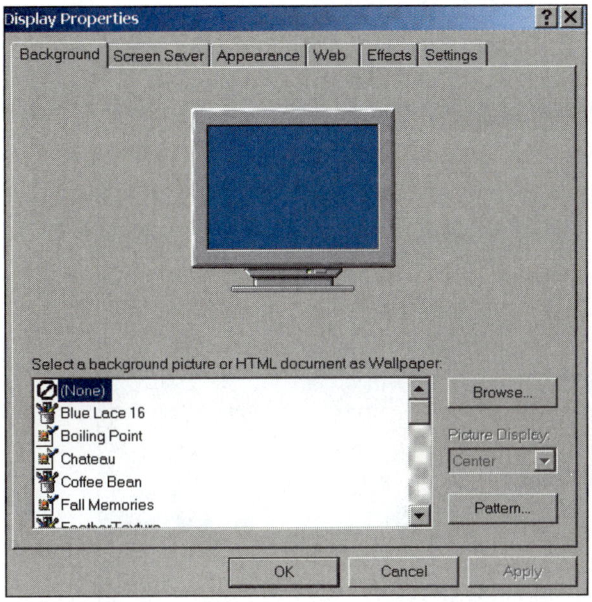

Changing the Desktop Background

The desktop background is customized at the Display Properties dialog box with the Background tab selected. Add a wallpaper background to the Windows desktop with options in the dialog box list box. Click any wallpaper option in the list box and preview the results in the preview screen. Wallpaper can be centered, tiled or stretched. Choose the display by clicking the down-pointing triangle at the right side of the Picture Display list box and then clicking the desired display. Choose the Tile option and the wallpaper covers the entire screen with a repeated series of images. Choose Center and the wallpaper is one image set in the middle of the screen or choose the Stretch option and the image is stretched across the entire screen. You can use the Browse button to select an HTML document from the network for your desktop background.

Add a pattern to the desktop with options from the Pattern dialog box. Display this dialog box by clicking the Pattern button located towards the bottom right corner of the Display Properties dialog box. The Pattern button is available only when the Picture Display option is set for Center.

If you want, you can choose (None) for both the wallpaper and pattern. This leaves the desktop one solid color. When you are satisfied with the pattern and wallpaper choices, click OK to set the changes and close the Display Properties dialog box.

Adding a Screen Saver

If your computer sits idle for periods of time, consider adding a screen saver. If a screen sits idle for a long period of time, you run the risk of burning any images onto the screen. (Fortunately, monitor technology has improved and burning images on the screen is becoming less of a problem.) A screen saver is a pattern that changes constantly, thus eliminating the problem of an image staying on the screen too long.

To add a screen saver, display the Display Properties dialog box and then click the Screen Saver tab. This displays the dialog box as shown in figure W.23.

FIGURE W.23 ***Display Properties Dialog Box with Screen Saver Tab Selected***

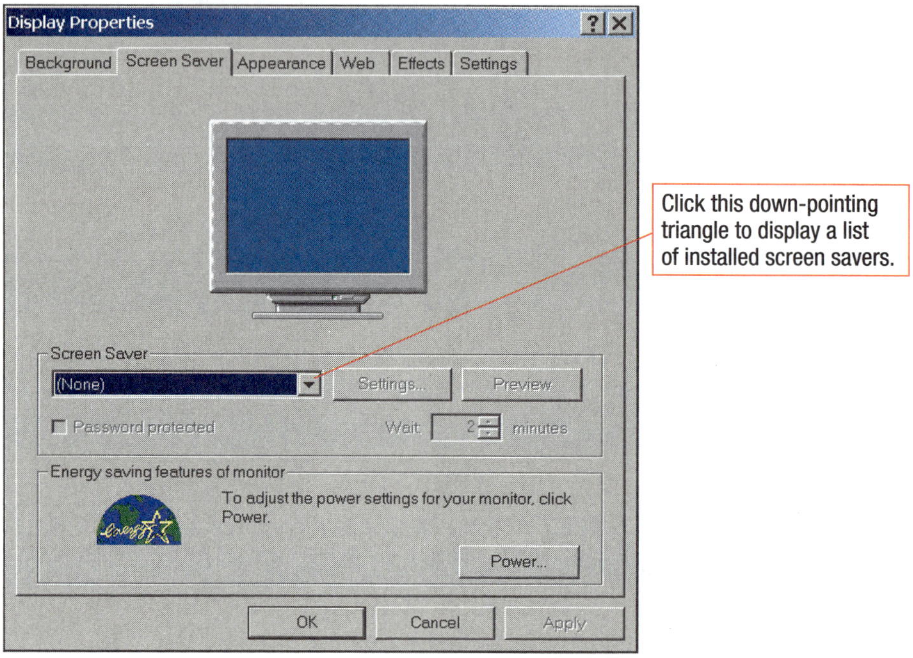

Click the down-pointing triangle at the right side of the Screen Saver list box to display a list of installed screen savers. Click a screen saver and a preview displays in the monitor located toward the top of the dialog box. Click the Preview button and the dialog box is hidden and the screen saver displays on your monitor. Move the mouse or click a button on the mouse and the dialog box will reappear.

Click the Settings button to display additional options for customizing a screen saver. Protect the screen saver with a password by clicking the Password protected check box. If a check mark appears in this check box, you must enter the correct password to clear the screen saver and return to the desktop.

If your computer's hardware is Energy Star compatible, the *Energy saving features of monitor* section is enabled. Click the Power button and a dialog box displays with options for choosing a power scheme appropriate to the way you use your computer. The dialog box also includes options for specifying how long the computer can be left unused before the monitor and hard disk are turned off and the system goes to standby or hibernate mode.

Changing Colors

Click the Appearance tab at the Display Properties dialog box and the dialog box displays as shown in figure W.24. At this dialog box, you can change the desktop scheme. Schemes are predefined collections of colors that are used in windows, menus, title bars, and system fonts. Windows 2000 loads with the Windows Standard scheme. Click the down-pointing triangle at the right side of the Scheme list box to display a list of available schemes. When you choose a scheme, the results are previewed in the sample dialog boxes.

FIGURE

W.24 ***Display Properties Dialog Box with Appearance Tab Selected***

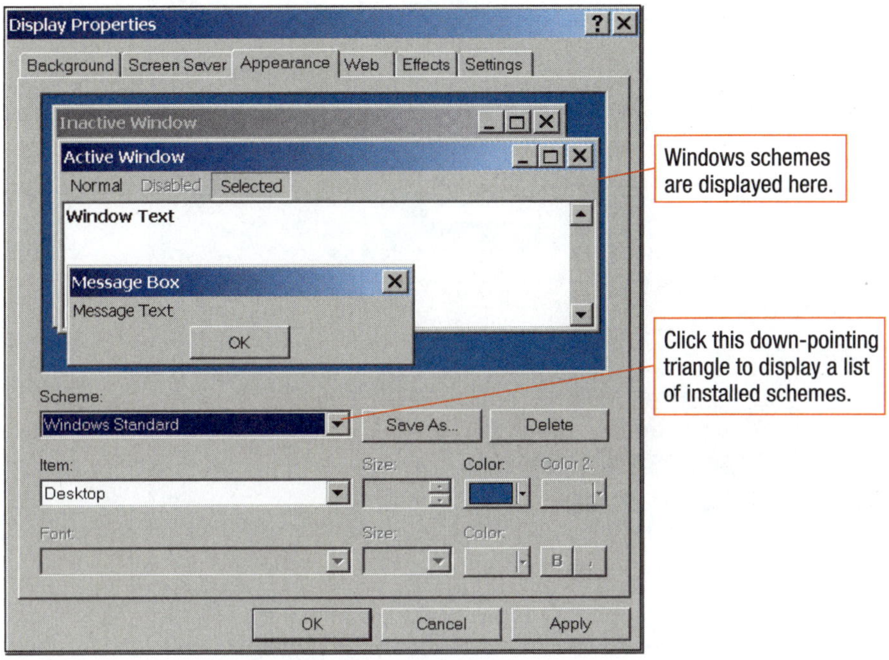

Schemes set the appearance of the entire operating system. If you want to set the desktop to a unique color, but leave the rest of the scheme intact, specify options at the Item drop-down list. Click the down-pointing triangle at the right side of the Item list box and then click the specific object to which you want the scheme applied.

Displaying Web Pages on the Desktop

Click the Web tab and the Display Properties dialog box displays. Windows uses your Internet browser to display Web pages and other Internet files on your desktop. Using the tab requires a working Internet connection.

Changing Desktop Icons

Click the Effects tab and the Display Properties dialog box displays. Use options from this dialog box to change desktop icons from the default icons used by Windows. Select the icon you want to change, click the Change Icon button, and select a new icon from the Current icon list box in the Change Icon dialog box. Use the Browse button to select an icon of your own design.

Changing Settings

Click the Settings tab at the Display Properties dialog box and the dialog box displays as shown in figure W.25. At this dialog box, you can set color and screen resolution.

FIGURE

W.25 ***Display Properties Dialog Box with Settings Tab Selected***

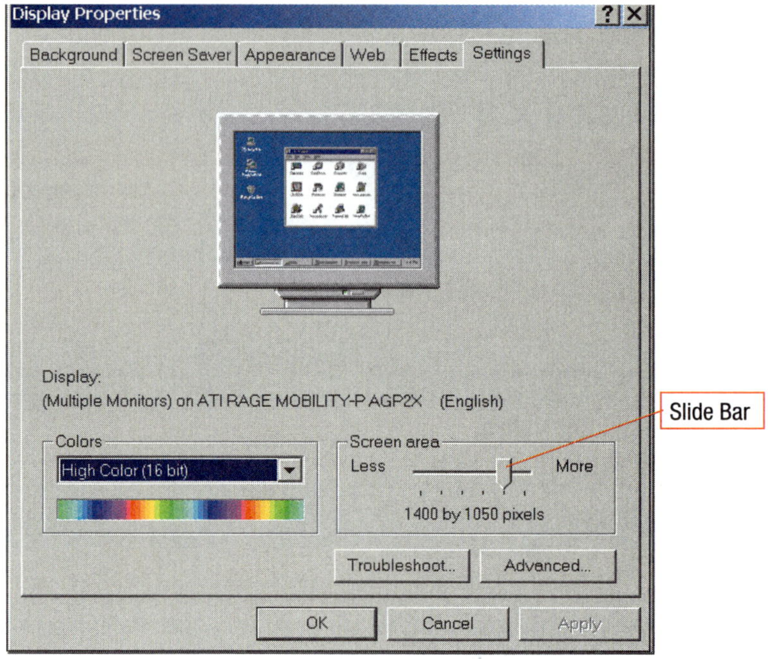

The Colors option determines how many colors are displayed on your monitor. The more colors that are shown, the more realistic the images will appear. However, a lot of computer memory is required to show thousands of colors. Your exact choice is determined by the specific hardware you are using. The Screen area slide bar sets the screen's resolution. The higher the number, the more you can fit onto your screen. Again, your actual values depend on your particular hardware. Clicking the Advanced button displays a dialog box with advanced display settings for changing font size.

exercise 10 — CUSTOMIZING THE DESKTOP

(Before completing this exercise, check with your instructor to determine if you can customize the desktop.)

1. At the Windows 2000 desktop, display the Display Properties dialog box by positioning the arrow pointer on an empty location on the desktop, clicking the *right* mouse button, and then clicking *Properties* at the pop-up menu.
2. At the Display Properties dialog box, add wallpaper to the desktop by completing the following steps:
   a. Make sure the Background tab is selected. (If it is not, click the Background tab.)
   b. Click *Blue Lace 16* in the Wallpaper list box. (If this option is not available, choose another wallpaper.)
   c. Make sure Center is selected in the Picture Display list box.
   d. Click OK to close the dialog box.
3. After viewing the desktop with the Blue Lace 16 wallpaper, add a pattern to fill in the space around the wallpaper by completing the following steps:
   a. Display the Display Properties dialog box.

b. At the Display Properties dialog box with the Background tab selected, click the Pattern button. (This displays the Pattern dialog box.)
c. Click *Paisley* in the Pattern list box. (If *Paisley* is not visible, click the down-pointing triangle in the Pattern list box until *Paisley* displays.)
d. Click OK to close the Pattern dialog box, and then click OK to close the Display Properties dialog box.

4. After viewing the desktop with the Blue Lace 16 wallpaper and the Paisley pattern applied, add a screen saver by completing the following steps:
   a. Display the Display Properties dialog box.
   b. At the Display Properties dialog box, click the Screen Saver tab. (If a screen saver is already selected in the Screen Saver list box, make a note of this screen saver name.)
   c. Click the down-pointing triangle at the right side of the Screen Saver list box.
   d. At the drop-down list that displays, click a screen saver that interests you. (A preview of the screen saver displays in the screen located toward the top of the dialog box.)
   e. Click a few other screen savers to see how they will display on the monitor.
   f. With a screen saver selected, click OK. (This closes the dialog box.)
   g. At the desktop the screen saver will display, by default, after the monitor has sat idle for 15 minutes.
5. Return all settings back to the default by completing the following steps:
   a. Display the Display Properties dialog box.
   b. Make sure the Background tab is selected.
   c. Click *(None)* in the Wallpaper list box.
   d. Click the Pattern button.
   e. At the Pattern dialog box, click *(None)* in the Pattern list box.
   f. Click OK to close the Pattern dialog box.
   g. Click the Screen Saver tab.
   h. At the Display Properties dialog box with the Screen Saver tab selected, click the down-pointing triangle at the right side of the Screen Saver list box, and then click *(None)*. (If a screen saver was selected before completing this exercise, return to that screen saver.)
   i. Click OK to close the Display Properties dialog box.

Exploring Windows 2000 Help Files

Windows 2000 includes an on-screen reference guide providing information, explanations, and interactive help on learning Windows features. The on-screen reference guide, referred to as "Help," contains complex files with hypertext used to access additional information by clicking a word or phrase. The Help feature can interact with open programs to help guide you through difficult tasks.

Using Windows Help Files

Display the Help window by clicking the Start button on the Taskbar and then click Help at the pop-up menu. The pane at the left side of the window contains four tabs—Contents, Index, Search, and Favorites. Click the Contents tab and help topics display in the list box below the tabs with each option preceded by a book icon as shown in figure W.26. Click a book icon and a list of subtopics appears. Click a subtopic that interests you and information about the topic displays in the pane at the right side of the window.

FIGURE

W.26 *Help Window with Contents Tab Selected*

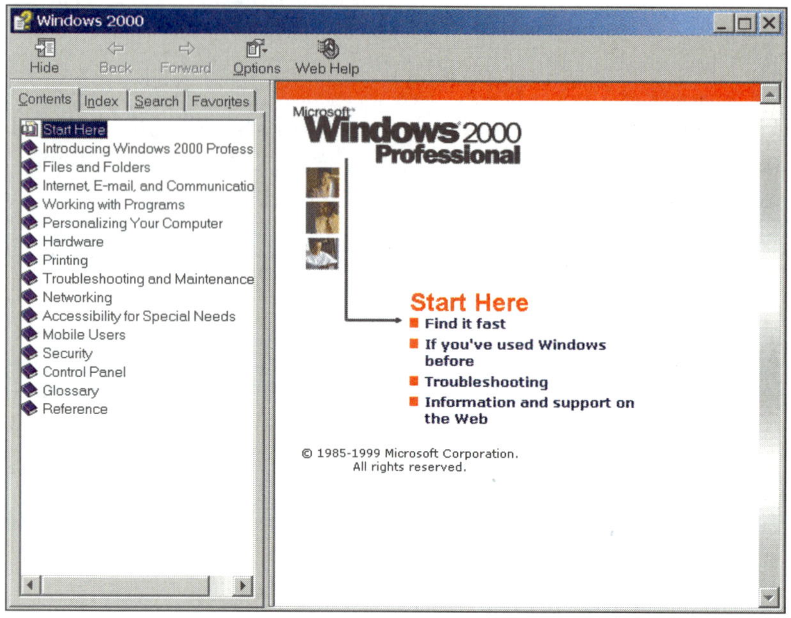

exercise 11

USING THE HELP TOPICS OR WINDOWS HELP DIALOG BOX WITH THE CONTENTS TAB SELECTED

(Depending on the type of installation completed on Windows, some of the Help categories may not be available. If some of the Help categories in exercise 11 do not display, experiment with other categories that interest you.)

1. At the Windows 2000 desktop, use the Help feature to learn about new Windows 2000 features by completing the following steps:
   a. Click the Start button located at the left side of the Taskbar.
   b. At the pop-up menu that displays, click *Help*.
   c. At the Help window, click the Contents tab. (Skip this step if the Contents tab is already selected.)
   d. Click *Introducing Windows 2000 Professional* located in the list box in the pane at the left side of the window. (This causes the book icon preceding *Introducing Windows 2000 Professional* to display as an open book and a list of subtopics to display below *Introducing Windows 2000 Professional*.)
   e. Click *What's new?* and information about new Windows 2000 features displays in the pane at the right side of the window.
   f. Click *Easier to use* (located in the pane at the right side of the window) and then read the information that displays below the topic.
   g. Click the other topics in the pane at the right side of the window and read the information supplied.
2. Close the Help window by clicking the Close button (displays with an X) that displays in the upper right corner of the window.

Click the Index tab and the Help window displays as shown in figure W.27. Key the desired feature, keyword, term, etc., in the *Type in the keyword to find* text box. Help displays a list of topics matching or related to the keyed text. Using the Help window with the Index tab selected is often easier than looking through the window with the Contents tab selected.

FIGURE W.27 **Help Window with Index Tab Selected**

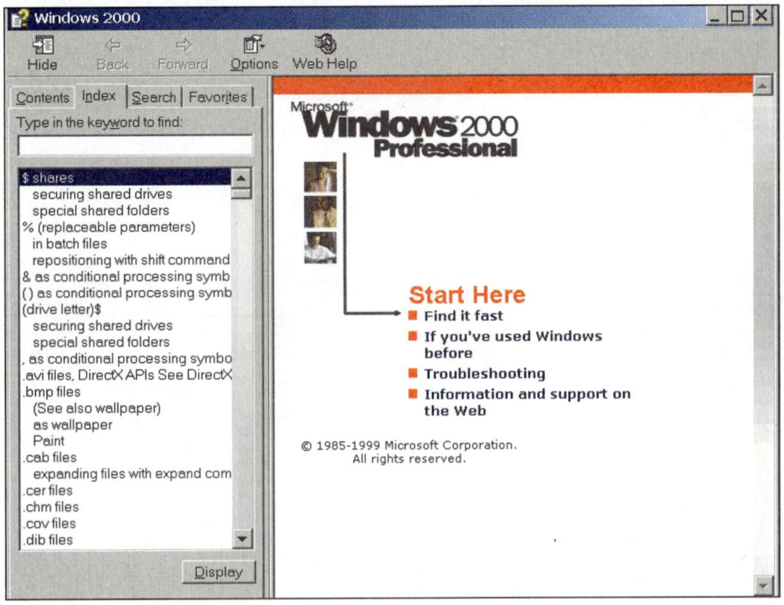

Use the Help window with the Search tab selected to search for a specific word, term, or phrase. At the Help window with the Search tab selected, as shown in figure W.28, key the desired word or phrase in the *Type in the keyword to find* list box and then press Enter or click the List Topics button.

FIGURE W.28 **Help Window with Search Tab Selected**

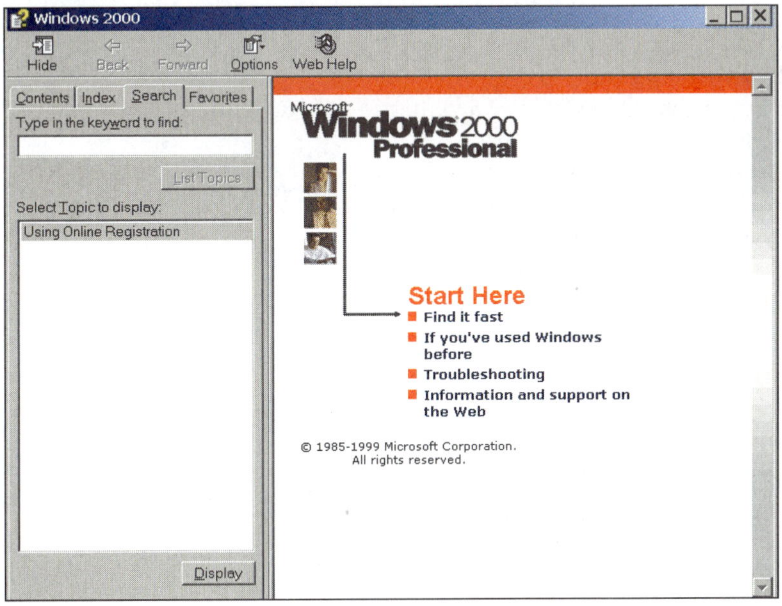

You can enter a word or phrase in the *Type in the keyword to find* list box. If you want to find help topics that contain a specific phrase, enclose the phrase in quotation marks. This tells Help to display only those topics that contain all the words in the phrase in the specific order.

If you repeatedly use a Help topic, you can add it to the Favorites tab. To do this, display the Help window and then display the desired topic. With the topic displayed in the pane at the right side of the window, click the Favorites tab. Click the Add button and the topic name is added to the list box located in the pane at the left side of the window. The next time you want to display the Help topic, display the Help window, click the Favorites tab, and then double-click the desired topic.

exercise 12

USING THE HELP WINDOW WITH THE INDEX TAB AND THE SEARCH TAB SELECTED

1. At the Windows 2000 desktop, use the Help feature to learn about deleting files and folders to the Recycle Bin by completing the following steps:
   a. Click the Start button and then click *Help* at the pop-up menu.
   b. At the Help window, click the Index tab.
   c. With the insertion point positioned in the *Type in the keyword to find* text box, key **deleting files**.
   d. At the list of topics that displays in the list box in the pane at the left side of the window, double-click the subtopic *Recycle Bin* that displays below the *deleting files* topic.
   e. At the Topics Found dialog box with the *Delete or restore files in the Recycle Bin* topic selected, click the Display button.
   f. Read the information that displays in the pane at the right side of the window.
   g. Click Related Topics that displays at the bottom of the pane at the right side of the window.
   h. At the pop-up list box that displays, click the *Remove items permanently when you delete them* topic.
   i. Read the information that displays in the pane at the right side of the window.
   j. Click the Close button (contains an X) that displays in the upper right corner of the Help window.
2. Use the Help feature to search for information on the Display Properties dialog box by completing the following steps:
   a. Click the Start button and then click *Help* at the pop-up menu.
   b. At the Help window, click the Search tab.
   c. Key **"Display Properties dialog box"** in the *Type in the keyword to find* text box. (Make sure you key the quotation marks.)
   d. Click the List Topics button.
   e. When a list of topics displays, double-click *Display overview*. (This displays the topic in the pane at the right side of the window with the phrase *Display Properties dialog box* selected.)
   f. Read the information that displays in the pane at the right side of the window.
   g. Select the text currently displayed in the *Type in the keyword to find* text box and then key **Display Properties dialog box** (without the quotation marks).
   h. Press Enter or click the List Topics button.
   i. Notice the list of topics that displays is different than the list that displayed for the previous search. Double-click one of the topics in the list and notice that the topic displays with one or more of the words in the phrase selected.
   j. Close the Help window.

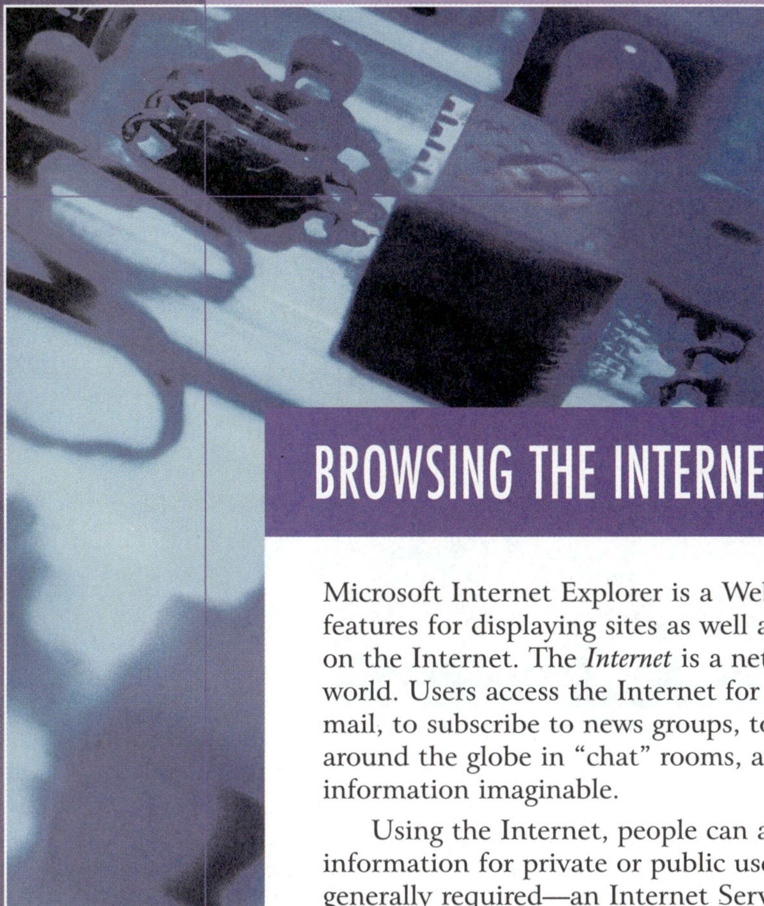

OFFICE XP

BROWSING THE INTERNET USING INTERNET EXPLORER

Microsoft Internet Explorer is a Web browser program with options and features for displaying sites as well as navigating and searching for information on the Internet. The *Internet* is a network of computers connected around the world. Users access the Internet for several purposes: to communicate using e-mail, to subscribe to news groups, to transfer files, to socialize with other users around the globe in "chat" rooms, and largely to access virtually any kind of information imaginable.

Using the Internet, people can access a phenomenal amount of information for private or public use. To use the Internet, three things are generally required—an Internet Service Provider (ISP), a program to browse the Web (called a *Web browser*), and a *search engine*. In this section, you will learn how to use the Internet Explorer Web browser to browse web sites, search for specific sites, and download a web page and image.

Browsing the Internet

You will use the Microsoft Internet Explorer Web browser to locate information on the Internet. Uniform Resource Locators, referred to as URLs, are the method used to identify locations on the Internet. The steps for browsing the Internet vary but generally include: opening Internet Explorer, keying the URL for the desired site, navigating the various pages of the site, printing web pages, and then closing Internet Explorer.

To launch Internet Explorer, double-click the Internet Explorer icon on the Windows desktop. Figure IE.1 identifies the elements of the Internet Explorer, version 5.5, window. The web page that displays in your Internet Explorer window may vary from what you see in Figure IE.1.

FIGURE IE.1 *Internet Explorer Window*

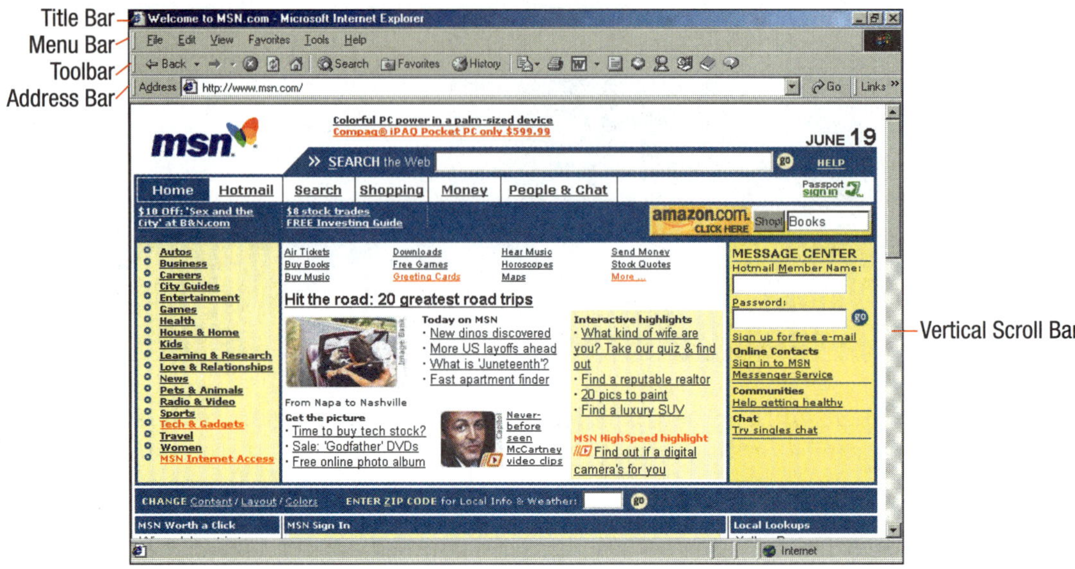

If you know the URL for the desired web site, click in the Address bar, key the URL, and then press Enter. In a few moments, the web site opening page displays in the Internet Explorer window. URLs (Uniform Resource Locators) are the method used to identify locations on the Internet. The format of a URL is *http://server-name.path*. The first part of the URL, *http* stands for HyperText Transfer Protocol, which is the protocol or language used to transfer data within the World Wide Web. The colon and slashes separate the protocol from the server name. The server name is the second component of the URL. For example, in the URL http://www.microsoft.com, the server name is *microsoft*. The last part of the URL specifies the domain to which the server belongs. For example, *.com* refers to "commercial" and establishes that the URL is a commercial company. Other examples of domains include *.edu* for "educational," *.gov* for "government," and *.mil* for "military."

exercise 1

BROWSING THE INTERNET WITH INTERNET EXPLORER

1. Make sure you are connected to the Internet through an Internet Service Provider and that the Windows desktop displays. (Check with your instructor to determine if you need to complete steps for accessing the Internet.)
2. Launch Microsoft Internet Explorer by double-clicking the Internet Explorer icon located on the Windows desktop.
3. At the Internet Explorer window, explore the web site for Yosemite National Park by completing the following steps:
   a. Click in the Address bar, key **www.nps.gov/yose** and then press Enter.

b. Scroll down the web site home page for Yosemite National Park by clicking the down-pointing triangle on the vertical scroll bar located at the right side of the Internet Explorer window.

c. Print the web site home page by clicking the Print button located on the Internet Explorer toolbar.

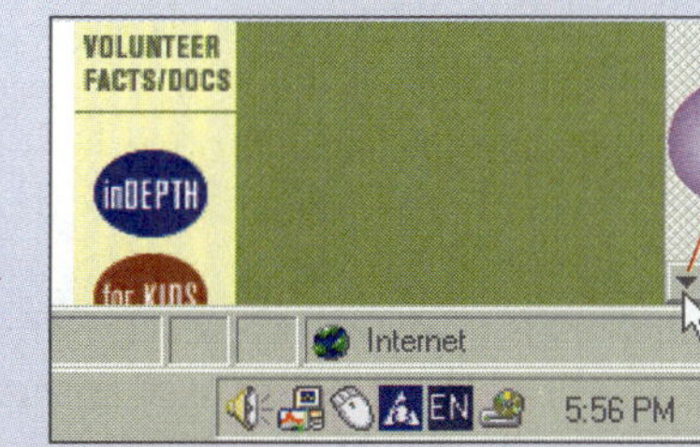

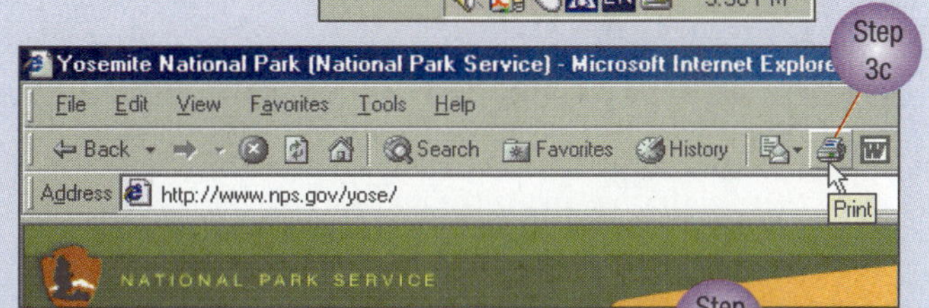

4. Explore the web site for Glacier National Park by completing the following steps:
   a. Click in the Address bar, key **www.nps.gov/glac** and then press Enter.
   b. Print the web site home page by clicking the Print button located on the Internet Explorer toolbar.

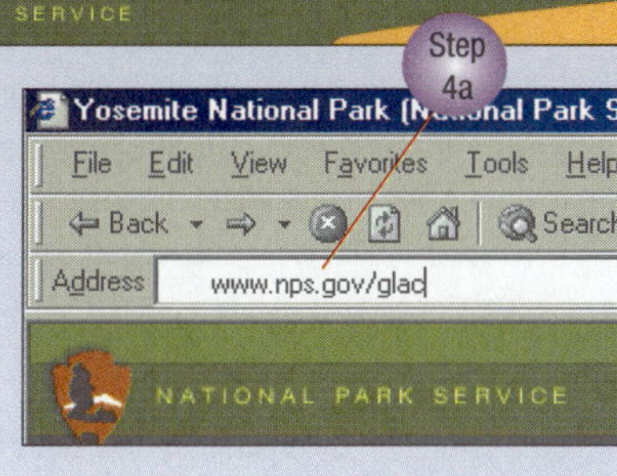

5. Close Internet Explorer by clicking the Close button (contains an X) located in the upper right corner of the Internet Explorer window. (You can also close Internet Explorer by clicking File on the Internet Explorer Menu bar and then clicking Close at the drop-down menu.)

Navigating Using Hyperlinks

Most web pages contain "hyperlinks" that you click to connect to another page within the web site or to another site on the Internet. Hyperlinks may display in a web page as underlined text in a specific color or as images or icons. To use a hyperlink, position the mouse pointer on the desired hyperlink until the mouse pointer turns into a hand, and then click the left mouse button. Use hyperlinks to navigate within and between sites on the Internet. The Internet Explorer toolbar contains a Back button that, when clicked, will take you back to the previous web page. If you click the Back button and then want to go back to the previous page, click the Forward button. By clicking the Back button, you can back your way out of hyperlinks and return to the web site home page.

exercise 2

VISITING WEB SITES AND NAVIGATING USING HYPERLINKS

1. Make sure you are connected to the Internet and then double-click the Internet Explorer icon on the Windows desktop.
2. At the Internet Explorer window, display the White House web page and navigate in the page by completing the following steps:
   a. Click in the Address bar, key **whitehouse.gov** and then press Enter.
   b. At the White House home web page, position the mouse pointer on the *History* hyperlink located towards the left side of the window until the pointer turns into a hand, and then click the left mouse button. (If this hyperlink is not available, click another hyperlink that interests you.)

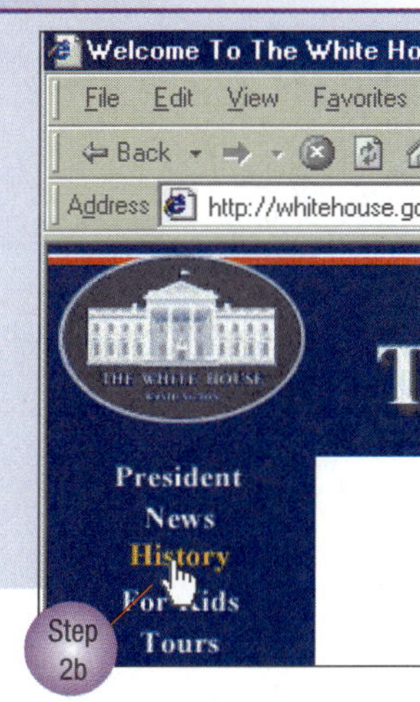

c. At the History web page, click the Back button.

d. At the White House home web page, click the Forward button to return to the History page.

e. Print the History page by clicking the Print button on the Internet Explorer toolbar.

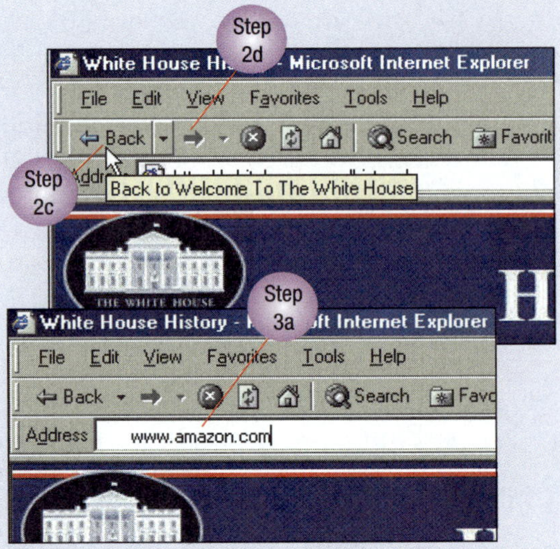

3. Display the Amazon.com web site and navigate in the site by completing the following steps:
   a. Click in the Address bar, key **www.amazon.com** and then press Enter.
   b. At the Amazon.com home page, click a hyperlink related to books.
   c. When a book web page displays, click the Print button on the Internet Explorer toolbar.
4. Close Internet Explorer by clicking the Close button (contains an X) located in the upper right corner of the Internet Explorer window.

Searching for Specific Sites

If you do not know the URL for a specific site or you want to find information on the Internet but do not know what site to visit, complete a search with a search engine. A search engine is a software program created to search quickly and easily for desired information. A variety of search engines are available on the Internet, each offering the opportunity to search for specific information. One method for searching for information is to click the Search button on the Internet Explorer toolbar. This displays a Search pane, as shown in figure IE.2 with options for completing a search. Another method for completing a search is to visit the web site home page for a search engine and use options at the site.

FIGURE IE.2 ***Internet Explorer Search Pane***

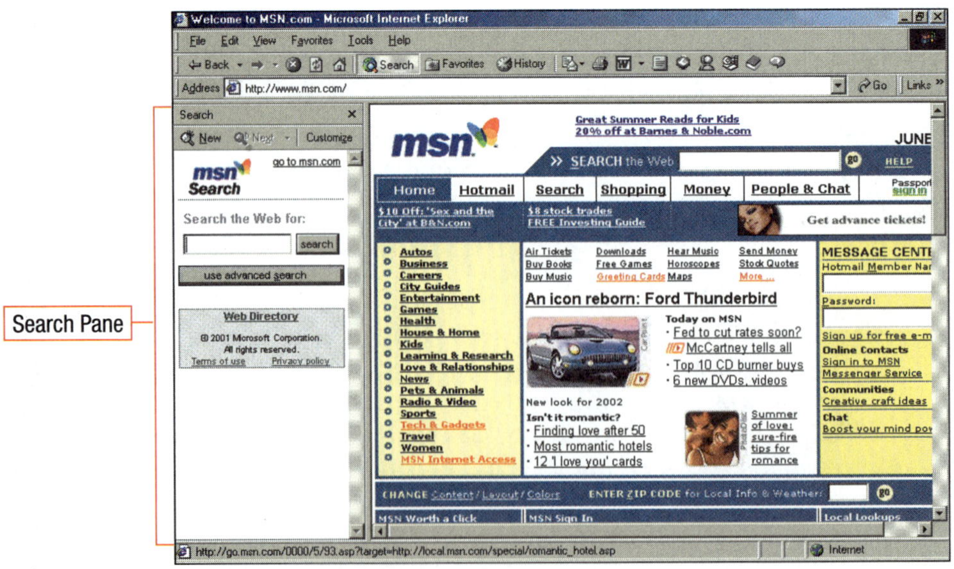

exercise 3

SEARCHING FOR SPECIFIC SITES ON THE WEB

1. Make sure you are connected to the Internet and then double-click the Internet Explorer icon on the Windows desktop.
2. At the Internet Explorer window, search for sites on Bluegrass music by completing the following steps:
   a. Click the Search button on the Internet Explorer toolbar. (This displays the Search pane at the left side of the window.)
   b. Click in the search text box, key **Bluegrass music** and then click the search button.
   c. When a list of sites displays in the Search pane, click a site that interests you.
   d. When the web site home page displays, click the Print button.

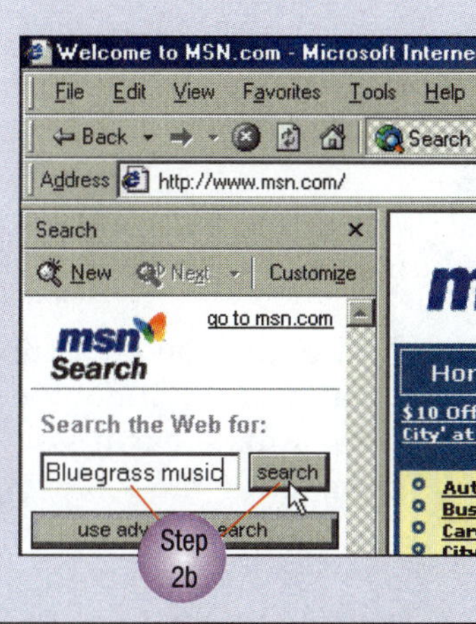

3. Click the Search button on the Internet Explorer toolbar to remove the Search pane.
4. Use the Yahoo search engine to find sites on Bluegrass music by completing the following steps:
   a. Click in the Address bar, key **www.yahoo.com** and then press Enter.
   b. At the Yahoo web site, click in the Search text box, key **Bluegrass music** and then click the Search button (or press Enter). (Notice that the sites displayed vary from the sites displayed in the earlier search.)
   c. Click hyperlinks until a Web site displays that interests you.
   d. When the site displays, click the Print button on the Internet Explorer toolbar.

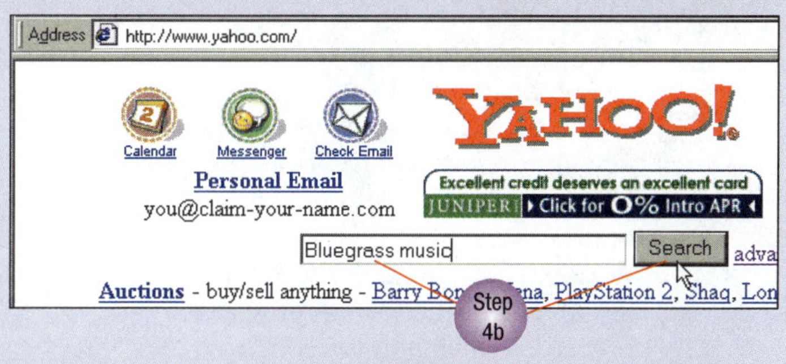

5. Use the Excite search engine to find sites on Jazz music by completing the following steps:
   a. Click in the Address bar, key **www.excite.com** and then press Enter.
   b. When the Excite web site home page displays, click in the Search text box, key **Jazz music** and then click the Search button.
   c. Click a site that interests you.
   d. When the web site home page displays, click the Print button on the Internet Explorer toolbar.

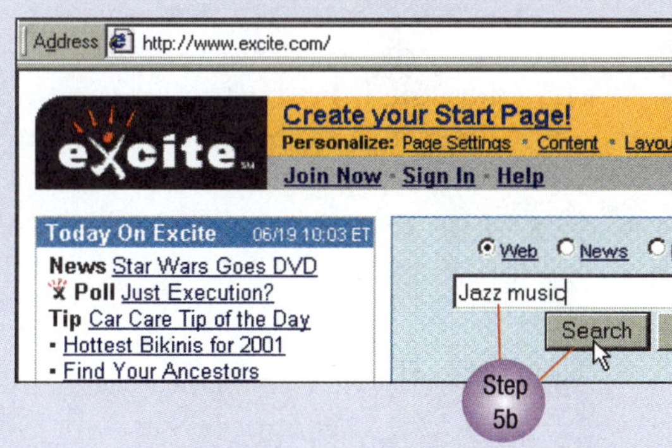

6. Close Internet Explorer.

Completing Advanced Searches for Specific Sites

The Internet contains a phenomenal amount of information. Depending on what you are searching for on the Internet and the search engine you use, some searches can result in several thousand "hits" (sites). Wading through a large number of sites can be very time consuming and counterproductive. Narrowing a search to very specific criteria can greatly reduce the number of hits for a search. To narrow a search, use the advanced search options offered by the search engine.

exercise 4 — NARROWING A SEARCH

1. Make sure you are connected to the Internet and then double-click the Internet Explorer icon on the Windows desktop.
2. Search for sites on skydiving in Oregon by completing the following steps:
   a. Click in the Address bar and then key **www.yahoo.com**.
   b. At the Yahoo web site home page, click the *advanced search* hyperlink.
   c. At the Search Options page, click in the search text box and then key **skydiving in Oregon**.
   d. Click the *An exact phrase match* option in the *Select a search method* section. (This limits the search to any web sites that contain the exact phrase "skydiving in Oregon.")
   e. Click the *Web Sites* option in the *Select a search area* section. (Clicking this option tells Yahoo to display only web sites that contain the exact phrase and not Yahoo categories.)
   f. Click the Search button.
   g. When the list of web sites displays, click a hyperlink that interests you.
   h. Click the Print button on the Internet Explorer toolbar to print the web page.
   i. Click the Back button on the Internet Explorer toolbar until the Yahoo Search Options page displays.

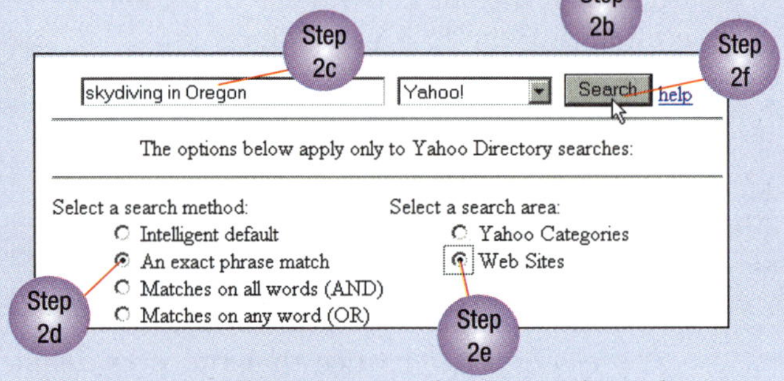

3. Search for specific sites on tandem skydiving and static line skydiving in Oregon by completing the following steps:
   a. Select the text currently displayed in the search text box and then key **skydiving Oregon tandem static line**.
   b. Click the *Matches on all words (AND)* option in the *Select a search method* section. (Clicking this option tells Yahoo to find web sites that contain all of the words keyed in the Search text box.)
   c. Make sure *Web Sites* is selected in the *Select a search area* section.
   d. Click the Search button.
   e. When the list of web sites displays, click a hyperlink that interests you, and then print the web page.
4. Close Internet Explorer.

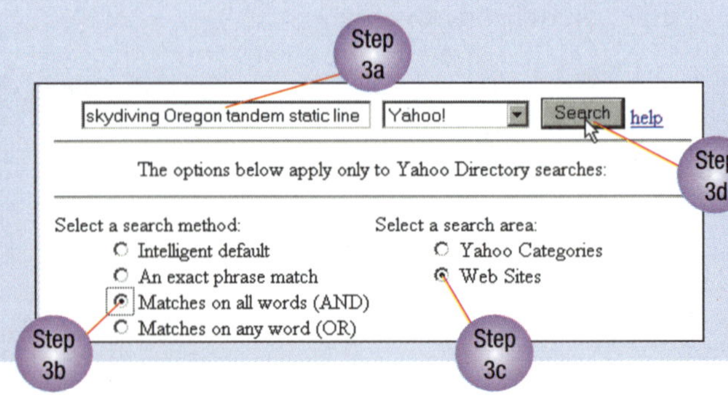

Downloading Images, Text, and Web Pages from the Internet

The image(s) and/or text that display when you open a web page as well as the web page itself can be saved as a separate file. This separate file can be viewed, printed, or inserted in another file. The information you want to save in a separate file is downloaded from the Internet by Internet Explorer and saved in a folder of your choosing with the name you specify. Copyright laws protect much of the information on the Internet. Before using information downloaded from the Internet, check the site for restrictions. If you do use information, make sure you properly cite the source.

exercise 5

DOWNLOADING IMAGES AND WEB PAGES

1. Make sure you are connected to the Internet and then double-click the Internet Explorer icon on the Windows desktop.
2. Download a Web page and image from the Banff National Park by completing the following steps:
   a. Use a search engine of your choosing to search for the Banff National Park web site.
   b. From the list of sites that displays, choose a site that contains information about Banff National Park and at least one image of the park.
   c. Insert a formatted disk in drive A. (Check with your instructor to determine if you should save the web page on a disk or save it into a folder on the hard drive or network.)
   d. Save the web page as a separate file by clicking File on the Internet Explorer Menu bar and then clicking Save As at the drop-down menu.
   e. At the Save Web Page dialog box, click the down-pointing triangle at the right side of the Save in option and then click *3½ Floppy (A:)* at the drop-down list. (This step may vary depending on where your instructor wants you to save the web page.)
   f. Click in the File name text box (this selects the text inside the box), key **Banff Web Page** and then press Enter.
3. Save the image as a separate file by completing the following steps:
   a. Right-click the image of the park. (The image that displays will vary from what you see to the right.)
   b. At the shortcut menu that displays, click Save Picture As.
   c. At the Save Picture dialog box, change the location to drive A (or the location specified by your instructor).

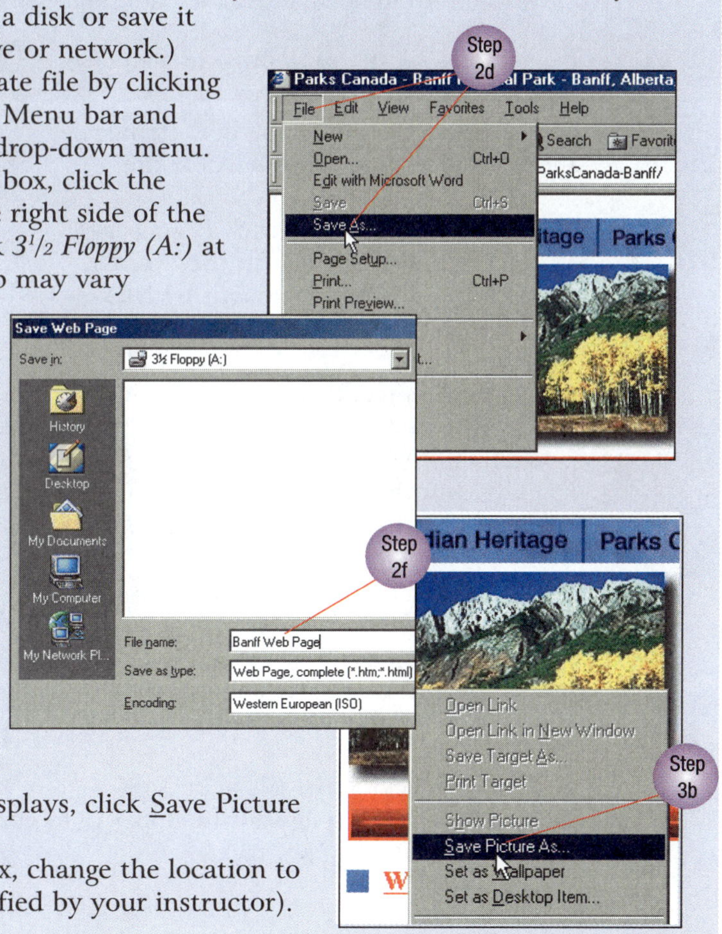

d. Click in the File name text box, key **Banff Image** and then press Enter.

4. Close Internet Explorer.

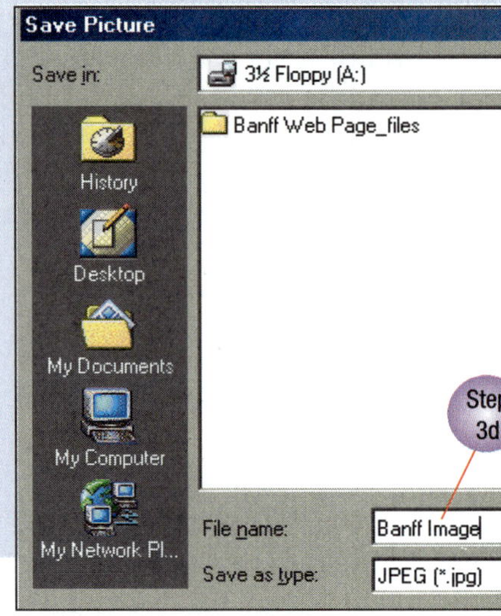

OPTIONAL exercise

OPENING THE SAVED WEB PAGE AND IMAGE IN A WORD DOCUMENT

1. Open Microsoft Word by clicking the Start button on the Taskbar, pointing to Programs, and then clicking Microsoft Word.
2. With Microsoft Word open, insert the Banff image in a document by completing the following steps:
   a. Click Insert on the Menu bar, point to Picture, and then click From File.
   b. At the Insert Picture dialog box, change the Look in option to drive A (or the location where you saved the Banff image) and then double-click *Banff Image*.
   c. When the image displays in the Word document, print the document by clicking the Print button on the Word Standard toolbar.
   d. Close the document by clicking File on the Menu bar and then clicking Close at the drop-down menu. At the message asking if you want to save the changes, click No.

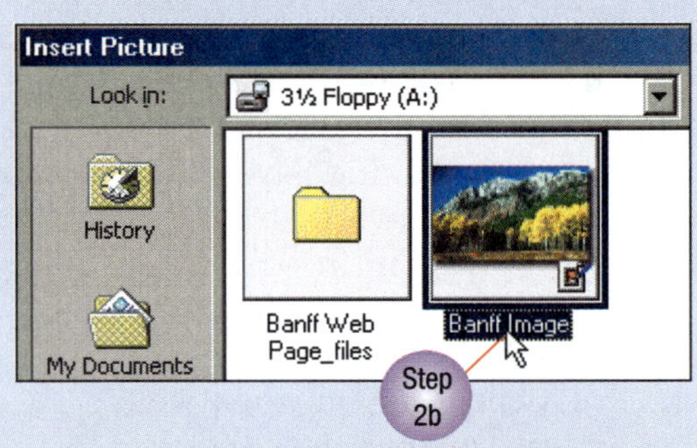

3. Open the Banff Web Page file by completing the following steps:
   a. Click File on the Menu bar and then click Open at the drop-down menu.
   b. At the Open dialog box, change the Look in option to drive A (or the location where you saved the Banff Web page), and then double-click *Banff Web Page*.
   c. Print the web page by clicking the Print button on the Word Standard toolbar.
   d. Close the *Banff Web Page* file by clicking File and then Close.
4. Close Word by clicking the Close button (contains an X) that displays in the upper right corner of the screen.

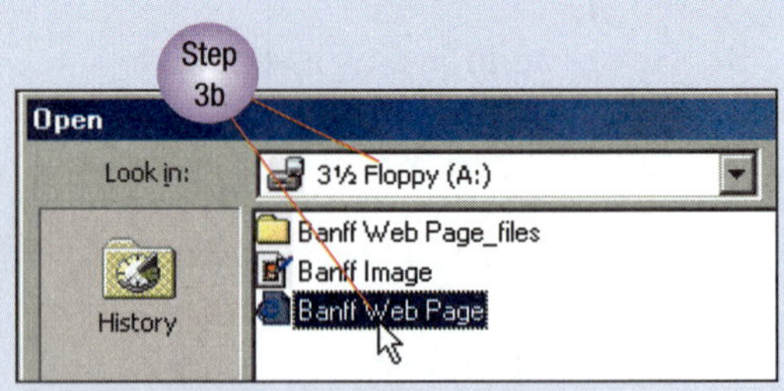

ACCESS

CORE LEVEL UNIT 1: CREATING TABLES, QUERIES, AND FILTERS

Creating a Database Table

Creating Relationships between Database Tables

Creating a Table Using a Wizard and Using Help

Performing Queries and Filtering Records

MICROSOFT® ACCESS 2002

CORE BENCHMARK MOUS SKILLS-UNIT 1

Reference No.	Skill	Pages
Ac2002-1	**Creating and Using Databases**	
Ac2002-1-1	Create Access databases	
	Create a database	C3-C29
Ac2002-1-2	Open database objects in multiple views	C13; C21; C25
Ac2002-1-3	Move among records	C118-C119
Ac2002-1-4	Format datasheets	C14-C16; C19
Ac2002-2	**Creating and Modifying Tables**	
Ac2002-2-1	Create and modify tables	
	Create a table in Design view	C4-C12
	Organize data in a table; determine fields	C4-C7
	Enter data in a table	C13-C16
	Print a table	C16-C18
	Change page setup - margins and orientation	C17-C18
	Create a table using a wizard	C61-C69
	Complete a spelling check	C70; C72
	Find and replace data	C70-C72
Ac2002-2-2	Add a pre-defined input mask to a field	C22-C23; C25-C27
Ac2002-2-3	Create Lookup fields	C23-C27
Ac2002-2-4	Modify field properties	
	Change field width	C19
	Add/delete a field; move a field	C21-C22; C27-C28
Ac2002-3	**Creating and Modifying Queries**	
Ac2002-3-1	Create and modify Select queries	
	Design a query	C85-C92
	Sort fields in a query	C92-C93
	Perform a query with the Simple Query Wizard	C93-C96
Ac2002-3-2	Add calculated fields to Select queries	C97-C98
Ac2002-5	**Viewing and Organizing Information**	
Ac2002-5-1	Enter, edit, and delete records	
	Enter data in a table	C13-C16
	Add/delete a record in a table	C20-C21
Ac2002-5-2	Create queries	C85-C98
Ac2002-5-3	Sort records	C29
Ac2002-5-4	Filter records	
	Filter by selection	C99-C100
	Filter by form	C100-C102
Ac2002-6	**Defining Relationships**	
Ac2002-6-1	Create one-to-many relationships	
	Create a one-to-many relationship	C37-C52
	Print a relationship	C48
	Edit and delete a relationship	C52
Ac2002-6-2	Enforce referential integrity	C45-C52

CHAPTER 1

CREATING A DATABASE TABLE

PERFORMANCE OBJECTIVES

Upon successful completion of chapter 1, you will be able to:

- **Design a database table**
- **Determine fields and assign data types in a database table**
- **Enter data in a database table**
- **Open, save, print, and close a database table**
- **Add and delete records in a database table**
- **Modify a database table by adding, deleting, or moving fields**
- **Use the Input Mask Wizard and the Lookup Wizard**

(Note: There are no data files to copy for this chapter.)

Managing information in a company is an integral part of operating a business. Information can come in a variety of forms, such as data on customers including names, addresses, and telephone numbers; product data; purchasing and buying data; information on services performed for customers or clients; and much more. Most companies today manage data using a database management system software program. Microsoft Office XP Professional includes a database management system software program called *Access*. With Access, you can organize, store, maintain, retrieve, sort, and print all types of business data.

As an example of how Access might be used to manage data in an office, suppose a bookstore decides to send a mailer to all customers who have purchased a certain type of book in the past month (such as autobiographies). The bookstore uses Access and maintains data on customers, such as names, addresses, types of books purchased, and types of books ordered. With this data in Access, the manager of the bookstore can easily select those customers who have purchased or ordered autobiographies in the past month and send a mailer announcing a visit by an author who has just completed writing an autobiography. The bookstore could also use the information to determine what types of books have been ordered by customers in the past few months and use this information to determine what inventory to purchase.

There are a multitude of uses for information in a database. This chapter contains just a few ideas. With a properly designed and maintained database management system, a company can operate smoothly with logical, organized, and useful information. The Access program displays in the Start pop-up menu preceded by a picture of a key, and a key is displayed in the Taskbar when Access is open. The key symbolizes the importance of managing and maintaining data to a company's survival and success.

HINT
Organize data in tables to minimize or eliminate duplication.

Organizing Data in a Database Table

Data is not very useful to a company if it is not organized in a logical manner. Organizing data in a manageable and logical manner allows the data to be retrieved and used for a variety of purposes.

Determining Fields

Microsoft Access is a database management system software program that allows you to design, create, input, maintain, manipulate, sort, and print data. Access is considered a relational database in which you organize data in related tables. In this chapter, you will be creating one table as part of a database file. In a later chapter, you will create a related table within the same database file.

HINT
A database table contains fields that describe a person, customer, client, object, place, idea, or event.

The first step in creating a table is to determine the fields. A field is one piece of information about a person, a place, or an item. For example, one field could be a customer's name, another field could be a customer's address, and another a customer number. All fields for one unit, such as a customer, are considered a record. For example, in exercise 1, a record is all the information pertaining to one employee of Premium Health Services. A collection of records becomes a database table.

When designing a database table, determine fields for information to be included on the basis of how you plan to use the data. When organizing fields, be sure to consider not only current needs for the data but also any future needs. For example, a company may need to keep track of customer names, addresses, and telephone numbers for current mailing lists. In the future, the company may want to promote a new product to customers from specific regions of the country. For this situation, a field that identifies regions must be included in the database. When organizing fields, consider all potential needs for the data but also try to keep the fields logical and manageable.

After deciding what data you want included in a database table, you need to determine field names. Consider the following guidelines when naming fields in a database table:

- Each field must contain a unique name.
- The name should describe the contents of the field.
- A field name can contain up to 64 characters.
- A field name can contain letters, numbers, spaces, and symbols except the period (.), comma (,), exclamation point (!), square brackets ([]), and grave accent (`).
- A field name cannot begin with a space.

In exercise 1, you will create a database table containing information on employees of a medical corporation. The fields in this table and the names you will give to each field are shown in figure 1.1.

FIGURE

1.1 *Field Information and Names for Exercise 1*

Employee Information	Field Name
I.D. number	*Emp #*
Last name	*Last Name*
First name	*First Name*
Middle initial	*Middle Initial*
Street address	*Street Address*
City	*City*
State	*State*
Zip Ccode	*Zip Code*
Date of hire	*Hire Date*
Department code	*Dept Code*

Assigning a Data Type to Fields

Part of the process of designing a database table includes specifying or assigning a data type to each field. The data type specifies the type of data you can enter in a field. Assigning a data type to fields helps maintain and manage the data and helps identify for anyone entering information into the field what type of data is expected. The data types that are available in Access along with a description of each and the field size are shown in figure 1.2.

HINT

Assign a data type for each field that determines the values that can be entered for the field.

FIGURE

1.2 *Data Types*

Assign this data type	*To this type of field*
Text	Assign to a field where text will be entered, such as names, addresses, and numbers that do not require calculations, such as telephone numbers, dates, Social Security numbers, and Zip Codes. A maximum number of 255 characters can be stored in a text data field; 50 characters is the default.
Memo	Assign to a field where more than 255 characters are needed. Up to 64,000 characters can be stored in a memo data field.
Number	Assign to a field where positive and/or negative numbers are to be entered for mathematical calculations, except calculations that involve money or require a high degree of accuracy. A maximum of 15 digits can be stored in a number data field.

Currency	Assign to a field where you do not want calculations rounded off during a calculation. A maximum of 15 digits can be stored in a currency data field.
Date/Time	Assign to a field where a date and/or time will be entered. Eight characters is the default.
AutoNumber	Create a field that automatically enters a number when a record is added. Three types of numbers can be generated: sequential numbers that change by one, random numbers, and replication ID numbers. A maximum of nine digits can be stored in an *AutoNumber* data field.
Yes/No	Assign to a field where data is to be limited to Yes or No, True or False, or On or Off.
OLE Object	Assign to an object such as an Excel spreadsheet or Word document linked to or embedded in an Access table. Up to 1 gigabyte of characters can be stored in the field.
Hyperlink	Assign to text or a combination of text and numbers stored as text and used as a hyperlink address. A hyperlink address can contain up to three parts and each part can contain up to 2,048 characters.
Lookup Wizard	Click this option to start the Lookup Wizard, which creates a *Lookup* field. When the wizard is completed, Access sets the data type based on the values selected during the wizard steps.

When designing a database table, determine the data type that is to be assigned to a field. The fields in exercise 1 will be assigned the data types and field sizes shown in figure 1.3.

FIGURE 1.3 ***Data Types for Exercise 1***

Field Name	**Data Type**
Emp #	Text (Field Size = 5)
Last Name	Text (Field Size = 30)
First Name	Text (Field Size = 30)
Middle Initial	Text (Field Size = 2)
Street Address	Text (Field Size = 30)
City	Text (Field Size = 20)
State	Text (Field Size = 2)
Zip Code	Text (Field Size = 5)
Dept Code	Text (Field Size = 2)
Hire Date	Date/Time

Data entered for some fields in exercise 1, such as *Zip Code,* will be numbers. These numbers, however, are not values and will not be used in calculations. This is why they are assigned the data type of Text (rather than Number or Currency).

During the process of creating the database table, field sizes are assigned. Each field is assigned a default field size as described in figure 1.2. You can, however, specify a maximum field size. For example, a Text data type sets the field size at 50 characters by default. For a field in exercise 1 such as the *Zip Code,* a specific maximum number can be assigned, such as 5 (if you are only using the five-number Zip Code). When assigning a field size, consider the data that will be entered in the field, and then shorten or lengthen the maximum number to accommodate any possible entries. For the *First Name* field or the *Last Name* field, for example, shortening the number to 30 would be appropriate, ensuring that all names would fit in the field. The two-letter state abbreviation will be used in the *State* field, so the number of characters is changed to 2.

Creating a Database Table

Once the fields, field names, and data types have been determined, you are ready to create the database table. To create a database table, you would follow these general steps:

1. Open Access. To do this, click the Start button on the Taskbar, point to *Programs*, and then click *Microsoft Access*.
2. At the blank Access screen, click the *Blank Database* hyperlink located in the New File Task Pane. (The New File Task Pane displays at the right side of the window as shown in figure 1.4.)
3. At the File New Database dialog box shown in figure 1.5, change to the drive where your disk is located, key a name for the database in the File name text box, and then press Enter or click the Create button.
4. At the Database window shown in figure 1.6, double-click *Create table in Design view* in the list box.
5. At the Table1 : Table window shown in figure 1.7, key the first field name in the Field Name text box, and then press Tab. (This moves the insertion point to the Data Type text box and inserts the word *Text*.)
6. With the insertion point positioned in the Data Type text box and the word *Text* inserted in the box, press Tab to move the insertion point to *Description* or change the data type and then press Tab.
7. With the insertion point positioned in the Description text box, key a description of the field, and then press Tab.
8. Continue keying field names, assigning a data type to each field, and keying a description of all fields.
9. When all fields have been keyed, click File and then Save, or click the Save button on the Table Design toolbar.
10. At the Save As dialog box shown in figure 1.8, key a name for the table in the top text box, and then press Enter or click OK.
11. A message displays telling you that no primary key is defined and asking if you want to create one. At this message, click No. (You will learn more about primary keys in chapter 2.)
12. Click File and then Close to close the database table.

HINT

Provide full descriptions of fields in a table if other users will be maintaining the database.

Save

FIGURE 1.4 *Microsoft Access Screen*

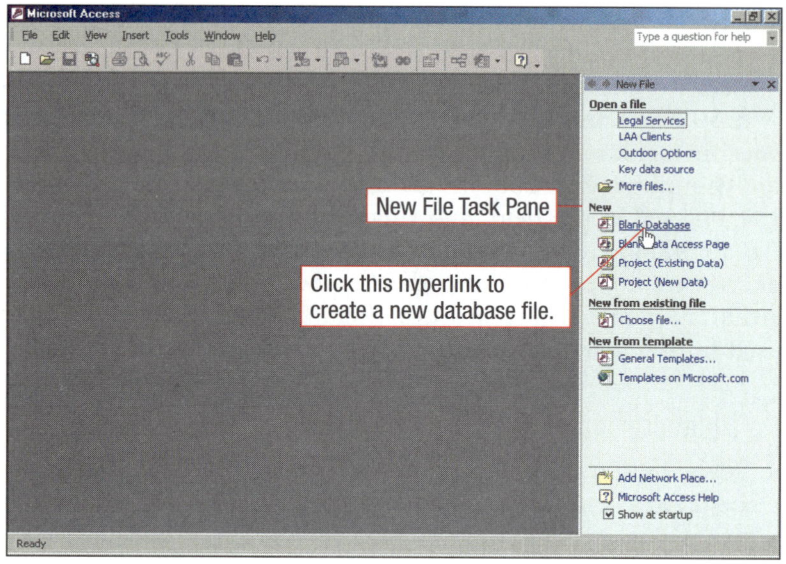

FIGURE 1.5 *File New Database Dialog Box*

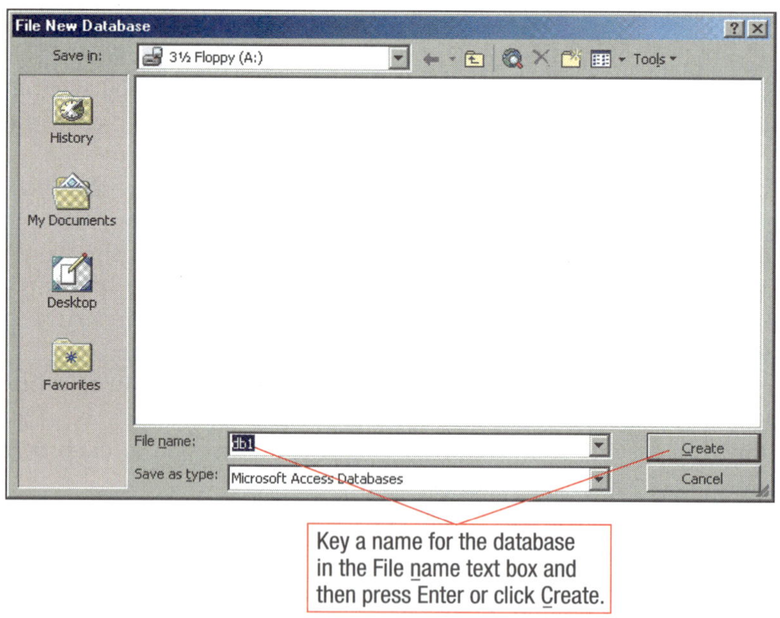

FIGURE 1.6 **Database Window**

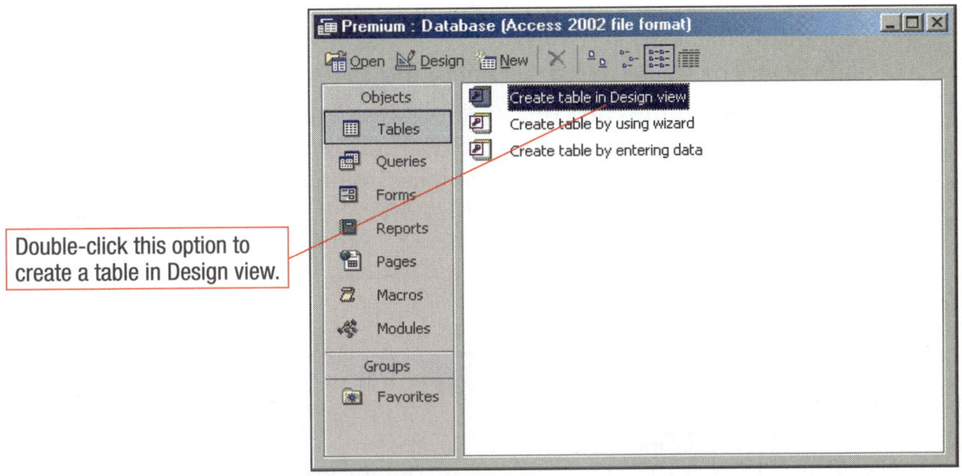

FIGURE 1.7 **Table1 : Table Window**

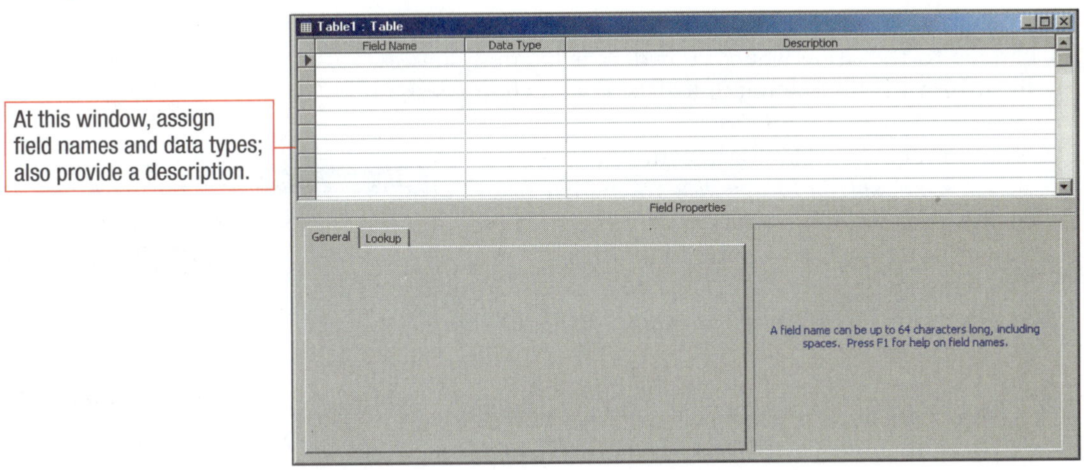

FIGURE 1.8 **Save As Dialog Box**

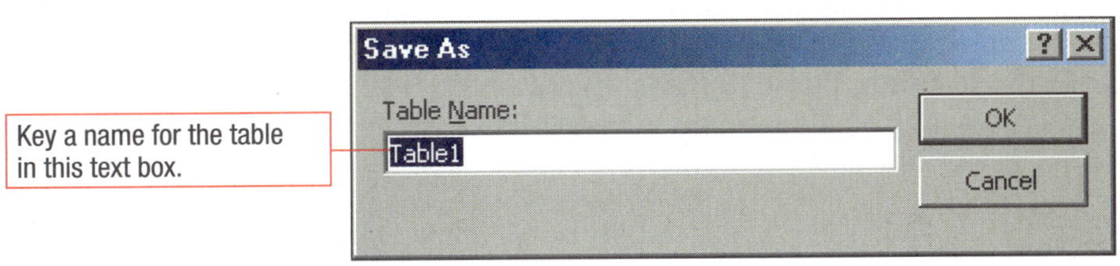

At the Table window shown in figure 1.7, field names are entered, data types are assigned, and descriptions are keyed. When assigning a data type, Access displays information in the bottom portion of the window in a section with the General tab selected. Information in this section can be changed to customize a data type for a field. For example, you can specify that only a maximum of two characters can be entered in the *Middle Initial* field.

A database file can contain more than one table. Tables containing related data are saved in the same database. In exercise 1, you will create a table named Employees that is part of the database file named Premium. In exercise 2, you will create another table as part of the Premium database that includes payroll information.

exercise 1

CREATING AN EMPLOYEES TABLE

(Note: Insert a blank formatted disk before completing exercise 1.)

1. Open Access by clicking the Start button on the Taskbar, pointing to *Programs*, and then clicking *Microsoft Access*.
2. At the blank Access screen, click the *Blank Database* hyperlink located in the New section of the New File Task Pane.
3. At the File New Database dialog box (see figure 1.5), change to the drive where your disk is located, key **Premium** in the File name text box, and then press Enter or click the Create button.
4. At the Premium : Database window, double-click *Create table in Design view* in the list box.
5. At the Table1 : Table window, key the fields shown in figure 1.9 by completing the following steps:
   a. Key **Emp #** in the Field Name text box and then press Tab.
   b. The word *Text* is automatically inserted in the Data Type text box. Change the field size from the default of 50 to 5. To do this, select *50* that displays after *Field Size* in the Field Properties section of the window and then key **5**.
   c. Position the I-beam pointer in the Description text box (for the *Emp #* field) and then click the left mouse button. (You can also press F6 to switch to the top of the window and then press Tab to move the insertion point to the Description text box.) Key **Employee number** in the Description text box and then press Tab.
   d. Key **Last Name** in the Field Name text box and then press Tab.
   e. Change the field size to 30 and then click in the Description text box for the *Last Name* field (or press F6 and then press Tab). Key **Employee last name** and then press Tab.
   f. Key **First Name** in the Field Name text box and then press Tab.

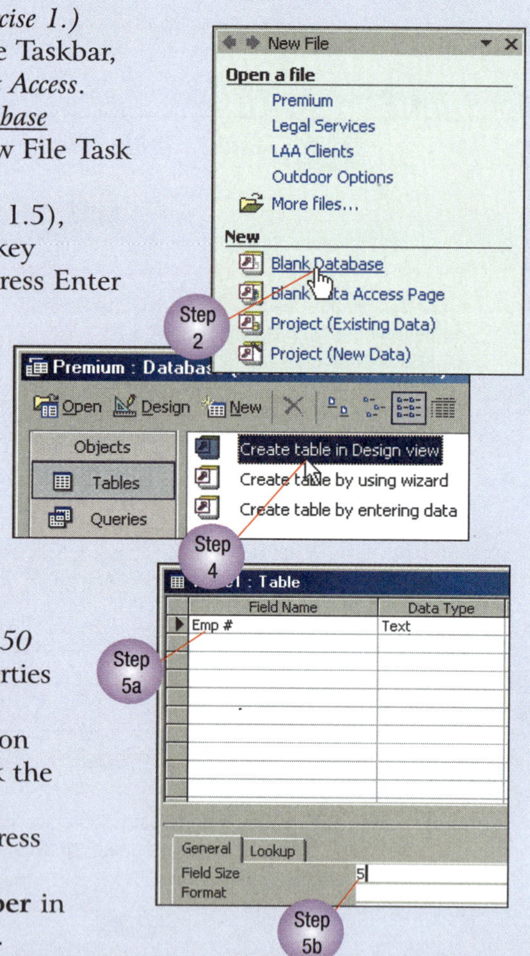

g. Change the field size to 30 and then click in the Description text box for the *First Name* field (or press F6 and then press Tab). Key **Employee first name** and then press Tab.

h. Continue keying the field names, data types, and descriptions as shown in figure 1.9. Refer to figure 1.3 for the text field sizes. To change the Data Type for the *Hire Date* field, click the down-pointing triangle after *Text* and then click *Date/Time* in the drop-down list.

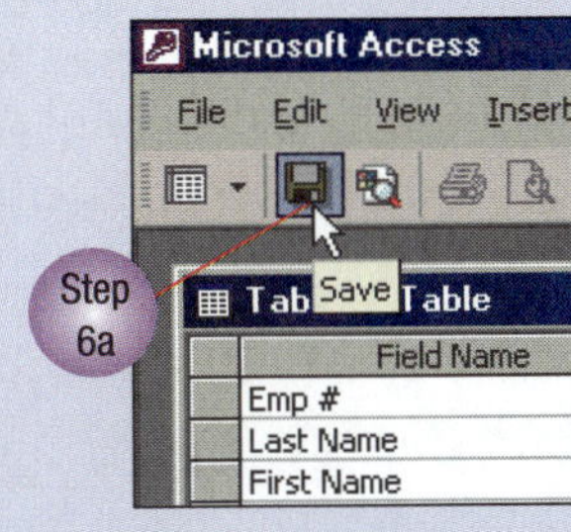

6. When all of the fields are entered, save the table by completing the following steps:
   a. Click the Save button on the Table Design toolbar.
   b. At the Save As dialog box, key **Employees** in the text box, and then press Enter or click OK.
   c. At the message telling you that no primary key is defined and asking if you want to create one, click No. (You will learn more about primary keys in chapter 2.)

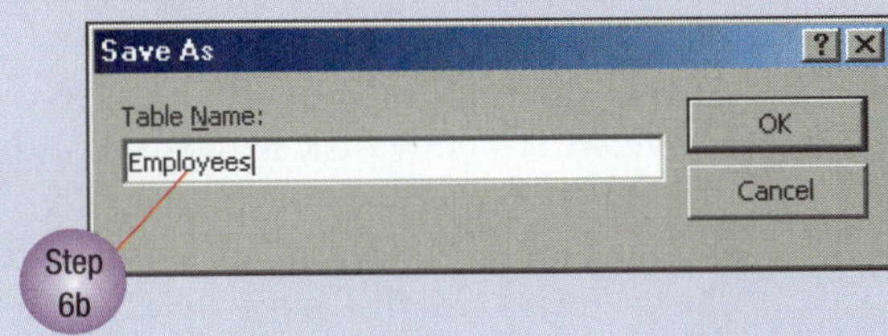

7. Close the Employees table by clicking File and then Close or clicking the Close button located in the upper right corner of the window.
8. Close the Premium database file by clicking File and then Close or clicking the Close button located in the upper right corner of the window at the right side of the Title bar.

FIGURE 1.9 *Exercise 1*

Table1 : Table

Field Name	Data Type	Description
Emp #	Text	Employee number
Last Name	Text	Employee last name
First Name	Text	Employee first name
Middle Initial	Text	Employee middle initial
Street Address	Text	Employee street address
City	Text	Employee city
State	Text	Employee state
Zip Code	Text	Employee Zip code
Dept Code	Text	Department code
Hire Date	Date/Time	Date of hire

In exercise 1, you saved the table containing the fields with the name Employees and then closed the Premium database file. Access automatically saves an open (or active) database on a periodic basis and also when the database is closed. If you are working with a database that is saved on a disk, never remove the disk while the database is open because Access saves the database periodically. If the disk is not in the drive when Access tries to save it, problems will be encountered and you run the risk of damaging the database. Exit (close) Access by clicking the Close button located in the upper right corner of the Access Title bar (contains an *X*) or by clicking File and then Exit.

The Employees table contains a *Dept Code* field. This field will contain a two-letter code identifying the department within the company. In exercise 2, you will create a table named Departments containing only two fields—the department

HINT

The active database is saved automatically on a periodic basis and also when the database is closed.

HINT

If you are working with a database file saved on a floppy disk, never remove the disk while the database file is open. If you do, Access will have problems when trying to automatically save the database.

code and the department name. Establishing a department code decreases the amount of data entered in the Employees table. For example, in an employee record, you key a two-letter code identifying the employee department rather than keying the entire department name. Imagine the time this saves when entering hundreds of employee records. This is an example of the power of a relational database.

exercise 2

CREATING A DEPARTMENT TABLE

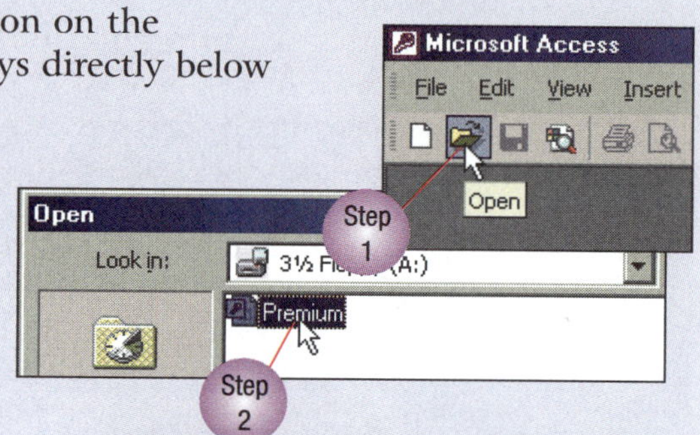

1. At the blank Access screen, click the Open button on the Database toolbar. (The Database toolbar displays directly below the Menu bar.)
2. At the Open dialog box, make sure the drive is active where your disk is located and then double-click *Premium* in the list box.
3. At the Premium : Database window, double-click *Create table in Design view* in the list box.

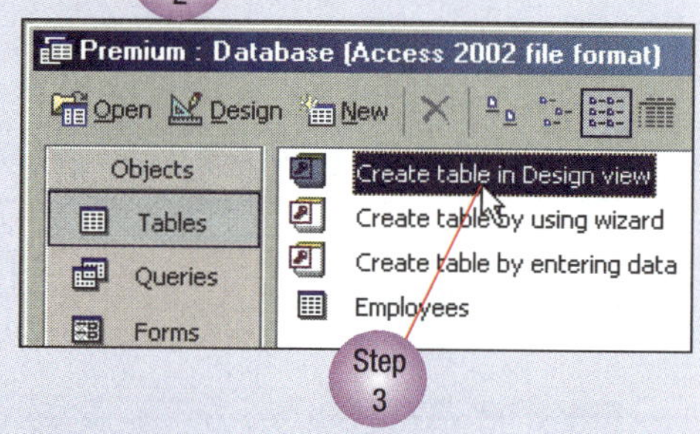

4. At the Table1 : Table window, key the fields shown in figure 1.10 by completing the following steps:
   a. Key **Dept Code** in the Field Name text box and then press Tab.
   b. Change the field size to 2 and then click in the Description text box for the *Dept Code* field.
   c. Key **Department code** in the Description text box and then press the Tab key.
   d. Key **Department** in the Field Name text box and then press Tab.
   e. Change the field size to 30 and then click in the Description text box for the *Department* field.
   f. Key **Department name** in the Description text box.
5. When all of the fields are entered, save the table by completing the following steps:

   a. Click the Save button on the Table Design toolbar.
   b. At the Save As dialog box, key **Departments** in the text box, and then press Enter or click OK.
   c. At the message telling you that no primary key is defined and asking if you want to create one, click No. (You will learn more about primary keys in chapter 2.)
6. Close the Departments table by clicking File and then Close or clicking the Close button located in the upper right corner of the window.
7. Close the Premium database file by clicking File and then Close or clicking the Close button located in the upper right corner of the window at the right side of the Title bar.

FIGURE 1.10 ***Exercise 2***

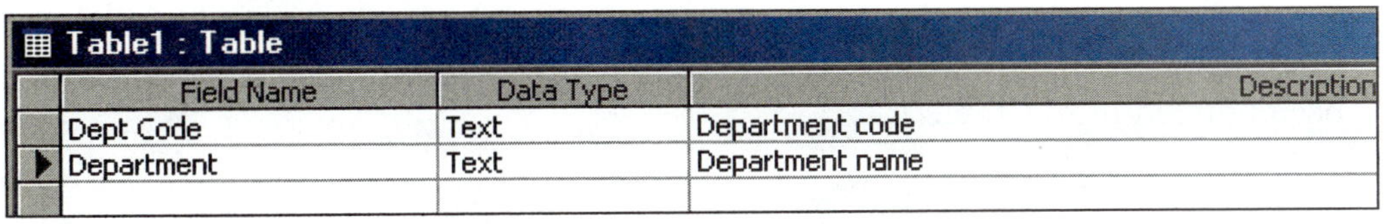

Table1 : Table

Field Name	Data Type	Description
Dept Code	Text	Department code
Department	Text	Department name

Entering Data in a Table

After a table has been designed with the necessary fields and has been created in Access, the next step is to input the data. One method for entering data into a table is to change to the Datasheet view. A table datasheet displays the contents of a table in rows and columns in the same manner as a Word table or Excel worksheet. Each row in a datasheet represents one record. In the Employees table of the Premium database, one record will contain the information for one employee.

Opening a Database File

Open

To open a database file, click the Open button on the Database toolbar or click File and then Open. At the Open dialog box, double-click the desired database file name in the Open dialog box list box.

Opening a Table

Open a database file and a database window displays similar to the one shown in figure 1.11. Open a specific table in the database file by double-clicking the table name in the list box.

HINT
Only one database file can be open at a time.

FIGURE 1.11 ***Premium : Database Window***

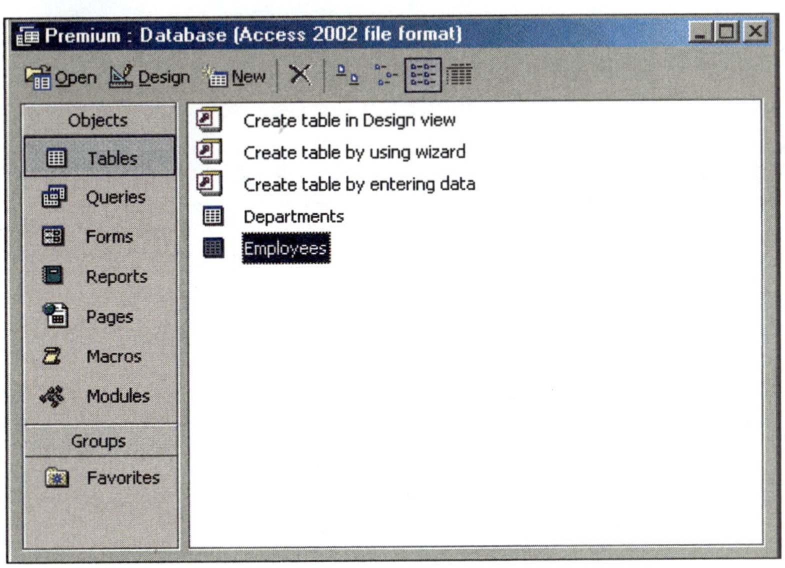

Entering Data in a Table

Open a table and the table displays in the Datasheet view. This is the view needed for entering data in the table. Key data for each field in the table, pressing Tab to move the insertion point from field to field. For example, the Employees table in the Premium database file will display as shown in figure 1.12. (Data has been entered in this table.)

FIGURE 1.12 ***Employees Table in Premium Database***

Employees table in the Premium database file.

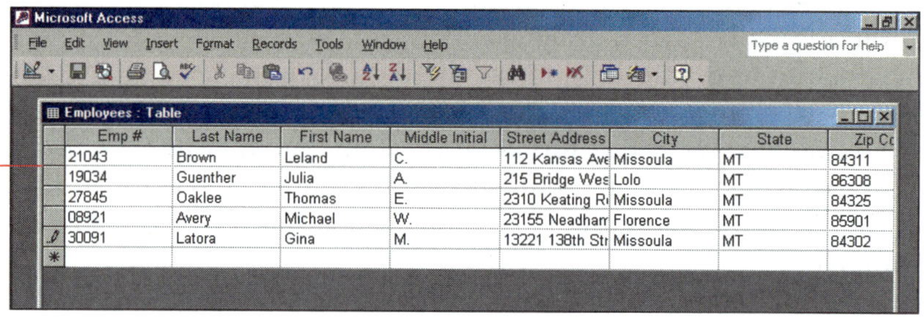

When you key data for the first field in the record, another row of cells is automatically inserted below the first row. Key the data for the first record, pressing Tab to move from field to field. The description you keyed for each field when creating the database table displays at the left side of the Access Status bar. This description reminds you of what data is expected in the field.

If you assigned the Yes/No data type to a field, a square displays in the field. This square can be left empty or a check mark can be inserted. If the field is asking a yes/no question, an empty box signifies "No" and a box with a check mark signifies "Yes." If the field is asking for a true/false answer, an empty box signifies "False" and a box with a check mark signifies "True." This field can also have an on/off response. An empty box signifies "Off" and a box with a check mark signifies "On." To insert a check mark in the box, tab to the field, and then press the spacebar or click in the box using the mouse.

When all records have been entered in the table, close the table and the table is automatically saved.

exercise 3

ENTERING DATA IN THE EMPLOYEES AND THE DEPARTMENTS TABLES

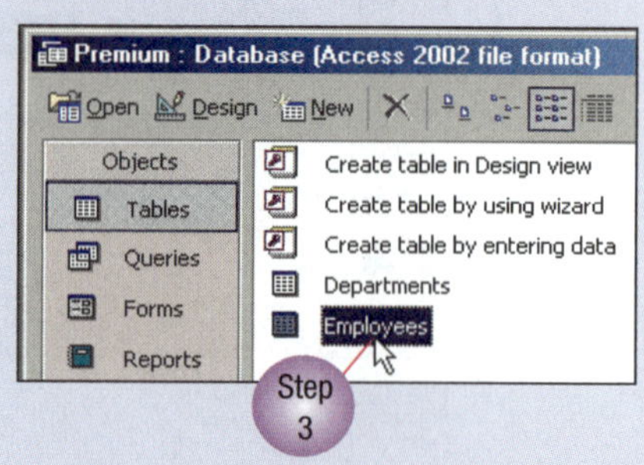

1. At the blank Access screen, click the Open button on the Database toolbar.
2. At the Open dialog box, make sure the drive is active where your disk is located, and then double-click *Premium* in the list box.
3. At the Premium : Database window, double-click *Employees* in the list box.
4. At the Employees : Table window, key the following data for five records in the specified fields. (Press Tab to move the insertion point to the next field or press

Shift + Tab to move the insertion point to the previous field. After entering data into the last field of a record, press Tab to go to the first field of a new record. You may notice a slight pause while the finished record is saved automatically. When keying data, not all of the data may be visible. You will adjust column widths in a later exercise.)

Emp #	=	**21043**
Last Name	=	**Brown**
First Name	=	**Leland**
Middle Initial	=	**C.**
Street Address	=	**112 Kansas Avenue**
City	=	**Missoula**
State	=	**MT**
Zip Code	=	**84311**
Dept Code	=	**PA**
Hire Date	=	**11/5/1995**

Emp #	=	**19034**
Last Name	=	**Guenther**
First Name	=	**Julia**
Middle Initial	=	**A.**
Street Address	=	**215 Bridge West**
City	=	**Lolo**
State	=	**MT**
Zip Code	=	**86308**
Dept Code	=	**MS**
Hire Date	=	**2/15/1990**

Emp #	=	**27845**
Last Name	=	**Oaklee**
First Name	=	**Thomas**
Middle Initial	=	**E.**
Street Address	=	**2310 Keating Road**
City	=	**Missoula**
State	=	**MT**
Zip Code	=	**84325**
Dept Code	=	**HR**
Hire Date	=	**6/8/1996**

Emp #	=	**08921**
Last Name	=	**Avery**
First Name	=	**Michael**
Middle Initial	=	**W.**
Street Address	=	**23155 Neadham Avenue**
City	=	**Florence**
State	=	**MT**
Zip Code	=	**85901**
Dept Code	=	**PA**
Hire Date	=	**11/5/1995**

Emp #	=	**30091**
Last Name	=	**Latora**
First Name	=	**Gina**
Middle Initial	=	**M.**
Street Address	=	**13221 138th Street**
City	=	**Missoula**
State	=	**MT**
Zip Code	=	**84302**
Dept Code	=	**HR**
Hire Date	=	**9/16/2000**

5. Close the Employees table by clicking File and then Close or by clicking the Close button in the upper right corner of the window. (The table is automatically saved.)
6. At the Premium : Database window, double-click *Departments* in the list box.

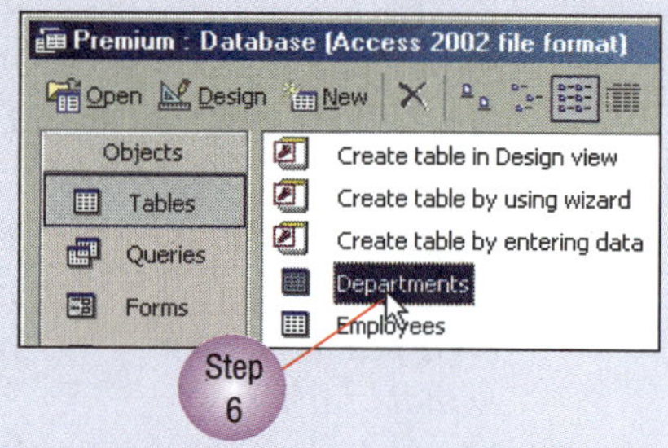

7. At the Departments : Table window, key the following data for four departments in the specified fields (press Tab to move the insertion point to the next field or press Shift + Tab to move the insertion point to the previous field):

Dept Code	=	**IS**
Department	=	**Information Services**
Dept Code	=	**HR**
Department	=	**Human Resources**
Dept Code	=	**MS**
Department	=	**Medical Services**
Dept Code	=	**PA**
Department	=	**Patient Accounts**

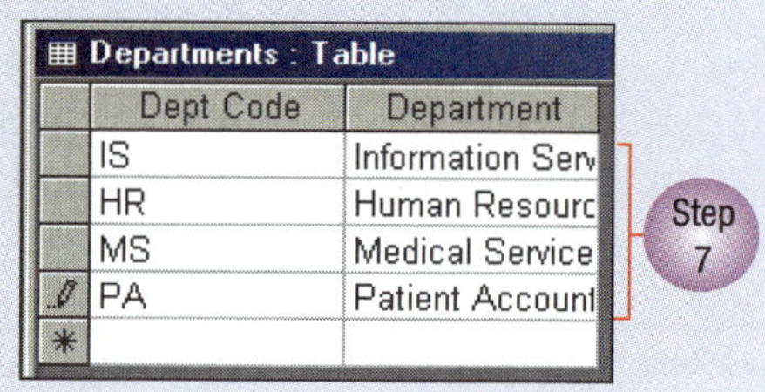

8. Close the Departments table by clicking File and then Close or by clicking the Close button in the upper right corner of the window title bar. (The table is automatically saved.)
9. Close the Premium database file by clicking File and then Close or by clicking the Close button in at the upper right corner of the window title bar.

Printing a Table

Print

Various methods are available for printing data in a table. One method for printing is to open the table and then click the Print button on the Table Datasheet toolbar. This sends the information directly to the printer without any formatting changes. In some fields created in the Employees table, this means that you would not be able to see all printed text in a field if all of the text did not fit in the field. For example, when keying the data in exercise 3, did you notice that the Street Address data was longer than the field column could accommodate? You can change the table layout to ensure that all data is visible. You will first print the Employees and Departments tables with the default settings, learn about changing the layout, and then print the tables again.

exercise 4

PRINTING THE EMPLOYEES AND DEPARTMENTS TABLES WITH THE DEFAULT SETTINGS

1. At the blank Access screen, open the Premium database file.
2. Open the Employees table.
3. Click the Print button on the Table Datasheet toolbar.
4. Close the Employees table.
5. Open the Departments table.
6. Click the Print button on the Table Datasheet toolbar.
7. Close the Departments table.
8. Close the Premium database file.

Look at the printing of the Employees table and notice how the order of records displays differently in the printing (and in the table) than the order in which the records were keyed. Access automatically sorted the records by the Zip Code in ascending order. Access automatically sorted the records in the Departments table alphabetically by department name. You will learn more about sorting later in this chapter.

Changing Page Setup

The Employees table printed on two pages in the Portrait orientation with default margins. The page orientation and page margins can be changed with options at the Page Setup dialog box with either the Margins or the Page tab selected. To display the Page Setup dialog box shown in figure 1.13, you would open the Employees or Departments table, and then click File and then Page Setup.

At the Page Setup dialog box with the Margins tab selected, notice that the default margins are 1 inch. Change these defaults by keying a different number in the desired margin text box. By default, the table name prints at the top center of the page. For example, when you printed the Employees table, *Employees* printed at the top of the page along with the current date (printed at the right side of the page). *Page 1* also printed at the bottom of the page. If you do not want the name of the table and the date as well as the page number printed, remove the check mark from the Print Headings option at the Page Setup dialog box with the Margins tab selected.

Change the table orientation at the Page Setup dialog box with the Page tab selected as shown in figure 1.14. To change to landscape orientation, click Landscape. You can also change the paper size with options in the Paper section of the dialog box and specify the printer with options in the Printer for (table name) section of the dialog box.

HINT
A table can be printed in landscape orientation.

FIGURE

1.13 *Page Setup Dialog Box with Margins Tab Selected*

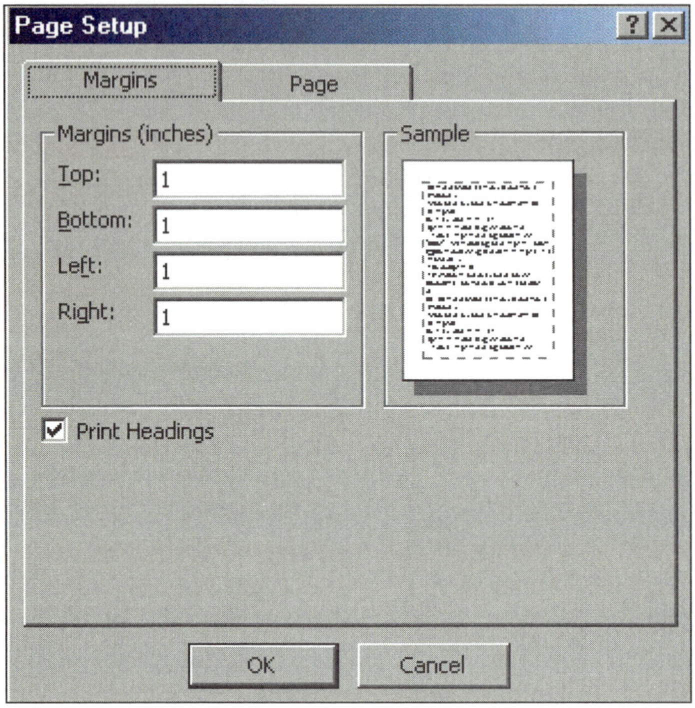

FIGURE

1.14 *Page Setup Dialog Box with Page Tab Selected*

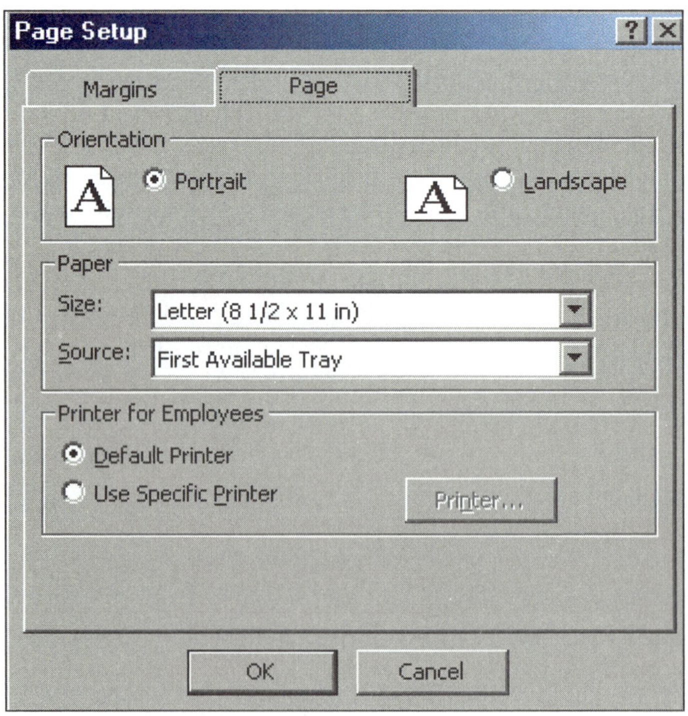

Changing Field Width

In the printing of the Employees table, not all of the data is visible in the *Street Address* field. You can remedy this situation by changing the width of the fields. Automatically adjust one field (column) in a table to accommodate the longest entry in the field by positioning the arrow pointer on the column boundary at the right side of the column until it turns into a double-headed arrow pointing left and right with a double line between and then double-clicking the left mouse button. Automatically adjust adjacent columns by selecting the columns first and then double-clicking on a column boundary. Save changes made to column widths by clicking the Save button on the Table Datasheet toolbar.

HINT

Automatically adjust column widths in an Access table in the same manner as adjusting column widths in an Excel worksheet.

exercise 5

CHANGING PAGE SETUP AND THEN PRINTING THE EMPLOYEES TABLE

1. Open the Premium database file and then open the Employees table.
2. Change the page margins and orientation by completing the following steps:
   a. Click File and then Page Setup.
   b. At the Page Setup dialog box, click the Page tab.
   c. At the Page Setup dialog box with the Page tab selected, click Landscape in the Orientation section.
   d. Click the Margins tab.
   e. At the Page Setup dialog box with the Margins tab selected, select *1* in the Top text box, and then key **2**.
   f. Click OK to close the dialog box.

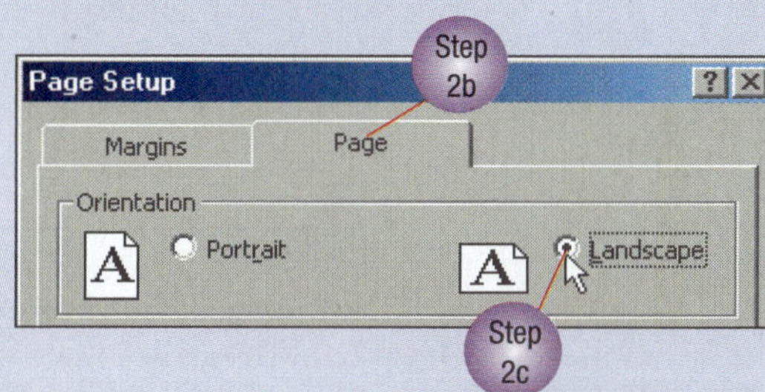

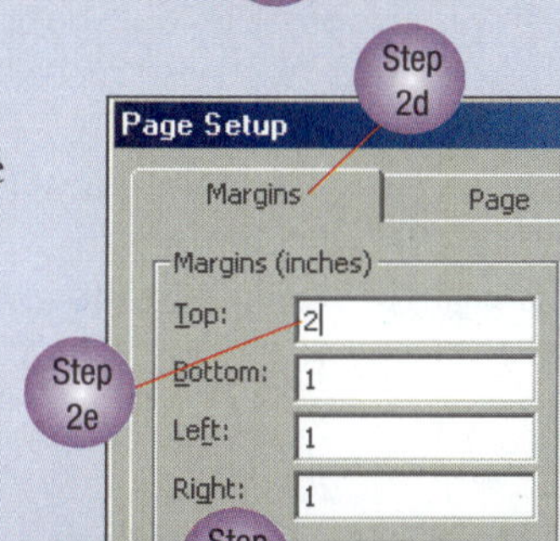

3. Automatically adjust all columns in the table to accommodate the longest entry by completing the following steps:
   a. Position the arrow pointer on the *Emp #* field name (the arrow pointer turns into a down-pointing black arrow).
   b. Hold down the left mouse button, drag the arrow pointer to the *Hire Date* field name, and then release the mouse button. (This selects all columns in the table.)
   c. Position the arrow pointer on one of the column boundaries until it turns into a double-headed arrow pointing left and right with a double line between, and then double-click the left mouse button. (If a column boundary is not visible, click the left scroll arrow at the left side of the horizontal scroll bar until a column boundary is visible.)
   d. Deselect the data by clicking in any field in the table.

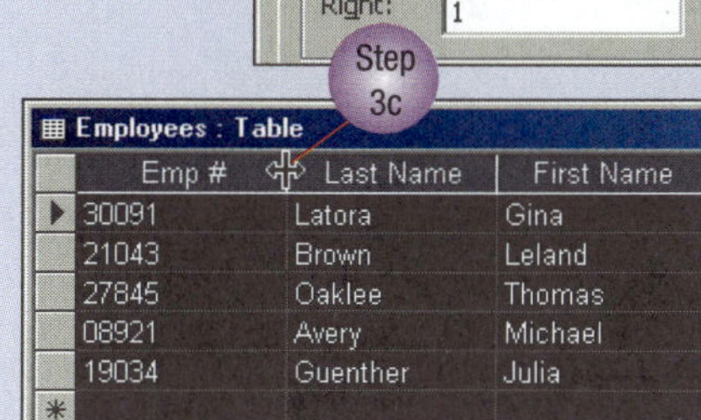

4. Save the database table layout by clicking the Save button on the Table Datasheet toolbar.
5. Send the table to the printer by clicking the Print button on the Table Datasheet toolbar.
6. Close the Employees table and then close the Premium database file.

Maintaining a Table

Once a database table is created, more than likely it will require maintenance. For example, newly hired employees will need to be added to the Employees table. An employee record may need to be deleted when an employee leaves the company. The type of maintenance required on a database table is related to the type of data stored in the table.

Adding a Record to a Table

New Record

Add a new record to an existing table by clicking the New Record button on the Table Datasheet toolbar. Key the data in the appropriate fields.

Deleting a Record in a Table

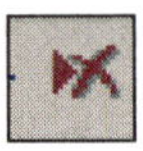

Delete Record

To delete an existing record in a table, click in any field in the row you want to delete, and then click the Delete Record button on the Table Datasheet toolbar. A message displays telling you that you will not be able to undo the delete operation and asking if you want to continue. At this message, click Yes.

exercise 6

ADDING AND DELETING RECORDS IN THE EMPLOYEES TABLE

1. Open the Premium database file and then open the Employees database table.
2. Add two new records to the table by completing the following steps:
   a. Click the New Record button on the Table Datasheet toolbar.

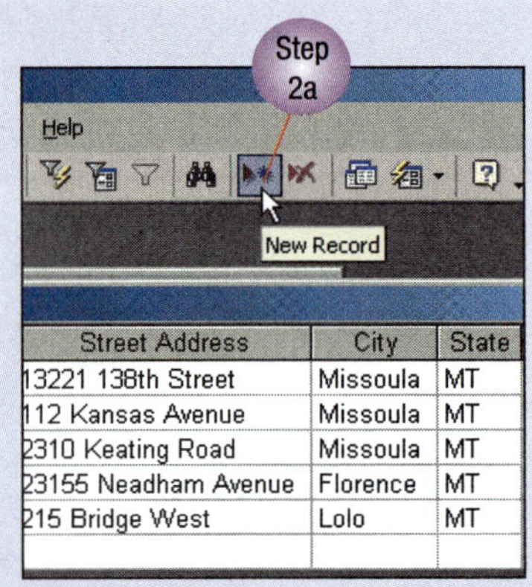

   b. Key the following data in the specified fields:

Emp #	=	**30020**
Last Name	=	**Pang**
First Name	=	**Brian**
Middle Initial	=	**R.**
Street Address	=	**15512 Country Drive**
City	=	**Lolo**
State	=	**MT**
Zip Code	=	**86308**
Dept Code	=	**IS**
Hire Date	=	**8/15/2002**

   c. Click the New Record button on the Table Datasheet toolbar (or, just press the Tab key).
   d. Key the following data in the specified fields:

Emp #	=	**30023**
Last Name	=	**Zajac**
First Name	=	**Elizabeth**
Middle Initial	=	**A.**
Street Address	=	**423 Corrin Avenue**
City	=	**Missoula**

State = **MT**
Zip Code = **84325**
Dept Code = **HR**
Hire Date = **8/15/2002**

3. Delete a record in the table by completing the following steps:
   a. Click anywhere in the last name *Guenther*.
   b. Click the Delete Record button on the Table Datasheet toolbar.
   c. At the message telling you that you will not be able to undo the delete operation and asking if you want to continue, click Yes.
4. Print the Employees table in landscape orientation. (You will need to change to the Landscape orientation at the Page Setup dialog box with the Page tab selected.)
5. Close the Employees table and then close the Premium database file.

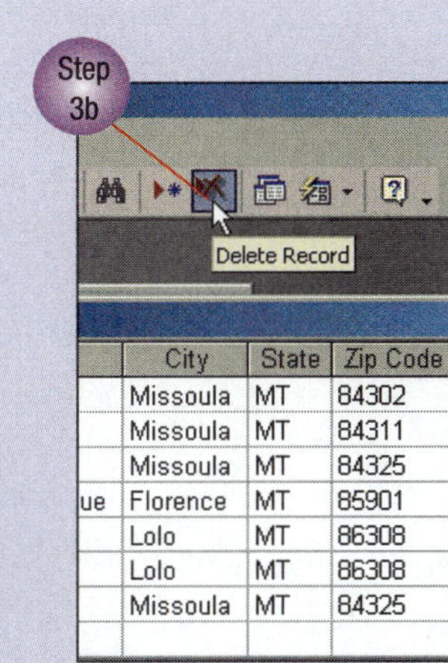

Modifying a Table

Maintaining a table involves adding and/or deleting records as needed. It can also involve adding, moving, changing, or deleting fields in the table. These types of changes modify the structure of the table and are done in the Design view. To display a table in the Design view, open the table, and then click the down-pointing triangle at the right side of the View button (first button from the left). When you click the down-pointing triangle, a drop-down menu displays with two viewing choices—Design View and Datasheet View. Click Design View to change the display of the table. In the Design view, *Field Name*, *Data Type*, and *Description* display at the top of the window and *Field Properties* displays toward the bottom of the window. In the Design view, you can add fields, remove fields, and change the order of fields.

View

In addition to clicking the down-pointing triangle at the right side of the View button, you can also just click the button. If the current view is the Datasheet view, clicking the button will change to the Design view. If the Design view is the current view, clicking the button will change to the Datasheet view. Save changes made to the table design by clicking the Save button on the Table Design toolbar.

Adding a Field

Situations change within a company, and a table must be flexible to accommodate changes that occur with new situations. Adding a field is a change that may need to be made to an existing table. For example, more information may be required to manage the data or an additional field may be needed for accounting purposes. Whatever the reason, being able to add a new field to an existing table is a necessity.

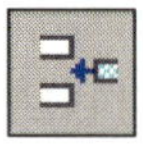

Insert Rows

Undo

Add a row for a new field to an existing table with a button on the Table Design toolbar, an option from the Insert drop-down menu, or a shortcut menu. To add a row for a new field, position the insertion point on any text in the row that will be immediately *below* the new field, and then click the Insert Rows button on the Table Design toolbar; click Insert, then Rows; or position the insertion point on any text in the row that will be immediately *below* the new field, click the *right* mouse button, and then click the left mouse button on *Insert Rows*. If you insert a row for a new field and then change your mind, immediately click the Undo button on the Table Design toolbar.

Deleting a Field

Delete a field in a table and all data entered in that field is also deleted. When a field is deleted it cannot be undone with the Undo button. Delete a field only if you are sure you really want it and the data associated with it completely removed from the table.

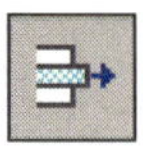

Delete Rows

To delete a field, open the table, and then change to the Design view. Position the insertion point in any text in the row containing the field you want deleted and then click the Delete Rows button on the Table Design toolbar, or click Edit, then Delete Rows. At the message asking if you want to permanently delete the field and all of the data in the field, click Yes.

Using the Input Mask Wizard

For some fields, you may want to control the data entered in the field. For example, in a *Zip Code* field, you may want the nine-digit Zip Code entered (rather than the five-digit Zip Code); or you may want the three-digit area code included in a telephone number. Use the *Input Mask* field property to set a pattern for how data is entered in a field. An input mask ensures that data in records conforms to a standard format. Access includes an Input Mask Wizard that guides you through creating an input mask.

After specifying the Field Size in the Field Properties section of the Table window, click the Input Mask text box. Run the Input Mask Wizard by clicking the button containing the three black dots that appears to the right of the Input Mask text box. This displays the first Input Mask Wizard dialog box as shown in figure 1.15. In the Input Mask list box, choose which input mask you want your data to look like, and then click the Next button. At the second Input Mask Wizard dialog box as shown in figure 1.16, specify the appearance of the input mask and the desired placeholder character, and then click the Next button. At the third Input Mask Wizard dialog, specify whether you want the data stored with or without the symbol in the mask, and then click the Next button. At the fourth dialog box, click the Finish button.

FIGURE 1.15 ***First Input Mask Wizard Dialog Box***

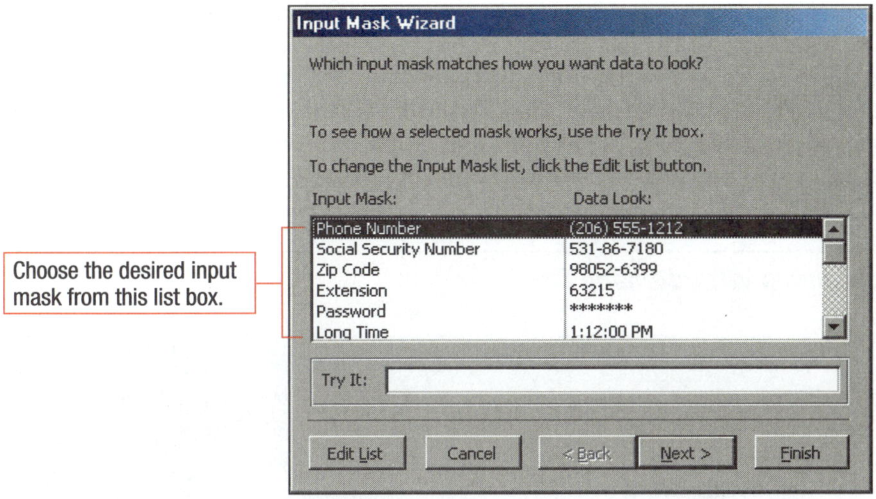

FIGURE 1.16 ***Second Input Mask Wizard Dialog Box***

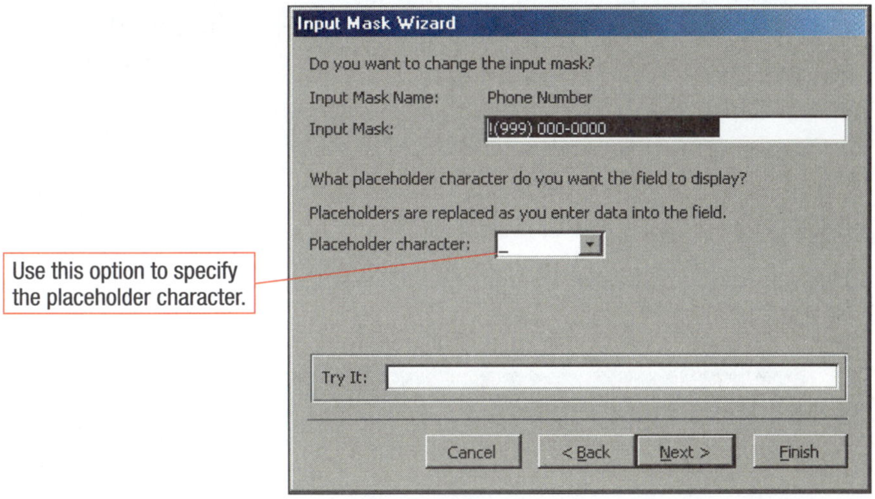

Using the Lookup Wizard

Like the Input Mask Wizard, you can use the Lookup Wizard to control the data entered in a field. Use the Lookup Wizard to confine the date entered into a field to a specific list of items. For example, in exercise 7 you will use the Lookup Wizard to restrict the new *Employee Category* field to one of three choices—*Salaried*, *Hourly*, and *Temporary*. When the user clicks in the field in the datasheet, a down-pointing triangle displays. The user clicks this triangle to display a drop-down list of available entries and then clicks the desired item.

Use the Lookup Wizard when assigning a data type to a field. Click in the Data Type text box and then click the down-pointing triangle that displays at the right side of the box. At the drop-down menu that displays, click *Lookup Wizard*.

This displays the first Lookup Wizard dialog box as shown in figure 1.17. At this dialog box, indicate that you want to enter the field choices by clicking the *I will type in the values that I want.* option, and then click the Next button. At the second Lookup Wizard dialog box shown in figure 1.18, click in the blank text box below *Col1* and then key the first choice. Press the Tab key and then key the second choice. Continue in this manner until all desired choices are entered and then click the Next button. At the third Lookup Wizard dialog box, make sure the proper name displays in the What label would you like for your lookup column? text box, and then click the Finish button.

FIGURE 1.17 **First Lookup Wizard Dialog Box**

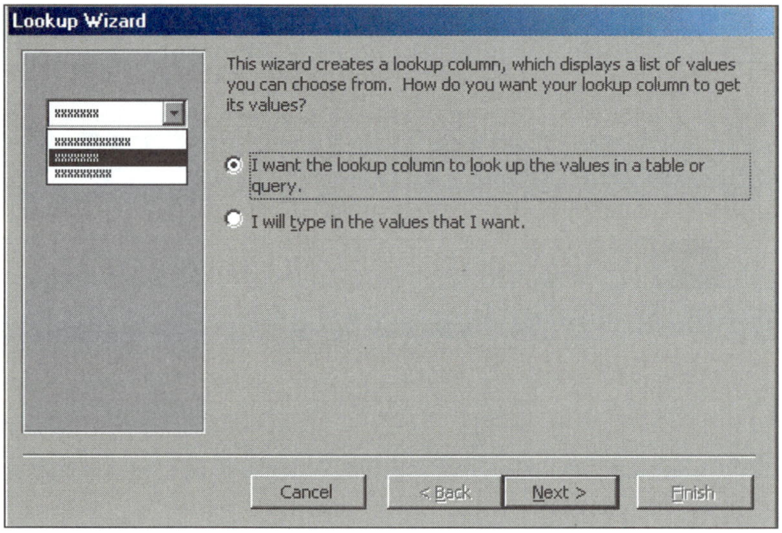

FIGURE 1.18 **Second Lookup Wizard Dialog Box**

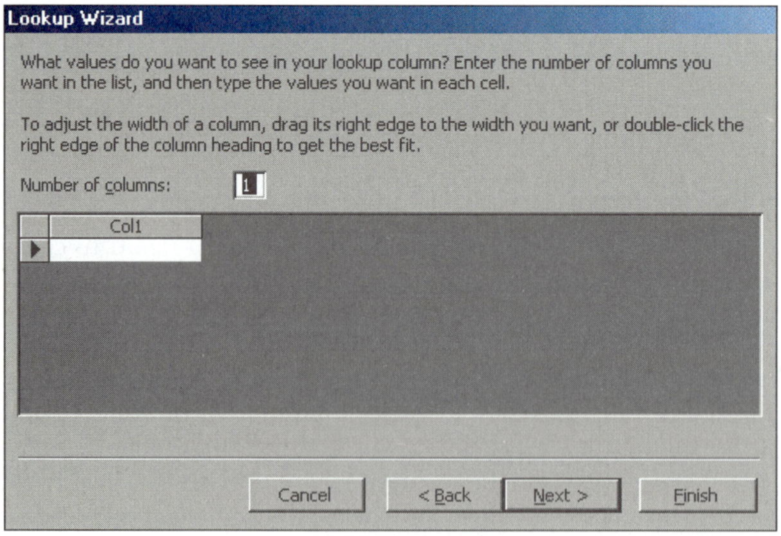

exercise 7

ADDING A FIELD TO AND DELETING A FIELD FROM THE EMPLOYEES TABLE

1. Open the Premium database file and then open the Employees table.
2. Add the field *Telephone* to the table by completing the following steps:
   a. Click the down-pointing triangle at the right side of the View button on the Table Datasheet toolbar (first button from the left).
   b. At the drop-down menu that displays, click *Design View*.
   c. Click anywhere in the text *Hire Date* that displays in the *Field Name* column. (You may need to scroll down the list to display this field.)
   d. Click the Insert Rows button on the Table Design toolbar.
   e. With the insertion point positioned in the new blank cell in the *Field Name* column, key **Telephone**.
   f. Press Tab (this moves the insertion point to the *Data Type* column).
   g. Select *50* that displays in the Field Size text box in the Field Properties section of the window and then key **14**.
   h. Click the Save button to save the table. (You must save the table before using the Input Mask Wizard.)
   i. Click in the Input Mask text box in the Field Properties section of the window.
   j. Click the button containing the three black dots that displays to the right of the Input Mask text box.
   k. At the first Input Mask Wizard dialog box, make sure *Phone Number* is selected in the Input Mask list box, and then click the Next button.
   l. At the second Input Mask Wizard dialog box, click the down-pointing triangle at the right side of the Placeholder character text box, and then click # at the drop-down list.
   m. Click the Next button.
   n. At the third Input Mask Wizard dialog box, click the *With the symbols in the mask, like this* option, and then click the Next button.
   o. At the fourth Input Mask Wizard dialog box, click the Finish button.
   p. Click in the *Description* column in the *Telephone* row and then key **Employee home telephone number**.

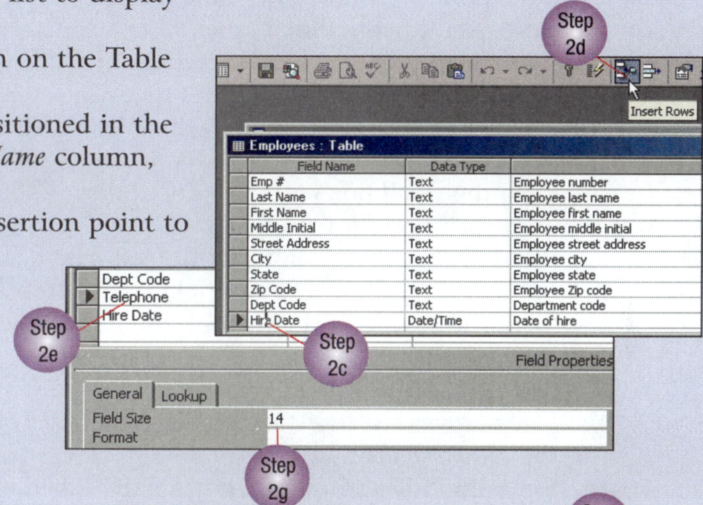

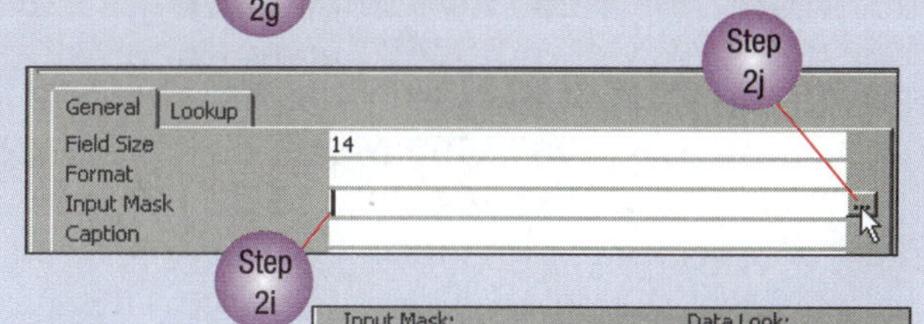

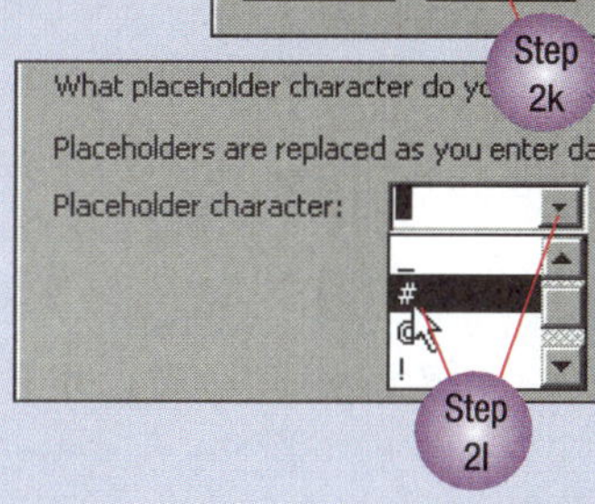

3. Delete the *Hire Date* row by completing the following steps:
   a. Click anywhere in the text *Hire Date* that displays in the *Field Name* column.
   b. Click the Delete Rows button on the Table Design toolbar.
   c. At the message asking if you want to permanently delete the field and the data in the field, click Yes.

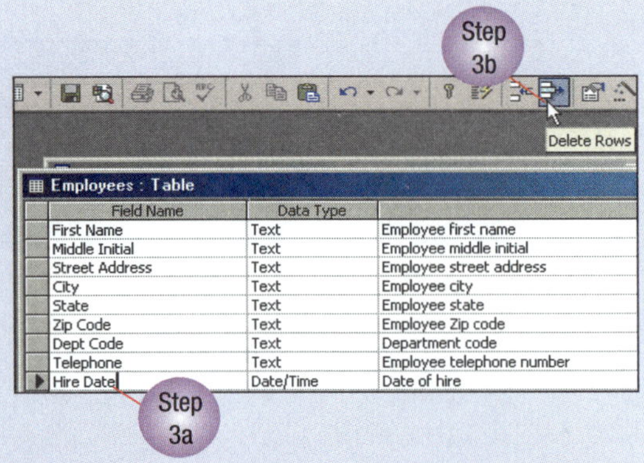

4. Click the Save button on the Table Design toolbar to save the modified table.
5. Add telephone numbers for the records in the Employees table by completing the following steps:
   a. Change to the Datasheet view by clicking the down-pointing triangle at the right side of the View button on the Table Design toolbar and then clicking *Datasheet View*.
   b. Drag the scroll box on the horizontal scroll bar to the right until the *Telephone* field is visible.
   c. Position the arrow pointer at the left side of the first blank cell below the new *Telephone* field until the arrow pointer turns into a thick, white plus symbol and then click the left mouse button. (This selects the entire cell.)
   d. Key **4065556841** and then press the down arrow key. (This moves the insertion point to the next blank cell in the *Telephone* column.)
   e. Key **4065557454** and then press the down arrow key.
   f. Key **4065553495** and then press the down arrow key.
   g. Key **4065557732** and then press the down arrow key.
   h. Key **4065550926** and then press the down arrow key.
   i. Key **4065554509** and then press the down arrow key.

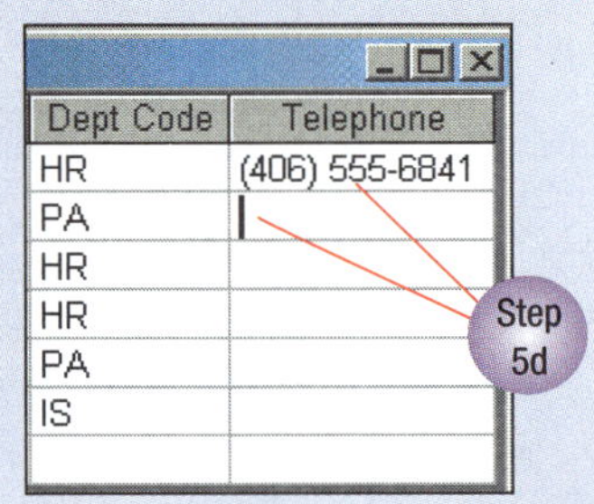

6. Click the Save button again on the Table Datasheet toolbar to save the table.
7. Add the field *Employee Category* and use the Lookup Wizard to specify field choices by completing the following steps:
   a. Change to the Design view by clicking the down-pointing triangle at the right side of the View button on the Table Design toolbar and then clicking *Design View*.
   b. Click anywhere in the text *Dept Code* that displays in the *Field Name* column.
   c. Click the Insert Rows button on the Table Design toolbar.
   d. With the insertion point positioned in the new blank cell in the *Field Name* column, key **Employee Category**.
   e. Press Tab (this moves the insertion point to the *Data Type* column).
   f. Click the down-pointing triangle at the right side of the text box and then click *Lookup Wizard* at the drop-down list.
   g. At the first Lookup Wizard dialog box, click the *I will type in the values that I want.* and then click the Next button.

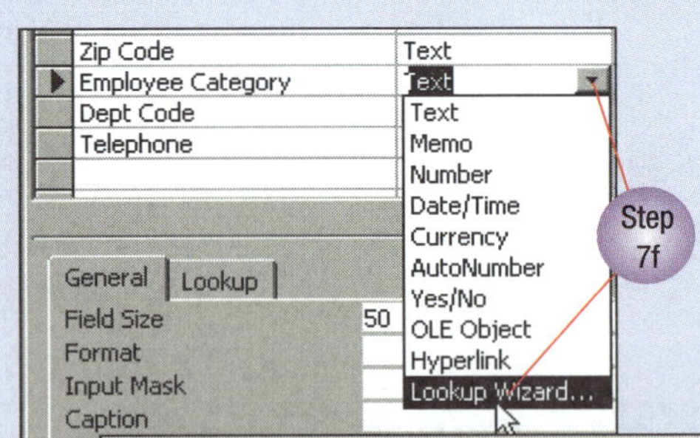

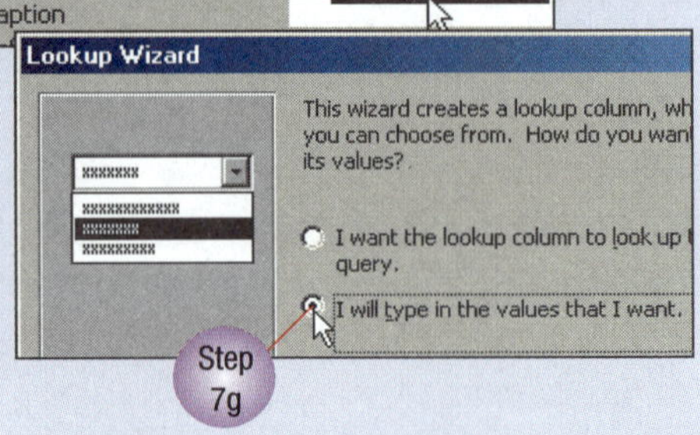

h. At the second Lookup Wizard dialog box, click in the blank text box below *Col1*, key **Salaried**, and then press Tab.
i. Key **Hourly** and then press Tab.
j. Key **Temporary**.
k. Click the Next button.
l. At the third Lookup Wizard dialog box, click the Finish button.
m. Click in the *Description* column in the *Employee Category* row and then key **Employee category**.

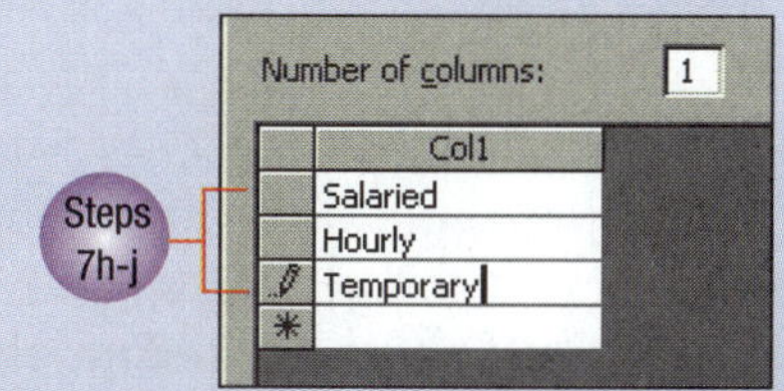

8. Click the Save button on the Table Design toolbar.
9. Insert information in the *Employee Category* for the records by completing the following steps:
   a. Change to the Datasheet view by clicking the down-pointing triangle at the right side of the View button on the Table Design toolbar and then clicking *Datasheet View*.
   b. Click in the first blank cell below the new *Employee Category* field.
   c. Click the down-pointing triangle at the right side of the cell and then click *Hourly* at the drop-down list.
   d. Click in next blank cell in the *Employee Category*, click the down-pointing triangle, and then click *Salaried* at the drop-down list.
   e. Continue entering information in the *Employee Category* by completing similar steps. Choose the following in the specified record:

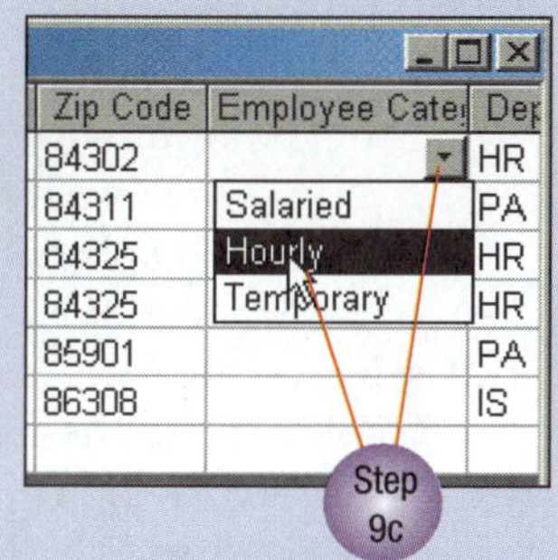

Third record	=	**Hourly**
Fourth record	=	**Hourly**
Fifth record	=	**Temporary**
Sixth record	=	**Salaried**

10. Click the Save button again on the Table Datasheet toolbar.
11. Print the table in landscape orientation with 0.5-inch left and right margins. (Change to the Landscape orientation at the Page Setup dialog box with the Page tab selected and then change to 0.5-inch left and right margins at the Page Setup dialog box with the Margins tab selected. [You must make the changes in this order.])
12. Close the Employees table and then close the Premium database file.

Moving a Field

You can move a field in a table to a different location. To do this, open the table, and then change to the Design view. Position the arrow pointer on the gray button at the left side of the field you want moved until the arrow pointer turns into a right-pointing black arrow and then click the left mouse button. This selects the entire row. Position the arrow pointer on the gray button at the left side of the selected row until it turns into the normal arrow pointer (white arrow pointing up and to the left). Hold down the left mouse button, drag the arrow pointer with the gray square attached until a thick gray line displays in the desired position, and then release the mouse button.

exercise 8

MOVING AND DELETING FIELDS IN THE EMPLOYEES TABLE

1. Open the Premium database file and then open the Employees table.
2. Move the *Last Name* field immediately below the *Middle Initial* field by completing the following steps:
   a. Click the down-pointing triangle at the right of the View button on the Table Datasheet toolbar and then click *Design View* at the drop-down menu.
   b. Position the arrow pointer on the gray button (this color may vary) at the left side of the *Last Name* field until it turns into a right-pointing black arrow and then click the left mouse button. (This selects the entire row.)
   c. Position the arrow pointer on the gray button at the left side of the selected row until it turns into the normal arrow pointer (white arrow pointing up and to the left).
   d. Hold down the left mouse button, drag the arrow pointer with the gray square attached until a black line displays between the *Middle Initial* field and the *Street Address* field, and then release the mouse button.

3. Move the *Telephone* field above the *Dept Code* field by completing the following steps:
   a. Select the row containing the *Telephone* field.
   b. Position the arrow pointer on the gray button at the left side of the selected row until it turns into the normal arrow pointer (white arrow pointing up and to the left).
   c. Hold down the left mouse button, drag the arrow pointer above the *Dept Code* field, and then release the mouse button.

4. Delete the *Middle Initial* field and the data in the field by completing the following steps:
   a. Position the insertion point anywhere in the text *Middle Initial*.
   b. Click the Delete Rows button on the Table Design toolbar.
   c. At the message asking if you want to permanently delete the field and the data in the field, click Yes.
5. Click the Save button on the Table Design toolbar to save the table.
6. Click the View button on the Table Design toolbar to change to the Datasheet view.
7. Print the Employees table in landscape orientation. (You will need to change to the Landscape orientation at the Page Setup dialog box with the Page tab selected.)
8. Close the Employees table and then close the Premium database file.

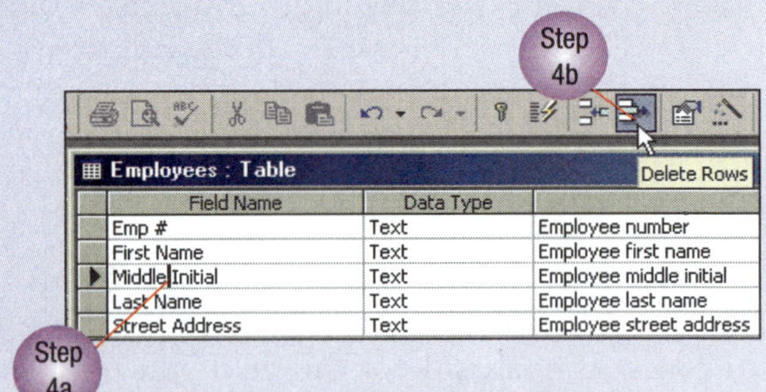

Sorting Records

The Table Datasheet toolbar contains two buttons you can use to sort data in records. Click the Sort Ascending button to sort from lowest to highest (or A-Z) on the field where the insertion point is located. Click the Sort Descending button to sort from highest to lowest (or Z-A).

exercise 9

SORTING RECORDS IN THE EMPLOYEES TABLE

1. Open the Premium database file and then open the Employees table.
2. Sort records in ascending order by city by completing the following steps:
   a. Click any city name in the table.
   b. Click the Sort Ascending button on the Table Datasheet toolbar.
   c. Print the Employees table in landscape orientation.

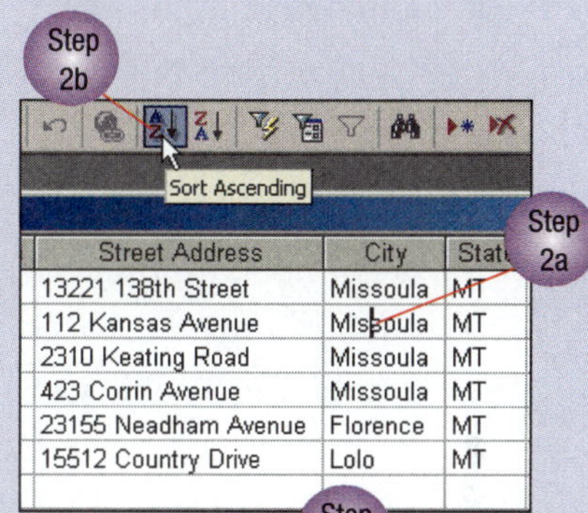

3. Sort records in descending order by employee number by completing the following steps:
   a. Click on any number in the *Emp #* field.
   b. Click the Sort Descending button on the Table Datasheet toolbar.
   c. Print the Employees table in landscape orientation.
4. Click the Save button to save the table.
5. Close the Employees table and then close the Premium database file.

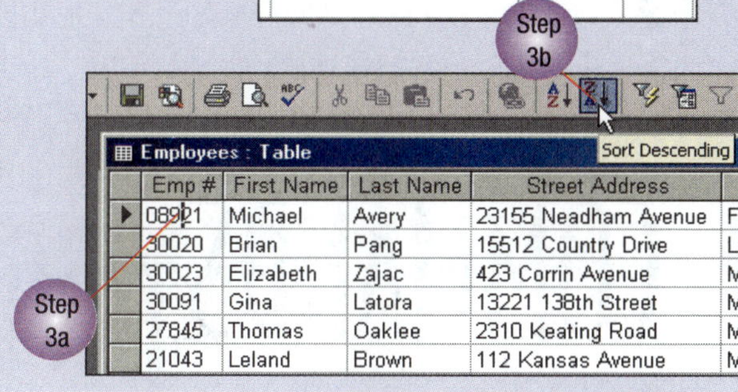

CHAPTER summary

- Microsoft Access is a database management system software program that will organize, store, maintain, retrieve, sort, and print all types of business data.
- Organize data in Access in related database tables in a database file.
- The first step in organizing data for a database table is determining fields. A field is one piece of information about a person, place, or item. All fields for one unit, such as an employee or customer, are considered a record.
- A field name should be unique and describe the contents of the field. It can contain up to 64 characters including letters, numbers, spaces, and some symbols.
- Part of the process of designing a database table is assigning a data type to each field, which helps maintain and manage data and helps identify what type of data is expected for the field. Data types include Text, Memo, Number, Currency, Date/Time, AutoNumber, and Yes/No.
- When assigning a data type, specific field sizes can be assigned to a field.

- Access automatically saves a database file on a periodic basis and also when the database file is closed.
- Open a database file when starting Access or open a database file at the Open dialog box.
- Enter data in a table in the Datasheet view. Key data in a field, pressing Tab to move to the next field or pressing Shift + Tab to move to the previous field.
- To permanently keep changes to a table's design or the layout of a datasheet, you will need to save the changes. Changes made to a record are saved when you leave the record.
- Print a table by opening the table and then clicking the Print button on the Table Datasheet toolbar.
- Change margins in a table at the Page Setup dialog box with the Margins tab selected.
- Change the page orientation and paper size and specify the printer with options at the Page Setup dialog box with the Page tab selected.
- Adjust field widths in a table in the same manner as column widths in an Excel worksheet. Double-click a column boundary to automatically adjust the width to accommodate the longest entry.
- Maintaining a table can include adding and/or deleting records.
- Modifying a table can include adding, moving, or deleting a field.
- Use the Input Mask Wizard to set a pattern for how data is entered in a field.
- Use the Lookup Wizard to confine data entered in a field to a specific list of items.
- Sort records in a table in ascending order with the Sort Ascending button on the Table Datasheet toolbar or in descending order with the Sort Descending button.

COMMANDS review

Command	Mouse/Keyboard
Open Access	Click Start, point to *Programs*, click *Microsoft Access*
Display Open dialog box	Click File, Open or click Open button on Database toolbar
Change view in table	Click View button on Table Design or Table Datasheet toolbar
Display Print dialog box	Open table; click File and then Print
Send table directly to printer	Open table; click Print button on Table Datasheet toolbar
Display Page Setup dialog box	Open table, click File and then Page Setup
Add record to a table	In Datasheet view, click New Record button on Table Datasheet toolbar
Delete record in a table	In Datasheet view, click Delete Record button on Table Datasheet toolbar
Add new field to a table	In Design view, click Insert Rows button on Table Design toolbar
Delete a field in a table	In Design view, click Delete Rows button on Table Design toolbar

Move a field in a table	In Design view, drag row containing field using the mouse
Use the Input Mask Wizard	In Design view, click in the Input Mask text box in the Field Properties section and then click the button containing three black dots that displays to the right of the Input Mask text box
Use the Lookup Wizard	In Design view, click in the desired cell in the *Data Type* column, click the down-pointing triangle that displays at the right side of the cell, and then click *Lookup Wizard*
Sort records in ascending order	In Datasheet view, click Sort Ascending button on Table Datasheet toolbar
Sort records in descending order	In Datasheet view, click Sort Descending button on Table Datasheet toolbar

CONCEPTS check

Completion: On a blank sheet of paper, indicate the correct term, symbol, or command for each item.

1. All fields for one unit, such as a customer, are considered to be this.
2. A field name can contain up to this number of characters.
3. Assign this data type to a field where more than 255 characters are needed.
4. Assign this data type to a field where you do not want calculations rounded off during a calculation.
5. You would probably assign this data type to a field that will contain telephone numbers.
6. In a field assigned the Yes/No data type, a check mark in the box in the field asking a yes/no question signifies this.
7. This view is used in a table to define field names and assign data types.
8. This is the view used in a table to enter data in fields.
9. Display this dialog box to change the page orientation.
10. This is the default left and right margin measurements for a table.
11. Add a new record to a table in this view.
12. Add a new field to a table in this view.
13. Use this wizard to set a pattern for how data is entered in a field.
14. Use this wizard to confine data entered in a field to a specific list of items.
15. Click the Sort Ascending button on this toolbar to sort records in ascending order.
16. Suppose you work for an insurance company and have been asked by your supervisor to design a table to keep track of client claims. This table should include the following information: client number (assigned in a separate table), the date of the claim, type of claim, and the amount of claim. Determine the fields you would use in this table and the data type you would assign to each and write out that information.

SKILLS check

Assessment 1

1. Use Access to create a database for a store that sells vitamins and other health aids. The table you create will keep track of what vitamins are ordered for the store. (This table assumes there are at least two other tables—one table containing information on suppliers and the other containing information on products. You will learn more about how tables are related in chapter 2.) Use the name of the store, Health Plus, as the database file name, and name the table Orders. (There is no primary key.) Create the following fields in the Orders table and assign the data type shown (you determine the Description):

Field Name		Data Type
Order #	=	Text (field size = 3)
Product Code	=	Text (field size = 2)
Supplier #	=	Text (field size = 2)
Date of Order	=	Date/Time
Amount of Order	=	Currency

2. Save the table and name it Orders.
3. Change to the Datasheet view and then enter the following data:

Order #	=	**214**
Product Code	=	**MT**
Supplier #	=	**10**
Date of Order	=	**4/5/2002**
Amount of Order	=	**$875.50**

Order #	=	**223**
Product Code	=	**PA**
Supplier #	=	**27**
Date of Order	=	**4/6/2002**
Amount of Order	=	**$1,005.45**

Order #	=	**241**
Product Code	=	**GS**
Supplier #	=	**10**
Date of Order	=	**4/8/2002**
Amount of Order	=	**$441.95**

Order #	=	**259**
Product Code	=	**AV**
Supplier #	=	**18**
Date of Order	=	**4/8/2002**
Amount of Order	=	**$772.00**

4. Automatically adjust the width of fields.
5. Save the Orders table again.
6. Print and then close the Orders table.

Assessment 2

1. With the Health Plus database file open, open the Orders table and then add the following records (remember to do this in the Datasheet view):

Order #	=	**262**
Product Code	=	**BC**
Supplier #	=	**27**
Date of Order	=	**4/9/2002**
Amount of Order	=	**$258.65**
Order #	=	**265**
Product Code	=	**VC**
Supplier #	=	**18**
Date of Order	=	**4/13/2002**
Amount of Order	=	**$1,103.45**

2. Delete the record for order number 241.
3. Print the table with a top margin of 2 inches.
4. Close the Orders table.

Assessment 3

1. With the Health Plus database file open, create a new table named Suppliers with the following fields and assign the data type shown (you determine the Description):

Field Name		**Data Type**
Supplier #	=	Text (field size = 2)
Supplier Name	=	Text (field size = 20)
Street Address	=	Text (field size = 30)
City	=	Text (field size = 20)
State	=	Text (field size = 2)
Zip Code	=	Text (field size = 10) Use the Input Mask Wizard to specify a nine-digit Zip Code. *(Hint: At the first Input Mask Wizard dialog box, click* Zip Code *in the Input Mask list box.)*

2. After creating and saving the table with the fields shown above, enter the following data in the table (remember to do this in the Datasheet view):

Supplier #	=	**10**
Supplier Name	=	**VitaHealth, Inc.**
Street Address	=	**12110 South 23rd**
City	=	**San Diego**
State	=	**CA**
Zip Code	=	**97432-1567**
Supplier #	=	**18**
Supplier Name	=	**Mainstream Supplies**
Street Address	=	**312 Evergreen Building**
City	=	**Seattle**
State	=	**WA**
Zip Code	=	**98220-2791**
Supplier #	=	**21**
Supplier Name	=	**LaVerde Products**

Street Address	=	**121 Vista Road**
City	=	**Phoenix**
State	=	**AZ**
Zip Code	=	**86355-6014**
Supplier #	=	**27**
Supplier Name	=	**Redding Corporation**
Street Address	=	**554 Ninth Street**
City	=	**Portland**
State	=	**OR**
Zip Code	=	**97466-3359**

3. Automatically adjust the width of fields.
4. Save the Suppliers table.
5. Change the page orientation to landscape and then print the table.
6. Close the Suppliers table.

Assessment 4

1. With the Health Plus database file open, open the Suppliers table.
2. Add the following fields and assign the data type as shown (remember to do this in the Design view):

Field Name		**Data Type**
Telephone	=	Text (field size = **14**) Use the Input Mask Wizard to specify that the area code surrounded by parentheses is to be included in the telephone number.
E-mail Address	=	Text (field size = **30**)
Supplier Type	=	Use the Lookup Wizard to create two categories for this field—*Wholesale* and *Retail*

3. Save the table, change to the Datasheet view, and then add the following information in the appropriate row (key the supplier telephone number, e-mail address, and insert the supplier type in the correct row).

Supplier	=	**LaVerde Products**
Telephone	=	**(602) 555-6775**
E-mail Address	=	**laverdep@emcp.com/gonet**
Supplier Type	=	*Wholesale*
Supplier	=	**VitaHealth, Inc.**
Telephone	=	**(619) 555-2388**
E-mail Address	=	**vitahealth@emcp.com/groupnet**
Supplier Type	=	*Retail*
Supplier	=	**Redding Corporation**
Telephone	=	**(503) 555-6679**
E-mail Address	=	**redding@emcp.com/opnet**
Supplier Type	=	*Retail*
Supplier	=	**Mainstream Supplies**
Telephone	=	**(206) 555-9005**
E-mail Address	=	**mainsupplies@emcp.com/msgt**
Supplier Type	=	*Wholesale*

4. Automatically adjust the width of fields to accommodate the longest entry.
5. Save the Suppliers table.

6. Change the page orientation to landscape, change the left and right margins to 0.3 inch, and then print the table.
7. Close the Suppliers table.

Assessment 5

1. With the Health Plus database file open, open the Orders table.
2. Change to the Design view and then move the fields around in the Orders table so they are displayed in this order:

   Order #
   Date of Order
   Amount of Order
   Product Code
   Supplier #

3. Save the table, change to the Datasheet view, and then sort the records in ascending order by *Supplier #*.
4. Save, print, and then close the Orders table.
5. Close the Health Plus database file.

CHAPTER 2

CREATING RELATIONSHIPS BETWEEN DATABASE TABLES

PERFORMANCE OBJECTIVES

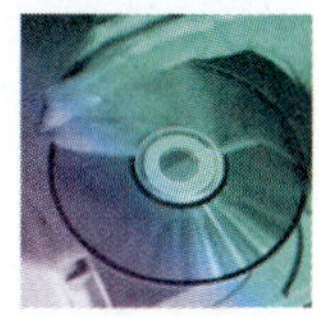

Southwest Insurance

Upon successful completion of chapter 2, you will be able to:

- **Create a table with a primary key and a foreign key**
- **Create a one-to-many relationship between tables**

Access is a relational database program that allows you to create tables that have a relation or connection to each other within the same database file. In chapter 1, you created a table containing information on employees and another containing department information. With Access, you can connect these tables through a common field that appears in both tables.

In this chapter you will learn how to identify a primary key field in a table that is unique to that table. In Access, data can be divided into logical groupings in tables for easier manipulation and management. Duplicate information is generally minimized in tables in the same database file. A link or relationship, however, should connect the tables. In this chapter, you will define primary keys and define relationships between tables.

Creating Related Tables

Generally, a database management system fits into one of two categories—either a file management system (also sometimes referred to as a *flat file database*) or a relational database management system. In a file management system, data is stored without indexing and sequential processing. This type of system lacks flexibility in manipulating data and requires the same data to be stored in more than one place.

In a relational database management system, like Access, relationships are defined between sets of data allowing greater flexibility in manipulating data and eliminating data redundancy (entering the same data in more than one place). In exercises in this chapter, you will define relationships between tables in the insurance company database file. Because these tables will be related, information on a client does not need to be repeated in a table on claims filed. If you used a flat file management system to maintain insurance records, you would need to repeat the client information for each claim filed.

Determining Relationships

Taking time to plan a database file is extremely important. Creating a database file with related tables takes even more consideration. You need to determine how to break down the required data and what tables to create to eliminate redundancies. One idea to help you determine the necessary tables in a database file is to think of the word "about." For example, an insurance company database will probably need a table "about" clients, another "about" the type of coverage, another "about" claims, and so on. A table should be about only one subject, such as a client, customer, department, or supplier.

Along with deciding on the necessary tables for a database file, you also need to determine the relationship between tables. The ability to relate, or "join," tables is part of what makes Access a relational database system. Figure 2.1 illustrates the tables and fields that either are or will become part of the Southwest Insurance database file. Notice how each table is about only one subject—clients, type of insurance, claims, or coverage.

FIGURE 2.1 ***Southwest Insurance Tables***

Clients table
Client #
Client
Street Address
City
State
Zip Code

Insurance table
License #
Client #
Insurance Code
Uninsured Motorist

Claims table
Claim #
Client #
License #
Date of Claim
Amount of Claim

Coverage table
Insurance Code
Type of Insurance

Some fields such as *Client #*, *License #*, and *Insurance Code* appear in more than one table. These fields are used to create a relationship between tables. For example, in exercise 2 you will create a relationship between the Clients table and the Insurance table with the *Client #* field.

Creating relationships between tables tells Access how to bring the information in the database file back together again. With relationships defined, you can bring information together to create queries, forms, and reports. (You will learn about these features in future chapters.)

Creating a Primary Field

HINT

You must enter a value in the primary key field in every record.

Before creating a relationship between tables, you need to define the primary key in a table. In a table, at least one field must be unique so that one record can be distinguished from another. A field (or several fields) with a unique value is considered a *primary key*. When a primary key is defined, Access will not allow duplicate values in the primary field. For example, the *Client #* field in the Clients table must contain a unique number (you would not assign the same client number to two different clients). If you define this as the primary key field, Access will not allow you to key the same client number in two different records.

In a field specified as a primary key, Access expects a value in each record in the table. This is referred to as *entity integrity*. If a value is not entered in a field, Access actually enters a *null value*. A null value cannot be given to a primary key field. Access will not let you close a database file containing a primary field with a null value.

To define a field as a primary key, open the table, and then change to the Design view. Position the insertion point somewhere in the row containing the field you want as the primary key and then click the Primary Key button on the Table Design toolbar. An image of a key is inserted at the beginning of the row identified as the primary key field. To define more than one field as a primary key, select the rows containing the fields you want as primary keys and then click the Primary Key button on the Table Design toolbar.

Primary Key

Creating a Foreign Key

A primary key field in one table may be a foreign key in another. For example, if you define the *Client #* field in the Clients table as the primary key, the *Client #* field in the Insurance table will then be considered a *foreign key*. The primary key field and the foreign key field form a relationship between the two tables. In the Clients table, each entry in the *Client #* field will be unique (it is the primary key), but the same client number may appear more than once in the *Client #* field in the Insurance table (such as a situation where a client has insurance on more than one vehicle).

Each table in figure 2.1 contains a unique field that will be defined as the primary key. Figure 2.2 identifies the primary keys and also foreign keys.

FIGURE

2.2 *Primary and Foreign Keys*

Clients table
Client # *(primary key)*
Client
Street Address
City
State
Zip Code

Claims table
Claim # *(primary key)*
Client # *(foreign key)*
License # *(foreign key)*
Date of Claim
Amount of Claim

Insurance table
License # *(primary key)*
Client # *(foreign key)*
Insurance Code *(foreign key)*
Uninsured Motorist

Coverage table
Insurance Code *(primary key)*
Type of Insurance

In exercise 1, you will create another table for the Southwest Insurance database file, enter data, and then define primary keys for the tables. In the section following exercise 1, you will learn how to create relationships between the tables.

exercise 1

CREATING A TABLE AND DEFINING PRIMARY KEYS

(Note: Delete from your disk any database files you created in chapter 1. In step 1, you will copy the Southwest Insurance database file from the CD that accompanies this textbook to your disk. You will then remove the read-only attribute from the Southwest Insurance database file on your disk. You need to remove this attribute before you can make changes to the database file.)

1. Copy the Southwest Insurance database file on the CD that accompanies this textbook to your disk, remove the read-only attribute, and then open the database file by completing the following steps:
   a. Insert the CD that accompanies this textbook into the drive.
   b. Copy the Southwest Insurance database file from the CD to your disk.
   c. Remove the read-only attribute from the Southwest Insurance database located on your disk by completing the following steps:
      1) In Access, display the Open dialog box with the drive active containing your disk.
      2) Click once on the Southwest Insurance database file name.
      3) Click the Tools button on the Open dialog box toolbar and then click Properties at the drop-down list.

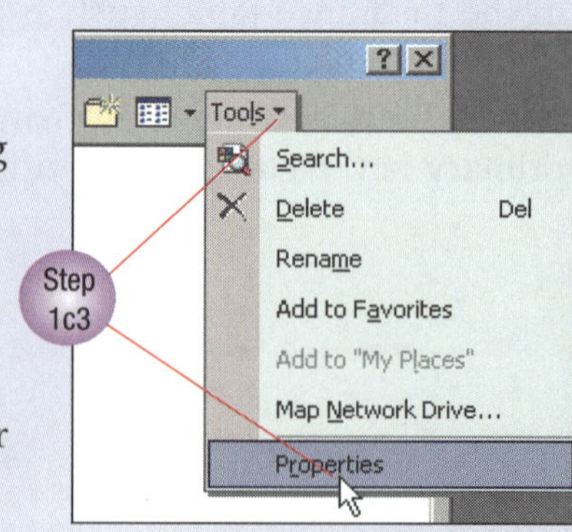

4) At the Southwest Insurance : Properties dialog box with the General tab selected, click Read-only in the Attributes section to remove the check mark.
5) Click OK to close the Southwest Insurance : Properties dialog box.

d. Open the Southwest Insurance database file.

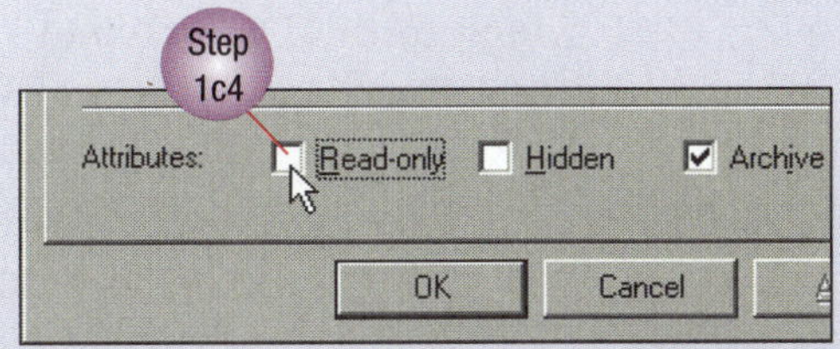

2. At the Southwest Insurance : Database window, create a new table by completing the following steps:
   a. Double-click *Create table in Design view* in the list box.
   b. At the Table1 : Table window, key the fields, assign the data types, and key the descriptions as shown below (for assistance, refer to chapter 1, exercise 1):

Field Name	**Data Type**	**Description**
License #	Text (Field Size = 7)	**Vehicle license number**
Client #	Text (Field Size = 4)	**Client number**
Insurance Code	Text (Field Size = 1)	**Insurance code**
Uninsured Motorist	Yes/No	**Uninsured motorist coverage**

(Note: To create the Yes/No data type for the Uninsured Motorist *field, click the down-pointing triangle at the right side of the* Data Type *field, and then click Yes/No at the drop-down list.)*

   c. Specify the *License #* as the primary key by completing the following steps:
      1) Click anywhere in the text *License #* (in the top row).
      2) Click the Primary Key button on the Table Design toolbar.

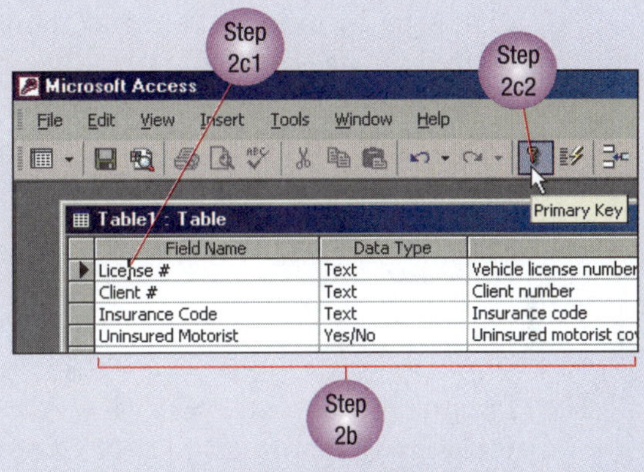

   d. Save the table by completing the following steps:
      1) Click the Save button on the Table Design toolbar.
      2) At the Save As dialog box, key **Insurance** in the Table Name text box, and then press Enter or click OK.
   e. Close the Insurance table by clicking File and then Close or by clicking the Close button located in the upper right corner of the window.

3. Define primary keys for the other tables in the database file by completing the following steps:
   a. At the Southwest Insurance : Database window, double-click *Claims* in the list box.
   b. With the Claims table open, click the View button on the Table Datasheet toolbar to switch to the Design view.
   c. Click anywhere in the text *Claim #* and then click the Primary Key button on the Table Design toolbar.
   d. Click the Save button on the Table Design toolbar.
   e. Close the Claims table.

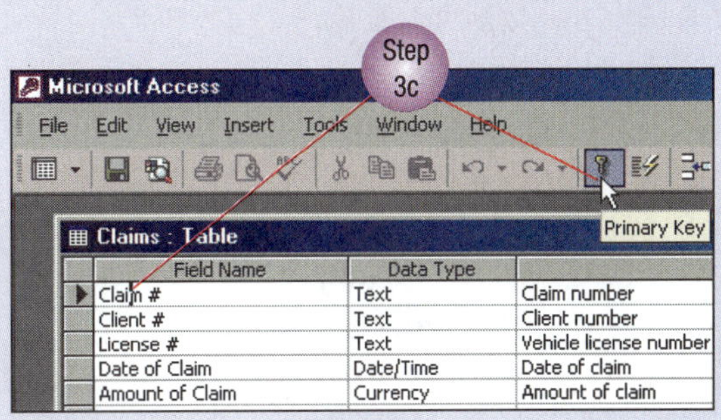

f. At the Southwest Insurance : Database window, double-click *Clients* in the list box.
g. With the Clients table open, click the View button on the Table Datasheet toolbar to switch to the Design view.
h. Click anywhere in the text *Client #* and then click the Primary Key button on the Table Design toolbar.
i. Click the Save button on the Table Design toolbar.
j. Close the Clients table.
k. At the Southwest Insurance : Database window, double-click *Coverage* in the list box.
l. With the Coverage table open, click the View button on the Table Datasheet toolbar to switch to the Design view.
m. Click anywhere in the text *Insurance Code* and then click the Primary Key button on the Table Design toolbar.
n. Click the Save button on the Table Design toolbar.
o. Close the Coverage table.

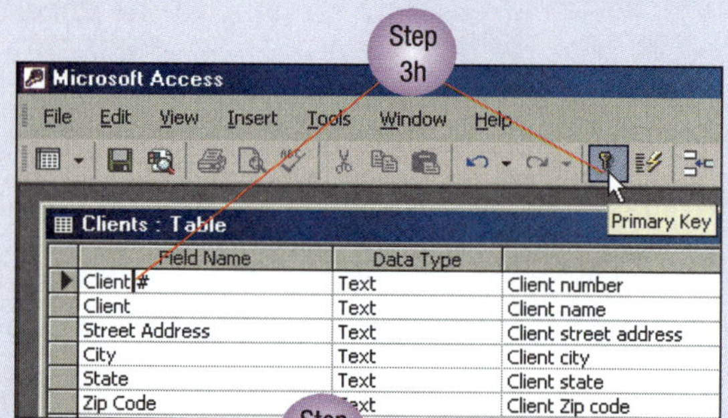

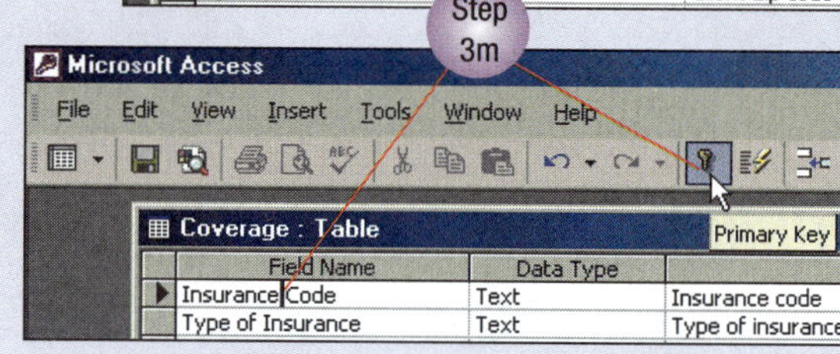

4. Open the Insurance table and then key the following data in the specified fields: (If the *Uninsured Motorist* field is Yes, insert a check mark in the field by pressing the spacebar. If the field is No, leave the check box blank.)

License #	=	**341 VIT**
Client #	=	**3120**
Insurance Code	=	**F**
Uninsured Motorist	=	**Yes**
License #	=	**776 ERU**
Client #	=	**9383**
Insurance Code	=	**F**
Uninsured Motorist	=	**No**
License #	=	**984 CWS**
Client #	=	**7335**
Insurance Code	=	**L**
Uninsured Motorist	=	**Yes**
License #	=	**877 BNN**
Client #	=	**4300**
Insurance Code	=	**L**
Uninsured Motorist	=	**Yes**
License #	=	**310 YTV**
Client #	=	**3120**
Insurance Code	=	**F**
Uninsured Motorist	=	**Yes**

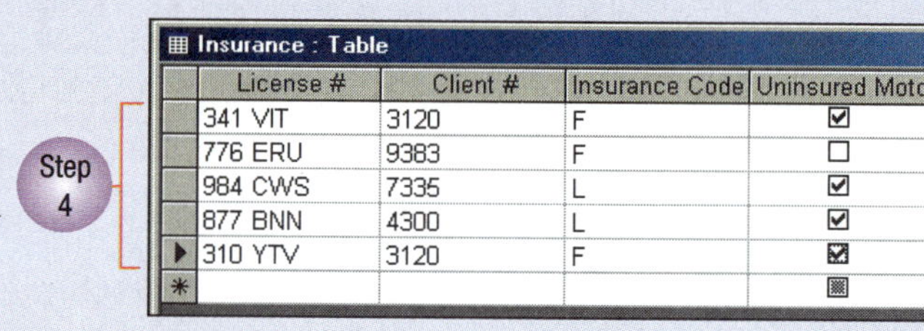

License #	Client #	Insurance Code	Uninsured Moto
341 VIT	3120	F	☑
776 ERU	9383	F	☐
984 CWS	7335	L	☑
877 BNN	4300	L	☑
310 YTV	3120	F	☑

5. Close the Insurance table.
6. Close the Southwest Insurance database file.

Establishing a Relationship between Tables

In Access, one table can be related to another, which is generally referred to as performing a *join*. When tables with a common field are joined, data can be extracted from both tables as if they were one large table. Another reason for relating tables is to ensure the integrity of the data. For example, in exercise 2, you will create a relationship between the Clients table and the Claims table. The relationship that is established will ensure that a client cannot be entered in the Claims table without first being entered in the Clients table. This also ensures that a claim is not processed on a person who is not a client of the insurance company. This type of relationship is called a one-to-many relationship, which means that one record in the Clients table will match zero, one, or many records in the Claims table.

In a one-to-many relationship, the table containing the "one" is referred to as the *primary table* and the table containing the "many" is referred to as the *related table*. Access follows a set of rules known as *referential integrity*, which enforces consistency between related tables. These rules are enforced when data is updated in related tables. The referential integrity rules ensure that a record added to a related table has a matching record in the primary table.

HINT

Defining a relationship between database tables is one of the most powerful features of a relational database management system.

HINT

Access provides a Table Analyzer that will analyze your tables and restructure them to better conform to relational theory. To use the Table Analyzer Wizard, click the Analyze button on the Database toolbar.

Creating a One-to-Many Relationship

A relationship is specified between existing tables in a database file. To create a one-to-many relationship, you would complete these basic steps:

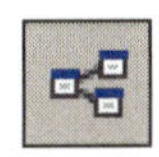

Relationships

1. Open the database file containing the tables to be related.
2. Click the Relationships button that displays at the right side of the Database toolbar; or click Tools and then Relationships. This displays the Show Table dialog box, as shown in figure 2.3.
3. At the Show Table dialog box, each table that will be related must be added to the Relationships window. To do this, click the first table name to be included, and then click Add. Continue in this manner until all necessary table names have been added to the Relationships window and then click the Close button.
4. At the Relationships window, such as the one shown in figure 2.4, use the mouse to drag the common field from the primary table (the "one") to the related table (the "many"). This causes the Edit Relationships dialog box to display as shown in figure 2.5.
5. At the Edit Relationships dialog box, check to make sure the correct field name displays in the Table/Query: and Related Table/Query: option boxes and the relationship type at the bottom of the dialog box displays as *"One-To-Many."*
6. Specify the relationship options by choosing Enforce Referential Integrity, as well as Cascade Update Related Fields and/or Cascade Delete Related Records. (These are explained in the text after these steps.)
7. Click the Create button. This causes the Edit Relationships dialog box to close and the Relationships window to display showing the relationship between the tables. In figure 2.6, the Clients box displays with a black line attached along with the number *1* (signifying the "one" side of the relationship). The black line is connected to the Claims box along with the infinity symbol ∞ (signifying the "many"

side of the relationship). The black line, called the *join line*, is thick at both ends if the enforce referential integrity option has been chosen. If this option is not chosen, the line is thin at both ends.

8. Click the Save button on the Relationship toolbar to save the relationship.
9. Close the Relationships window by clicking the Close button that displays at the right side of the Title bar.

FIGURE 2.3 **Show Table Dialog Box**

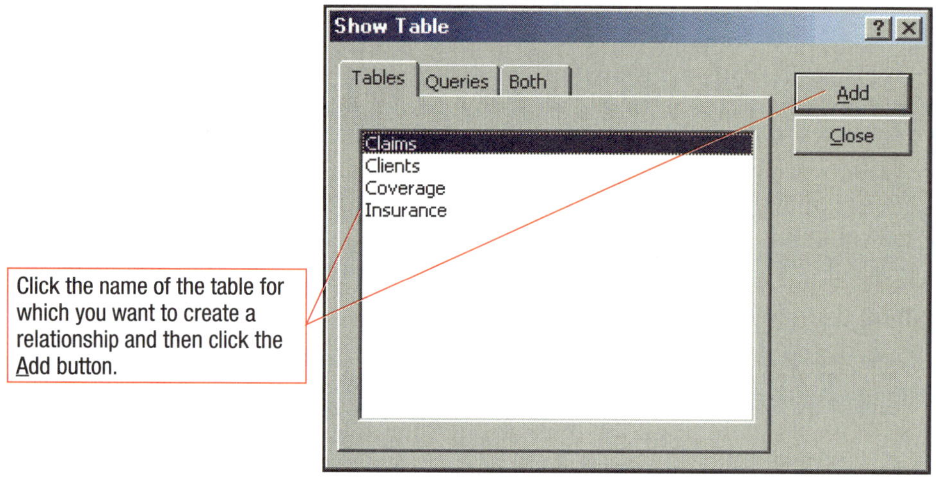

FIGURE 2.4 **Relationships Window**

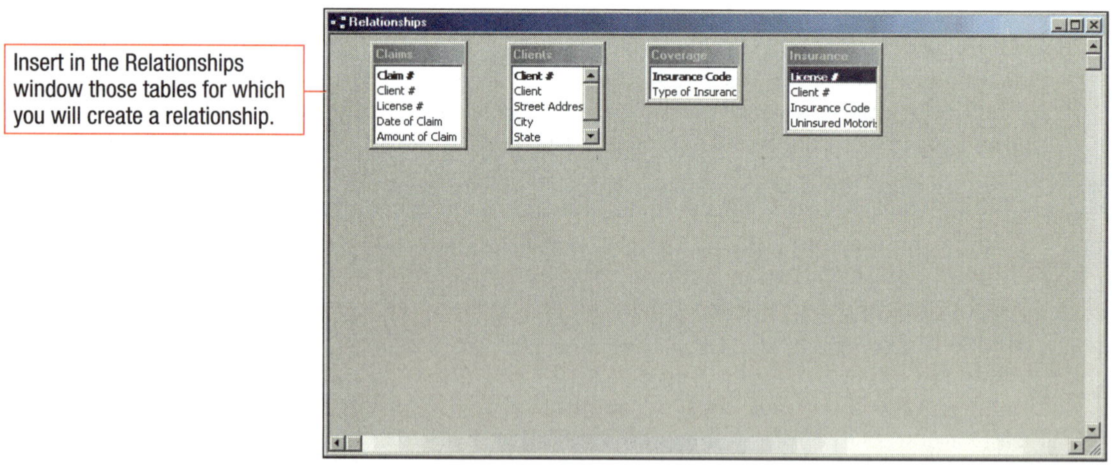

FIGURE

2.5 *Edit Relationships Dialog Box*

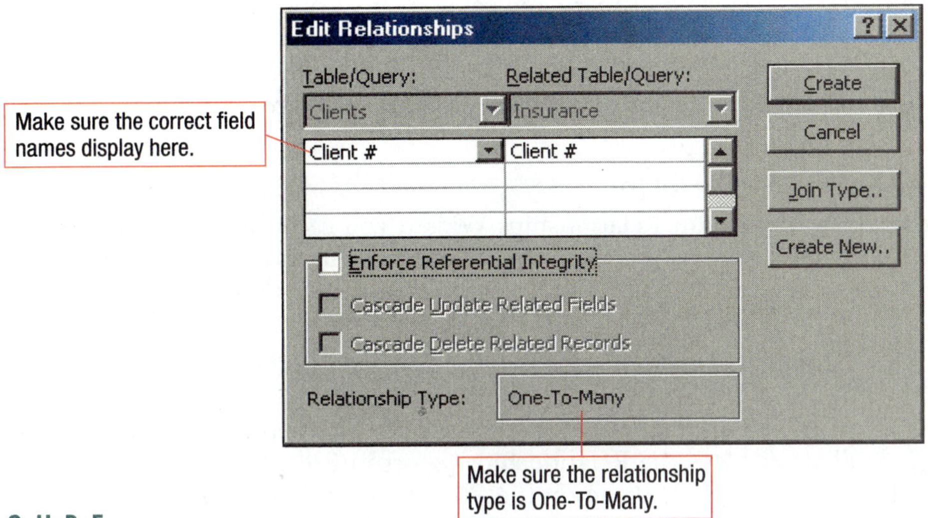

FIGURE

2.6 *One-to-Many Relationship*

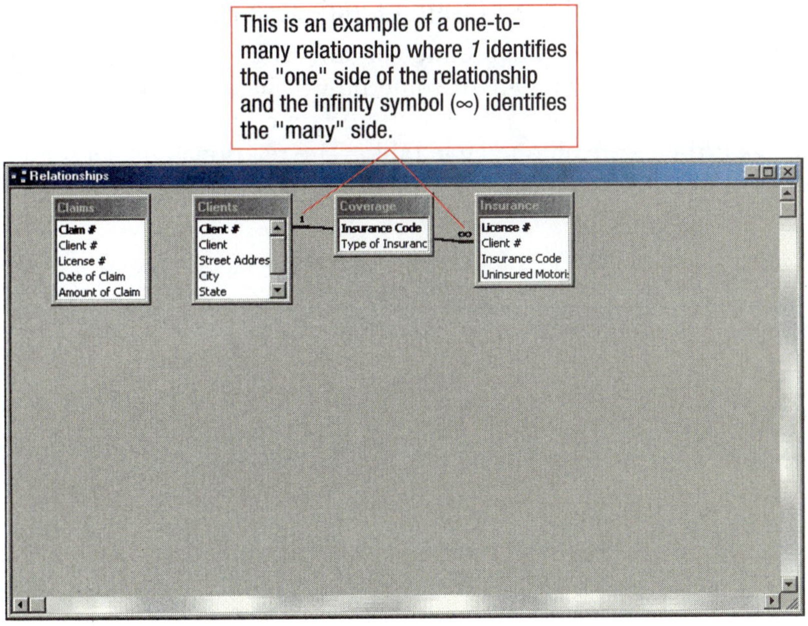

Specifying Referential Integrity

In step 6, the referential integrity of the relationship was established. Choose Enforce Referential Integrity at the Edit Relationships dialog box to ensure that the relationships between records in related tables are valid. Referential integrity can be set if the field from the primary table is a primary key and the related fields have the same data type. When referential integrity is established, a value for the primary key must first be entered in the primary table before it can be entered in the related table.

HINT

Referential integrity makes sure that a record exists in the "one" table before the record can be entered in the "many" table.

If you select only Enforce Referential Integrity and the related table contains a record, you will not be able to change a primary key value or delete a primary key value in the primary table. If you choose Cascade Update Related Fields, you will be able to change a primary key value in the primary table and Access will automatically update the matching value in the related table. Choose Cascade Delete Related Records and you will be able to delete a record in the primary table and Access will delete any related records in the related table.

Printing Table Relationships

Access contains a Print Relationships Wizard you can use to print a report displaying the relationships between tables. To print a report of relationships between tables in a database file, you would complete these steps:

1. Open the database.
2. Display the Relationships window by clicking the Relationships button on the Database toolbar.
3. At the Relationships window, click File and then Print Relationships. (This displays the Relationships report in Print Preview.)
4. Click the Print button on the Print Preview toolbar to send the report to the printer.
5. Click the Close button to close Print Preview.

Print

Relating Tables in the Southwest Insurance Database File

The Southwest Insurance database file contains the four tables shown in figure 2.1. Each table contains data about something—clients, insurance, claims, and coverage. You can relate these tables so that data can be extracted from more than one table as if they were all one large table. The relationships between the tables are identified in figure 2.7.

FIGURE 2.7 ***Relationships between Southwest Insurance Tables***

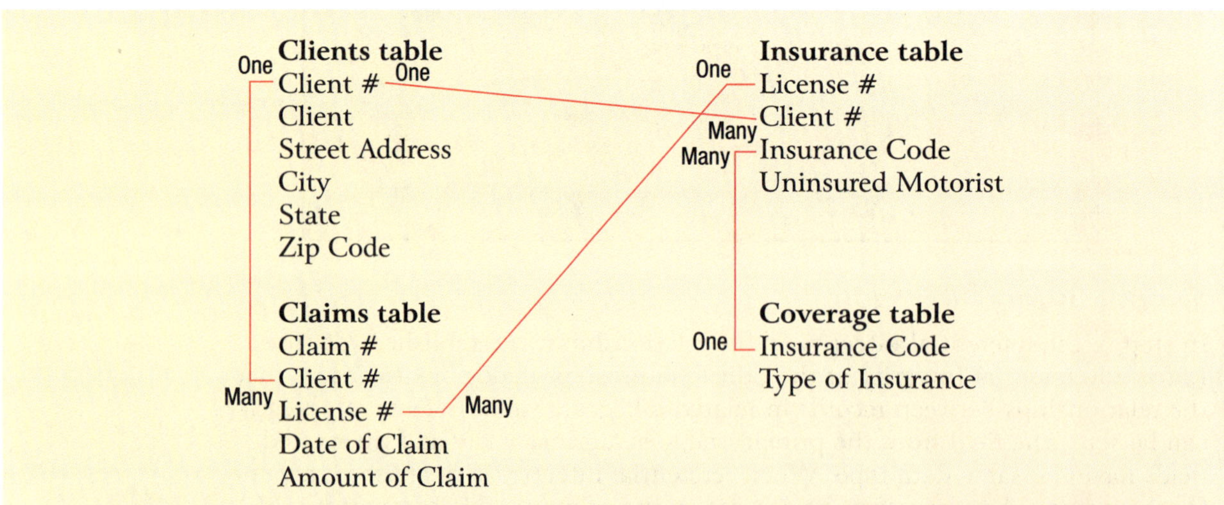

In the relationships shown in figure 2.7, notice how the primary key is identified as the "one" and the foreign key is identified as the "many." Relate these tables so you can extract information from more than one table. For example, you can design a report about claims that contains information on claims as well as information on the clients submitting the claims.

exercise 2

CREATING A ONE-TO-MANY RELATIONSHIP BETWEEN TWO TABLES

1. Create a one-to-many relationship between the Clients table and the Claims table by completing the following steps:
   a. Open the Southwest Insurance database file.
   b. Click the Relationships button that displays towards the right side of the Database toolbar.

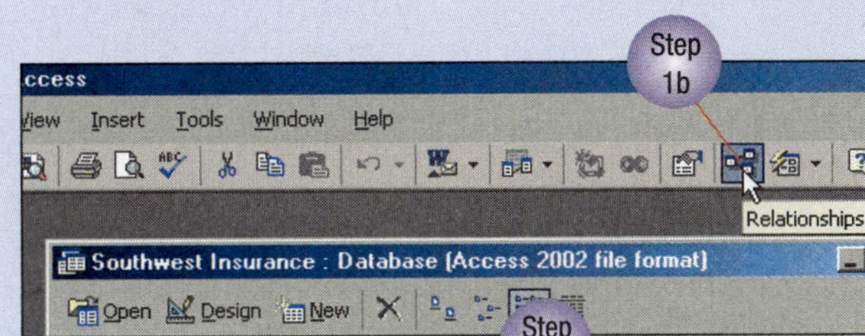

   c. At the Show Table dialog box, add the Clients and Claims tables to the Relationships window by completing the following steps:
      1) Click *Clients* in the list box and then click Add.
      2) Click *Claims* in the list box and then click Add.

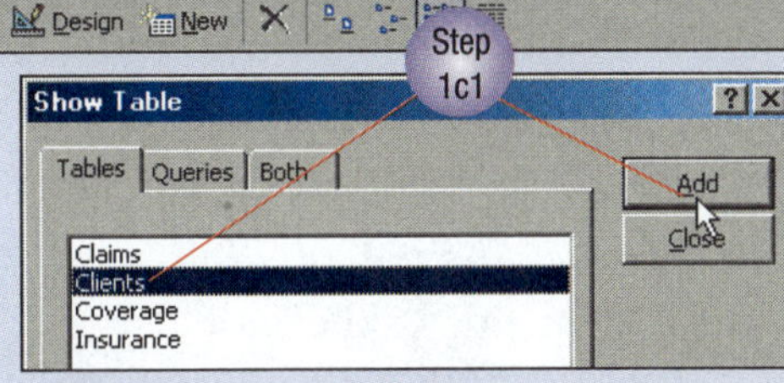

   d. Click the Close button to close the Show Table dialog box.
   e. At the Relationships window, drag the *Client #* field from the Clients table to the Claims table by completing the following steps:
      1) Position the arrow pointer on the *Client #* field that displays in the Clients box.
      2) Hold down the left mouse button, drag the arrow pointer (with a field icon attached), to the *Client #* field in the Claims box, and then release the mouse button. (This causes the Edit Relationships dialog box to display.)

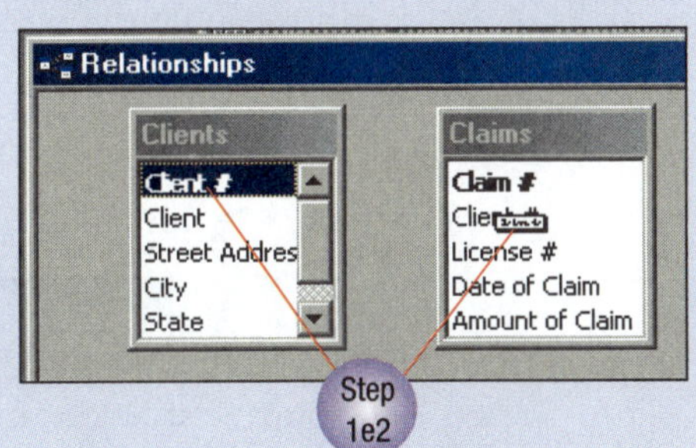

   f. At the Edit Relationships dialog box, make sure *Client #* displays in the Table/Query: and Related Table/Query: option boxes and the relationship type at the bottom of the dialog box displays as *"One-To-Many."*
   g. Enforce the referential integrity of the relationship by completing the following steps:
      1) Click Enforce Referential Integrity. (This makes the other two options available.)
      2) Click Cascade Update Related Fields.
      3) Click Cascade Delete Related Records.

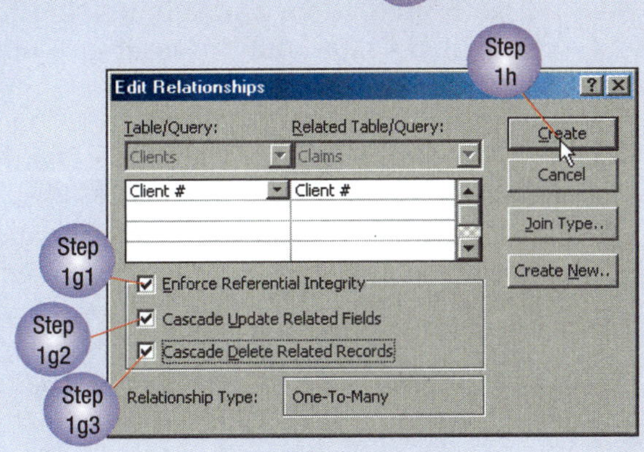

h. Click the Create button. (This causes the Edit Relationships dialog box to close and the Relationships window to display showing a thick black line connecting Clients to Claims. At the Clients side, a *"1"* will appear and an infinity symbol ∞ will display at the Claims side of the thick black line.)

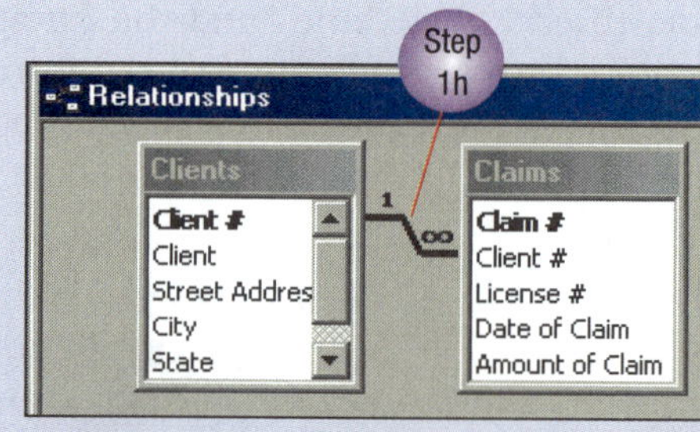

i. Click the Save button on the Relationship toolbar to save the relationship.

j. Print the relationships by completing the following steps:

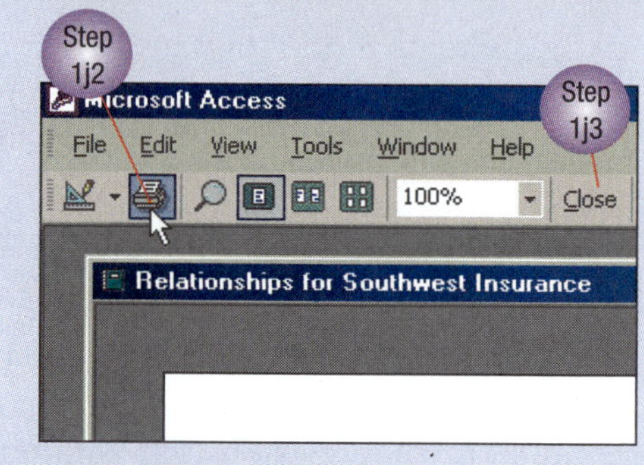

1) At the Relationships window, click File and then Print Relationships. (This displays the Relationships report in Print Preview.)
2) Click the Print button on the Print Preview toolbar.
3) Click the Close button to close Print Preview.
4) At the Report window, click the Close button (contains an *X*) located in the upper right corner of the window.
5) At the message asking if you want to save changes to the design of the report, click No.

k. Close the Relationships window by clicking the Close button that displays at the right side of the Title bar.

2. Close the Southwest Insurance database file.

Once a relationship has been established between tables, clicking the Relationships button causes the Relationships window to display (rather than the Show Table dialog box). To create additional relationships, click Relationships on the Menu bar and then click Show Table. This displays the Show Table dialog box where you can specify the tables you need for creating another relationship.

exercise 3

CREATING ADDITIONAL ONE-TO-MANY RELATIONSHIPS BETWEEN TABLES

1. Open the Southwest Insurance database file.
2. Create another one-to-many relationship between the Clients table and the Insurance table by completing the following steps:
   a. Click the Relationships button that displays towards the right side of the Database toolbar.
   b. At the Relationships window, click Relationships on the Menu bar and then click Show Table at the drop-down menu.
   c. At the Show Table dialog box, click *Insurance* in the list box, and then click the Add button. (You do not need to add the Clients table because it was added in exercise 2.)

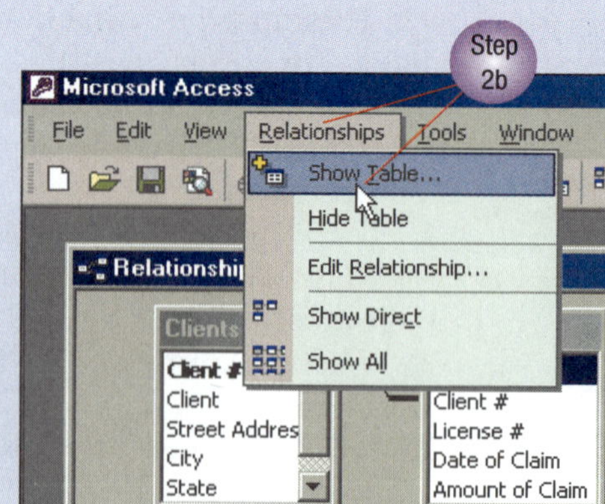

d. Click the Close button to close the Show Table dialog box.

e. At the Relationships window, drag the *Client #* field from the Clients table to the Insurance table by completing the following steps:

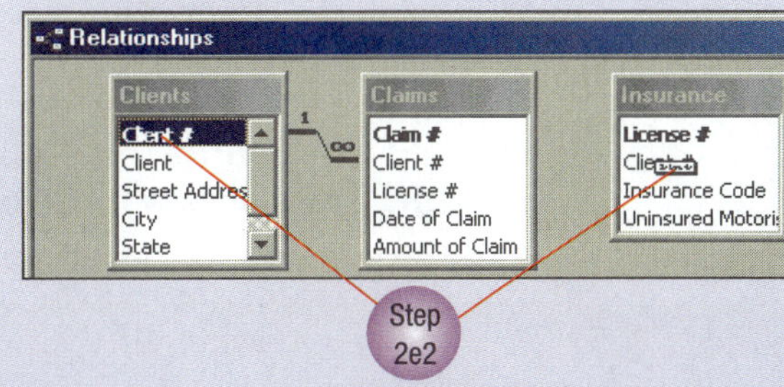

1) Position the arrow pointer on the *Client #* field that displays in the Clients box.
2) Hold down the left mouse button, drag the arrow pointer (with a field icon attached), to the *Client #* field in the Insurance box, and then release the mouse button. (This causes the Edit Relationships dialog box to display.)

f. At the Edit Relationships dialog box, make sure *Client #* displays in the Table/Query: and Related Table/Query: option boxes and the relationship type at the bottom of the dialog box displays as *"One-To-Many."*

g. Enforce the referential integrity of the relationship by completing the following steps:

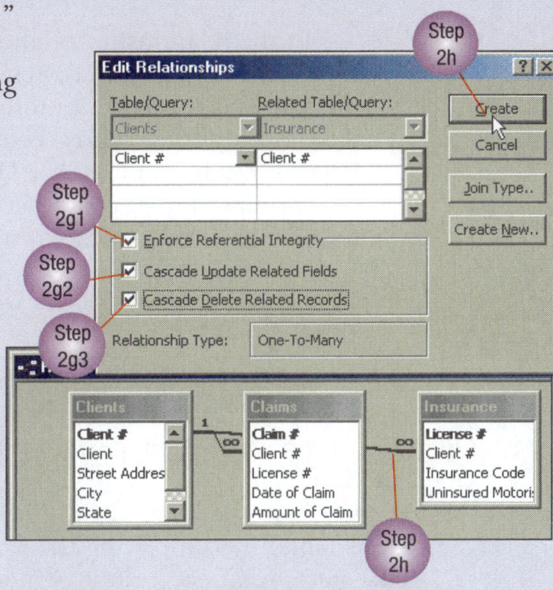

1) Click Enforce Referential Integrity. (This makes the other two options available.)
2) Click Cascade Update Related Fields.
3) Click Cascade Delete Related Records.

h. Click the Create button. (This causes the Edit Relationships dialog box to close and the Relationships window to display showing a thick black line connecting Clients to Insurance. At the Clients side, a *"1"* will appear and an infinity symbol ∞ will display at the Insurance side of the thick black line.)

i. Click the Save button on the Relationship toolbar to save the relationship.

j. With the Relationships window still open, create the following one-to-many relationships by completing steps similar to those in 2b through 2i:
1) Create a relationship between *License #* in the Insurance table and the Claims table. (*License #* in the Insurance table is the "one" and *License #* in the Claims table is the "many.") At the Edit Relationships dialog box, be sure to choose Enforce Referential Integrity, Cascade Update Related Fields, and Cascade Delete Related Records.
2) Add the Coverage table to the Relationships window and then create a relationship between *Insurance Code* in the Insurance table and the Coverage table. (*Insurance Code* in the Coverage table is the "one" and *Insurance Code* in the Insurance table is the "many.") At the Edit Relationships dialog box, be sure to choose Enforce Referential Integrity, Cascade Update Related Fields, and Cascade Delete Related Records.

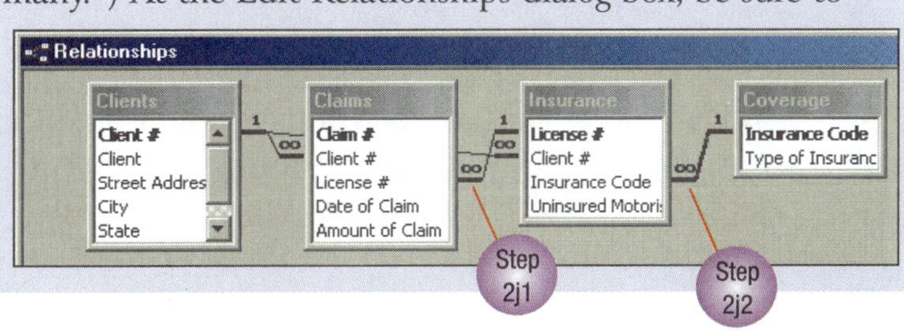

k. Click the Save button on the Relationship toolbar.
l. Print the relationships by completing the following steps:
    1) At the Relationships window, click File and then Print Relationships. (This displays the Relationships report in Print Preview.)
    2) Click the Print button on the Print Preview toolbar.
    3) Click the Close button to close Print Preview.
    4) At the Report window, click the Close button (contains an *X*) located in the upper right corner of the window.
    5) At the message asking if you want to save changes to the design of the report, click No.
m. Close the Relationships window by clicking the Close button that displays at the right side of the Title bar.

3. Close the Southwest Insurance database file.

In the relationship established in exercise 2, a record must first be added to the Clients table before a related record can be added to the Claims table. This is because you chose the Enforce Referential Integrity option at the Edit Relationships dialog box. Because you chose the two options Cascade Update Related Fields and Cascade Delete Related Records, records in the Clients table (the primary table) can be updated and/or deleted and related records in the Claims table (related table) will automatically be updated or deleted.

exercise 4

UPDATING FIELDS AND ADDING AND DELETING RECORDS IN RELATED TABLES

1. Open the Southwest Insurance database file.
2. Open the Clients table.
3. Change two client numbers in the Clients table (Access will automatically change it in the Claims table) by completing the following steps:
    a. Make sure the Clients : Table window displays in the Datasheet view.
    b. Click once in the *Client #* field for Paul Vuong containing the number *4300*.
    c. Change the number from *4300* to *4308*.
    d. Click once in the *Client #* field for Vernon Cook containing the number *7335*.
    e. Change the number from *7335* to *7325*.
    f. Click the Save button on the Table Datasheet toolbar.
    g. Close the Clients table.
    h. Open the Claims table. (Notice that the client numbers for Vernon Cook and Paul Vuong automatically changed.)
    i. Close the Claims table.

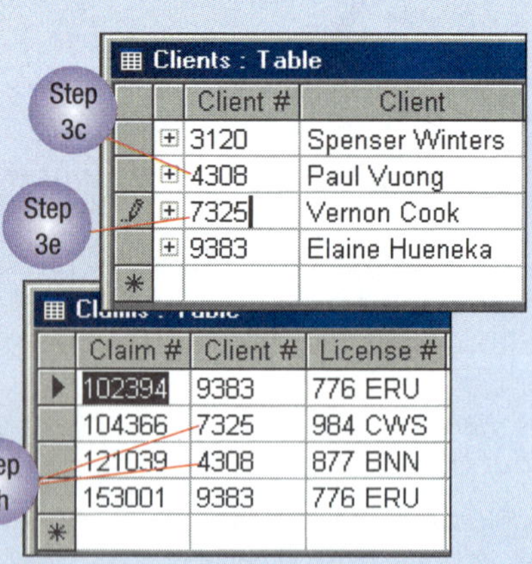

4. Open the Clients table, make sure the table displays in Datasheet view, and then add the following records at the end of the table:

Client #	=	**5508**
Client	=	**Martina Bentley**
Street Address	=	**6503 Taylor Street**

City = **Scottsdale**
State = **AZ**
Zip Code = **85889**

Client # = **2511**
Client = **Keith Hammond**
Street Address = **21332 Janski Road**
City = **Glendale**
State = **AZ**
Zip Code = **85310**

5. With the Clients table still open, delete the record for Elaine Hueneka. At the message telling you that relationships that specify cascading deletes are about to cause records in this table and related tables to be deleted, click Yes.
6. Save, print, and then close the Clients table.
7. Open the Insurance table, make sure the table displays in Datasheet view, and then add the following records at the end of the table:

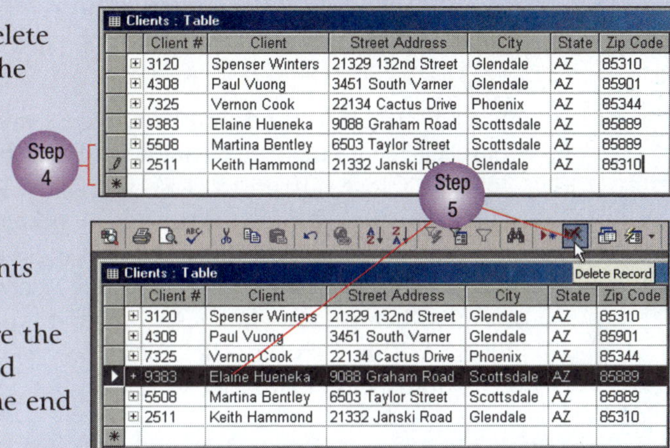

Client #	Client	Street Address	City	State	Zip Code
3120	Spenser Winters	21329 132nd Street	Glendale	AZ	85310
4308	Paul Vuong	3451 South Varner	Glendale	AZ	85901
7325	Vernon Cook	22134 Cactus Drive	Phoenix	AZ	85344
9383	Elaine Hueneka	9088 Graham Road	Scottsdale	AZ	85889
5508	Martina Bentley	6503 Taylor Street	Scottsdale	AZ	85889
2511	Keith Hammond	21332 Janski Road	Glendale	AZ	85310

License # = **422 RTW**
Client # = **5508**
Insurance Code = **L**
Uninsured Motorist = **Yes**

License # = **130 YWR**
Client # = **5508**
Insurance Code = **F**
Uninsured Motorist = **No**

License # = **795 GRT**
Client # = **2511**
Insurance Code = **L**
Uninsured Motorist = **Yes**

8. Print and then close the Insurance table.
9. Open the Claims table, make sure the table displays in Datasheet view, and then add the following record:

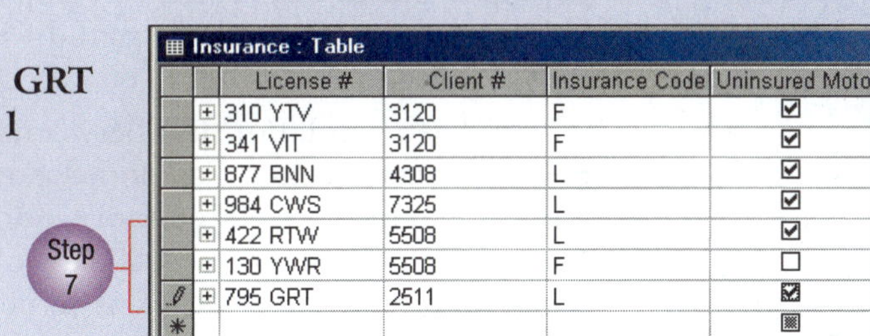

License #	Client #	Insurance Code	Uninsured Moto
310 YTV	3120	F	☑
341 VIT	3120	F	☑
877 BNN	4308	L	☑
984 CWS	7325	L	☑
422 RTW	5508	L	☑
130 YWR	5508	F	☐
795 GRT	2511	L	☑

Claim # = **130057**
Client # = **2511**
License # = **795 GRT**
Date of Claim = **3/4/2002**
Amount of Claim = **$186.40**

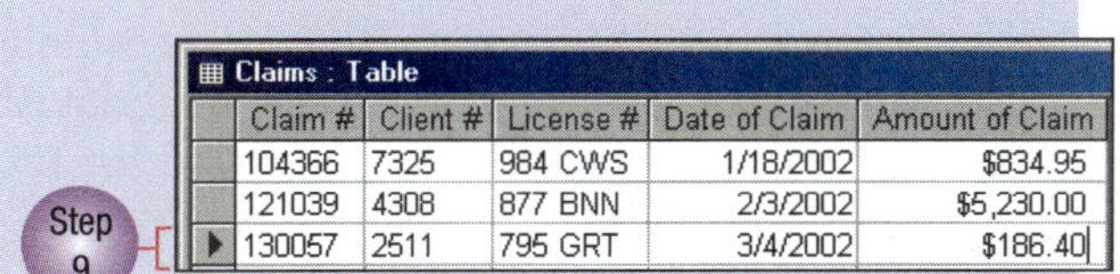

Claim #	Client #	License #	Date of Claim	Amount of Claim
104366	7325	984 CWS	1/18/2002	$834.95
121039	4308	877 BNN	2/3/2002	$5,230.00
130057	2511	795 GRT	3/4/2002	$186.40

10. Print the Claims table.
11. With the Claims table still open, try to enter a record for a client who has not been entered in the Clients table by completing the following steps (Access will not allow this because of the one-to-many relationship that was established in exercise 2):
    a. Add the following record to the Claims table:

Claim #	=	201221
Client #	=	5824
License #	=	640 TRS
Date of Claim	=	3/11/2002
Amount of Claim	=	$895.25

    b. Click OK to close the Microsoft Access message box.
    c. Click the Save button on the Table Datasheet toolbar.
    d. Click the Close button to close the Claims table. This causes a message to display telling you that the record cannot be added or changed because a related record is required in the Clients table. At this message, click OK.
    e. A message displays warning you that Access cannot save the table, that closing the object will cause the changes to be lost, and asking if you want to close the database object. At this warning, click Yes.
12. Close the Southwest Insurance database file.

Editing and Deleting a Relationship

HINT
The Relationships window will display any relationship that has been defined between tables.

Changes can be made to a relationship that has been established between tables. The relationship can also be deleted. To edit a relationship, open the database file containing the tables with the relationship, and then click the Relationships button on the Database toolbar; or click Tools and then Relationships. This displays the Relationships window with the related tables displayed in boxes. Position the arrow pointer on the thin portion of one of the black lines that connects the related tables and then click the *right* mouse button. This causes a pop-up menu to display. At this pop-up menu, click the left mouse button on Edit Relationship. This displays the Edit Relationships dialog box such as the one shown in figure 2.5, where you can change the current relationship.

To delete a relationship between tables, display the related tables in the Relationships window. Position the arrow pointer on the thin portion of the black line connecting the related tables and then click the *right* mouse button. At the pop-up menu that displays, click the left mouse button on Delete. At the message asking if you are sure you want to permanently delete the selected relationship from your database, click Yes.

Displaying Related Records in a Subdatasheet

When a relationship is established between tables, you can view and edit fields in related tables with a subdatasheet. Figure 2.8 displays the Clients table with the subdatasheet displayed for the client Spenser Winters. The subdatasheet displays the fields in the Insurance table related to Spenser Winters. Use this subdatasheet to view information and also to edit information in the Clients table a well as the

Insurance table. Changes made to fields in a subdatasheet affect the table and any related table.

A plus symbol (+) displays before each record in the Clients table shown in figure 2.8. Access automatically inserts plus symbols before each record in a table that is joined to another table by a one-to-many relationship.

FIGURE 2.8 ***Table with Subdatasheet Displayed***

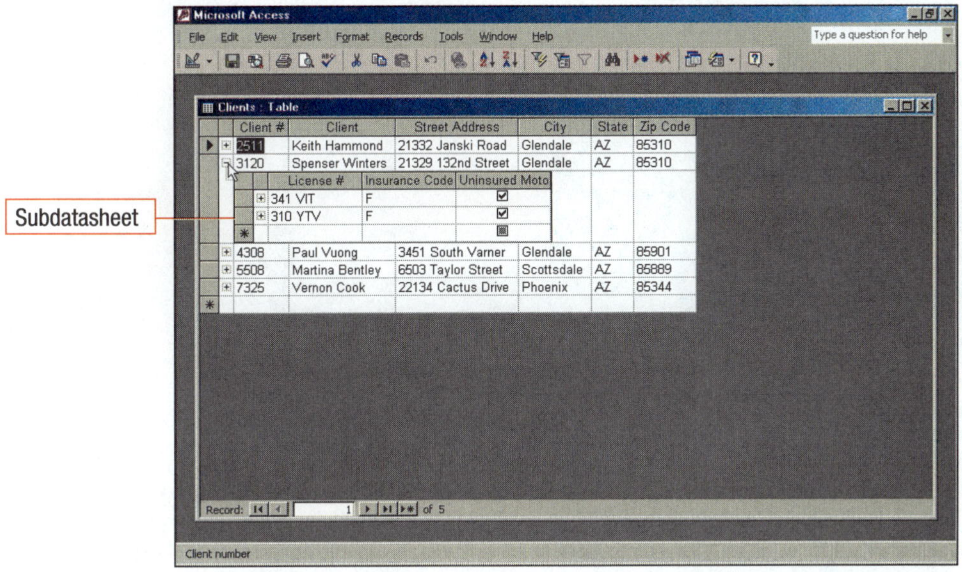

To create a subdatasheet, display the table that is the "one" in the one-to-many relationship. Click the plus symbol preceding the record for which you want to display fields in a related table. This displays the Insert Subdatasheet dialog box shown in figure 2.9. At this dialog box, click the desired table in the list box, and then click OK. The subdatasheet is inserted below the record and contains fields from the related table. To remove the subdatasheet, click the minus sign preceding the record. (The plus symbol turns into the minus symbol when a subdatasheet displays.)

FIGURE

2.9 *Insert Subdatasheet Dialog Box*

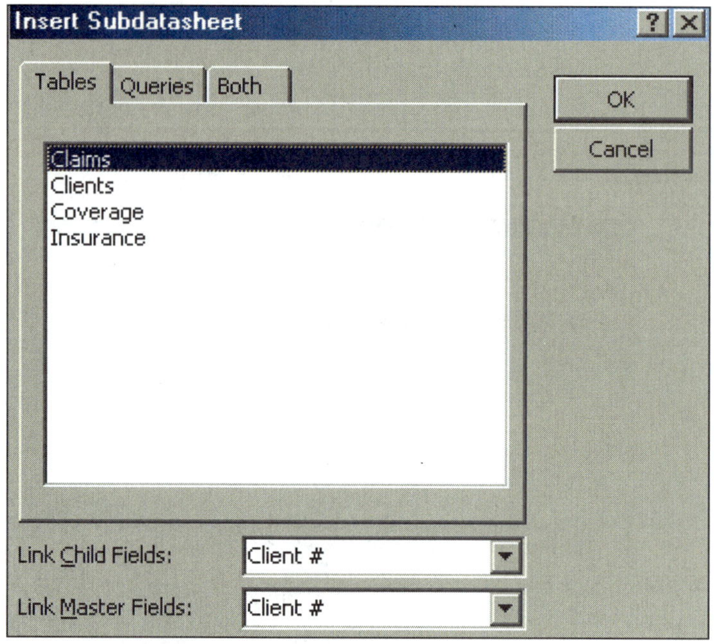

Specify a different subdatasheet in a table by clicking the Insert option on the Menu bar and then clicking Subdatasheet. This displays the Insert Subdatasheet dialog box shown in figure 2.9 where you can specify the desired table.

exercise 5

VIEWING AND EDITING A SUBDATASHEET

1. Open the Southwest Insurance database file.
2. Open the Clients table.
3. Display a subdatasheet with fields in the Claims table by completing the following steps:
   a. Click the plus symbol that displays at the left side of the first row (the row for Keith Hammond).
   b. At the Insert Subdatasheet dialog box, click *Claims* in the list box, and then click OK.
4. Display subdatasheets for each of the remaining records by clicking the plus symbol that displays before each of the remaining four rows.
5. Remove subdatasheets for each record by clicking the minus symbol that displays before each record.
6. Suppose that the client, Vernon Cook, has moved to a new address and purchased insurance for a new car. Display the Insurance subdatasheet and make changes to fields in the Clients table and the Insurance table by completing the following steps:

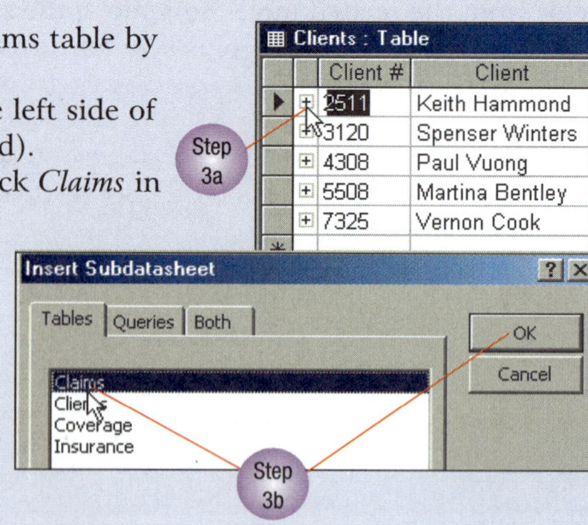

a. Click Insert on the Menu bar and then click Subdatasheet at the drop-down menu.
b. At the Insert Subdatasheet dialog box, click *Insurance* in the list box, and then click OK.
c. Click the plus symbol at the beginning of the row for Vernon Cook.
d. Change his street address from *22134 Cactus Drive* to *1230 South Mesa*.
e. Change his Zip Code from *85344* to *86201*.
f. Add the following information in the second row in the Insurance subdatasheet:

License #	=	**430 DWT**
Insurance Code	=	**F**
Uninsured Motorist	=	**Yes**

g. Click the Save button on the Table Datasheet toolbar.
h. Close the Clients table.

7. Open the Clients table, print it, and then close it.
8. Open the Insurance table, print it, and then close it.
9. Close the Southwest Insurance database file.

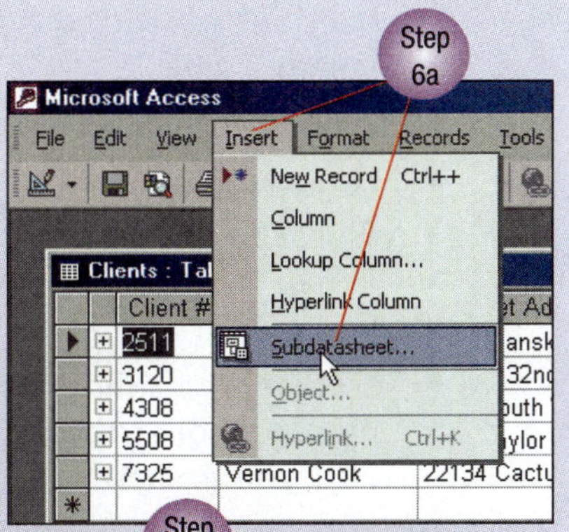

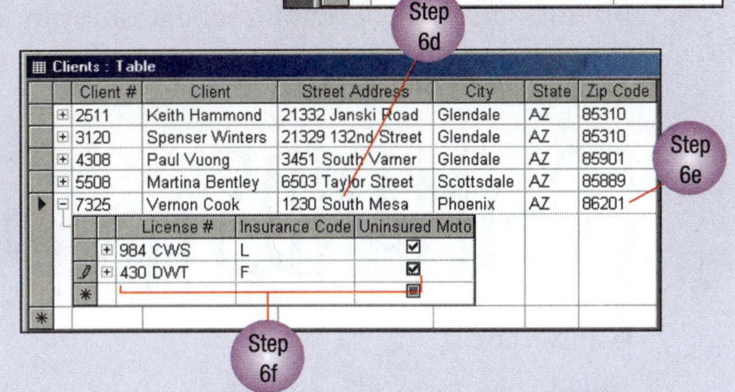

CHAPTER summary

- Access is a relational database software program where database tables can be created that have a relation or connection to one another.
- When planning a table, take time to determine how to break down the required data and what relationships will need to be defined to eliminate data redundancies.
- In a table, at least one field must be unique so that one record can be distinguished from another. A field with a unique value is considered a primary key.
- In a field defined as a primary key, duplicate values are not allowed in the primary field and Access also expects a value in each record in the primary key field.
- Define a primary key field with the Primary Key button on the Table Design toolbar.
- A primary key field included in another table is referred to as a foreign key. Unlike a primary key field, a foreign key field can contain duplicate data.
- In Access, one table can be related to another by performing a join. When tables that have a common field are joined, data can be extracted from both tables as if they were one large table.

- A one-to-many relationship can be created between tables in a database file. In this relationship, a record must be added to the "one" table before it can be added to the "many" table.
- A relationship between tables can be edited and/or deleted.
- Access contains a Print Relationships Wizard you can use to print a report displaying the relationships between tables.
- When a relationship is established between tables, you can view and edit fields in related tables with a subdatasheet.
- To display a subdatasheet, display the Insert Subdatasheet dialog box (by clicking the plus symbol at the beginning of a record or by clicking Insert and then Subdatasheet), click the desired table in the list box, and then click OK.
- Turn off the display of a subdatasheet by clicking the minus symbol at the beginning of a record.

COMMANDS review

Command	Mouse/Keyboard
Identify primary key in table	Position insertion point in row in table, click Primary Key button on Table Design toolbar
Display Edit Relationships dialog box	At the Relationships window, drag common field from primary table to related table
Print database relationships	At Relationships window, click File and then Print Relationships; then click Print button on Print Preview toolbar
Display Insert Subdatasheet dialog box	Click plus symbol at beginning of a record in a related table; or, click Insert and then Subdatasheet

CONCEPTS check

Completion: On a blank sheet of paper, indicate the correct term, symbol, or character for each description.

1. A primary key field must contain unique data while this type of key field can contain duplicate data.
2. In Access, one table can be related to another, which is generally referred to as performing this.
3. In a one-to-many relationship, the table containing the "one" is referred to as this.
4. In a one-to-many relationship, the table containing the "many" is referred to as this.

5. In a one-to-many relationship, Access follows a set of rules that enforces consistency between related tables and is referred to as this.
6. In related tables, this number displays near the black line next to the primary table.
7. In related tables, this symbol displays near the black line next to the related table.
8. The black line that connects related tables is referred to as this.
9. Click this symbol at the beginning of a record in a related table to display the Insert Subdatasheet dialog box.
10. Turn off the display of a subdatasheet by clicking this symbol that displays at the beginning of the record.
11. Suppose you have created a table named Committees within the database file named Members. The Committees table contains a field named *Committee Name* that you decide should be identified as the primary key field. List the steps you would complete to identify *Committee Name* as the primary key field (you are beginning at a blank Access screen).
12. List the steps you would complete to create a one-to-many relationship between the Member Information table and the Committees table in the Members database file. The primary key field in the Member Information table is *Member #*. (You are beginning at the Members : Database window.)

SKILLS check

Assessment 1

1. Use Access to create a database for keeping track of books. Name the database file Books. Name the first table you create Author Information and include the following fields in the table (you determine the data type, field size, and description):

   Field Name
   Author # (primary key)
   First Name
   Last Name
   Middle Initial

2. After creating the table with the fields shown above and defining the primary key, save the table and name it Author Information. Switch to Datasheet view and then enter the following data in the table:

   Author # = **1**
   First Name = **Branson**
   Last Name = **Walters**
   Middle Initial = **A.**

   Author # = **2**
   First Name = **Christiana**
   Last Name = **Copeland**
   Middle Initial = **M.**

   Author # = **3**
   First Name = **Shirley**
   Last Name = **Romero**
   Middle Initial = **E.**

Author #	=	**4**
First Name	=	**Jeffrey**
Last Name	=	**Fiedler**
Middle Initial	=	**R.**

3. Automatically adjust the width of columns.
4. Save, print, and then close the Author Information table.
5. At the Books database file, create another table with book information with the following fields (you determine the data type, field size, and description):

   Field Name
   ISBN (primary key)
   Author #
   Title
   Category Code
   Price

6. After creating the table with the fields shown above and defining the primary key, save the table and name it Book Information. Switch to Datasheet view and then enter the following data in the table:

ISBN	=	**12-6543-9008-7**
Author #	=	**4**
Title	=	**Today's Telecommunications**
Category Code	=	**B**
Price	=	**$34.95**
ISBN	=	**09-5225-5466-6**
Author #	=	**2**
Title	=	**Marketing in the Global Economy**
Category Code	=	**M**
Price	=	**$42.50**
ISBN	=	**23-9822-7645-0**
Author #	=	**1**
Title	=	**International Business Strategies**
Category Code	=	**B**
Price	=	**$45.00**
ISBN	=	**08-4351-4890-3**
Author #	=	**3**
Title	=	**Technological Advances**
Category Code	=	**B**
Price	=	**$36.95**

7. Automatically adjust the width of columns (to accommodate the longest entry).
8. Save, print, and then close the Book Information table.
9. At the Books database file, create another table with category information with the following fields (you determine the data type, field size, and description):

   Field Name
   Category Code (primary key)
   Category

10. After creating the table with the fields shown above and defining the primary key, save the table and name it Category. Switch to Datasheet view and then enter the following data in the table:

Category Code	=	**B**
Category	=	**Business**
Category Code	=	**M**
Category	=	**Marketing**

11. Print and then close the Category table.
12. Close the Books database file.

Assessment 2

1. Open the Books database file and then create the following relationships:
   a. Create a one-to-many relationship with the *Author #* field in the Author Information table the "one" and the *Author #* field in the Book Information table the "many." (At the Edit Relationships dialog box, choose Enforce Referential Integrity, Cascade Update Related Fields, and Cascade Delete Related Records.)
   b. Create a one-to-many relationship with the *Category Code* field in the Category table the "one" and the *Category Code* field in the Book Information table the "many." (At the Edit Relationships dialog box, choose Enforce Referential Integrity, Cascade Update Related Fields, and Cascade Delete Related Records.)
2. Print the relationships.
3. After creating, saving, and printing the relationships, add the following record to the Author Information table:

Author #	=	**5**
First Name	=	**Glenna**
Last Name	=	**Zener-Young**
Middle Initial	=	**A.**

4. Adjust the column width for the *Last Name* field.
5. Save, print, and then close the Author Information table.
6. Add the following records to the Book Information table:

ISBN #	=	**23-8931-0084-7**
Author #	=	**2**
Title	=	**Practical Marketing Strategies**
Category	=	**M**
Price	=	**$28.50**
ISBN #	=	**87-4009-7134-6**
Author #	=	**5**
Title	=	**Selling More**
Category	=	**M**
Price	=	**$40.25**

7. Print and then close the Book Information table.
8. Close the Books database file.

CHAPTER 3

CREATING A TABLE USING A WIZARD AND USING HELP

PERFORMANCE OBJECTIVES

Upon successful completion of chapter 3, you will be able to:

- **Create a table using the Table Wizard**
- **Complete a spelling check on data in a table**
- **Find specific records in a table**
- **Find specific data in a table and replace with other data**
- **Use the Help feature**

(Note: There are no data files to copy for this chapter.)

Access, like other programs in the Microsoft Office suite, contains a variety of wizards you can use to design and create tables, reports, forms, and so on. In this chapter, you will learn how to use the Table Wizard to prepare a table. Access contains a spelling check feature as well as a find and replace feature. Use the spelling checker to find misspelled words in a table and use the find and replace feature to find specific records in a table or find specific data in a table and replace with other data. Microsoft Office contains an on-screen reference manual containing information on features and commands for each program within the suite. In this chapter, you will learn to use the Help feature to display information about Access.

Creating a Table Using the Table Wizard

Access contains a Table Wizard you can use to design a table. The wizard helps you design a table by offering possible field choices with data types already assigned. If the Table Wizard does not offer the exact field name you require, you can edit a field name to personalize it.

> **HINT**
> Before using the Table Wizard, you must create the database file into which you will save the table.

To use the Table Wizard, create a new database file. At the new database window, double-click the *Create table by using wizard* option in the list box. This displays the first Table Wizard dialog box shown in figure 3.1. At this dialog box, specify whether the table is designed for a business or personal use, choose a sample table from the Sample Tables list box, and choose the desired fields.

HINT

Choose the table that most closely matches the type of data you are managing.

At the second Table Wizard dialog box, shown in figure 3.2, key a name for the table and then specify if you want the wizard to set the primary key or if you want to set it. At the third Table Wizard dialog box, shown in figure 3.3, specify what you want to do after the wizard creates the table—modify the table design, enter data directly into the table, or enter data into the table using a form the wizard creates.

FIGURE 3.1 *First Table Wizard Dialog Box*

HINT

Each field offered by the Table Wizard has the appropriate data type assigned to it.

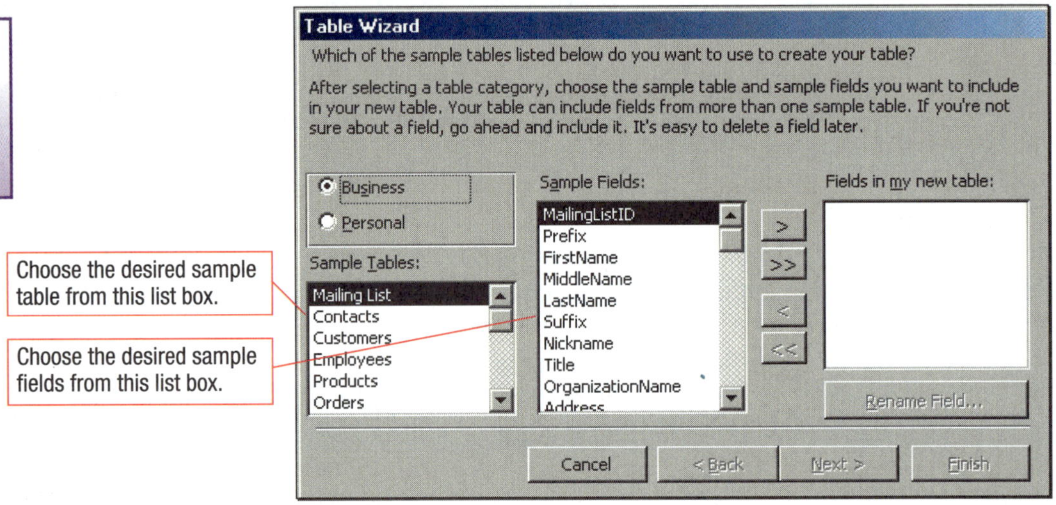

FIGURE 3.2 *Second Table Wizard Dialog Box*

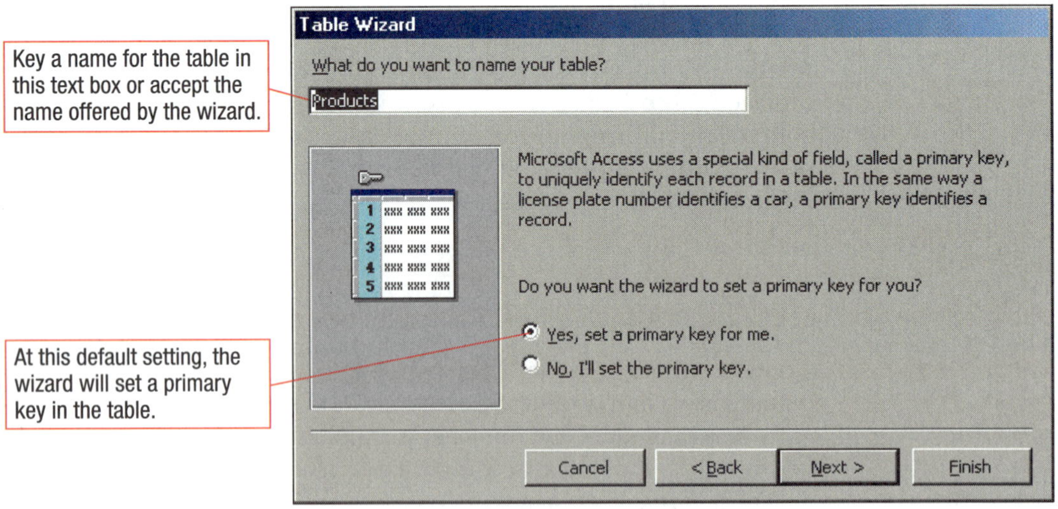

FIGURE

3.3 *Third Table Wizard Dialog Box*

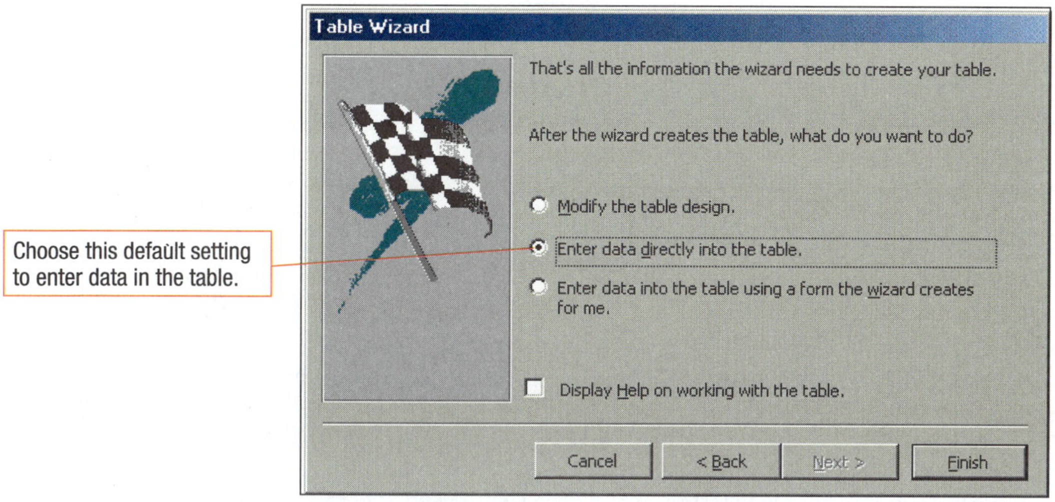

exercise 1

USING A TABLE WIZARD TO CREATE A TABLE

(Note: Delete from your disk any database files you created in chapter 2.)

1. Create a table for information on products used in MedSafe Clinic by completing the following steps:
   a. Start at the blank Access window and then click the New button on the Database toolbar or click File and then New. (This displays the New File Task Pane.)
   b. At the New File Task Pane, click the *Blank Database* hyperlink.
   c. At the File New Database dialog box, make sure the proper drive is selected, key **MedSafe Clinic** in the File name text box, and then press Enter or click the Create button.
   d. At the MedSafe Clinic : Database window, double-click *Create table by using wizard* in the list box.

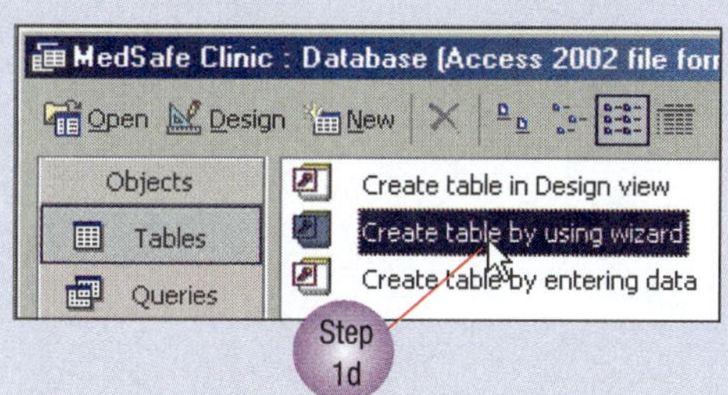

   e. At the first Table Wizard dialog box (refer to figure 3.1), click *Products* in the Sample Tables list box. (This changes the fields in the Sample Fields list box.)
   f. Choose some of the sample fields in the Sample Fields list box and add them to the Fields in my new table list box by completing the following steps:
      1) With *ProductID* already selected in the Sample Fields list box, click the button containing the greater than symbol (>) that displays between the Sample Fields list box and the Fields in my new table list box. (This inserts *ProductID* in the Fields in my new table list box and also selects *ProductName* in the Sample Fields list box.)
      2) With *ProductName* selected in the Sample Fields list box, click the button containing the > symbol. (This adds *ProductName* to the Fields in my new table list box.)
      3) Click once on *SupplierID* in the Sample Fields list box and then click the button containing the > symbol.
      4) Click once on *UnitsInStock* in the Sample Fields list box and then click the button containing the > symbol.

5) With *UnitsOnOrder* already selected in the Sample Fields list box, click the button containing the > symbol.

6) With *UnitPrice* already selected in the Sample Fields list box, click the button containing the > symbol.

7) With *ReorderLevel* already selected in the Sample Fields list box, click the button containing the > symbol.

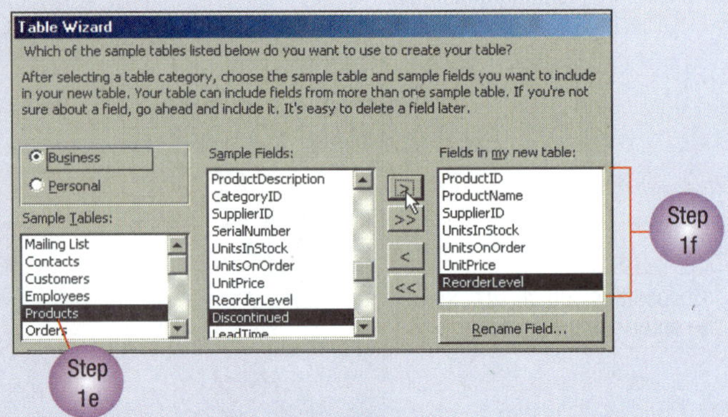

g. Click the Next button located at the bottom of the dialog box.

h. At the second Table Wizard dialog box (refer to figure 3.2), the wizard offers the name *Products* for the table name and also will set a primary key for the table. These choices are appropriate so click the Next button at the bottom of the dialog box.

i. At the third Table Wizard dialog box (refer to figure 3.3), the wizard has already selected *Enter data directly into the table*. This is appropriate for this exercise, so click the Finish button that displays at the bottom right corner of the dialog box.

j. At the Products : Table window shown in figure 3.4, notice that *AutoNumber* automatically displays in the *Product ID* field. This is because the Table Wizard assigned the data type AutoNumber to the field. (Access will insert a *1* in this field as soon as you key data into the second field in the Products table.) Press Tab to move the insertion point to the next field *(Product Name)*.

k. Key the following in the specified fields (do not key anything in the *Product ID* field; simply press the Tab key and let Access insert the number):

Product Name	=	**Latex gloves**
Supplier ID	=	**3**
Units In Stock	=	**243**
Units On Order	=	**0**
Unit Price	=	**0.50**
Reorder Level	=	**200**

Product Name	=	**Syringes**
Supplier ID	=	**1**
Units In Stock	=	**58**
Units On Order	=	**75**
Unit Price	=	**0.35**
Reorder Level	=	**75**

Product Name	=	**1-inch gauze pads**
Supplier ID	=	**4**
Units In Stock	=	**144**
Units On Order	=	**0**
Unit Price	=	**0.05**
Reorder Level	=	**125**

Product Name = **Tongue depressors**
Supplier ID = **1**
Units In Stock = **85**
Units On Order = **100**
Unit Price = **0.03**
Reorder Level = **100**

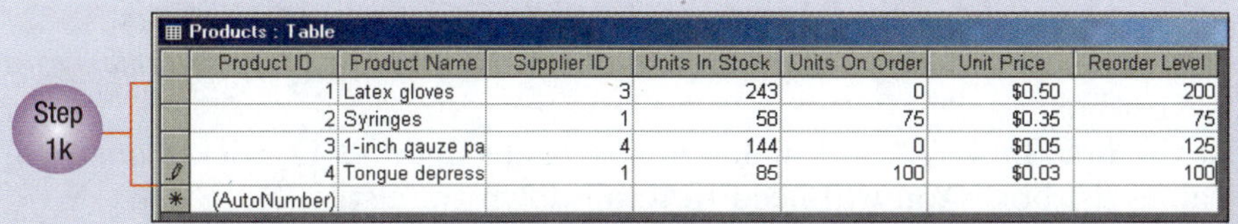

Product ID	Product Name	Supplier ID	Units In Stock	Units On Order	Unit Price	Reorder Level
1	Latex gloves	3	243	0	$0.50	200
2	Syringes	1	58	75	$0.35	75
3	1-inch gauze pa	4	144	0	$0.05	125
4	Tongue depress	1	85	100	$0.03	100
(AutoNumber)						

l. Automatically adjust the column widths for all columns containing data.
m. After entering the data and adjusting the column widths, click the Save button on the Table Datasheet toolbar.

2. Change the page orientation to landscape and then print the Products table.
3. Close the Products table.
4. Close the MedSafe Clinic database file.

FIGURE 3.4 ***Products : Table Window***

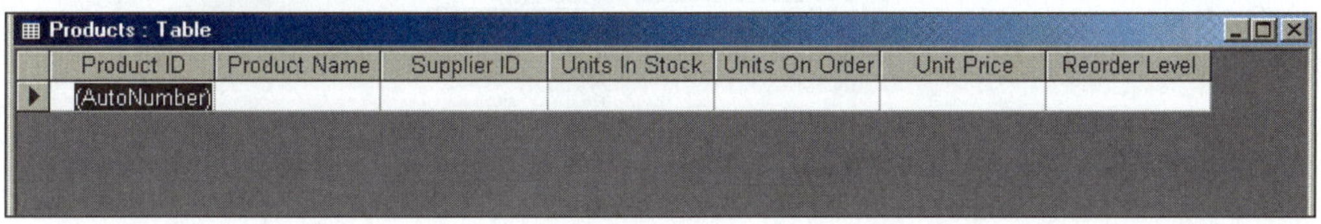

Product ID	Product Name	Supplier ID	Units In Stock	Units On Order	Unit Price	Reorder Level
(AutoNumber)						

In exercise 1, step 1f, you added fields to the Fields in my new table list box by selecting the desired field in the Sample Fields list box and then clicking the button containing the greater than symbol (>). Other buttons display by the button containing the greater than symbol. Click the button containing two greater than symbols (>>) and all fields in the Sample Fields list box are inserted in the Fields in my new table list box. If you want to remove a field from the Fields in my new table list box, select the field, and then click the button containing the less than symbol (<). Click the button containing two less than symbols (<<) to remove all fields from the Fields in my new table list box.

HINT

Rename a field by clicking the field in the Fields in my table list box, clicking the Rename Field button, keying the new name, and then clicking OK.

The MedSafe Clinic database file created in exercise 1 contains only one table. Use the Table Wizard to create other tables within the same database file. In exercise 2, you will use the Table Wizard to create a table containing information about suppliers used by MedSafe Clinic.

When a second or subsequent table is created in a database file using the Table Wizard, a relationship can be created between tables. In exercise 2, you will be creating a one-to-many relationship using the Table Wizard. The Suppliers table you create in exercise 2 will be identified as the "one" and the Products table you created in exercise 1 will be identified as the "many."

exercise 2

CREATING ANOTHER TABLE AND RELATING TABLES USING THE TABLE WIZARD

1. Create a table for suppliers used by MedSafe Clinic by completing the following steps:
   a. At the blank Access window, click the Open button on the Database toolbar; or click File and then Open.
   b. At the Open dialog box, double-click *MedSafe Clinic* in the list box.
   c. At the MedSafe Clinic : Database window, double-click *Create table by using wizard* in the list box.
   d. At the first Table Wizard dialog box (refer to figure 3.1), click *Suppliers* in the Sample Tables list box. (You will need to scroll down the list.)
   e. Add the following fields in the Sample Fields list box to the Fields in my new table list box (for help, refer to exercise 1, step 1f):

      SupplierID
      SupplierName
      Address
      City
      StateOrProvince
      PostalCode (Note: This is in a different order than shown in the Sample Fields list box.)
      PhoneNumber
      EmailAddress

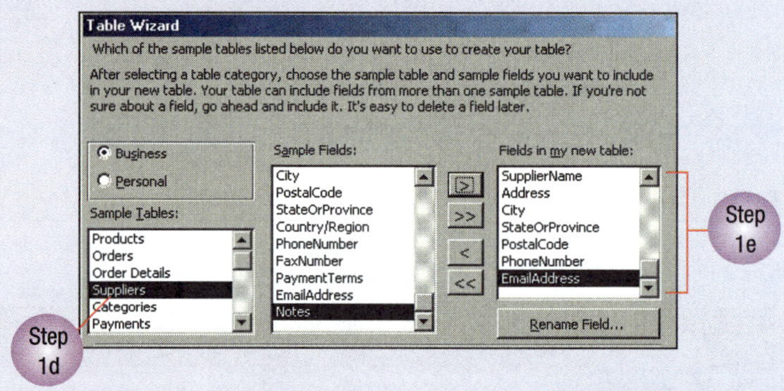

   f. After inserting the fields above in the Fields in my new table list box, click the Next button located at the bottom of the dialog box.
   g. At the second Table Wizard dialog box, the wizard offers the name *Suppliers* for the table name and also will set a primary key for the table. These choices are appropriate so click the Next button at the bottom of the dialog box.
   h. At the third Table Wizard dialog box shown in figure 3.5, create a one-to-many relationship between Suppliers (the "one") and Products (the "many") by completing the following steps:
      1) Click the Relationships button that displays toward the bottom right side of the dialog box.
      2) At the Relationships dialog box shown in figure 3.6, click the option button that displays before the *One record in the 'Suppliers' table will match many records in the 'Products' table* option.
      3) Click OK to close the dialog box.

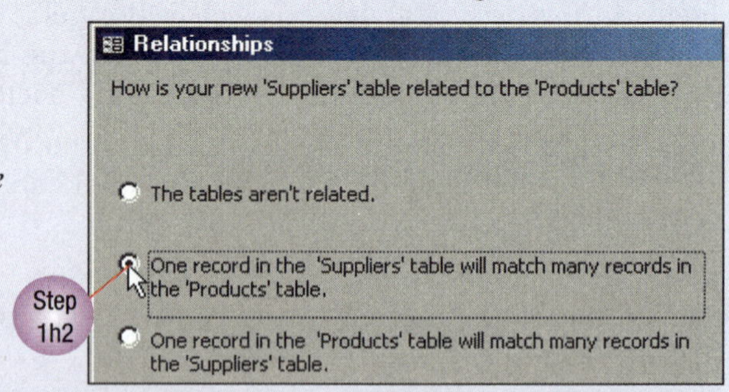

   i. At the Table Wizard dialog box, click Next.
   j. At the Table Wizard dialog box telling you that the wizard has all of the information it needs to create the table, make sure *Enter data directly into the table.* is selected, and then click Finish.
   k. At the Suppliers : Table window, key the following in the specified fields (the table wizard will automatically insert a number in the *Supplier ID* field):

Supplier Name = **Robicheaux Suppliers**
Address = **3200 Linden Drive**
City = **Baton Rouge**
State = **LA**
Postal Code = **70552**
Phone Number = **(318) 555-3411**
E-mail Address = **robi@emcp.com/med**

Supplier Name = **Quality Medical Supplies**
Address = **211 South Fourth Avenue**
City = **Tampa**
State = **FL**
Postal Code = **33562**
Phone Number = **(813) 555-8900**
E-mail Address = **qms@emcp.com/med**

Supplier Name = **Peachtree Medical Supplies**
Address = **764 Harmon Way**
City = **Atlanta**
State = **GA**
Postal Code = **73780**
Phone Number = **(404) 555-6474**
E-mail Address = **peachmed@emcp.com/med**

Supplier Name = **Lafferty Company**
Address = **12031 Ruston Way**
City = **Atlanta**
State = **GA**
Postal Code = **73125**
Phone Number = **(404) 555-8225**
E-mail Address = **lafferty@emcp.com/med**

Step 1k

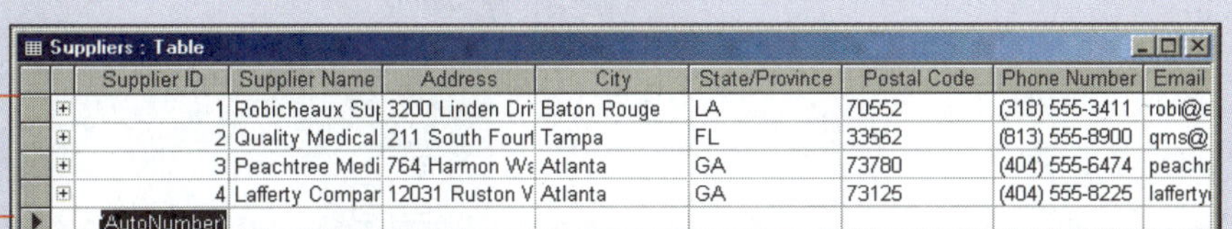

Suppliers : Table

Supplier ID	Supplier Name	Address	City	State/Province	Postal Code	Phone Number	Email
1	Robicheaux Su	3200 Linden Dri	Baton Rouge	LA	70552	(318) 555-3411	robi@e
2	Quality Medical	211 South Fourt	Tampa	FL	33562	(813) 555-8900	qms@
3	Peachtree Medi	764 Harmon W	Atlanta	GA	73780	(404) 555-6474	peachr
4	Lafferty Compar	12031 Ruston V	Atlanta	GA	73125	(404) 555-8225	lafferty
(AutoNumber)							

l. Automatically adjust the column widths for all columns containing data.
m. Click the Save button on the Table Datasheet toolbar to save the Suppliers table.

2. Change the page orientation to landscape, change the left and right margins to 0.3 inches, and then print the Suppliers table.
3. Close the Suppliers table.
4. Close the MedSafe Clinic database file.

FIGURE 3.5 *Third Table Wizard Dialog Box*

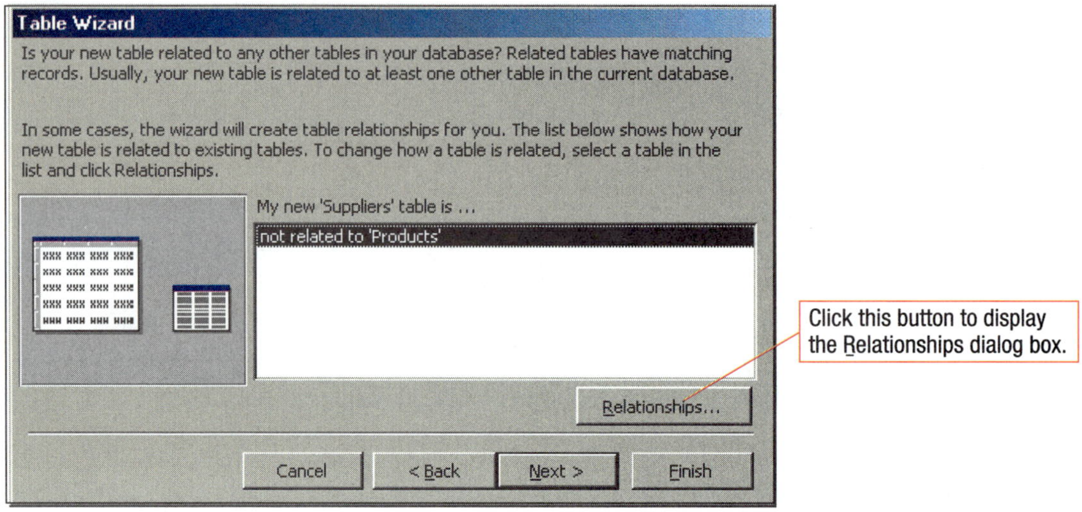

FIGURE 3.6 *Relationships Dialog Box*

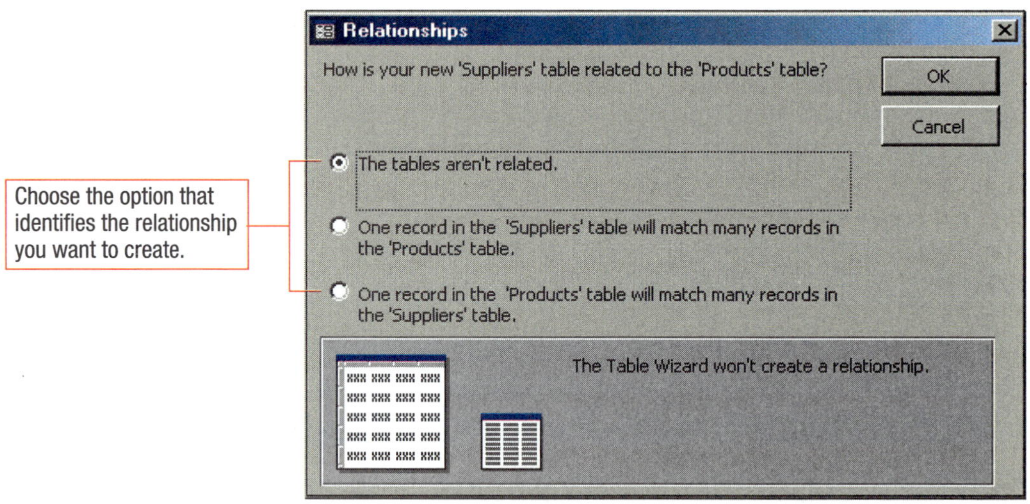

In exercise 2, a one-to-many relationship was created between the Suppliers and Products tables. In this relationship, a record for a supplier must first be created in the Suppliers table before the supplier number can be used in a record in the Products table. In exercise 3, you will add a new supplier to the Suppliers table and then use that supplier in a record in the Products table.

exercise 3

ADDING RECORDS TO THE SUPPLIERS AND PRODUCTS TABLES

1. Open the MedSafe Clinic database file.
2. Open the Suppliers table.
3. With Suppliers open in Datasheet view, add the following record at the end of the table:

Supplier Name	=	**National Products**
Address	=	**2192 Second Street**
City	=	**Little Rock**
State	=	**AR**
PostalCode	=	**72203**
Phone Number	=	**(501) 555-0551**
E-mail Address	=	**natprod@emcp.com/med**

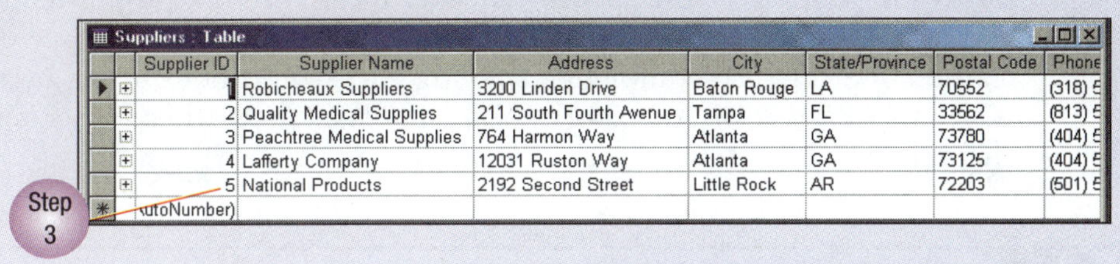

Supplier ID	Supplier Name	Address	City	State/Province	Postal Code	Phone
1	Robicheaux Suppliers	3200 Linden Drive	Baton Rouge	LA	70552	(318) 5
2	Quality Medical Supplies	211 South Fourth Avenue	Tampa	FL	33562	(813) 5
3	Peachtree Medical Supplies	764 Harmon Way	Atlanta	GA	73780	(404) 5
4	Lafferty Company	12031 Ruston Way	Atlanta	GA	73125	(404) 5
5	National Products	2192 Second Street	Little Rock	AR	72203	(501) 5
utoNumber)						

4. Change the page orientation to landscape, change the left and right margins to 0.3 inches, and then print the Suppliers table.
5. Close the Suppliers table.
6. Open the Products table and then add the following records at the end of the table:

Product Name	=	**Cotton swabs**
Supplier ID	=	**5**
Units In Stock	=	**1345**
Units On Order	=	**1000**
Unit Price	=	**0.03**
Reorder Level	=	**1500**

Product Name	=	**Thermometer covers**
Supplier ID	=	**2**
Units In Stock	=	**414**
Units On Order	=	**250**
Unit Price	=	**0.02**
Reorder Level	=	**450**

7. Delete the record for tongue depressors.
8. Adjust the column width for *Product Name*.
9. Save the Products table.
10. Change the page orientation to landscape and then print the Products table.
11. Close the Products table.
12. Close the MedSafe Clinic database file.

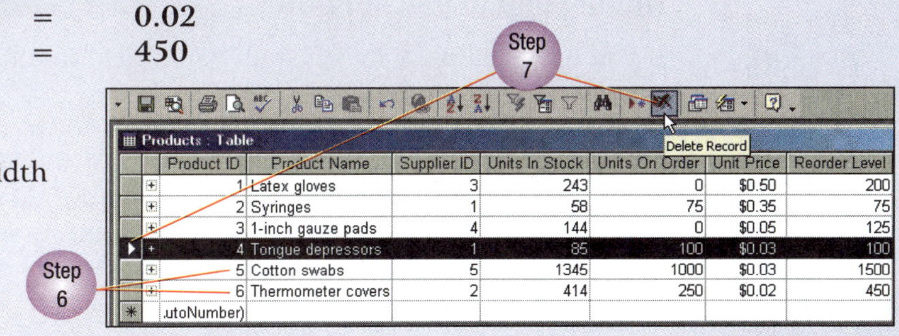

Product ID	Product Name	Supplier ID	Units In Stock	Units On Order	Unit Price	Reorder Level
1	Latex gloves	3	243	0	$0.50	200
2	Syringes	1	58	75	$0.35	75
3	1-inch gauze pads	4	144	0	$0.05	125
4	Tongue depressors	1	85	100	$0.03	100
5	Cotton swabs	5	1345	1000	$0.03	1500
6	Thermometer covers	2	414	250	$0.02	450
utoNumber)						

Completing a Spelling Check

HINT
You can also begin spell checking by clicking Tools and then Spelling or by pressing F7.

Spelling

The spelling checker feature in Access finds misspelled words and offers replacement words. It also finds duplicate words and irregular capitalizations. When you spell check an object in a database file such as a table, the spelling checker compares the words in your table with the words in its dictionary. If a match is found, the word is passed over. If there is no match for the word, the spelling checker selects the word and offers replacement suggestions.

To complete a spelling check, open the desired table in Datasheet view, and then click the Spelling button on the Table Datasheet toolbar. If the spelling checker does not find a match for a word in your table, the Spelling dialog box displays with replacement options. Figure 3.7 displays the Spelling dialog box with the word *Montain* selected and possible replacements displayed in the Suggestions list box. At the Spelling dialog box, you can choose to ignore the word (for example, if the spelling checker has selected a proper name), change to one of the replacement options, or add the word to the dictionary or AutoCorrect feature. You can also complete a spelling check on other objects in a database file such as a query, form, or report. (You will learn about these objects in future chapters.)

FIGURE 3.7 ***Spelling Dialog Box***

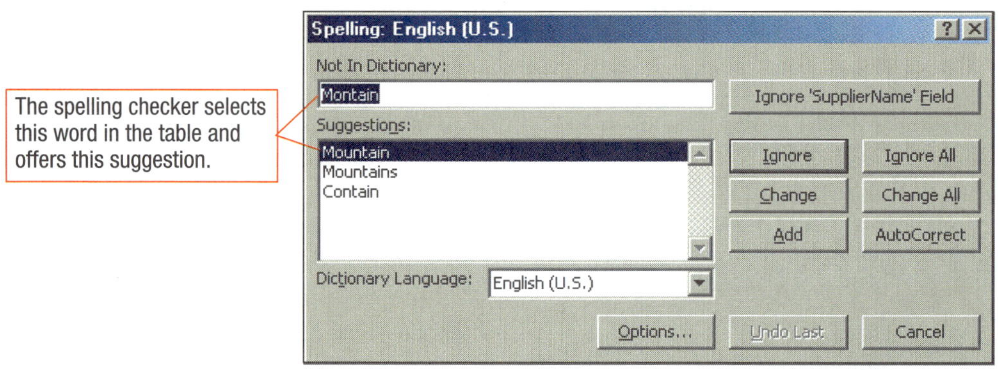

Finding and Replacing Data

Find

If you need to find a specific entry in a field in a table, consider using options at the Find and Replace dialog box with the Find tab selected as shown in figure 3.8. Display this dialog box by clicking the Find button on the Table Datasheet toolbar or by clicking Edit and then Find. At the Find and Replace dialog box, enter the data for which you are searching in the Find What text box. By default, Access will look in the specific column where the insertion point is positioned. Click the Find Next button to find the next occurrence of the data or click the Cancel button to remove the Find and Replace dialog box.

HINT
Press Ctrl + F to display the Find and Replace dialog box with the Find tab selected.

FIGURE 3.8 *Find and Replace Dialog Box with Find Tab Selected*

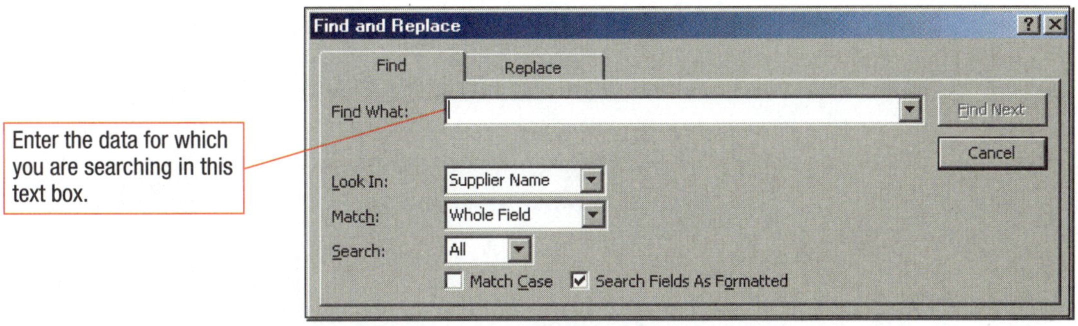

The Look In option defaults to the column where the insertion point is positioned. You can choose to look in the entire table by clicking the down-pointing triangle at the right side of the option and then clicking the table name at the drop-down list. The Match option has a default setting of *Whole Field*. You can change this to *Any Part of Field* or *Start of Field*. The Search option has a default setting of *All*, which means that Access will search all data in a specific column. This can be changed to *Up* or *Down*. If you want to find data that contains specific uppercase and lowercase letters, insert a check mark in the Match Case check box.

You can use the Find and Replace dialog box with the Replace tab selected as shown in figure 3.9 to search for specific data and replace with other data. Display this dialog box by clicking the Find button on the Table Datasheet toolbar and then clicking the Replace tab. Or you can display this dialog box by clicking Edit and then Replace.

HINT

Press Ctrl + H to display the Find and Replace dialog box with the Replace tab selected.

FIGURE 3.9 *Find and Replace Dialog Box with Replace Tab Selected*

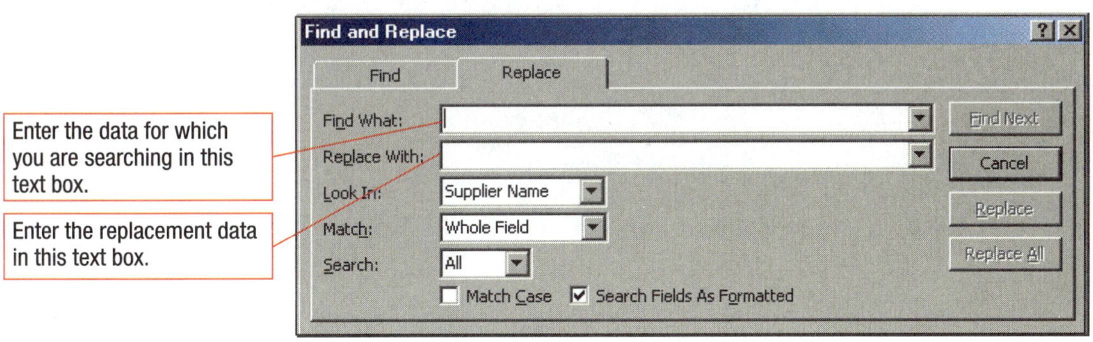

exercise 4 CHECKING THE SPELLING AND FINDING SPECIFIC DATA IN A TABLE

1. Open the MedSafe Clinic database file.
2. Open the Suppliers table.
3. With Suppliers open in Datasheet view, add the following record at the end of the table. (Key the misspelled words as shown below. You will correct the spelling in a later step.)

Supplier Name	=	**Blue Montain Supplies**
Address	=	**9550 Unaversity Avenue**
City	=	**Little Rock**
State	=	**AR**
Postal Code	=	**72209**
Phone Number	=	**(501) 555-4400**
E-mail Address	=	**bluemtn@emcp.com/med**

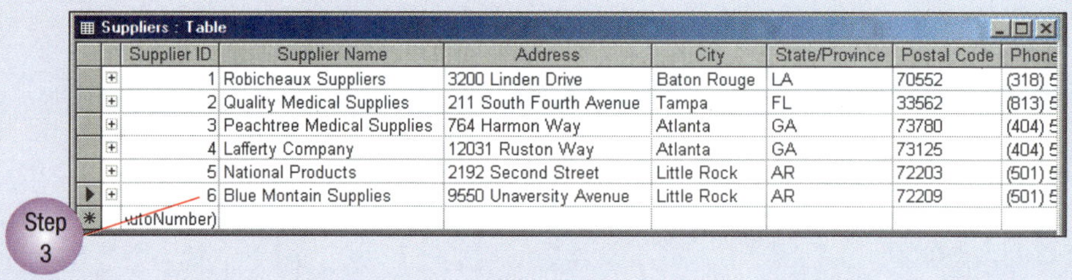

4. Complete a spelling check on the table by completing the following steps:
   a. With the Suppliers table open in Datasheet view, click in the first entry in the *SupplierID* column.
   b. Click the Spelling button on the Table Datasheet toolbar.
   c. The spelling checker selects the name *Robicheaux*. This is a proper name, so click the Ignore button to tell the spelling checker to leave the name as written.

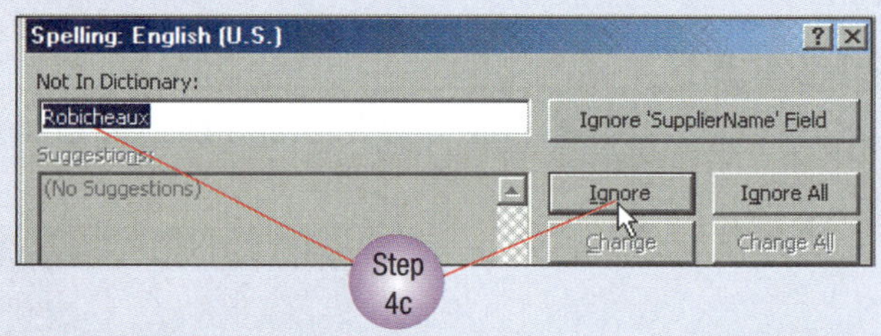

   d. The spelling checker selects *Montain*. The proper spelling *(Mountain)* is selected in the Suggestions list box, so click the Change button.
   e. The spelling checker selects *Unaversity*. The proper spelling *(University)* is selected in the Suggestions list box, so click the Change button.
   f. At the message telling you that the spelling check is complete, click the OK button.

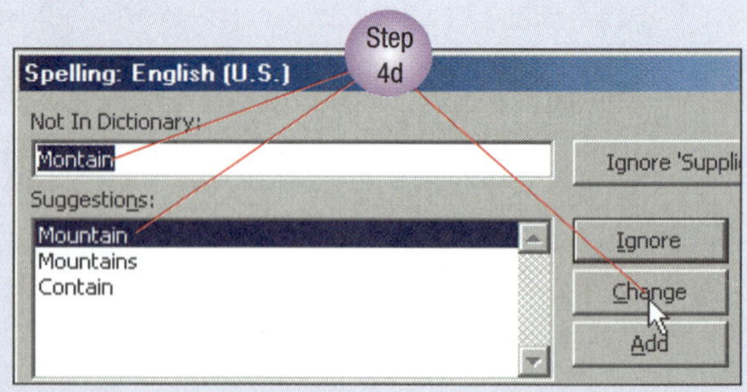

5. Find any records containing the two-letter state abbreviation *GA* by completing the following steps:
   a. Click in the first entry in the *State/Province* column.

b. Click the Find button on the Table Datasheet toolbar.

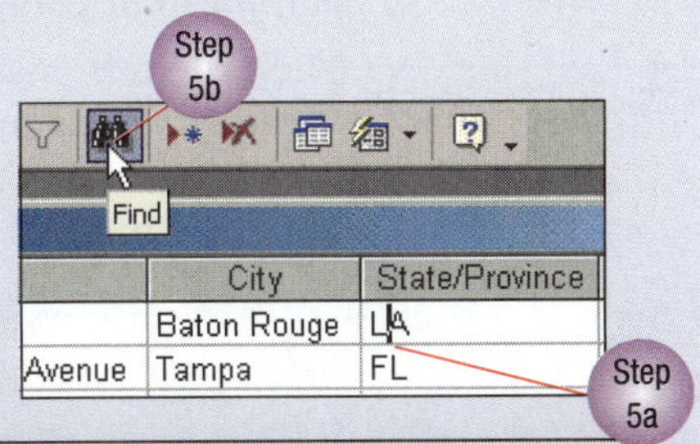

c. At the Find and Replace dialog box with the Find tab selected, key **GA** in the Find What text box.

d. Click the Find Next button. (Access finds and selects the first occurrence of *GA*. If the Find and Replace dialog box covers the data, drag the dialog box to a different location on the screen.)

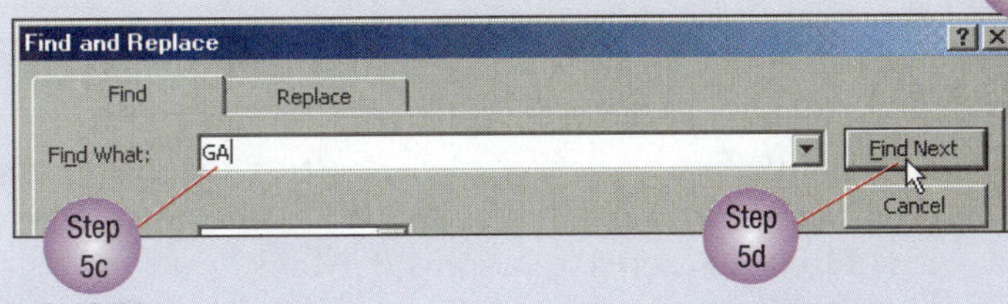

e. Continue clicking the Find Next button until a message displays telling you that Access has finished searching the records. At this message, click OK.

f. Click the Cancel button to close the Find and Replace dialog box.

6. Suppose Quality Medical Supplies has changed its telephone number. Complete the following steps to find the current telephone number and replace it with the new telephone number:
   a. Click in the first entry in the *Telephone* column.
   b. Click Edit and then Replace.
   c. At the Find and Replace dialog box with the Replace tab selected, key **(813) 555-8900** in the Find What text box.
   d. Press the Tab key. (This moves the insertion point to the Replace With text box.
   e. Key **(863) 555-2255** in the Replace With text box.
   f. Click the Find Next button.
   g. When Access selects the telephone number *(813) 555-8900*, click the Replace button.
   h. Click the Cancel button to close the Find and Replace dialog box.

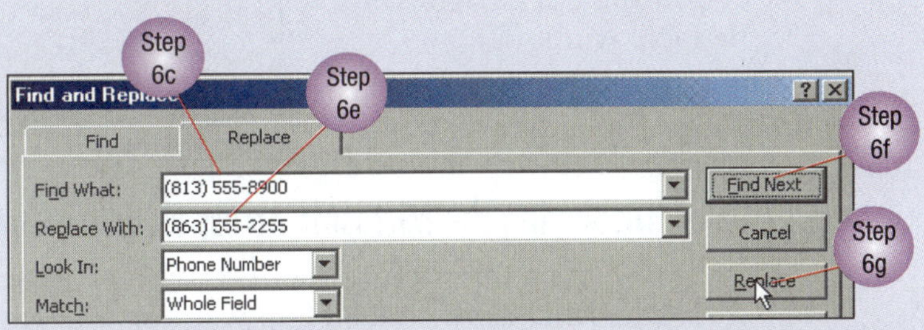

7. Change the page orientation to landscape, change the left and right margins to 0.3 inches, and then print the Suppliers table.
8. Close the Suppliers table.
9. Close the MedSafe Clinic database file.

Using Help

The Access Help feature is an on-screen reference manual containing information about all Access features and commands. The Access Help feature is similar to the Windows Help and the Help features in Word, Excel, and PowerPoint. Get help using the Ask a Question button on the Menu bar, the Office Assistant, or from the Help Topics window.

Getting Help Using the Ask a Question Button

Ask a Question

Click the text inside the Ask a Question button located at the right side of the Menu bar (this removes the text), key a help question, and then press Enter. A list of topics matching key words in your question displays below the Ask a Question button. Click the desired topic and a Help window displays with information about the topic.

exercise 5

GETTING HELP USING THE ASK A QUESTION BUTTON

1. At a blank Access screen, click the text inside the Ask a Question button located at the right side of the Menu bar.
2. Key **How do I create an Input Mask?**.
3. Press the Enter key.
4. From the list of topics that displays below the Ask a Question button, click the *About creating input masks to control how data is entered in a field or control* option.
5. When the Help window displays, click the *Show All* hyperlink that displays in the upper right corner of the window. (This expands the topics in the window.)
6. Read the information in the Help window and then click the Close button (contains an *X*) located in the upper right corner of the Help window.

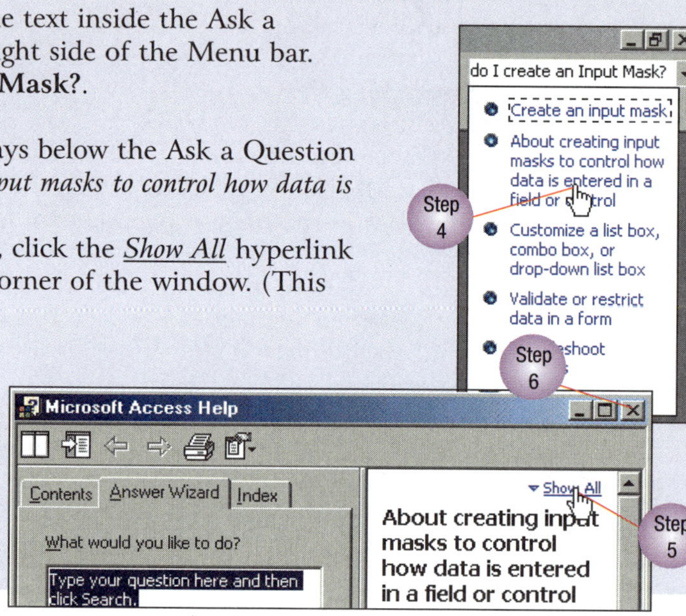

Displaying the Microsoft Access Help Window

Microsoft Access Help

Keying a question in the Ask a Question button and then pressing Enter displays the Microsoft Access Help window. You can also display this Help window by clicking the Microsoft Access Help button on the Database toolbar, clicking Help and then Microsoft Access Help, or clicking the *Microsoft Access Help* hyperlink in the New File Task Pane.

Using Buttons at the Help Window

Auto Tile

Show

Forward

The Help window contains a toolbar with buttons. Click the Auto Tile button and all open windows are tiled so each window displays next to each other. Click the Auto Tile button and it changes to the Untile button. Click the Show button to expand the window and display three tabs—Contents, Answer Wizard, and Index. If you move to various help items, click the Back button to return to the previous window. Click the Forward button to move forward to a help item. Click the Print button to send the Help information to the printer. Click the Options button and a drop-down menu displays with many of the same features as the buttons. For example, there is a Show Tabs option that will expand the window and Back and Forward options that do the same thing as the Back and Forward buttons. Additional options include Home, Stop, Refresh, Internet Options, and Print.

Using Options at the Expanded Help Window

Back

The Help window toolbar contains a Show button. Click the Show button and the window expands as shown in figure 3.10. Three tabs display in the expanded window—Contents, Answer Wizard, and Index.

Print

Options

FIGURE 3.10 ***Expanded Microsoft Access Help Window***

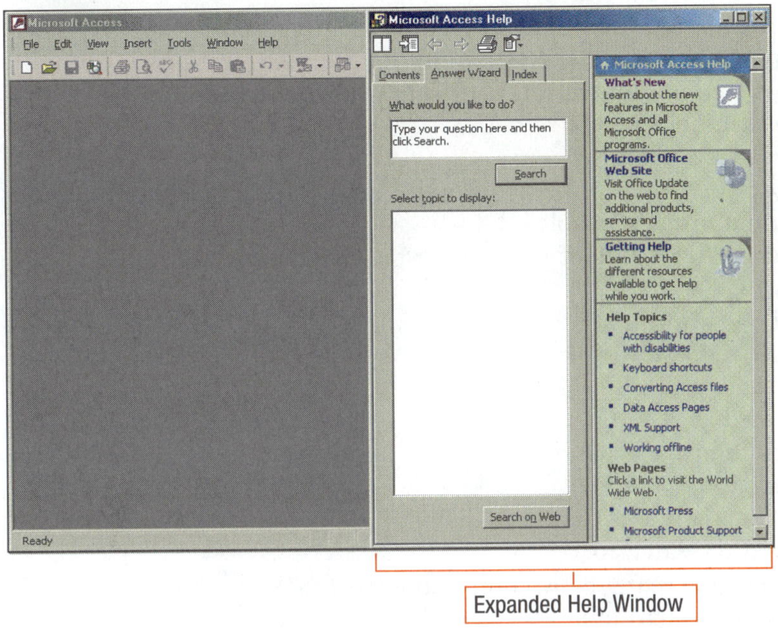

HINT
Press F1 to display the Microsoft Access Help window.

Select the Contents tab at the expanded Microsoft Access Help window and a variety of categories display preceded by an icon of a closed book. Most of these categories contain additional categories. To display these additional categories, double-click a category. This causes the closed book icon to change to an open book icon and the additional categories to display below the selected category.

Click the Answer Wizard tab and a text box displays preceded by the question *"What would you like to do?"* Key your question in the text box and then click the Search button. This displays a list of categories in the Select topic to display list box. Click a topic in the list box, and information about the topic displays at the right side of the window.

With the Index tab selected, enter a keyword in the Type keywords list box, and then click the Search button. Topics related to the keyword display in the Choose a topic list box. Click a topic in this list box and information about that topic displays at the right side of the window. You can also scroll through the Or choose keywords list box to display the desired topic. The topics in this list box are alphabetized.

In some situations, the Help window will display a list of topics. If you want to expand the topics and display all of the information related to each topic, click the *Show All* hyperlink located in the upper right corner of the Help window. (The *Show All* hyperlink changes to the *Hide All* hyperlink.)

HINT
Click Help, About Microsoft Access, and then click the System Info button to display information about your computer such as your processor type, operating system, memory, and hard disk space.

exercise 6

GETTING HELP FROM THE EXPANDED HELP WINDOW

1. Use the Help feature with the Contents tab selected to find information on creating tables by completing the following steps:
   a. Click the Microsoft Access Help button on the Database toolbar.
   b. At the Help window, click the Show button to expand the window. (Skip this step if the window is already expanded.)
   c. Click the Contents tab. (Skip this step if the Contents tab is already selected.)
   d. Click the plus symbol that displays before the *Microsoft Access Help* option in the list box. (Skip this step if a minus symbol displays before the option.)
   e. Click the plus symbol that precedes the *Tables* option.
   f. Click the *About tables* option. (This displays information about tables in the pane at the right side of the Help window.)
   g. Display all of the information in the pane at the right side of the Window by clicking the *Show All* hyperlink located in the upper right corner of the window and then read the information.

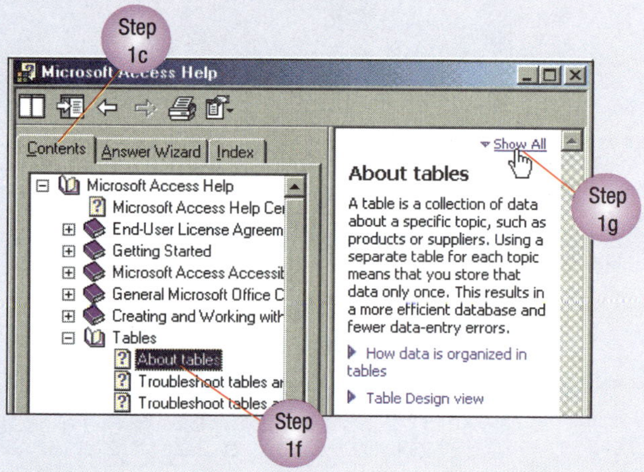

2. Use the Help feature with the Answer Wizard tab selected to search for information on changing margins by completing the following steps:
   a. Click the Answer Wizard tab.
   b. Key **How do I change margins?** in the What would you like to do? text box and then click the Search button.
   c. When information displays in the pane at the right, click the *Show All* hyperlink and then read the information.

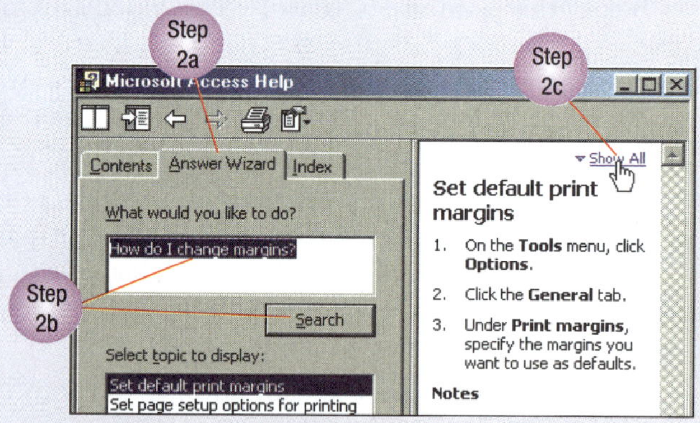

3. Use the Help feature with the Index tab selected to search for information on data types by completing the following steps:
   a. Click the Index tab.
   b. Key **datatype** in the Type keywords text box and then press Enter. (The Help feature automatically changes *datatype* to *DataType;*.)
   c. Read the information that displays in the pane at the right side of the window.

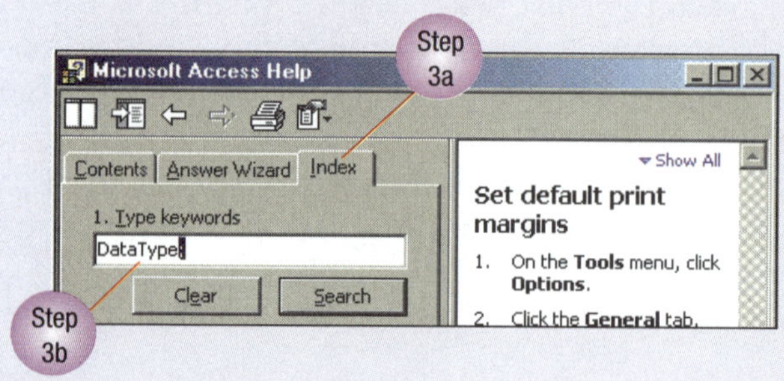

4. Click the Close button (contains an *X*) that displays in the upper right corner of the Help window.

Getting Help from the Office Assistant

The Office Assistant provides information about specific topics. Display the Office Assistant by clicking Help and then Show the Office Assistant. To get help, click the Office Assistant and a help box displays above the assistant as shown in figure 3.11. Key a question about a specific feature in the text box and then click the Search button. The Office Assistant displays a list of related topics. At this list, click the desired topic and information displays in the Help window. After reading the information, click the Close button (contains an *X*) located in the upper right corner of the Help window.

FIGURE 3.11 ***Office Assistant Help Box***

To turn off the display of the Office Assistant, click Help and then Hide the Office Assistant. This only hides the assistant. If you click Help and then Microsoft Access Help, the Office Assistant will display again. To permanently turn off the display of the Office Assistant, click the Office Assistant and then click the Options button. At the Office Assistant dialog box, click in the Use the Office Assistant check box to remove the check mark, and then click OK.

exercise 7

GETTING HELP FROM THE OFFICE ASSISTANT

1. At a blank Access screen, use the Office Assistant to read information on adjusting the row height in a table datasheet by completing the following steps:
   a. Click Help and then Show the Office Assistant.
   b. Click the Office Assistant.
   c. Key **How do I increase the row height in a table datasheet?**.
   d. Click the Search button.
   e. At the list that displays in the yellow box, click *Resize a column or row*. (When you position the arrow pointer on the topic, the pointer turns into a hand.)

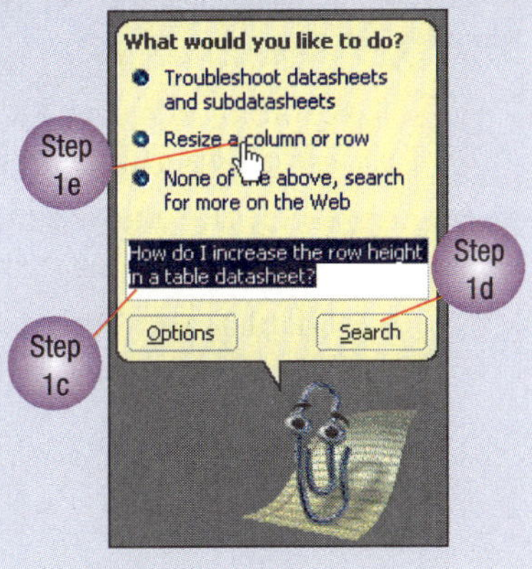

f. Click the *Show All* hyperlink that displays in the upper right corner of the Help window and then read the information that displays in the window.
g. Click the Close button (contains an *X*) located in the upper right corner of the Microsoft Access Help window.

2. Turn off the display of the Office Assistant permanently by completing the following steps:
   a. Click the Office Assistant. (This displays the Help box above the assistant.)
   b. Click the Options button.
   c. At the Office Assistant dialog box, click in the Use the Office Assistant check box to remove the check mark.
   d. Click OK.

Step 2c

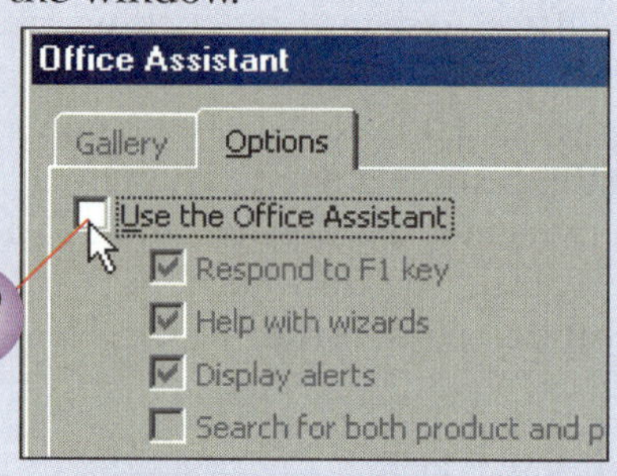

CHAPTER summary

- Access contains a Table Wizard that helps create tables.
- The Table Wizard offers possible field choices with data types already assigned.
- When a second or subsequent table is created in a database file using the Table Wizard, a relationship can be created between the tables.
- Use the spelling checker to find misspelled words in a table.
- The spelling checker compares the words in a table with words in its dictionary. If a match is found, the word is passed over. If no match is found, spelling checker will select the word and offer possible replacements.
- Begin the spelling checker by clicking the Spelling button on the Table Datasheet toolbar.
- Use options at the Find and Replace dialog box with the Find tab selected to search for specific field entries in a table. Display this dialog box by clicking the Find button on the Table Datasheet toolbar or by clicking Edit and then Find.
- Use options at the Find and Replace dialog box with the Replace tab selected to search for specific data and replace with other data. Display this dialog box by clicking Edit and then Replace.
- Get Help from the Access Help feature by keying a question in the Ask a Question button located at the right side of the Menu bar.
- Display the Help window by clicking the Microsoft Access Help button on the Database toolbar, clicking Help and then Microsoft Access Help, or by clicking the *Microsoft Access Help* hyperlink in the New File Task Pane.
- Click the Show button to expand the Help window. The expanded Microsoft Access Help window displays with three tabs—Contents, Answer Wizard, and Index.
- Display the Office Assistant by clicking Help and then Show the Office Assistant.
- Turn off the display of the assistant by clicking Help and then Hide the Office Assistant.
- Turn off the display of the Office Assistant permanently by clicking the Office Assistant and then clicking the Options button. At the Office Assistant dialog box, click the *Use the Office Assistant* option to remove the check mark, and then click OK.

COMMANDS review

Command	Mouse/Keyboard
Begin Table Wizard	At database window, double-click *Create table by using wizard*
Begin the spelling checker	Click Spelling button on Table Datasheet toolbar
Display Find and Replace dialog box with Find tab selected	Click Find button on Table Datasheet toolbar or click Edit and then Find
Display Find and Replace dialog box with Replace tab selected	Click Edit and then Replace
Display Microsoft Access Help window	Click Microsoft Access Help button on Database toolbar; click Help and then Microsoft Access Help; or click *Microsoft Access Help* hyperlink in the New File Task Pane
Display Office Assistant	Click Help, Show the Office Assistant
Display Office Assistant dialog box	Click Office Assistant and then click Options button

CONCEPTS check

Completion: On a blank sheet of paper, indicate the correct term, symbol, or character.

1. Click this button at the first Table Wizard dialog box to add *all* of the selected fields in the Sample Fields list box to the Fields in my new table list box.
2. Click this button at the first Table Wizard dialog box to remove *all* of the fields in the Fields in my new table list box.
3. When a second or subsequent table is created in a database file using the Table Wizard, this can be created between the database tables.
4. Click this button on the Table Datasheet toolbar to begin the spelling checker.
5. Click this button on the Table Datasheet toolbar to display the Find and Replace dialog box with the Find tab selected.
6. Use options at the Find and Replace dialog box with this tab selected to search for specific data and replace with other data.
7. Key a help question inside this button located at the right side of the Menu bar.
8. Click this button on the Help window toolbar to expand the Help window to display three tabs.
9. Click this tab at the Help window and a text box displays preceded by the question *"What would you like to do?"*

SKILLS check

Assessment 1

1. Use the Table Wizard to create two tables in a database file named Lafferty Company. Create the first table with the following specifications:
   a. At the first Table Wizard dialog box, click *Employees* in the Sample Tables list box.
   b. Insert the following fields located in the Sample Fields list box to the Fields in my new table list box:

      EmployeeID
      FirstName
      MiddleName
      LastName
      Title
      Extension

   c. At the second Table Wizard dialog box, accept the table name of *Employees* offered by the wizard and allow the wizard to set a primary key.
   d. At the third Table Wizard dialog box, leave *Enter data directly into the table* selected, and then click Finish.
   e. Key the following data in the specified fields (the *Employee ID* field will automatically be assigned a number):

First Name	=	**Samantha**
Middle Name	=	**Lee**
Last Name	=	**Murray**
Title	=	**Account Manager**
Extension	=	**412**
First Name	=	**Ralph**
Middle Name	=	**Edward**
Last Name	=	**Sorrell**
Title	=	**Director**
Extension	=	**432**
First Name	=	**Cheryl**
Middle Name	=	**Janet**
Last Name	=	**Plaschka**
Title	=	**Assistant Director**
Extension	=	**549**
First Name	=	**Brandon**
Middle Name	=	**Michael**
Last Name	=	**Perrault**
Title	=	**Administrative Assistant**
Extension	=	**653**

First Name	=	**Leland**
Middle Name	=	**John**
Last Name	=	**Nitsche**
Title	=	**Account Manager**
Extension	=	**894**

f. Complete a spelling check on the table. (Assume proper names are spelled correctly.)
g. Adjust the column widths.
h. Save the Employees table.
i. Change the orientation to landscape and then print the table.
j. Close the Employees table.

2. Create a second table with the following specifications:
   a. At the first Table Wizard dialog box, click *Expenses* in the Sample Tables list box. (You will need to scroll down the list to display *Expenses*.)
   b. Insert the following fields located in the Sample Fields list box to the Fields in my new table list box:

      ExpenseID
      EmployeeID
      ExpenseType
      PurposeofExpense
      AmountSpent
      DateSubmitted

   c. At the second Table Wizard dialog box, accept the table name of *Expenses* offered by the wizard and let the wizard set the primary key.
   d. At the third Table Wizard dialog box, create a one-to-many relationship where one record in the Employees table will match many records in the Expenses table. *(Hint: You must click the Relationships button at the third Table Wizard dialog box.)*
   e. At the fourth Table Wizard dialog box, leave *Enter data directly into the table* selected, and then click Finish.
   f. Key the following data in the specified fields (the *Expense ID* field will automatically be assigned a number):

Employee ID	=	**1**
Expense Type	=	**Travel**
Purpose of Expense	=	**Marketing Conference**
Amount Spent	=	**$215.75**
Date Submitted	=	**2/4/03**

Employee ID	=	**2**
Expense Type	=	**Lodging**
Purpose of Expense	=	**Finance Conference**
Amount Spent	=	**$568.50**
Date Submitted	=	**2/10/03**

Employee ID	=	**3**
Expense Type	=	**Travel**
Purpose of Expense	=	**Management Workshop**
Amount Spent	=	**$422.70**
Date Submitted	=	**2/12/03**

Employee ID	=	**1**
Expense Type	=	**Business Dinner**
Purpose of Expense	=	**Customer Relations**
Amount Spent	=	**$124.90**
Date Submitted	=	**2/16/03**

Employee ID	=	**4**
Expense Type	=	**Printing**
Purpose of Expense	=	**Promotional Literature**
Amount Spent	=	**$96.00**
Date Submitted	=	**2/18/03**

Employee ID	=	**1**
Expense Type	=	**Travel**
Purpose of Expense	=	**Customer Contact**
Amount Spent	=	**$184.35**
Date Submitted	=	**2/19/03**

g. Complete a spelling check on the table.
h. Adjust the column widths.
i. Save the Expenses table.
j. Change the orientation to landscape and then print the table.
k. Close the Expenses table.

Assessment 2

1. Open the Employees table in the Lafferty Company database file and then add the following records:

First Name	=	**Laurie**
Middle Name	=	**Jean**
Last Name	=	**Noviello**
Title	=	**Account Manager**
Extension	=	**568**

First Name	=	**Roderick**
Middle Name	=	**Earl**
Last Name	=	**Lobdell**
Title	=	**Assistant Director**
Extension	=	**553**

2. Delete the record for Leland John Nitsche.
3. Print the table in landscape orientation.
4. Close the Employees table.
5. Open the Expenses table and then add the following records:

Employee ID	=	**4**
Expense Type	=	**Printing**
Purpose of Expense	=	**Product Brochure**
Amount Spent	=	**$510.00**
Date Submitted	=	**2/22/03**

Employee ID	=	**5**
Expense Type	=	**Travel**
Purpose of Expense	=	**Customer Contact**

Amount Spent	=	$75.20
Date Submitted	=	2/23/03

6. Print the Expenses table in landscape orientation.
7. Close the Expenses table.

Assessment 3

1. Open the Employees table in the Lafferty Company database file.
2. Make the following changes:
   a. Find the one occurrence of *Noviello* and replace with *Orson*.
   b. Find all occurrences of *Account Manager* and replace with *Sales Director*.
3. Print the table in landscape orientation.
4. Close the Employees table.
5. Close the Lafferty Company database file.

Assessment 4

1. In chapter 2, you learned to create a one-to-many relationship between tables. In Access, a many-to-many relationship can also be created between tables. Use the Access Help feature to read and print information on creating a many-to-many relationship between tables.
2. After reading the information, open Microsoft Word, and then create a memo to your instructor and include the following:
   a. Description of a many-to-many relationship.
   b. Steps to create a many-to-many relationship.
   c. At least one example of a situation in which a many-to-many relationship would be useful.
3. Save the Word document and name it Access C03 SA04.
4. Print and then close Access C03 SA04.

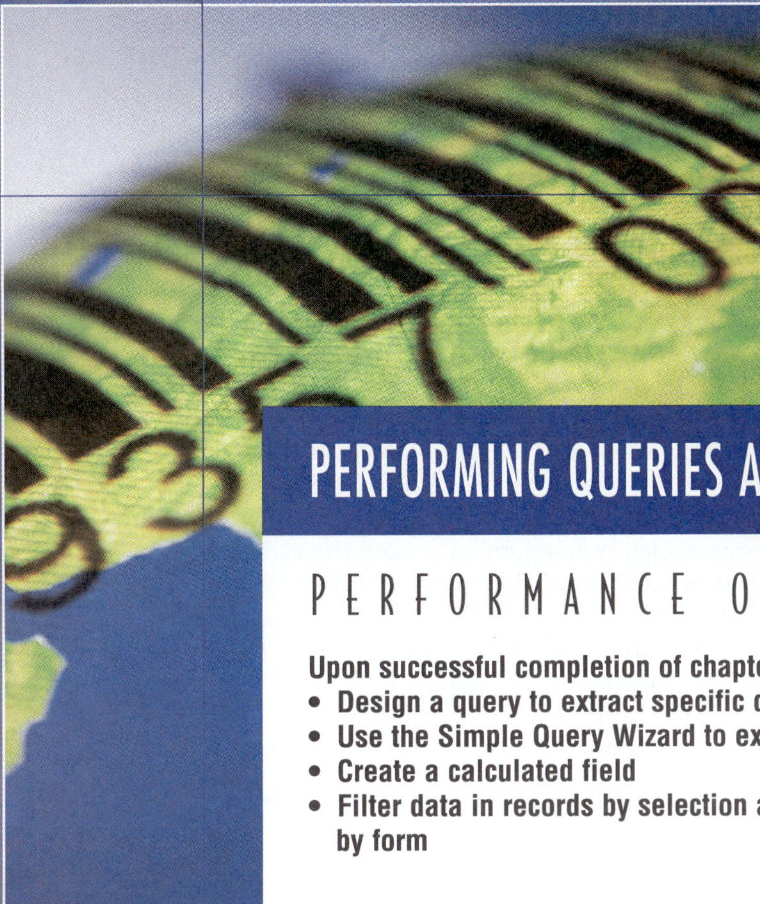

CHAPTER 4

PERFORMING QUERIES AND FILTERING RECORDS

PERFORMANCE OBJECTIVES

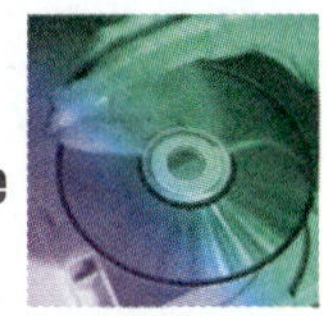

Upon successful completion of chapter 4, you will be able to:

- **Design a query to extract specific data from a table**
- **Use the Simple Query Wizard to extract specific data from a table**
- **Create a calculated field**
- **Filter data in records by selection and by form**

Outdoor Options • Legal Services

One of the primary uses of a database file is to extract specific information from the database. A company might need to know such information as: How much inventory is currently on hand? What products have been ordered? What accounts are past due? What customers live in a particular city? This type of information can be extracted from a table by completing a query. You will learn how to perform a variety of queries on tables in this chapter.

Access provides a Filter By Selection button and a Filter By Form button, which you can use to temporarily isolate specific records in a table. Like a query, a filter lets you select specific field values from a table. You will learn to use these two buttons to isolate specific data in tables.

Performing Queries

Being able to extract (pull out) specific data from a table is one of the most important functions of a database. Extracting data in Access is referred to as performing a "query." The word *query* means to ask a question. Access provides several methods for performing a query. You can design your own query, use a Simple Query Wizard, or use complex query wizards. In this chapter, you will learn to design your own query and use the Simple Query Wizard.

Designing a Query

Designing a query consists of identifying the table from which you are gathering data, the field or fields from which the data will be drawn, and the criteria for selecting the data. To design a query and perform the query, you would follow these basic steps:

1. Open the database file.
2. At the database file window, click the Queries button on the Objects bar shown in figure 4.1.
3. Double-click *Create query in Design view* in the list box.
4. At the Show Table dialog box with the Tables tab selected as shown in figure 4.2, select the table you want included in the query, and then click the Add button. Add any other tables required for the query. When all tables have been added, click the Close button.
5. At the Query1 : Select Query window shown in figure 4.3, use the mouse to drag the first field to be included in the query from the table box in the top of the window to the first empty Field text box. If more than one field is to be included in the query, continue dragging field names from the box in the top to the Field text boxes.
6. To establish a criterion, click inside the Criteria text box in the column containing the desired Field name, and then key the criterion.
7. With the fields and criteria established, click the Run button located on the Query Design toolbar.
8. Access searches the specified table for records that match the criteria and then displays those records in the Query1 : Select Query window.
9. If the query will be used in the future, save the query and name it. If you do not need the query again, close the Query1 : Select Query window without saving it.

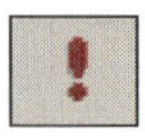

Run

HINT
A query can be saved.

FIGURE 4.1 ***Objects Bar***

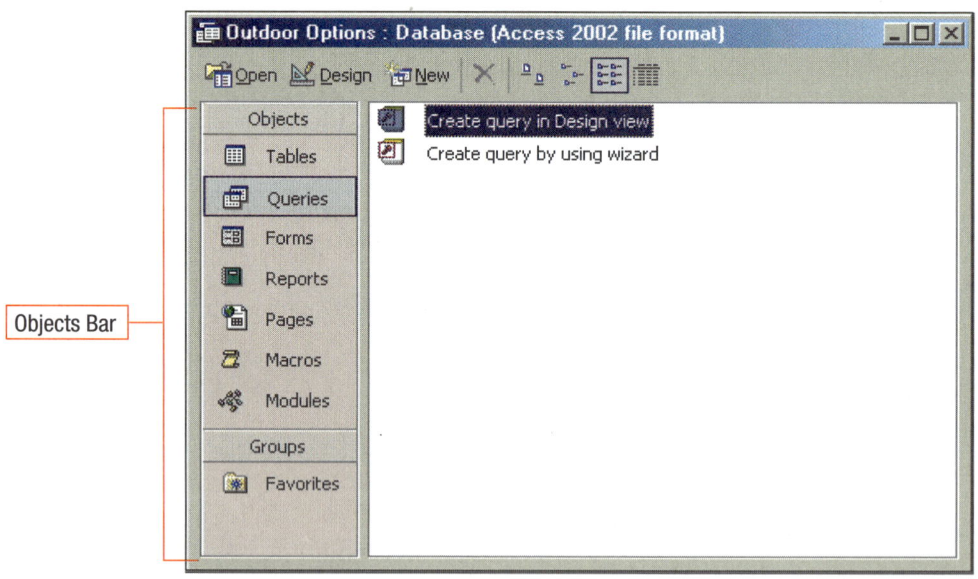

FIGURE 4.2 ***Show Table Dialog Box***

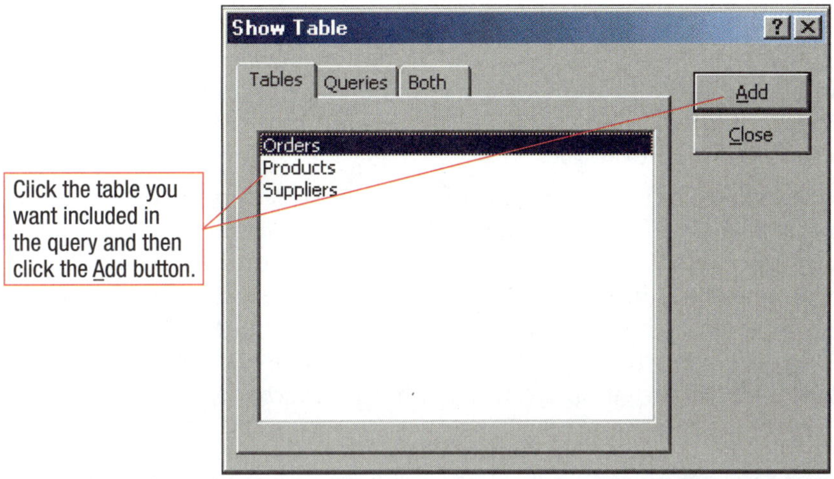

FIGURE 4.3 ***Query1 : Select Query Window***

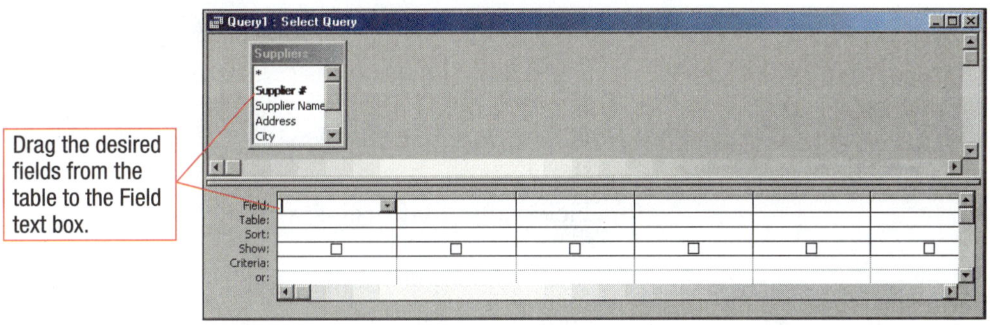

In step 5, the mouse is used to drag fields from the table box in the top of the window to the first empty Field text box in the lower part of the window. As an example, suppose you wanted to find out how many purchase orders were issued on a specific date. To do this, you would drag the *PurchaseOrderID* field from the table to the first Field text box, and then drag the *OrderDate* field from the table to the second Field text box. In this example, both fields are needed so the purchase order ID is displayed along with the specific order date. After dragging the fields, you would then insert the criterion. The criterion for this example would be something like *#1/15/2002#*. After the criterion is inserted, click the Run button on the Query Design toolbar and the results of the query are displayed on the screen.

Establishing Query Criteria

A query does not require that specific criteria are established. In the example described earlier, if the criterion for the date was not included, the query would "return" (*return* is the term used for the results of the query) all Purchase Order numbers with the dates. While this information may be helpful, you could easily find this information in the table. The value of performing a query is to extract specific information from a table. To do this, you must insert a criterion like the one described in the example.

HINT

Include only those fields in a query for which you want to enter criteria or that you want to display.

Access makes writing a criterion fairly simple because it inserts the necessary symbols in the criterion. If you key a city such as *Vancouver* in the Criteria text box and then press Enter, Access changes the criterion to *"Vancouver"*. The quotation marks are inserted by Access and are necessary for the query to run properly. You can either let Access put the proper symbols in the Criteria text box, or you can key the criterion with the symbols. Figure 4.4 shows some criteria examples including what is keyed and what is returned.

FIGURE 4.4 ***Criteria Examples***

Keying this criteria	***Returns this***
"Smith"	Field value matching *Smith*
"Smith" or "Larson"	Field value matching either *Smith* or *Larson*
Not "Smith"	Field value that is not *Smith* (the opposite of "Smith")
"S*"	Field value that begins with *S* and ends in anything
"*s"	Field value that begins with anything and ends in *s*
"[A-D]*"	Field value that begins with *A* through *D* and ends in anything
#01/01/2002#	Field value matching the date 01/01/2002
< #04/01/2002#	Field value less than (before) 04/01/2002
> #04/01/2002#	Field value greater than (after) 04/01/2002
Between #01/01/2002 And #03/31/2002	Any date between 01/01/2002 and 03/31/2002

In figure 4.4, notice the quotation marks surrounding field values (such as "Smith"). If you do not key the quotation marks when keying the criterion, Access will automatically insert them. The same is true for the pound symbol (#). Notice in figure 4.4 that the pound symbol (#) was used around dates. If you do not key the pound symbol around a date, Access will automatically insert the symbols. Access automatically inserts the correct symbol when you press the Enter key after keying the query criteria.

In the criteria examples, the asterisk was used as a wildcard indicating any character. This is consistent with many other software programs where the asterisk is used as a wildcard character. The less than and greater than symbols were used in two of the criteria examples. These symbols can be used for fields containing numbers, values, dates, amounts, and so forth. In the next several exercises, you will be designing queries to extract specific information from different tables in database files.

exercise 1

PERFORMING QUERIES ON TABLES

(Note: Delete from your disk any database files you created in chapter 3.)

1. Copy the Outdoor Options database file from the CD that accompanies this textbook to your disk. Remove the read-only attribute from the Outdoor Options database file.
2. Open the Outdoor Options database file.
3. Extract records of those suppliers located in Vancouver by completing the following steps:
   a. Click the Queries button on the Objects bar.
   b. Double-click *Create query in Design view* in the list box.
   c. At the Show Table dialog box with the Tables tab selected (see figure 4.2), click *Suppliers* in the list box, click the Add button, and then click the Close button.

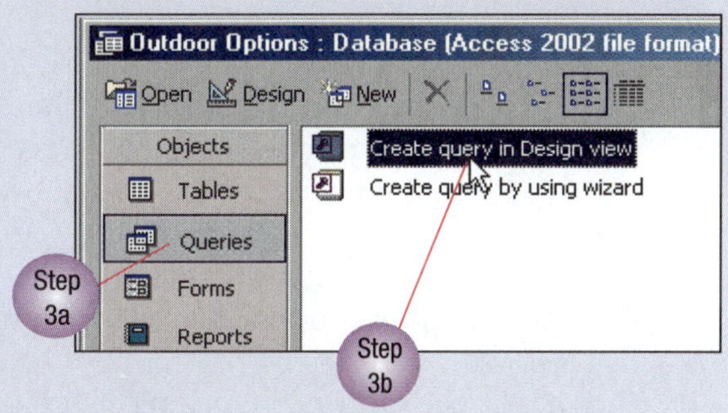

   d. Drag fields from the table box to the Field text boxes by completing the following steps:
      1) Position the arrow pointer on the *Supplier Name* field in the table list box located toward the top of the window, hold down the left mouse button, drag the field icon to the first Field text box in the lower portion of the window, and then release the mouse button. (When you release the mouse button, Access automatically inserts the table name *Suppliers* in the Table: text box and inserts a check box with a check mark in the Show text box.)
      2) Drag the *Street Address* field in the table list box to the next Field text box (to the right of *Supplier Name*).
      3) Drag the *City* field in the table list box to the next Field text box (to the right of *Street Address*).
      4) Scroll down the table list box until *Province* displays and then drag the *Province* field in the table list box to the next Field text box (to the right of *City*).
      5) Drag the *Postal Code* field in the table list box to the next Field text box (to the right of *Province*).
   e. Insert the criterion text telling Access to display only those suppliers located in Vancouver by completing the following steps:

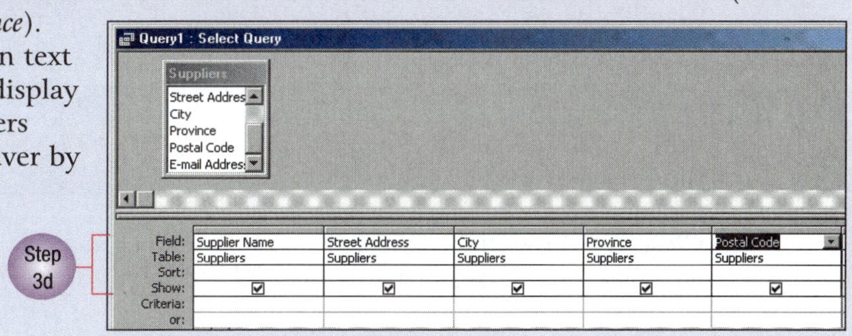

1) Position the I-beam pointer in the Criteria text box in the *City* column and then click the left mouse button. (This positions the insertion point inside the text box.)

2) Key **Vancouver** and then press Enter. (This changes the criteria to "Vancouver").

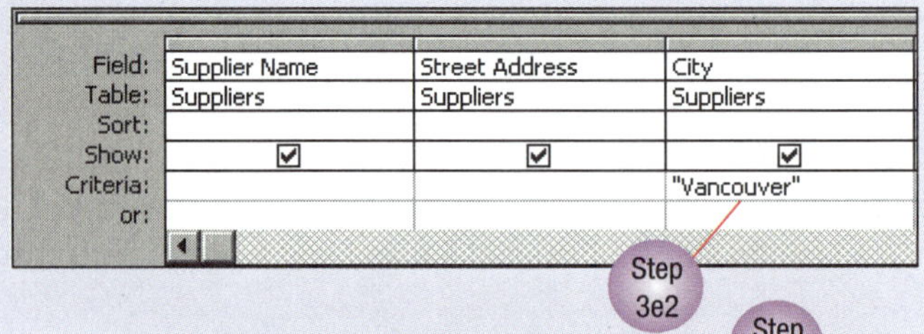

f. Return the results of the query by clicking the Run button on the Query Design toolbar.

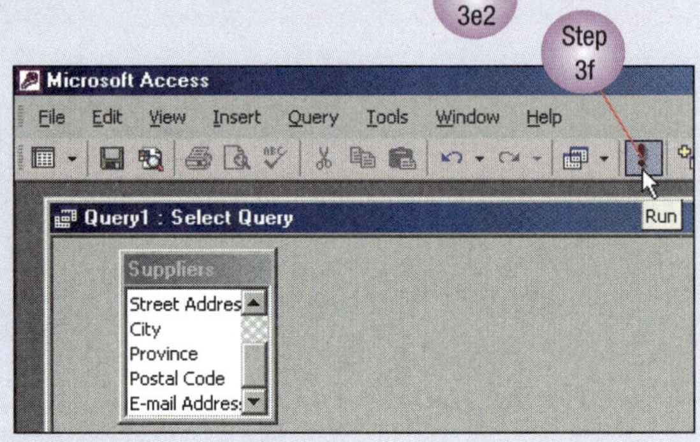

g. Save the results of the query by completing the following steps:

1) Click the Save button on the Query Datasheet toolbar.

2) At the Save As dialog box, key **Vancouver Query** and then press Enter or click OK.

h. Print the results of the query by clicking the Print button on the Query Datasheet toolbar.

i. Close Vancouver Query.

4. Extract those product records with units on order greater than zero by completing the following steps:

a. At the Outdoor Options : Database window, double-click *Create query in Design view*.

b. At the Show Table dialog box, click *Products* in the list box, click the Add button, and then click the Close button.

c. At the Query1 : Select Query window, drag the *Product* field from the table list box to the first Field text box.

d. Scroll down the table list box until *Units on Order* displays and then drag *Units on Order* to the second Field text box (to the right of *Product*).

e. Insert the query criteria by completing the following steps:

1) Position the I-beam pointer in the Criteria text box in the *Units on Order* column and then click the left mouse button. (This positions the insertion point inside the text box.)

2) Key **>0** and then press Enter. (Make sure you key a zero and not a capital *O*.)

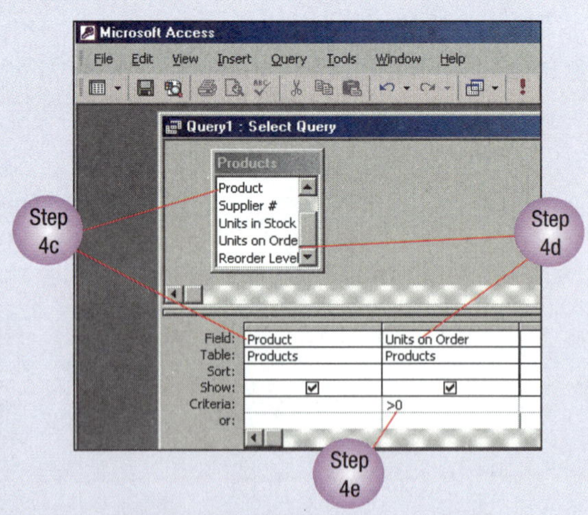

f. Return the results of the query by clicking the Run button on the Query Design toolbar.

g. Save the query and name it Units on Order Query.

h. Print the results of the query by clicking the Print button on the Query Datasheet toolbar.

i. Close Units on Order Query.

5. Extract those orders greater than $1,500 by completing the following steps:

a. At the Outdoor Options : Database window, double-click *Create query in Design view*.

b. At the Show Table dialog box, click *Orders* in the list box, click the Add button, and then click the Close button.
c. At the Query1 : Select Query window, drag the *Order #* field from the table list box to the first Field text box.
d. Drag the *Product #* field to the second Field text box (to the right of *Order #*).
e. Scroll down the table list box until *Amount* is visible and then drag the *Amount* field to the third Field text box (to the right of *Product #*).
f. Insert the query criteria by completing the following steps:
   1) Position the I-beam pointer in the Criteria text box in the *Amount* column and then click the left mouse button. (This positions the insertion point inside the text box.)
   2) Key **>1500** and then press Enter. (Make sure you key zeros and not capital *O*s.)

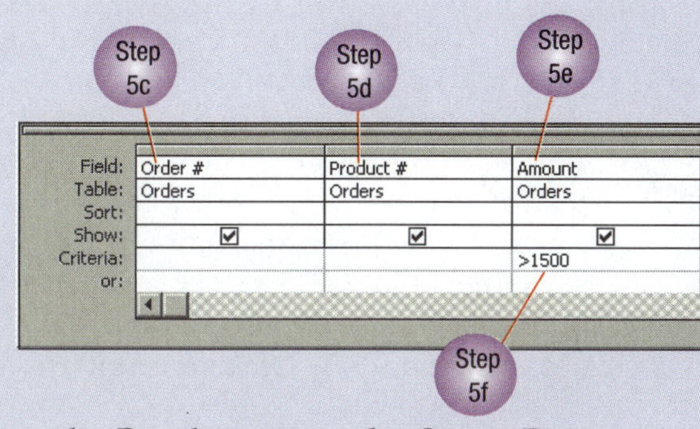

g. Return the results of the query by clicking the Run button on the Query Design toolbar.
h. Save the query and name it Orders Over $1500 Query.
i. Print the results of the query by clicking the Print button on the Query Datasheet toolbar.
j. Close Orders Over $1500 Query.

6. Close the Outdoor Options database file.

In exercise 1, you performed several queries on specific tables. A query can also be performed on fields from more than one table. In exercise 2, you will be performing queries on related tables.

HINT
A query can be performed on two or more tables that are joined in a relationship.

exercise 2

PERFORMING A QUERY ON RELATED TABLES

1. Open the Outdoor Options database file.
2. Extract information on products ordered between February 20 and February 28, 2002, and include the supplier's name by completing the following steps:
   a. Click the Queries button on the Objects bar.
   b. Double-click *Create query in Design view*.
   c. At the Show Table dialog box, click *Products* in the list box and then click the Add button.
   d. Click *Suppliers* in the Show Table dialog box list box and then click the Add button.
   e. Click *Orders* in the list box, click the Add button, and then click the Close button.
   f. At the Query1 : Select Query window, drag the *Product* field from the Products table list box to the first Field text box.
   g. Drag the *Supplier Name* field from the Suppliers table list box to the second Field text box.
   h. Drag the *Order Date* field from the Orders table list box to the third Field text box. (You will need to scroll down the list box to display the *Order Date* field.)

i. Insert the query criteria by completing the following steps:
   1) Position the I-beam pointer in the Criteria text box in the *Order Date* column and then click the left mouse button. (This positions the insertion point inside the text box.)
   2) Key **Between 2/20/2002 and 2/28/2002** and then press Enter. (Make sure you key zeros and not capital *O*s.)
j. Return the results of the query by clicking the Run button on the Query Design toolbar.
k. Save the query and name it February 20-28 Orders Query.
l. Print and then close the query.

3. Close the Outdoor Options database file.

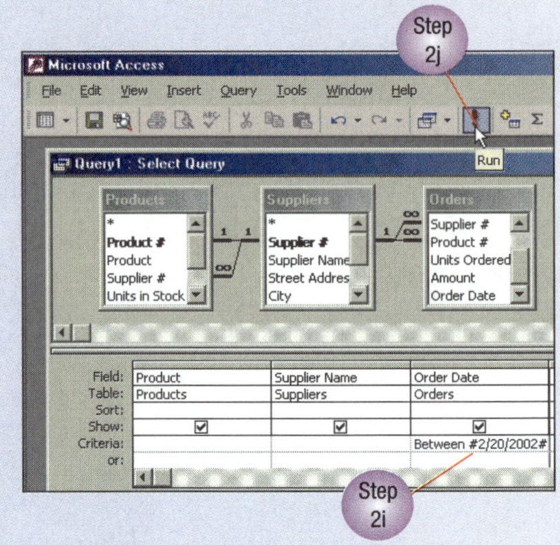

Sorting Fields in a Query

When designing a query, the sort order of a field or fields can be specified. Notice in figure 4.3 that there is a Sort text box. Click inside one of the columns in the Sort text box and a down-pointing triangle displays at the right of the field. Click this down-pointing triangle and a drop-down menu displays with the choices *Ascending*, *Descending*, and *(not sorted)*. Click Ascending to sort from lowest to highest or click Descending to sort from highest to lowest.

exercise 3 PERFORMING A QUERY ON RELATED TABLES AND SORTING IN ASCENDING ORDER

1. Open the Outdoor Options database file.
2. Extract information on orders less than $1,500 by completing the following steps:
   a. Click the Queries button on the Objects bar.
   b. Double-click *Create query in Design view*.
   c. At the Show Table dialog box, click *Products* in the list box and then click the Add button.
   d. Click *Orders* in the list box, click the Add button, and then click the Close button.
   e. At the Query1 : Select Query window, drag the *Product #* field from the Products table list box to the first Field text box.
   f. Drag the *Supplier #* field from the Products table list box to the second Field text box.
   g. Drag the *Units Ordered* field from the Orders table list box to the third Field text box.
   h. Drag the *Amount* field from the Orders table list box to the fourth Field text box. (You will need to scroll down the list box to display the *Amount* field.)
   i. Insert the query criterion by completing the following steps:
      1) Position the I-beam pointer in the Criteria text box in the *Amount* column and then click the left mouse button.

2) Key **<1500** and then press Enter. (Make sure you key zeros and not capital *O*s.)

j. Sort the *Amount* field values from lowest to highest by completing the following steps:

   1) Position the insertion point in the Sort text box in the *Amount* column and then click the left mouse button. (This will cause a down-pointing triangle to display at the right side of the text box.)

   2) Click the down-pointing triangle at the right side of the Sort text box and then click *Ascending*.

k. Return the results of the query by clicking the Run button on the Query Design toolbar.

l. Save the query and name it Orders Less Than $1500 Query.

m. Print and then close the query.

3. Close the Outdoor Options database file.

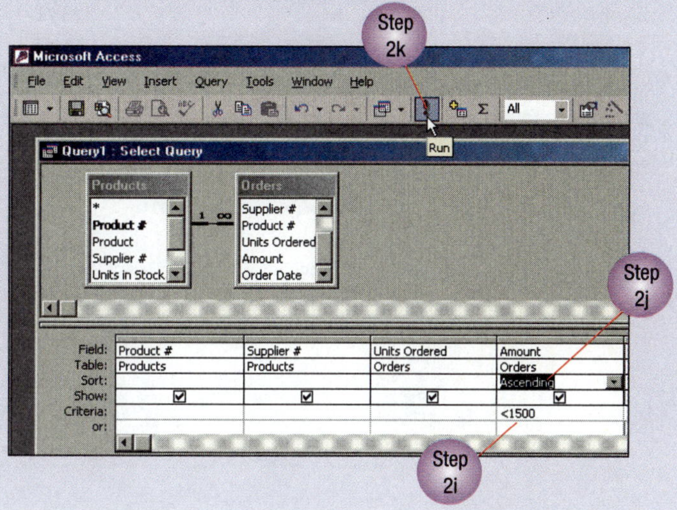

Performing a Query with the Simple Query Wizard

The Simple Query Wizard provided by Access guides you through the steps for preparing a query. To use this wizard, open the database file, click the Queries button on the Objects bar, and then double-click the *Create query by using wizard* option in the list box. Or, click the New button and then, at the New Query dialog box, double-click *Simple Query Wizard* in the list box. At the first Simple Query Wizard dialog box, as shown in figure 4.5, specify the table(s) in the Tables/Queries option box. After specifying the table, insert the fields you want included in the query in the Selected Fields list box, and then click the Next button.

HINT

Use the Simple Query Wizard to walk you through the steps for preparing a query.

FIGURE 4.5 *First Simple Query Wizard Dialog Box*

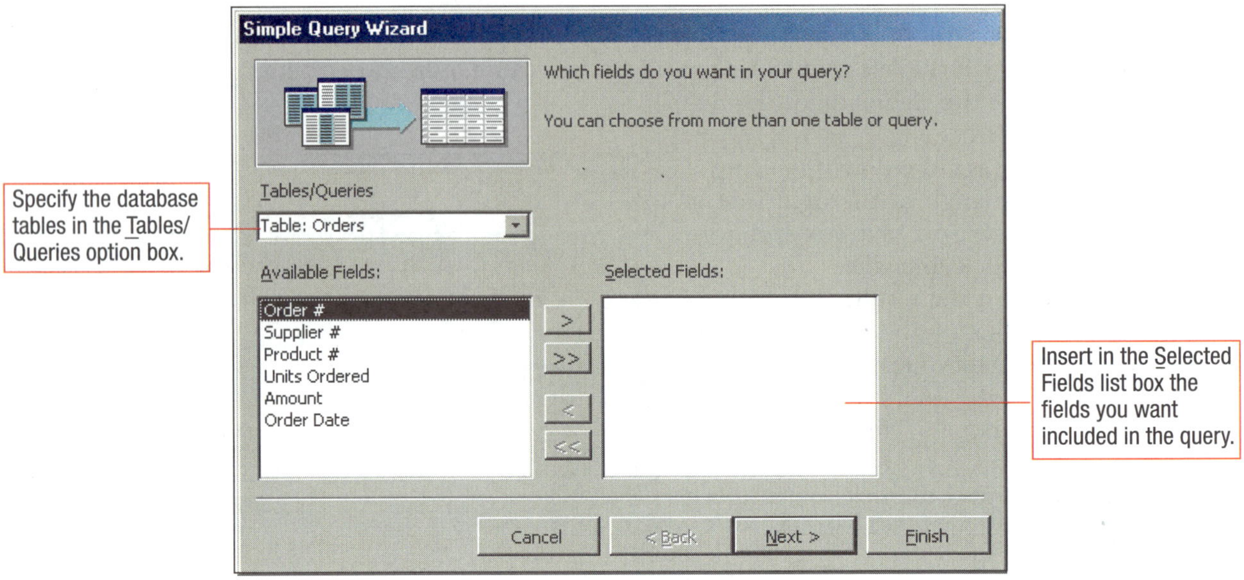

At the second Simple Query Wizard dialog box, specify whether you want a detail or summary query, and then click the Next button. At the third (and last) Simple Query Wizard dialog box, shown in figure 4.6, key a name for the completed query or accept the name provided by the wizard. At this dialog box, you can also specify that you want to open the query to view the information or modify the query design. If you want to extract specific information, be sure to choose the *Modify the query design* option. After making any necessary changes, click the Finish button.

FIGURE 4.6 *Last Simple Query Wizard Dialog Box*

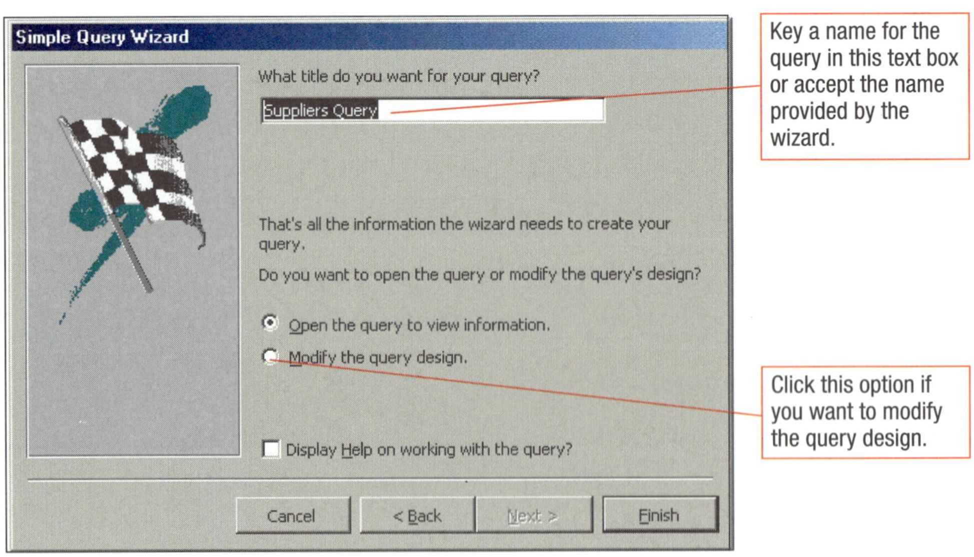

If you do not modify the query design in the last Simple Query Wizard dialog box, the query displays all records for the fields identified in the first Simple Query Wizard dialog box. In exercise 4 you will be performing a query without modifying the design, and in exercise 5 you will be modifying the query design.

exercise 4

PERFORMING A QUERY WITH THE SIMPLE QUERY WIZARD

1. Open the Outdoor Options database file.
2. Perform a query with the Simple Query Wizard by completing the following steps:
   a. Click the Queries button on the Objects bar.
   b. Double-click the *Create query by using wizard* option in the list box.
   c. At the first Simple Query Wizard dialog box, click the down-pointing triangle at the right of the Tables/Queries option box, and then click *Table: Suppliers*.
   d. With *Supplier #* selected in the Available Fields list box, click the button containing the greater than symbol. (This inserts the *Supplier #* field in the Selected Fields list box.)
   e. With *Supplier Name* selected in the Available Fields list box, click the button containing the greater than symbol.
   f. Click the down-pointing triangle at the right of the Tables/Queries option box and then click *Table: Orders*.
   g. Click *Product #* in the Available Fields list box and then click the button containing the greater than symbol.
   h. Click *Amount* in the Available Fields list box and then click the button containing the greater than symbol.
   i. Click the Next button.
   j. At the second Simple Query Wizard dialog box, click the Next button.
   k. At the last Simple Query Wizard dialog box, click the Finish button.
3. When the results of the query are returned, print the results.
4. Close the Suppliers Query : Select Query window.
5. Close the Outdoor Options database file.

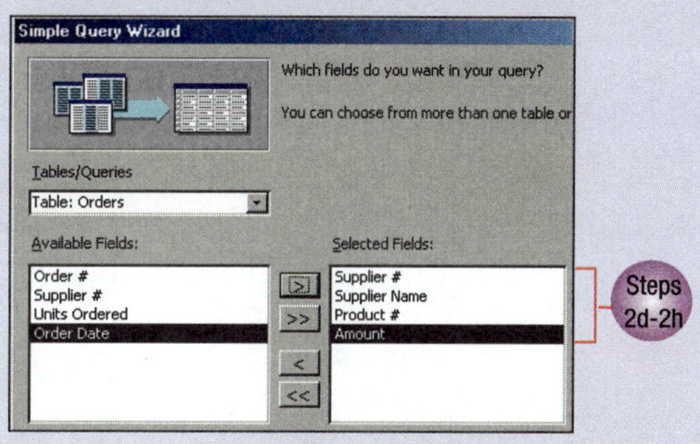

To extract specific information when using the Simple Query Wizard, tell the wizard that you want to modify the query design. This displays a window where you can insert query criteria.

exercise 5 PERFORMING AND MODIFYING A QUERY WITH THE SIMPLE QUERY WIZARD

1. Open the Outdoor Options database file.
2. Perform a query with the Simple Query Wizard and modify the query by completing the following steps:
   a. Click the Queries button on the Objects bar.
   b. Double-click the *Create query by using wizard* option in the list box.
   c. At the first Simple Query Wizard dialog box, click the down-pointing triangle at the right of the Tables/Queries option box, and then click *Table: Suppliers*.
   d. Insert the following fields in the Selected Fields list box:

      Supplier Name
      Street Address
      City
      Province
      Postal Code

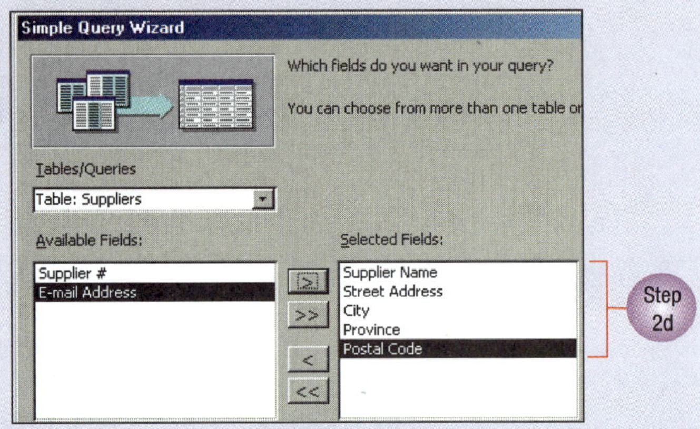

   e. Click the Next button.
   f. At the second Simple Query Wizard dialog box, click the *Modify the query design* option, and then click the Finish button.
   g. At the Suppliers Query1 : Select Query window, insert the query criteria by completing the following steps:
      1) Click in the Criteria text box in the *City* column.
      2) Key **Not Vancouver** and then press Enter.
   h. Specify that the fields are to be sorted in ascending order by Postal Code by completing the following steps:
      1) Click in the Sort text box in the *Postal Code* column (you may need to scroll to see this column).

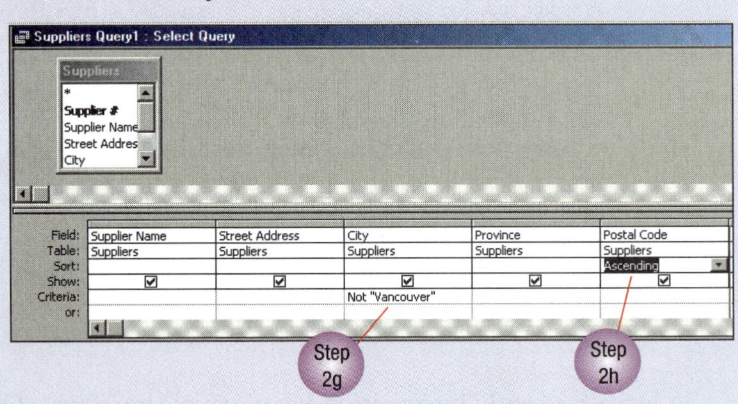

      2) Click the down-pointing arrow that displays at the right side of the text box and then click *Ascending*.
   i. Click the Run button on the Query Design toolbar. (Those suppliers not located in Vancouver will display and the records will display in ascending order by Postal Code.)
   j. With the results of the query returned, print the query.
   k. Click the Save button to save the query. (Access automatically saves the query with the name Suppliers Query1.)
   l. Close the query.
3. Close the Outdoor Options database file.

Creating a Calculated Field

A calculated control uses a mathematical equation to determine the contents that are displayed in the control object. In a query, you can insert a calculated field that performs mathematical equations. Insert a calculated field in the Field text box when designing a query. To insert a calculated field, click in the desired fields text box. Key the desired field name followed by a colon and then key the equation. For example, to multiply Unit Price by Units Ordered and name the field *Total Amount*, you would key **Total Amount:[Unit Price]*[Units Ordered]** in the Field text box.

exercise 6

CREATING A CALCULATED FIELD IN A QUERY

1. Open the Outdoor Options database file.
2. Perform a query with the Simple Query Wizard and modify the query by completing the following steps:
   a. Click the Queries button on the Objects bar.
   b. Double-click the *Create query by using wizard* option in the list box.
   c. At the first Simple Query Wizard dialog box, click the down-pointing triangle at the right of the Tables/Queries option box, and then click *Table: Suppliers*.
   d. Insert the *Supplier Name* field in the Selected Fields list box.
   e. Click the down-pointing triangle at the right of the Tables/Queries option box, click *Table: Products*, and then insert the following fields in the Selected Fields list box:

      Product
      Units in Stock
      Units on Order

   f. Click the Next button.
   g. At the second Simple Query Wizard dialog box, click the Next button.
   h. At the last Simple Query Wizard dialog box, click the *Modify the query design* option, and then click the Finish button.
   i. At the Suppliers Query2 : Select Query window, insert a calculated field that calculates the total number of units by completing the following steps:
      1) Click in the fifth Field text box.
      2) Key **Total:[Units in Stock]+[Units on Order]** and then press Enter.
   j. Click the Run button on the Query Design toolbar. (All records will display with the total of the units in stock and on order displayed.)

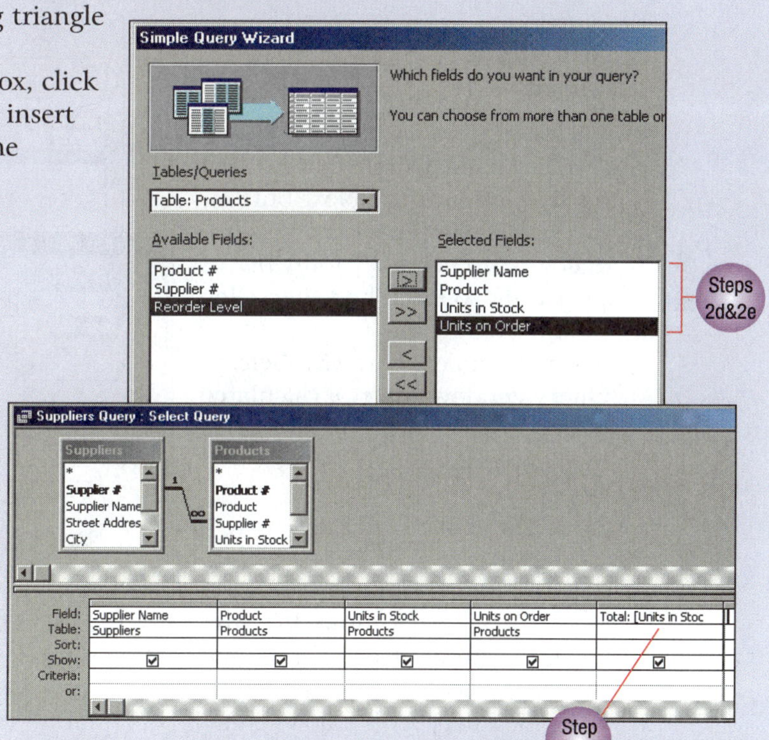

k. With the results of the query returned, print the query.
l. Click the Save button to save the query with the default name (Suppliers Query2.)
m. Close the query.

3. Close the Outdoor Options database file.

exercise 7

CREATING A CALCULATED FIELD IN A QUERY THAT CALCULATES UNIT PRICE

1. Open the Outdoor Options database file.
2. Perform a query with the Simple Query Wizard and modify the query by completing the following steps:
   a. Click the Queries button on the Objects bar.
   b. Double-click the *Create query by using wizard* option in the list box.
   c. At the first Simple Query Wizard dialog box, click the down-pointing triangle at the right of the Tables/Queries option box, and then click *Table: Suppliers*.
   d. Insert the *Supplier Name* field in the Selected Fields list box.
   e. Click the down-pointing triangle at the right of the Tables/Queries option box, click *Table: Orders*, and then insert the following fields in the Selected Fields list box:

      Order #
      Units Ordered
      Amount

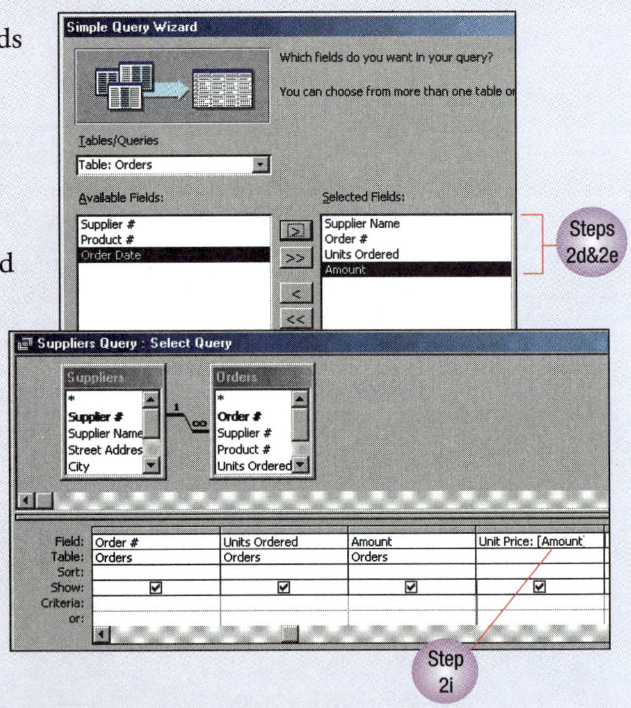

   f. Click the Next button.
   g. At the second Simple Query Wizard dialog box, click the Next button.
   h. At the last Simple Query Wizard dialog box, click the *Modify the query design* option, and then click the Finish button.
   i. At the Suppliers Query3 : Select Query window, insert a calculated field that calculates the unit price by completing the following steps:
      1) Click in the fifth Field text box.
      2) Key **Unit Price:[Amount]/[Units Ordered]** and then press Enter.
   j. Click the Run button on the Query Design toolbar. (All records will display with the unit price calculated for each order.)
   k. Save the query with a new name by completing the following steps:
      1) Click File and then Save As.
      2) At the Save As dialog box, key **Unit Price Query** and then press Enter or click OK.
   l. Print and then close the query.
3. Close the Outdoor Options database file.

Filtering Data

You can place a set of restrictions, called a *filter*, on records in a table or form to temporarily isolate specific records. A filter, like a query, lets you select specific field values in a table or form. Data can be filtered by selection or by form.

Using Filter By Selection

Filter By Selection

With the Filter By Selection button that displays on the Table Datasheet toolbar, you can select specific data in a field and then tell Access to display only those records containing the selected data. For example, if you want to display only those records for a specific Supplier #, select the supplier number in the appropriate table, and then click the Filter By Selection button on the Table Datasheet toolbar. Only those records matching the selected data are displayed on the screen.

Apply Filter

The Table Datasheet toolbar contains a button named Apply Filter. When a filter is applied by selection, this button changes to Remove Filter (and also displays with a blue border). If you want to remove the filter and display the original data in the table, click the Remove Filter button on the Table Datasheet toolbar.

exercise 8

USING FILTER BY SELECTION TO DISPLAY SPECIFIC DATA IN A TABLE

1. Open the Outdoor Options database file.
2. At the Outdoor Options : Database window, click the Tables button on the Objects bar.
3. Open the Products table by double-clicking *Products* in the list box.
4. Use the Filter By Selection button to display only those records with no units on order by completing the following steps:
   a. Select a 0 (zero) in one of the fields in the Units on Order column.
   b. Click the Filter By Selection button on the Table Datasheet toolbar. (This displays only those records with no units on order.)
   c. Sort the records in ascending order by the supplier number by completing the following steps:
      1) Click in any field in the *Supplier #* column.
      2) Click the Sort Ascending button on the Table Datasheet toolbar.
   d. Print the table.

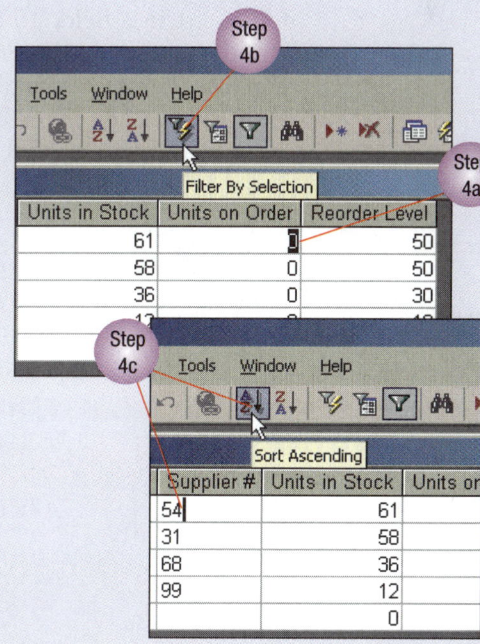

e. After printing the table, click the Remove Filter button on the Table Datasheet toolbar (this redisplays all records in the table).
5. Close the Products table without saving the changes to the design.
6. Open the Suppliers table by double-clicking *Suppliers* in the list box.
7. Use the Filter By Selection button to display only those records of suppliers in Burnaby by completing the following steps:
    a. Select *Burnaby* in one of the fields in the *City* column.
    b. Click the Filter By Selection button on the Table Datasheet toolbar.
    c. Print the table in landscape orientation.
    d. After printing the table, click the Remove Filter button on the Table Datasheet toolbar (this redisplays all records in the table).
8. Close the Suppliers table without saving changes to the design.
9. Close the Outdoor Options database file.

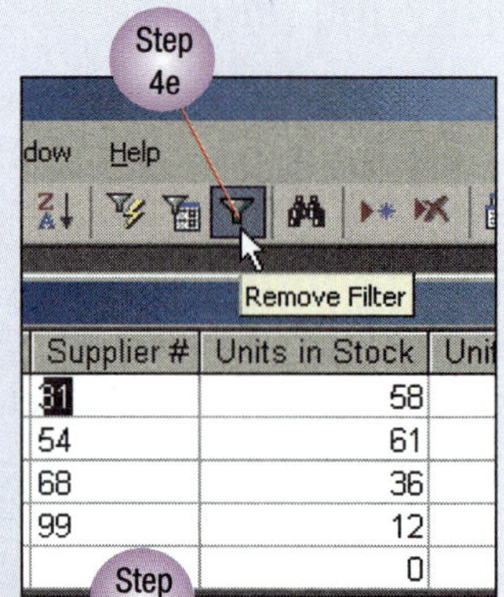

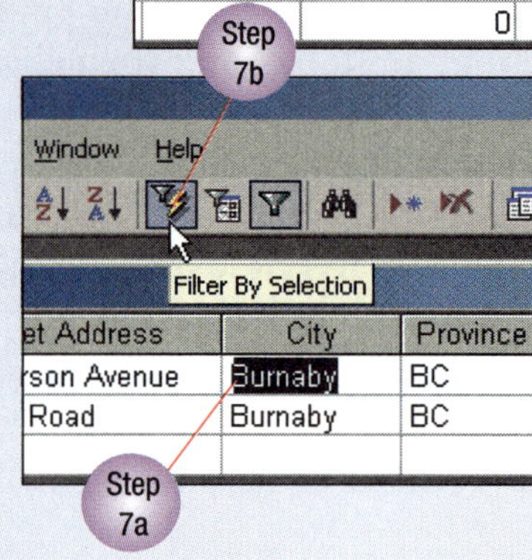

Using Filter By Form

Filter By Form

The Table Datasheet toolbar contains a Filter By Form button that, when clicked, displays the table with a blank record. You set the values you want filtered records to contain at this blank record. Figure 4.7 shows a blank record for the Orders table in the Outdoor Options database file. At the Orders : Filter By Form window displayed in figure 4.7, notice that two tabs display toward the bottom. The Look for tab is active by default and tells Access to look for whatever data you insert in a field. To display only those records for supplier number 68, you would click inside the *Supplier #* field. This causes a down-pointing triangle to display. Click this triangle and then click *68* at the drop-down menu. To filter the records, click the Filter By Form button on the Table Datasheet toolbar and only those records for supplier number 68 are displayed on the screen.

FIGURE 4.7 *Orders : Filter By Form Window*

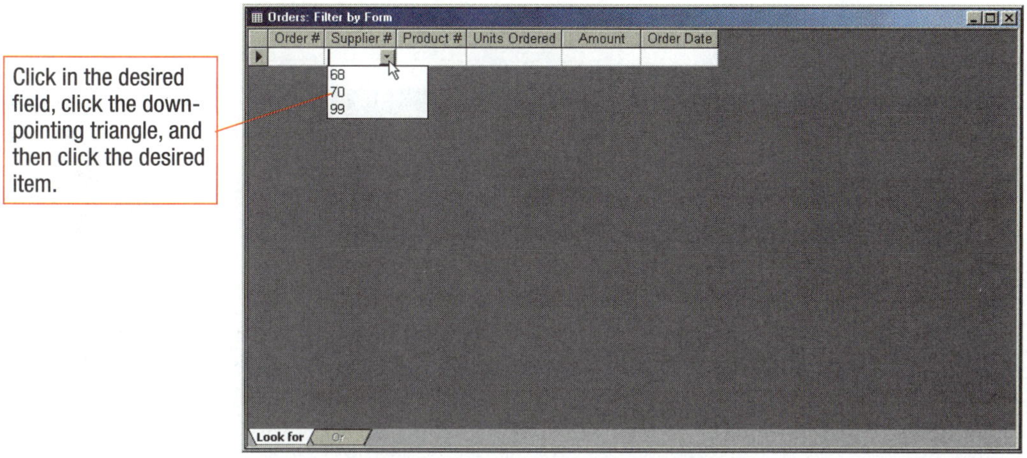

exercise 9

USING FILTER BY FORM TO DISPLAY SPECIFIC RECORDS

1. Open the Outdoor Options database file.
2. At the Outdoor Options : Database window, click the Tables button on the Objects bar, and then double-click *Orders* in the list box.
3. Use the Filter By Form button to display only those records containing supplier number 68 in the *Supplier #* field by completing the following steps:
   a. Click the Filter By Form button on the Table Datasheet toolbar.
   b. At the blank record, click in the *Supplier #* field.
   c. Click the down-pointing triangle at the right side of the *Supplier #* field and then click *68* at the drop-down menu.
   d. Click the Apply Filter button on the Table Datasheet toolbar.
   e. Print the records.

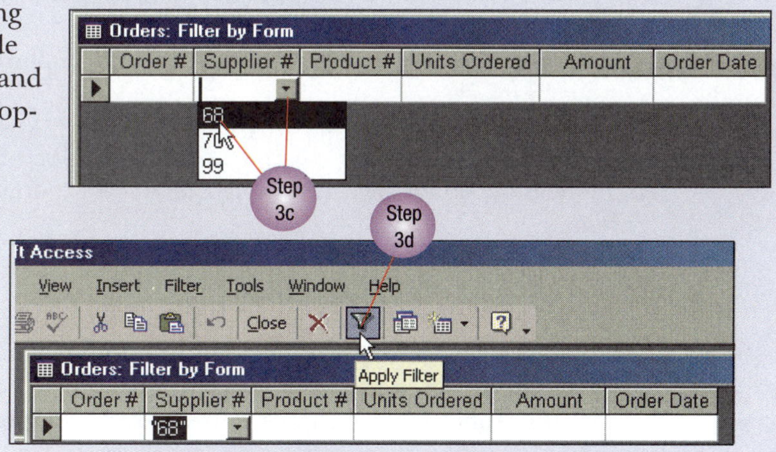

4. Close the Orders : Table window without saving the changes to the design.
5. At the Outdoor Options : Database window, double-click *Products* in the list box.
6. Use the Filter By Form button to display only those records containing supplier number 99 in the *Supplier #* field by completing the following steps:
   a. Click the Filter By Form button on the Table Datasheet toolbar.
   b. At the blank record, click in the *Supplier #* field.

c. Click the down-pointing triangle at the right side of the *Supplier #* field and then click *99* at the drop-down menu.
d. Click the Apply Filter button on the Table Datasheet toolbar.
e. Print the records.

7. Close the Products : Table window without saving the changes to the design.
8. Close the Outdoor Options database file.

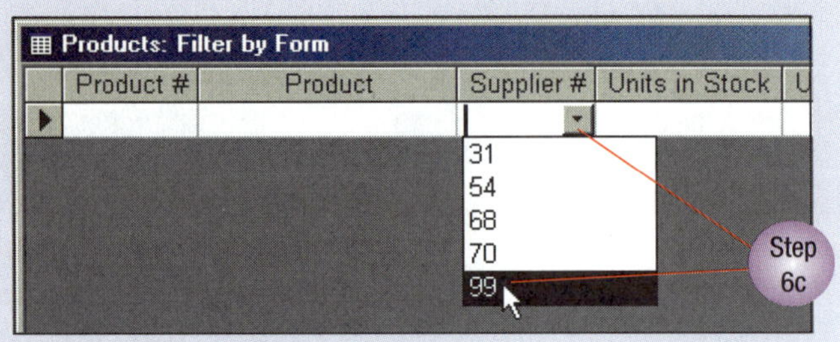

HINT

Data can be filtered on two or more field values.

A tab displays at the bottom of the Orders : Filter By Form window shown in figure 4.7 with the word *Or*. Click this tab if you want to filter on two field values. When you click the Or tab, another blank record displays below the first one. As an example of when you would use the Or tab, suppose you wanted to display only those records for supplier # 68 *or* supplier # 31. You would insert *68* in the *Supplier #* field of the first blank record, click the Or button, and then insert *31* in the *Supplier #* field in the second blank record. As another example, in a table containing suppliers' addresses, you could display only those records for suppliers located in Burnaby *or* Port Moody.

exercise 10

USING FILTER BY FORM TO FILTER ON TWO FIELD VALUES

1. Open the Outdoor Options database file.
2. At the Outdoor Options : Database window, click the Tables button on the Objects bar, and then double-click *Suppliers* in the list box.
3. Use the Filter By Form button to display only those records for suppliers in Port Moody *or* Burnaby by completing the following steps:
   a. Click the Filter By Form button on the Table Datasheet toolbar.
   b. At the blank record, click in the *City* field.
   c. Click the down-pointing triangle at the right side of the *City* field and then click *Port Moody* at the drop-down menu.
   d. Click the Or tab located toward the bottom of the Suppliers: Filter By Form window.
   e. At the new blank record, click the down-pointing triangle at the right side of the *City* field, and then click *Burnaby* at the drop-down menu.
   f. Click the Apply Filter button on the Table Datasheet toolbar.
   g. Print the records in landscape orientation.

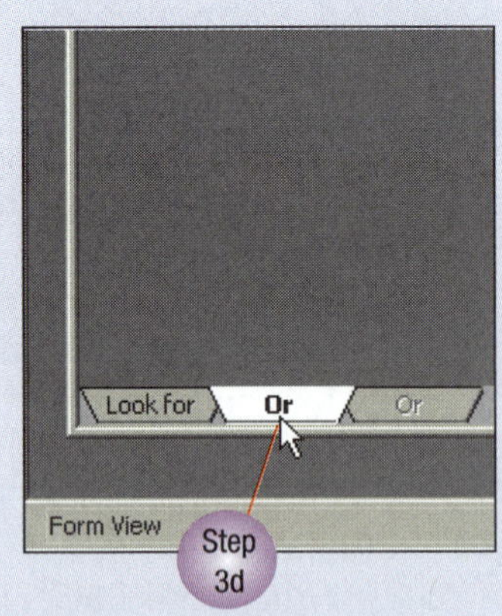

4. Close the Suppliers : Table window without saving the changes to the design.
5. Close the Outdoor Options database file.

CHAPTER summary

- Being able to extract specific information is one of the most important functions of a database. Data can be extracted from an Access database file by performing a query, which can be done by designing a query or using the Simple Query Wizard.
- Designing a query consists of identifying the table, the field or fields from which the data will be drawn, and the criteria for selecting the data.
- During the designing of a query, write the criterion (or criteria) for extracting the specific data. Access inserts any necessary symbols in the criterion when the Enter key is pressed.
- In a criterion, quotation marks surround text values and pound symbols (#) surround dates. The asterisk (*) can be used as a wildcard symbol.
- A query can be performed on fields within one table or on fields from related tables.
- When designing a query, the sort order of a field or fields can be specified.
- The Simple Query Wizard guides you through the steps for preparing a query. A query designed by the Simple Query Wizard can be modified.
- A calculated field can be inserted in a Field text box when designing a query.
- A set of restrictions, called a filter, can be set on records in a table or form. A filter lets you select specific field values.
- Filter specific data in a field with the Filter By Selection button that displays on the Table Datasheet toolbar.
- Click the Filter By Form button on the Table Datasheet toolbar and a blank record is displayed. Set the values you want filtered records to contain at this blank record.
- When a filter is done by selection or by form, the Apply Filter button on the Table Datasheet toolbar changes to Remove Filter.

COMMANDS review

Command	Mouse/Keyboard
Display Show Table dialog box	Open database file, click Queries on the Objects bar, and then double-click *Create query in Design view* in the list box
Begin Simple Query Wizard	Open database file, click Queries on the Objects bar, and then double-click *Create query by using wizard* in the list box
Filter specific data	Open table, select specific data, click Filter By Selection button on Table Datasheet toolbar
Filter by form	Open table, click Filter By Form button, at blank record specify data, and then click Apply Filter button on Table Datasheet toolbar
Remove filter	Click Remove Filter button on Table Datasheet toolbar

CONCEPTS check

Completion: On a blank sheet of paper, indicate the correct term, symbol, or command for each item.

1. A query can be performed by designing your own query or using this wizard.
2. This is the term used for the results of the query.
3. This is the symbol Access will automatically insert around a text value when establishing criteria for a query.
4. This is the symbol Access will automatically insert around a date when establishing criteria for a query.
5. Use this symbol when establishing criteria to indicate a wildcard character.
6. This is the criterion you would key to return field values greater than $500.
7. This is the criterion you would key to return field values that begin with the letter *L*.
8. This is the criterion you would key to return field values that are not in Oregon.
9. A set of restrictions placed on records in a table or form is referred to as this.
10. Click this button on the Table Datasheet toolbar to display only those records containing the selected data.
11. Click this tab, located at the bottom of the Filter By Form window, to filter on two field values.
12. List the steps you would complete to display only those records with order dates between February 15, 2002, and February 20, 2002, in the Orders table located in the Outdoor Options database file.

SKILLS check

Assessment 1

1. Copy the Legal Services database file from the CD that accompanies this textbook to your disk. Remove the read-only attribute from the Legal Services database file.
2. Open the Legal Services database file.
3. Design the following queries on data in the Legal Services database file:
   a. Extract records from the Billing table with the following specifications:
      1) Include the fields *Billing #*, *Client ID*, and *Category* in the query.
      2) Extract those records with the SE category.
      3) Save the query and name it SE Category Billing Query.
      4) Print and then close the query.
   b. Extract records from the Billing table with the following specifications:
      1) Include the fields *Billing #*, *Client ID*, and *Date*.
      2) Extract those records in the *Date* field with dates between 6/7/2002 and 6/9/2002.
      3) Save the query and name it June 7-9 Billing Query.
      4) Print and then close the query.
   c. Extract records from the Clients table with the following specifications:
      1) Include the fields *First Name*, *Last Name*, and *City*.
      2) Extract those records with any city other than Kent in the *City* field.
      3) Save the query and name it Not Kent Clients Query.
      4) Print and then close the query.
4. Close the Legal Services database file.

Assessment 2

1. Open the Legal Services database file.
2. Extract information from two tables with the following specifications:
   a. Include the fields *Billing #*, *Client ID*, *Date*, and *Rate #* from the Billing table.
   b. Include the field *Rate* from the Rates table.
   c. Extract those records with a rate number greater than 2.
   d. Save the query and name it Rate Greater Than 2 Query.
   e. Print and then close the query.
3. Extract information from three tables with the following specifications:
   a. Include the field *Attorney* from the Attorneys table.
   b. Include the fields *First Name* and *Last Name* from the Clients table.
   c. Include the fields *Attorney ID*, *Date,* and *Hours* from the Billing table.
   d. Extract those records with an Attorney ID of 12.
   e. Save the query and name it Attorney Query.
   f. Print and then close the query.
4. Close the Legal Services database file.

Assessment 3

1. Open the Legal Services database file.
2. Use the Simple Query Wizard to extract specific information from two tables with the following specifications:
   a. At the first Simple Query Wizard dialog box, include the following fields:
      From the Attorneys table: *Attorney ID* and *Attorney*
      From Categories table: *Category Name*
      From Billing table: *Hours*
   b. At the second Simple Query Wizard dialog box, click Next.
   c. At the third Simple Query Wizard dialog box, click the *Modify the query design* option, and then click the Finish button.
   d. At the query window, key **14** in the Criteria text box in the *Attorney ID* column.
   e. Run the query.
   f. Save the query with the default name.
   g. Print and then close the query.
3. Close the Legal Services database file.

Assessment 4

1. Open the Legal Services database file.
2. Open the Clients table and then use the Filter By Selection button on the Table Datasheet toolbar to display the following records:
   a. Display only those records of clients who live in Renton. When the records of clients in Renton display, print the results (in landscape orientation), and then click the Remove Filter button.
   b. Display only those records of clients with the Zip Code of 98033. When the records of clients with the Zip Code 98033 display, print the results (in landscape orientation), and then click the Remove Filter button.
3. Close the Clients table without saving the changes.
4. Open the Billing table and then use the Filter By Selection button on the Table Datasheet toolbar to display the following records:
   a. Display only those records with a Category of CC. Print the CC records and then click the Remove Filter button.
   b. Display only those records with an Attorney ID of 12. Print the records and then click the Remove Filter button.
5. Close the Billing table without saving the changes.
6. Close the Legal Services database file.

Assessment 5

1. Open the Legal Services database file.
2. Open the Clients table and then use the Filter By Form button to display clients in Auburn or Renton. (Be sure to use the Or tab at the very bottom of the table.) Print the table and then click the Remove Filter button.
3. Close the Clients table without saving the changes.
4. Open the Billing table and then use the Filter By Form button to display categories G or P. Print the table and then click the Remove Filter button.
5. Close the Billing table without saving the changes.
6. Close the Legal Services database file.

Assessment 6

1. Use the Access Help feature to learn how to hide fields in a query's result.
2. After reading the information on hiding fields, complete the following steps:
   a. Open the Legal Services database file.
   b. Design the following query:
      1) At the Show Table dialog box, add the Billing table, the Clients table, and the Rates table.
      2) At the Query1 : Select Query window, drag the following fields to Field text boxes:

         Clients table:
         First Name
         Last Name

         Billing table:
         Hours

         Rates table:
         Rate

      3) Insert in the fifth Field text box the calculated field *Total:[Hours]*[Rate].*
      4) Hide the *Hours* and the *Rate* fields.
   c. Run the query.
   d. Print the query and then close it without saving it.
3. Close the Legal Services database file.

WORK IN Progress

Creating Tables, Queries, and Filters

ASSESSING proficiency

In this unit, you have learned to design and create database files, modify data in tables, and create a one-to-many relationship between tables. You also learned how to create a table using the Table Wizard, perform queries on data in tables, and filter records in a table.

(Note: Before completing unit assessments, delete any database files from your disk.)

Assessment 1

1. Use Access to create tables for Cornerstone Catering. Name the database file Cornerstone. Create a table named Employees that includes the following fields (you determine the field name, data type, field size, and description):

    Employee # (primary key)
    First Name
    Last Name
    Cell Phone Number

2. After creating the table, save it and name it Employees. Switch to Datasheet view and then enter the following data in the appropriate fields:

    Employee #: **10**
    First Name: **Erin**
    Last Name: **Jergens**
    Cell Phone Number: **(505) 555-3193**

    Employee #: **19**
    First Name: **Martin**
    Last Name: **Vaughn**
    Cell Phone Number: **(505) 555-4461**

    Employee #: **14**
    First Name: **Mikio**
    Last Name: **Ogami**
    Cell Phone Number: **(505) 555-1087**

    Employee #: **24**
    First Name: **Shawn**
    Last Name: **Kettering**
    Cell Phone Number: **(505) 555-3885**

3. Print and then close the Employees table.
4. Create a table named Plans that includes the following fields:

    Plan Code (primary key)
    Plan

5. After creating the table, save it and name it Plans. Switch to Datasheet view and then enter the following data in the appropriate fields:

    Plan Code: **A**
    Plan: **Sandwich Buffet**

    Plan Code: **C**
    Plan: **Hot Luncheon Buffet**

Plan Code: **B**
Plan: **Cold Luncheon Buffet**

Plan Code: **D**
Plan: **Combination Dinner**

6. Print and then close the Plans table.
7. Create a table named Prices that includes the following fields (you determine the field name, data type, field size, and description [except as shown]):

   Price Code (primary key)
   Price Per Person (identify this data type as *Currency*)

8. After creating the table, save it and name it Prices. Switch to Datasheet view and then enter the following data in the appropriate fields:

   Price Code: **1**
   Price Per Person: **$11.50**

   Price Code: **2**
   Price Per Person: **$12.75**

   Price Code: **3**
   Price Per Person: **$14.50**

   Price Code: **4**
   Price Per Person: **$16.00**

   Price Code: **5**
   Price Per Person: **$18.00**

9. Print and then close the Prices table.
10. Create a table named Clients that includes the following fields (you determine the field name, data type, field size, and description):

    Client # (primary key)
    Client Name
    Street Address
    City
    State
    Zip Code
    Telephone

11. After creating the table, save it and name it Clients. Switch to Datasheet view and then enter the following data in the appropriate fields:

    Client #: **104**
    Client Name: **Sarco Corporation**
    Street Address: **340 Cordova Road**
    City: **Santa Fe**
    State: **NM**
    Zip Code: **87510**
    Telephone: **(505) 555-3880**

    Client #: **155**
    Client Name: **Creative Concepts**
    Street Address: **1046 Market Street**
    City: **Los Alamos**
    State: **NM**
    Zip Code: **87547**
    Telephone: **(505) 555-1200**

    Client #: **218**
    Client Name: **Allenmore Systems**
    Street Address: **7866 Second Street**
    City: **Espanola**
    State: **NM**
    Zip Code: **87535**
    Telephone: **(505) 555-3455**

    Client #: **286**
    Client Name: **Sol Enterprises**
    Street Address: **120 Cerrillos Road**
    City: **Santa Fe**
    State: **NM**
    Zip Code: **87560**
    Telephone: **(505) 555-7700**

12. Print and then close the Clients table.

13. Create a table named Events that includes the following fields (you determine the data type, field size, and description [except as shown]):

    Event # (primary key; identify this data type as AutoNumber)
    Client #
    Employee #
    Date (identify this data type as Date/Time)
    Plan Code
    Price Code
    Number of People (identify this data type as Number)

14. After creating the table, save it and name it Events. Switch to Datasheet view and then enter the following data in the appropriate fields:

    Event #: (AutoNumber)
    Client #: 218
    Employee #: 14
    Date: 7/3/2002
    Plan Code: B
    Price Code: 3
    Number of People: 250

    Event #: (AutoNumber)
    Client #: 104
    Employee #: 19
    Date: 7/6/2002
    Plan Code: D
    Price Code: 5
    Number of People: 120

    Event #: (AutoNumber)
    Client #: 155
    Employee #: 24
    Date: 7/8/2002
    Plan Code: A
    Price Code: 1
    Number of People: 300

    Event #: (AutoNumber)
    Client #: 286
    Employee #: 10
    Date: 7/10/2002
    Plan Code: C
    Price Code: 4
    Number of People: 75

    Event #: (AutoNumber)
    Client #: 218
    Employee #: 14
    Date: 7/14/2002
    Plan Code: C
    Price Code: 4
    Number of People: 50

15. Adjust the columns so that the report prints on one page. Print and then close the Events table.

Assessment 2

1. With the Cornerstone database file open, create the following one-to-many relationships:
    a. *Client #* in the Clients table is the "one" and *Client #* in the Events table is the "many."
    b. *Employee #* in the Employees table is the "one" and *Employee #* in the Events table is the "many."
    c. *Plan Code* in the Plans table is the "one" and *Plan Code* in the Events table is the "many."
    d. *Price Code* in the Prices table is the "one" and *Price Code* in the Events table is the "many."
2. Save and then print the relationships.

Assessment 3

1. With the Cornerstone database file open, open the Plans table in Datasheet view and then add the following record at the end of the table:

   Plan Code: **E**
   Plan: **Hawaiian Luau Buffet**

2. Print and then close the Plans table.
3. Open the Events table in Datasheet view and then add the following record at the end of the table:

   Event #: (AutoNumber)
   Client #: **104**
   Employee #: **19**
   Date: **7/18/2002**
   Plan Code: **E**
   Price Code: **5**
   Number of People: **125**

4. Print and then close the Events table.

Assessment 4

1. With the Cornerstone database file open extract records from the Events table with the following specifications:
   a. Include the fields *Client #*, *Date*, and *Plan Code*.
   b. Extract those records with a Plan Code of C.
   c. Print and then close the query without saving it.
2. Extract records from the Clients table with the following specifications:
   a. Include the fields *Client Name*, *City*, and *Telephone*.
   b. Extract those records with a city of Santa Fe.
   c. Print and then close the query without saving it.
3. Extract information from two tables with the following specifications:
   a. From the Clients table, include the fields *Client Name* and *Telephone*.
   b. From the Events table, include the field *Date*, *Plan Code*, and *Number of People*.
   c. Extract those records with a date between July 10 and July 25, 2002.
   d. Print the query and then close it without saving it.

Assessment 5

1. With the Cornerstone database file open, open the Events database table and then use the Filter By Selection button on the Table Datasheet toolbar to display the following records:
   a. Display only those records with an Employee # of 14. When the records display, print the results, and then click the Remove Filter button.
   b. Display only those records with a Price Code of 4. When the records display, print the results, and then click the Remove Filter button.
2. Close the Events table without saving the changes.

3. Open the Clients table and then use the Filter By Form button to display clients in Espanola or Los Alamos. (Be sure to use the Or tab at the very bottom of the table.) Print the results and then click the Remove Filter button.
4. Close the Clients table without saving the changes.
5. Open the Events table and then use the Filter By Form button to display Plan Code A or C. Print the results and then click the Remove Filter button.
6. Close the Events table without saving the changes.
7. Close the Cornerstone database file.

WRITING activity

The following activity gives you the opportunity to practice your writing skills along with demonstrating an understanding of some of the important Access features you have mastered in this unit. Use correct grammar, appropriate word choices, and clear sentence constructions.

Activity 1

The manager of Cornerstone Catering has asked you to add information to the Cornerstone database file on employee payroll. You need to create another table that will contain information on payroll. The manager wants the table to include the following (you determine the appropriate field name, data type, field size, and description):

Employee #: **10**
Status: **Full-time**
Monthly Salary: **$1,650**

Employee #: **19**
Status: **Part-time**
Monthly Salary: **$840**

Employee #: **14**
Status: **Part-time**
Monthly Salary: **$600**

Employee #: **24**
Status: **Full-time**
Monthly Salary: **$1,800**

Print and then close the payroll table. Open Word and then write a report to the manager detailing how you created the table. Include a title for the report, steps on how the table was created, and any other pertinent information. Save the completed report and name it U01 Act01. Print and then close U01 Act01.

INTERNET project

Vehicle Search

In this activity you will search the Internet for information on different vehicles before doing actual test drives. Learning about a major product, such as a vehicle, can increase your chances of finding a good buy, can potentially guide you away from a poor purchase, and can help speed up the process of narrowing the search to the type of vehicle that will meet your needs. Before you begin, list the top five criteria you would look for in a vehicle. For example, it must be a 4-door vehicle, needs to be 4-wheel drive, etc.

Using key search words, find at least two Web sites that list vehicle reviews. Use the search engines provided within the different review sites to find vehicles that fulfill the criteria you listed to meet your particular needs. Create a database file in Access and create a table in that file that will contain the results from your vehicle search. Design the table keeping in mind what type of data you need to record for each vehicle that meets your requirements. Include at least the make, model, year, price, description, and special problems in the table. Also include the ability to rate the vehicle as poor, fair, good, or excellent. You will decide on the rating of each vehicle depending on your findings.

JOB study

Mobile Home Park Project

In this activity you are working in the office of a large mobile home park. The manager of the park has asked you to find a way to document information about the people living in the park so that she can better meet their needs. For example, when road work has to be done, she would like to know which patrons would have difficulty in parking their cars a long distance from their homes. When utility workers are scheduled to be in the park, she would like to notify the children's parents of any potentially dangerous situations.

The mobile home lots are numbered 1 through 200 and each are rated by size and location for rent as either standard or premium. The manager has asked you to record for each lot number, the names and phone numbers of the residents, whether or not it is a premium lot, whether or not there are any disabled individuals living in the home, the number of children living in the home, and the date the individuals occupied the lot. Create a database file and a table within the file to store the information. Enter 10 records to test the table. (Make up the data for the table.) Create a query for all lots where children live and another query for all lots with disabled individuals. For each query, provide the residents names and phone numbers, and then print the results. The queries should be saved with appropriate names for later use.

ACCESS

CORE LEVEL UNIT 2: CREATING FORMS AND REPORTS

Creating Forms

Creating Reports, Mailing Labels, and Charts

Importing and Exporting Data

Creating Web Pages and Using Database Wizards

MICROSOFT® ACCESS 2002

CORE BENCHMARK MOUS SKILLS-UNIT 2

Reference No.	Skill	Pages
Ac2002-1	**Creating and Using Databases**	
Ac2002-1-1	Create Access databases	
	Create a database with the Database Wizard	C192-C199
Ac2002-4	**Creating and Modifying Forms**	
Ac2002-4-1	Create and display forms	
	Create a form using AutoForm	C118-C120
	Print a form	C118-C120
	Create a form using the Form Wizard	C121-C125
	Create a form with related tables	C125-C126
	Create a form in Design view	C126-137
Ac2002-4-2	Modify form properties	
	Add/delete records	C119-C120
	Move, resize, format, align, control objects	C127-C132
	Add a form header and form footer	C133-C135
	Add a calculated control	C135-C137
Ac2002-7	**Producing Reports**	
Ac2002-7-1	Create and format reports	
	Create report using AutoReport	C143-C144
	Create a report using the Report Wizard	C144-C149
	Create a report based on two tables	C149-C150
	Create a report in Design view	C150-C155
	Add a report header and report footer	C152-C155
Ac2002-7-2	Add calculated controls to reports	
	Add, move, resize, and customize control objects	C150-C155
Ac2002-7-3	Preview and print reports	C144; C148; C150
Ac2002-8	**Integrating with Other Applications**	
Ac2002-8-1	Import data to Access	
	Import data to a new table	C177-C178
	Linking data to a new table	C178-C179
Ac2002-8-2	Export data from Access	
	Export data to Excel	C167-C169
	Export data to Word	C170-C176
Ac2002-8-3	Create a simple data access page	C187-C192

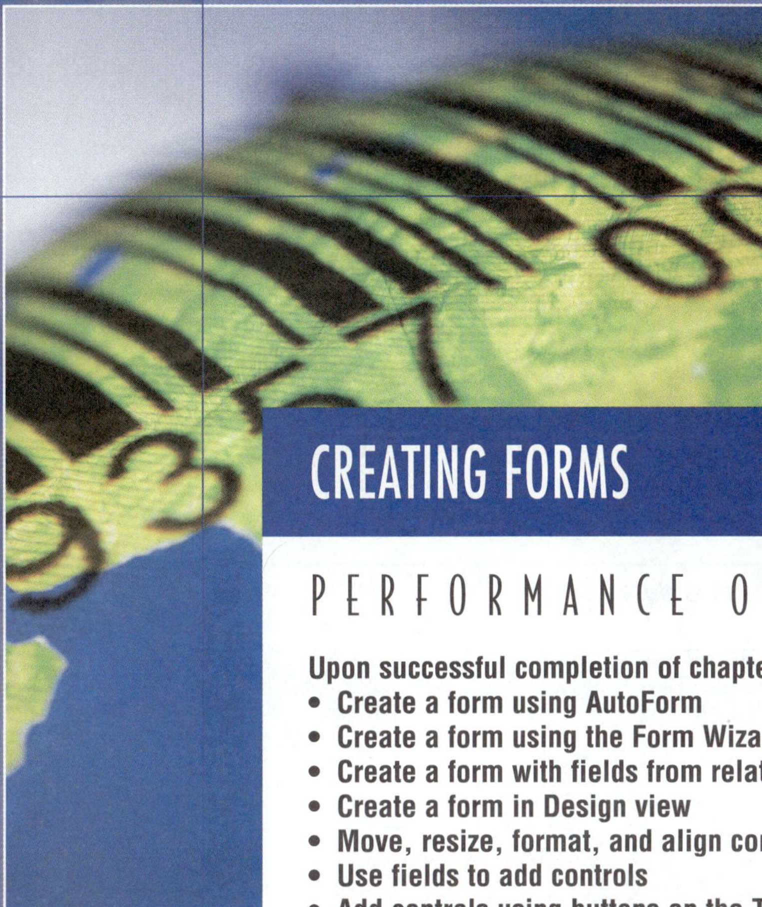

CHAPTER 5

CREATING FORMS

PERFORMANCE OBJECTIVES

Upon successful completion of chapter 5, you will be able to:

- **Create a form using AutoForm**
- **Create a form using the Form Wizard**
- **Create a form with fields from related tables**
- **Create a form in Design view**
- **Move, resize, format, and align control objects**
- **Use fields to add controls**
- **Add controls using buttons on the Toolbox**
- **Add a Form Header and Form Footer to a form**
- **Add a calculated control to a form**

Outdoor Options

In this chapter, you will learn to create a form from tables, improving the data display and making data entry easier. Access offers several methods for presenting data on the screen for easier data entry. You can create a form using the AutoForm and the Form Wizard. You can also create a form in Design view and then edit control objects in the form.

Creating a Form

Access offers a variety of options for presenting data in a more easily read and attractive format. When entering data in a table at the Datasheet view, multiple records are displayed at the same time. If a record contains several fields, you may not be able to view all fields within a record at the same time. If you create a form, generally all fields for a record are visible at one time.

HINT
Use a form to easily enter, edit, and/or view data.

Several methods are available for creating a form. In this section, you will learn how to use AutoForm to insert existing data into a form, use the Form Wizard to create a form, and use the Form Wizard to create a form with fields from related tables.

HINT
A form allows you to focus on a single record at a time.

HINT
After creating a form, save it before working with it.

New Object

Creating a Form Using AutoForm

Data in a table can be viewed, added, or edited in the Datasheet view. You can perform these functions on data inserted in a form. The advantage to a form is that the functions are generally easier to perform because the data is easier to read. Access offers the AutoForm feature, which automatically copies data in a table and creates a form. To use the AutoForm feature, click the down-pointing triangle at the right side of the New Object button on the Database toolbar, and then click AutoForm at the drop-down list. AutoForm automatically creates a form and inserts it on the screen.

In exercise 1, you will be using AutoForm to create a form for data contained in the Orders table, which is part of the Outdoor Options database file. When AutoForm creates the form, the first record will display as shown in figure 5.1.

FIGURE 5.1 *Form Created from Data in Orders Table*

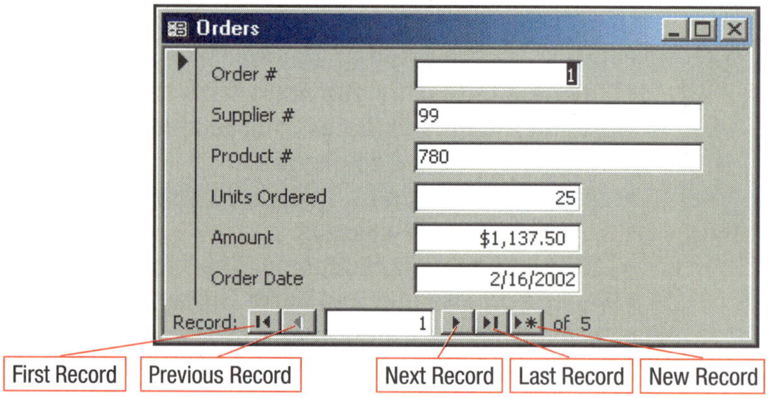

HINT
You can use the keyboard to display specific records. Press Page Down to move forward a single record or press Page Up to move back a single record. Press Ctrl + Home to display the first record or press Ctrl + End to display the last record.

Navigation buttons display along the bottom of the first Orders record. The function each button performs is shown in figure 5.1. Using these navigation buttons, you can display the first record in the table, the previous record, the next record, the last record, and a new record.

Printing a Form

Print a form in the same manner as a table. If desired, changes can be made to the page margins and/or page orientation at the Page Setup dialog box. To display this dialog box, click File and then Page Setup. Print all records in the form by clicking the Print button on the Database toolbar. If you want to print a specific record, display the desired record, and then display the Print dialog box by clicking File and then Print. At the Print dialog box, click the Selected Record(s) option, and then click OK.

exercise 1

CREATING A FORM WITH THE ORDERS TABLE

(Note: Delete any database files from your disk.)

1. Copy the Outdoor Options database file from the CD that accompanies this textbook to your disk. Remove the read-only attribute from the Outdoor Options database file.
2. Open the Outdoor Options database file.
3. Use the AutoForm feature to create a form with the data in the Orders table by completing the following steps:
   a. At the Outdoor Options : Database window, click *Orders* in the list box.
   b. Click the down-pointing triangle at the right of the New Object button on the Database toolbar.
   c. At the drop-down menu that displays, click the AutoForm option.
   d. When the first record displays, display the next record by clicking the button toward the bottom of the Orders form (see figure 5.1) that contains a right-pointing triangle.
   e. Practice displaying different records using the navigation buttons along the bottom of the Orders form.
4. Save the form by completing the following steps:
   a. Click the Save button on the Form View toolbar.
   b. At the Save As dialog box, with *Orders* inserted in the Form Name dialog text box, click OK.
5. Print all records in the form by clicking the Print button on the Form View toolbar.
6. Close the Orders form.
7. Close the Outdoor Options database file.

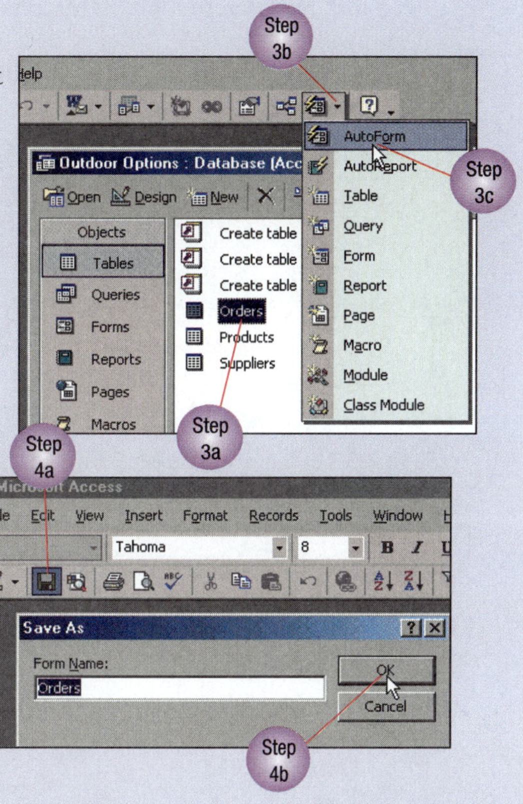

Adding/Deleting Records

Navigate through records in a form using the navigation buttons that display along the bottom of the form, as shown in figure 5.1. Add a new record to the form by clicking the New Record button that displays along the bottom of the form and contains a right-pointing triangle followed by an asterisk. You can also add a new record to a form by clicking the New Record button on the Form View toolbar that displays towards the top of the screen.

New Record

To delete a record, display the record, and then click the Delete Record button on the Form View toolbar. At the message telling you that the record will be deleted permanently, click Yes.

Delete Record

exercise 2

ADDING AND DELETING RECORDS IN A FORM

1. Open the Outdoor Options database file.
2. At the Outdoor Options : Database window, click the Forms button on the Objects bar located at the left side of the window.
3. Double-click *Orders* in the list box.
4. With Orders open and the first record showing, add new records and delete an existing record by completing the following steps:

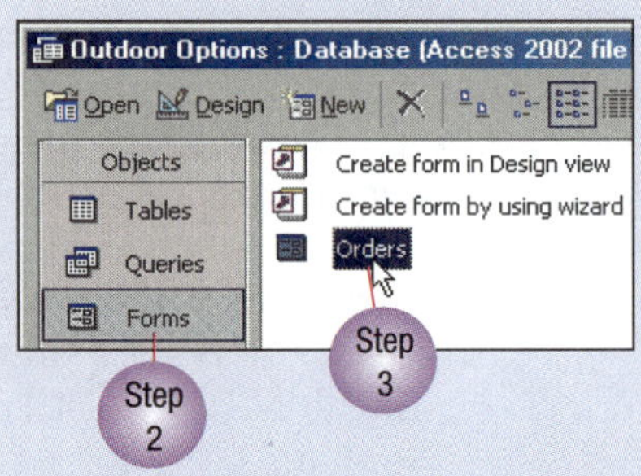

   a. Click the New Record button located toward the bottom of the first record.
   b. At the new blank record, key the following information in the specified fields (move to the next field by pressing Tab or Enter; move to the previous field by pressing Shift + Tab):

Order #	=	(automatically inserted)
Supplier #	=	**54**
Product #	=	**103**
Units Ordered	=	**10**
Amount	=	**$573.25**
Order Date	=	**2/22/2002**

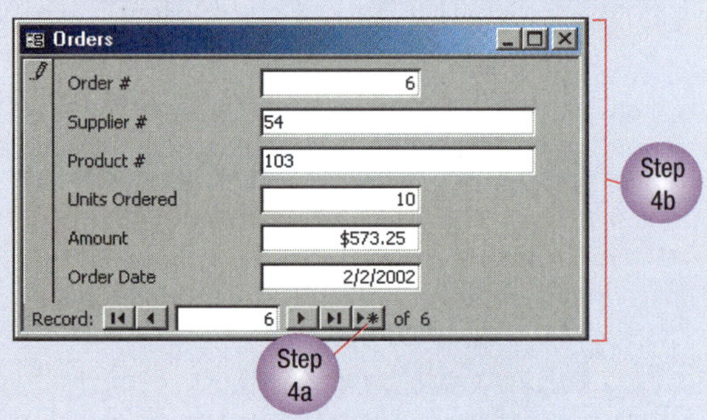

   c. After keying the information for the new record, press the Tab key to display the next new record (you can also click the New Record button), and then key the following information in the specified fields:

Order #	=	(automatically inserted)
Supplier #	=	**99**
Product #	=	**647**
Units Ordered	=	**5**
Amount	=	**$325.00**
Order Date	=	**2/22/2002**

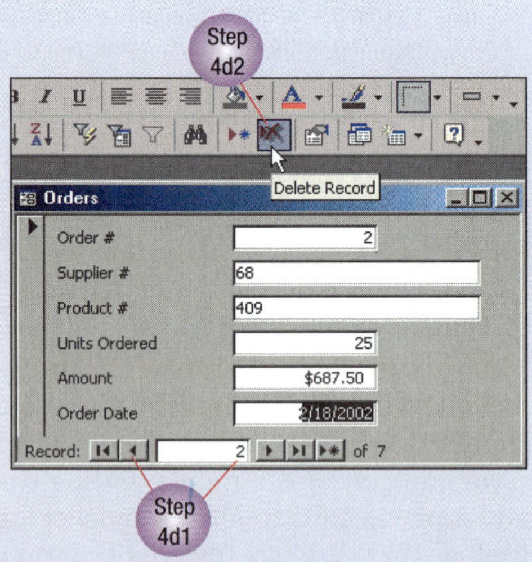

   d. Delete the second record by completing the following steps:
      1) Click the button toward the bottom of the record that displays with a left-pointing triangle until Record 2 displays.
      2) With Record 2 displayed, click the Delete Record button on the Form View toolbar.
      3) At the message telling you that you will not be able to undo the delete operation, click Yes.
   e. Click the Save button on the Form View toolbar.
   f. Change the top and bottom margins to 0.5 and 0.5, and then print all records in the form by clicking the Print button on the Form View toolbar.
   g. Close the Orders form.
5. Close the Outdoor Options database file.

Creating a Form Using the Form Wizard

Access offers a Form Wizard that will guide you through the creation of a form. The Form Wizard offers more formatting choices than the AutoForm feature. To create a form using the Form Wizard, open the database file containing the table for which you want to create a form. At the database window, click the Forms button on the Objects bar, and then click the New button on the window toolbar. At the New Form dialog box shown in figure 5.2, double-click *Form Wizard* in the list box and the first Form Wizard dialog box displays as shown in figure 5.3.

HINT

The Form Wizard is a general-purpose wizard that provides more flexibility than the AutoForm choices.

FIGURE 5.2 ***New Form Dialog Box***

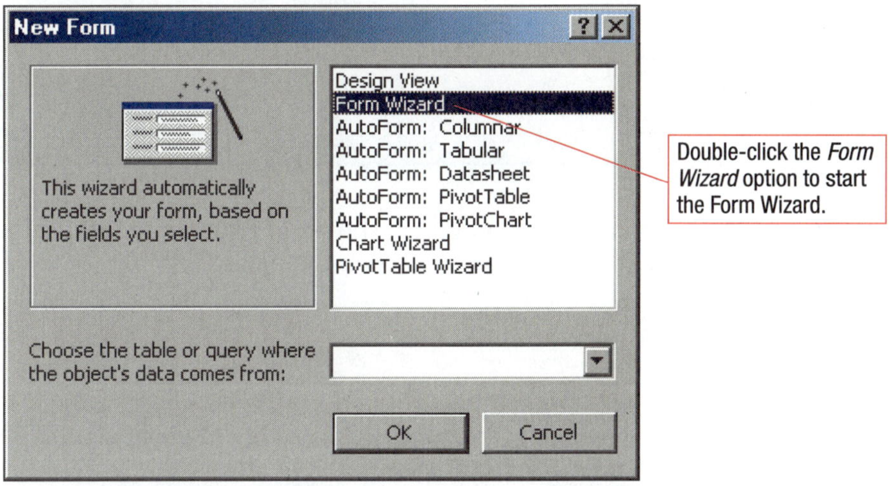

At the first Form Wizard dialog box, specify the table and then the fields you want included in the form. To select the table, click the down-pointing triangle at the right side of the Tables/Queries option box, and then click the desired table. Select the desired field in the Available Fields list box, click the button containing the greater than symbol (>), and the field is inserted in the Selected Fields list box. Continue in this manner until all desired fields are inserted in the Selected Fields list box. If you want to insert all fields into the Selected Fields list box at one time, click the button containing the two greater than symbols (>>). After specifying fields, click the Next button.

HINT

The Form Wizard automates the creating of a form and lets you specify some or all of the fields to be used in the form.

FIGURE 5.3 **First Form Wizard Dialog Box**

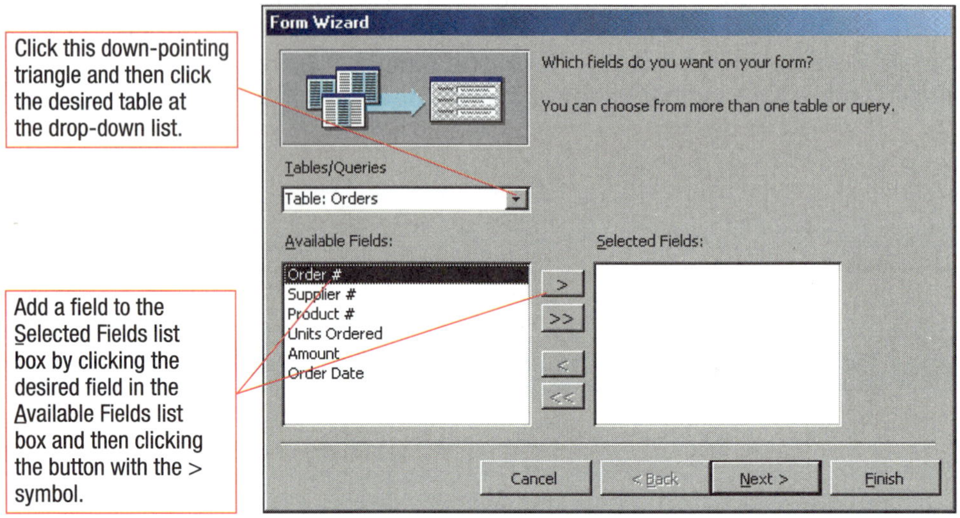

At the second Form Wizard dialog box, shown in figure 5.4, specify the layout for the records. After choosing the layout, click the Next button.

FIGURE 5.4 **Second Form Wizard Dialog Box**

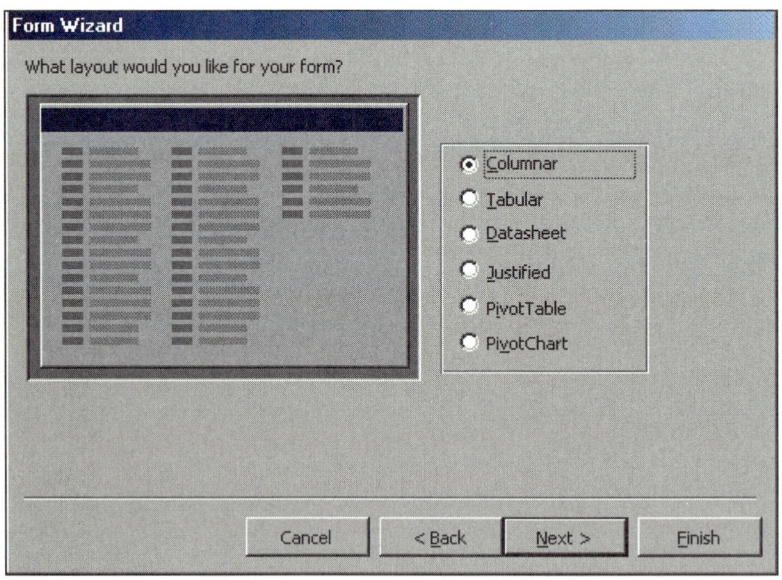

One of the advantages offered by the Form Wizard is the ability to choose from a variety of formats. At the third Form Wizard dialog box, shown in figure 5.5, you choose a format style, such as *Blends*, *Blueprint*, *Expedition*, *Industrial*, and so forth. Click a format style and the results of the style are shown in the preview box. After selecting the desired format style, click the Next button.

FIGURE 5.5 *Third Form Wizard Dialog Box*

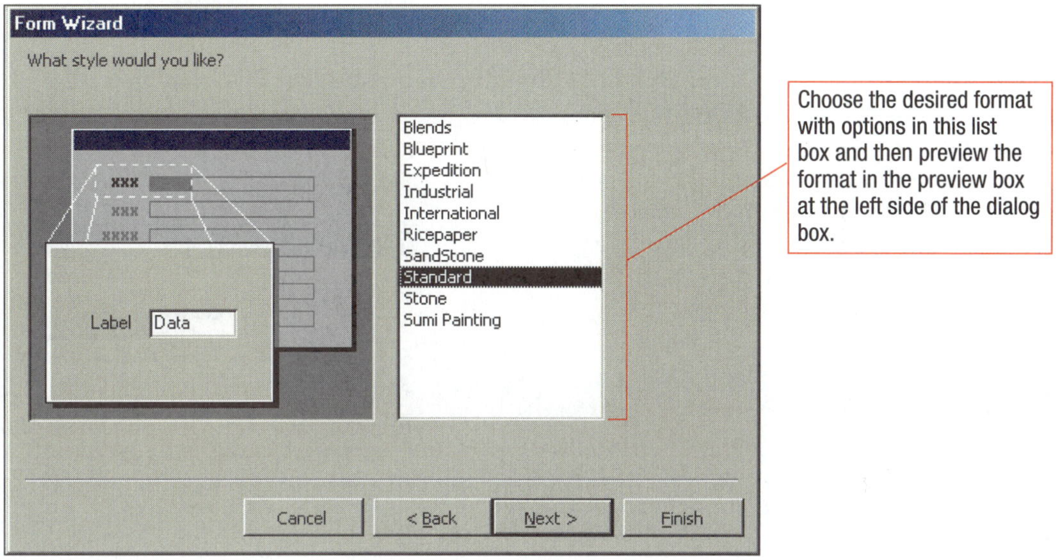

At the last Form Wizard dialog box, shown in figure 5.6, the Form Wizard offers a title for the form and also provides the option *Open the form to view or enter information*. Make any necessary changes in this dialog box and then click the Finish button.

FIGURE 5.6 *Fourth Form Wizard Dialog Box*

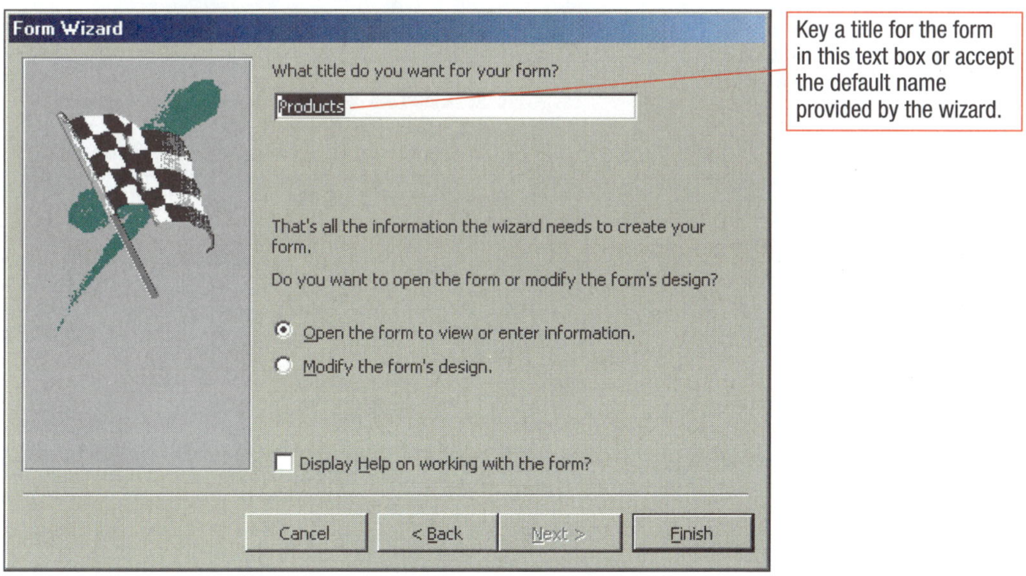

exercise 3 — CREATING A FORM USING THE FORM WIZARD

1. Open the Outdoor Options database file.
2. At the Outdoor Options : Database window, click the Forms button on the Objects bar located at the left side of the window.
3. Delete the Orders form you created in exercise 1 by completing the following steps:
   a. Position the arrow pointer on *Orders* in the list box and then click the *right* mouse button.
   b. At the shortcut menu that displays, click the left mouse button on Delete.
   c. At the question asking if you want to permanently delete the form, click Yes.
4. At the Outdoor Options : Database window with the Forms button selected, create a form with the Form Wizard by completing the following steps:
   a. Click the New button on the window toolbar.
   b. At the New Form dialog box, double-click the *Form Wizard* option in the list box.
   c. At the first Form Wizard dialog box, click the down-pointing triangle at the right side of the Tables/Queries option box, and then click *Table: Products* at the drop-down list and click OK.
   d. Specify that you want all fields included in the form by clicking the button containing the two greater than symbols (>>), and then clicking the Next button.
   e. At the second Form Wizard dialog box, click the Next button. (This leaves the layout at the default of Columnar.)
   f. At the third Form Wizard dialog box, click the *International* option in the list box, and then click the Next button.
   g. At the fourth Form Wizard dialog box, leave the options at the default, and then finish the form by clicking the Finish button.
5. When the first record is shown in the form, click the New Record button, and then add the following records:

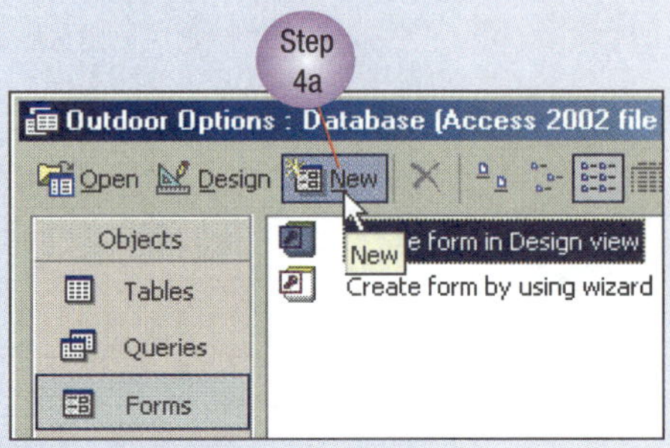

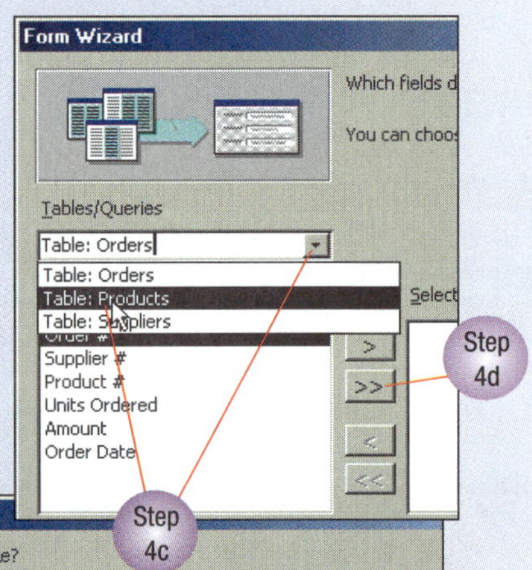

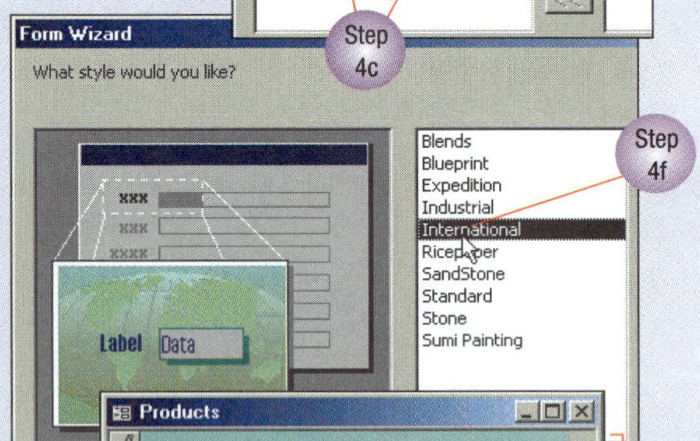

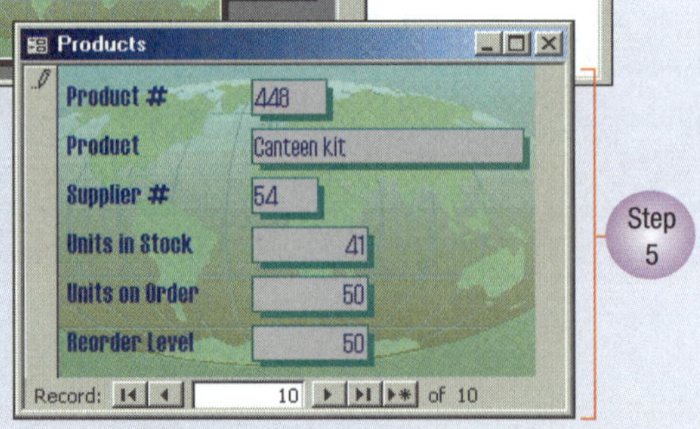

Product #	=	**448**
Product	=	**Canteen kit**
Supplier #	=	**54**
Units in Stock	=	**41**
Units on Order	=	**50**
Reorder Level	=	**50**
Product #	=	**302**
Product	=	**Pocket warmer**
Supplier #	=	**31**

Units in Stock	=	13
Units on Order	=	15
Reorder Level	=	15

6. Delete the record containing information on ski goggles. (At the warning message, click Yes.)
7. Click the Save button on the Form View toolbar.
8. Click the Print button to print all records in the form.
9. Close the form by clicking the Close button in the upper right corner of the record.
10. Close the Outdoor Options database file.

Creating a Form with Related Tables

The forms you have created so far in this chapter have included all of the fields from one table. Forms can also be created with fields from tables that are connected by a one-to-many relationship. You can use the Form Wizard to create a form with fields from related tables. At the first Form Wizard dialog box (see figure 5.3), choose fields from the selected table and then choose fields from a related table. To change to the related table, click the down-pointing triangle at the right of the Tables/Queries option box, and then click the name of the desired table.

exercise 4 — CREATING A FORM WITH RELATED TABLES

1. Create a form that includes fields from the Products table and fields from the Suppliers table by completing the following steps:
   a. Open the Outdoor Options database file.
   b. At the Outdoor Options : Database window, click the Forms button on the Objects bar.
   c. Click the New button on the window toolbar.
   d. At the New Form dialog box, double-click *Form Wizard* in the list box.
   e. At the first Form Wizard dialog box, click the down-pointing triangle at the right of the Tables/Queries option box, and then click *Table: Products*.
   f. Complete the following steps to insert fields in the Selected Fields list box:
      1) With *Product #* selected in the Available Fields list box, click the button containing the greater than symbol (>).
      2) With *Product* selected in the Available Fields list box, click the button containing the greater than symbol (>).
      3) Click *Units in Stock* in the Available Fields list box and then click the button containing the greater than symbol (>).
      4) Click the down-pointing triangle at the right of the Table/Queries option box and then click *Table: Suppliers*.
      5) With *Supplier #* selected in the Available Fields list box, click the button containing the greater than symbol (>).
      6) With *Supplier Name* selected in the Available Fields list box, click the button containing the greater than symbol (>).
      7) Click *E-mail Address* in the Available Fields list box and then click the button containing the greater than symbol (>).

8) Click the Next button.

g. At the second Form Wizard dialog box, make sure *by Products* is selected in the list box that displays in the upper left corner of the dialog box, and then click the Next button.

h. At the third Form Wizard dialog box, click the Next button.

i. At the fourth Form Wizard dialog box, click *Blends* in the format style list box, and then click the Next button.

j. At the fifth Form Wizard dialog box, key the name **Units in Stock**, and then click the Finish button.

2. When the first record displays, print the record by displaying the Print dialog box, clicking Selected Record(s) in the Print Range section, and then clicking OK.
3. Close the form by clicking the Close button.
4. Close the Outdoor Options database file.

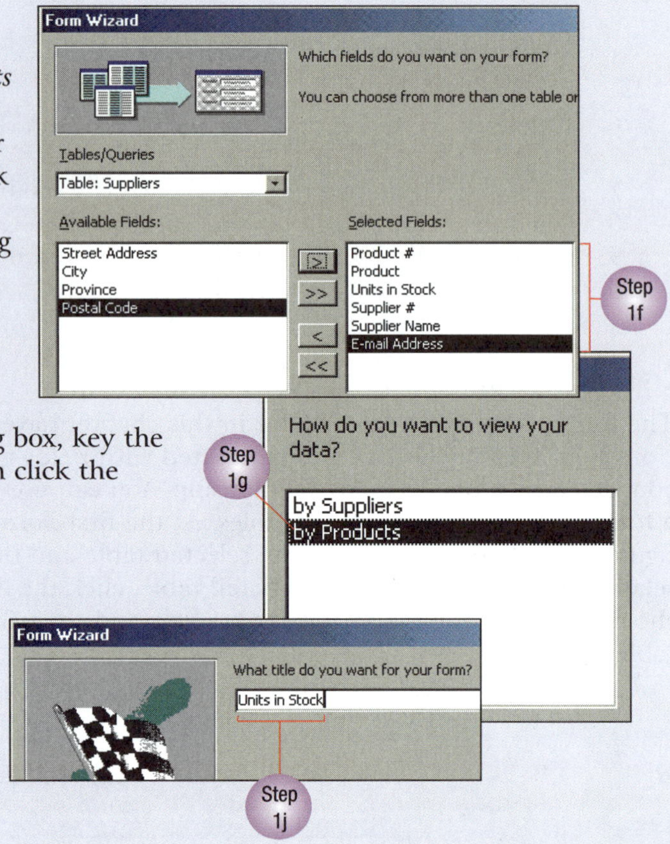

Creating a Form in Design View

A form is comprised of a series of controls, which are objects that display titles or descriptions, accept data, or perform actions. In the forms you created in this chapter, the AutoForm feature or the Form Wizard created the controls for the form using fields from the tables. Another method for creating a form is to use the Design view. To display the Design view, as shown in figure 5.7, click the Forms button on the Objects bar, and then double-click the *Create form in Design view* option in the list box. In the Design view, you can use fields from a table to create controls in the Design grid and you can also add controls with buttons on the Toolbox palette. The Toolbox palette, shown in figure 5.7, appears automatically in the Design view.

FIGURE

5.7 ***Form in Design View***

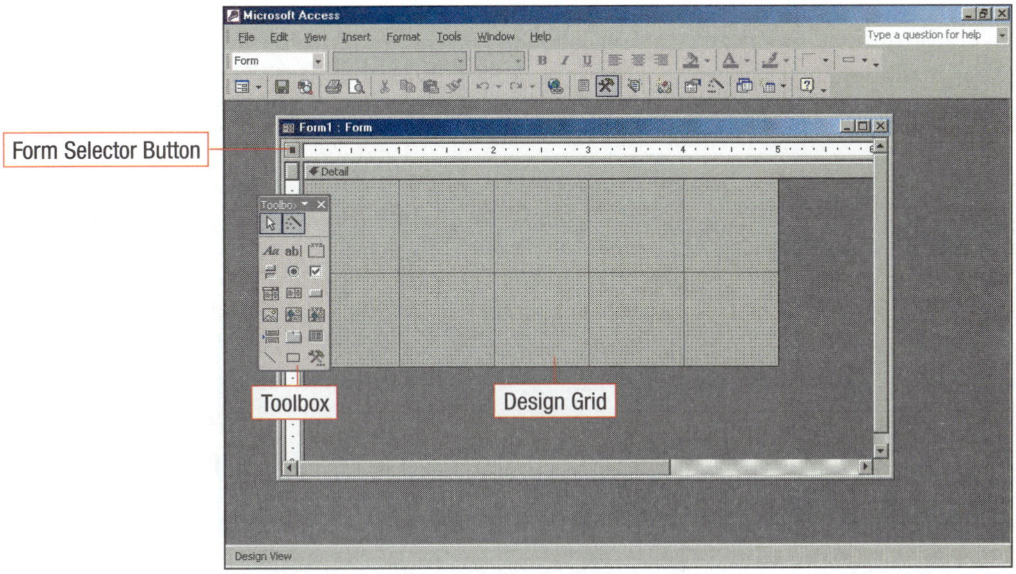

A form in Design view contains three sections—Form Header, Detail, and Form Footer. The Detail section is the only section that displays by default. (You will learn more about the Form Header and Form Footer sections later in this chapter.) The Detail section of the form in Design view is set up as a grid. Use the rulers along the top and left side of the section and the lines and dots that make up the grid to precisely position fields and controls.

Using Fields to Add Controls

Form Selector

Associate a table with the form to use fields to create controls. To associate a table, right-click the Form1 : Form title bar and then click Properties at the shortcut menu. This displays the Form properties sheet. (You can also display the Form properties sheet by double-clicking the Form Selector button that displays in the upper left corner of the Design grid.) At the Form properties sheet, click the All tab, and then click in the Record Source text box. Click the down-pointing triangle that displays at the right side of the option box and then click the desired table. This displays the table fields in a field list box. (If the field list box does not display, click the Field List button on the Form Design toolbar.) Using the mouse, drag the desired field from the field list box to the Design grid.

Field List

Moving Control Objects

When a field is moved to the Design grid, a label control containing the field name and a text box control used to accept data are placed adjacent to each other on the grid. The label control containing the field name is included for descriptive purposes so that the user knows which data to key into the corresponding text box.

The label control and its corresponding text box control for a field can be moved individually or together to another location on the form. To move the two control objects together, click one of the objects. This inserts eight sizing handles around the object you clicked with a large black handle displaying in the upper left corner as shown in figure 5.8. The adjacent object displays with one large black sizing handle in the upper left corner. Position the arrow pointer on the border of the control object containing the eight sizing handles (on the border, not on a sizing handle) until the pointer turns into a hand. Hold down the left mouse button and then drag the objects to the desired position. Move multiple control objects at the same time by holding down the Shift key while clicking each object. You can also select multiple control objects by drawing a border around the desired control objects.

FIGURE 5.8 ***Selected Control Objects***

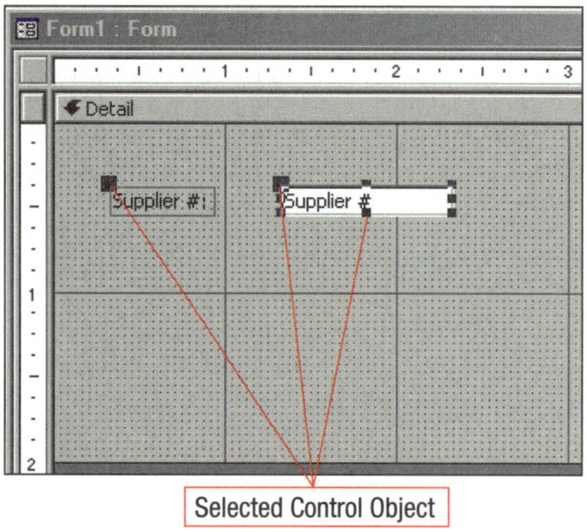

To move a control object separately from the adjacent object, position the mouse pointer on the large black handle that displays in the upper left corner of the object, hold down the left mouse button, and then drag the object to the desired position.

Resizing Control Objects

Increase or decrease the size of a selected control object using the sizing handles that display around the object. Drag the middle sizing handles at the left or right edge to make the control wider or narrower; drag the middle sizing handles at the top or bottom to make the control taller or shorter; and use the corner sizing handles to resize the object both horizontally and vertically at the same time.

Formatting Control Objects

Customize the formatting of selected control objects with options at the properties sheet. (The name of the properties sheet will vary depending on what is selected.) With the All tab selected, all formatting options are available. Click the Format tab to display only formatting options such as options to change the font size, font style, font color, foreground color, background color, and caption. Click in a text box for some options and a button containing three black dots displays at the right side. Click this button to display additional formatting choices.

Aligning Control Objects

Control objects inserted in the Design grid align with horizontal and vertical lines in the grid. This is because the Snap to Grid effect is on by default. Even with the Snap to Grid effect on, you may want to control the alignment of control objects. To align control objects, select the desired objects, and then click the Format option on the Menu bar. At the drop-down menu that displays, point to the Align option, and then click the desired alignment at the side menu.

exercise 5

CREATING AND FORMATTING A FORM IN DESIGN VIEW

1. Open the Outdoor Options database file.
2. At the Outdoor Options : Database window, click the Forms button on the Objects bar.
3. Create a form in Design view as shown in figure 5.9 by completing the following steps:
   a. Double-click the *Create form in Design view* option in the list box.
   b. At the Design grid, right-click on the Form1 : Form title bar and then click Properties at the shortcut menu.

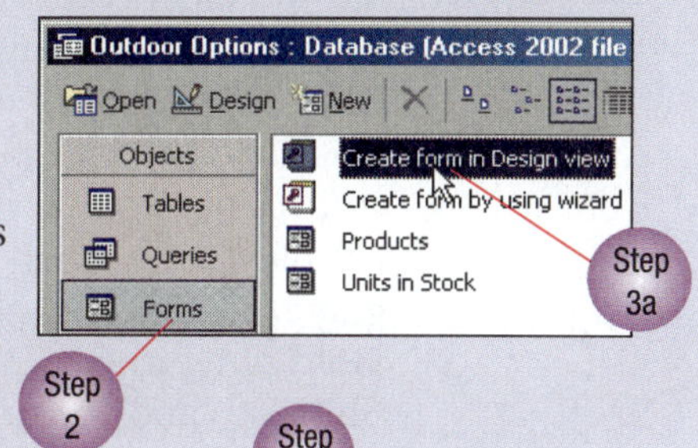

   c. At the Form properties sheet, click the All tab.
   d. At the Form properties sheet with the All tab selected, click in the Record Source text box, and then click the down-pointing triangle that displays at the right side of the text box.
   e. At the drop-down list that displays, click *Suppliers*.

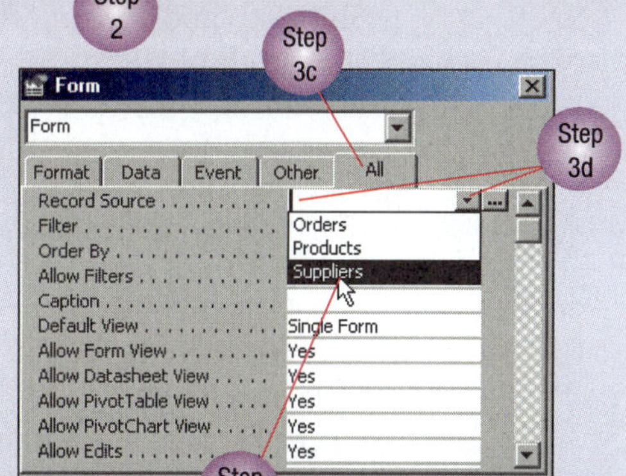

   f. Drag the *Supplier #* field from the field list box to the Design grid to the approximate location shown below. (You will be aligning the control objects later in this exercise.) (You may need to move the properties sheet and the Toolbox palette in order to place the objects in the desired location.)
   g. Drag the remaining fields from the field list box to the Design grid to the approximate locations shown below. (You will be formatting the control objects later in this exercise.) (Since all necesary fields have been added to the form, close the field list box by clicking the Close button in the upper right corner of the box.)

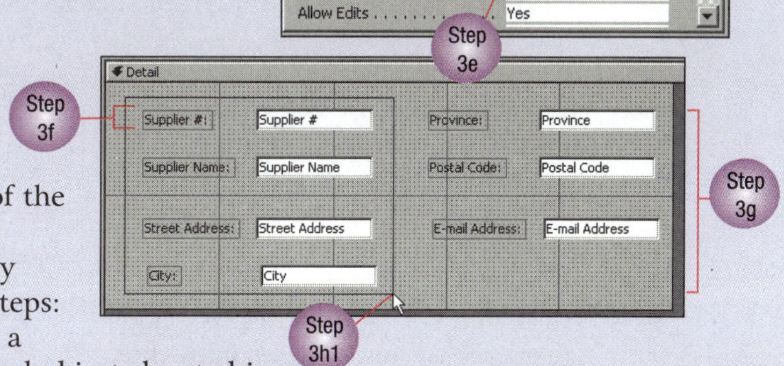

   h. Align the control objects by completing the following steps:
      1) With the mouse, draw a border around all control objects located in the first column. (This selects the control objects.)
      2) With the control objects selected, click Format on the Menu bar, point to Align, and then click Right at the side menu.
      3) With the mouse, draw a border around all control objects located in the second column.

4) Click Format on the Menu bar, point to Align, and then click Right at the side menu.
5) If the control objects are not positioned in the locations shown in figure 5.9, select and then drag the object to the desired position.

i. Change the *Supplier #:* caption by completing the following steps:
1) Click the *Supplier #:* label control object (displays with a gray background).
2) Click in the Caption text box in the Label properties sheet. (The Form properties sheet became the Label properties sheet when the label control object was selected.) (You may need to scroll up the list to display the Caption text box.)
3) Edit the text in the Caption text box so it displays as *Supplier Number:*.
4) Click anywhere in the Design grid outside a control object to deselect the object.

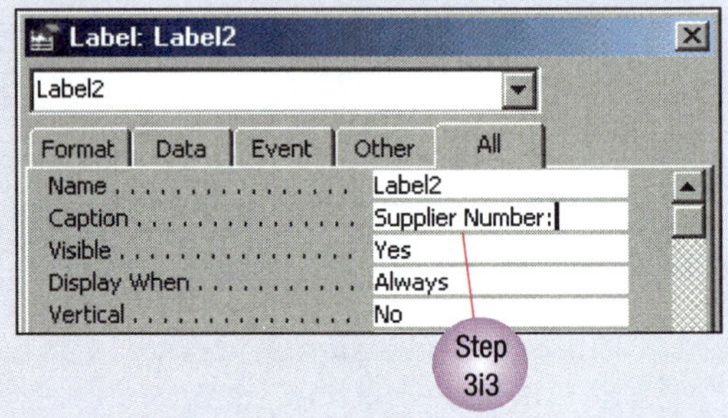

j. Format the label control objects by completing the following steps:
1) Click the *Supplier Number* label control object (displays with a gray background).
2) Hold down the Shift key and then click each of the remaining label control objects (objects that display with a gray background).

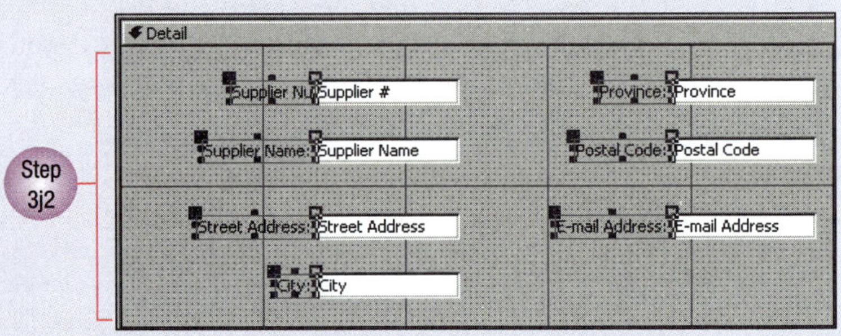

3) Click in the Fore Color text box in the Multiple selection properties sheet. (The Label properties sheet became the Multiple selection properties sheet when you selected the labels.) (You will need to scroll down the list to display the Fore Color text box.)
4) Click the button containing three black dots that displays at the right side of the text box.
5) At the color palette that displays, click the turquoise color (fifth color from the left in the top row), and then click OK to close the palette. (The color will not be visible in the Design grid until you choose another option.)
6) Click in the Back Color text box and then click the button containing three black dots.

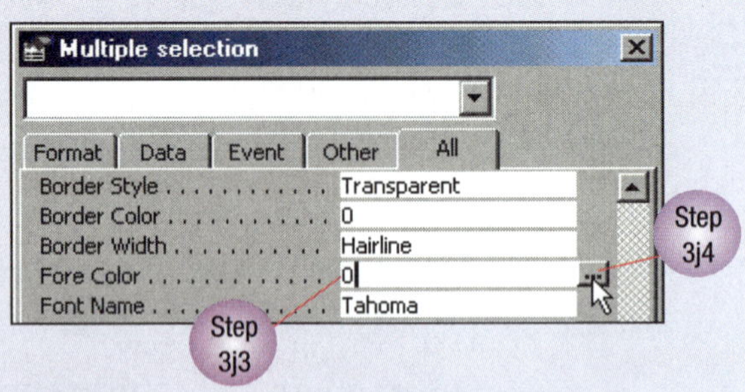

7) At the color palette that displays, click the blue color (sixth color from the left in the fourth row from the top), and then click OK to close the palette.
8) Click in the Font Name text box in the properties sheet and then click the down-pointing triangle that displays at the right side of the text box.

9) At the drop-down list that displays, scroll up the list to display *Arial* and then click *Arial*.
10) Click in the Font Size text box, click the down-pointing triangle that displays at the right, and then click *10*.
11) Click in the Font Weight text box, click the down-pointing triangle that displays at the right, and then click *Bold*.

k. Click in the Design grid outside a control object to deselect the objects.

l. Resize each of the label control objects so the label name displays completely. (To do this, select the label control object and then use the middle sizing handle at the left side of the object to increase the width.)

m. Format the text control objects by completing the following steps:
1) Click the *Supplier #* text control object (contains a white background).
2) Hold down the Shift key and then click each of the remaining text control objects (objects that display with a white background).
3) Click in the Fore Color text box in the Multiple selection properties sheet, click the button containing three black dots, click the blue color (sixth color from the left in the fourth row), and then click OK.

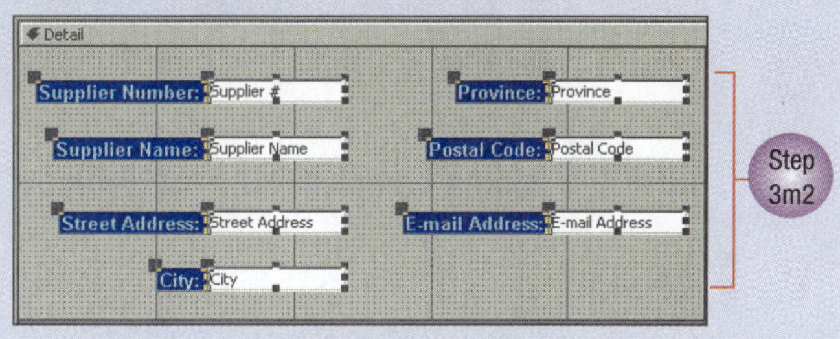

4) Click in the Back Color text box, click the button containing three black dots, click the turquoise color (fifth color from the left in the top row), and then click OK.
5) Click in the Font Name text box, click the down-pointing triangle that displays at the right, and then click *Arial* at the drop-down list. (You will need to scroll up the list to display *Arial*.)
6) Click in the Font Size text box, click the down-pointing triangle that displays at the right, and then click *10*.
7) Click in the Font Weight text box, click the down-pointing triangle that displays at the right, and then click *Bold*.

n. Click in the Design grid outside a control object to deselect the objects.

4. Close the properties sheet. (To do this, click the Close button that displays in the upper right corner of the sheet [contains an *X*].)
5. View the form in Form view by clicking the View button on the Form Design toolbar.
6. Save the form and name it Suppliers Form.
7. Print the currently displayed form by completing the following steps:
   a. Click File and then Print.
   b. At the Print dialog box, click the Selected Record(s) option in the Print Range section.
   c. Click OK.
8. Close the Suppliers Form.
9. Close the Outdoor Options database file.

FIGURE 5.9 *Exercise 5*

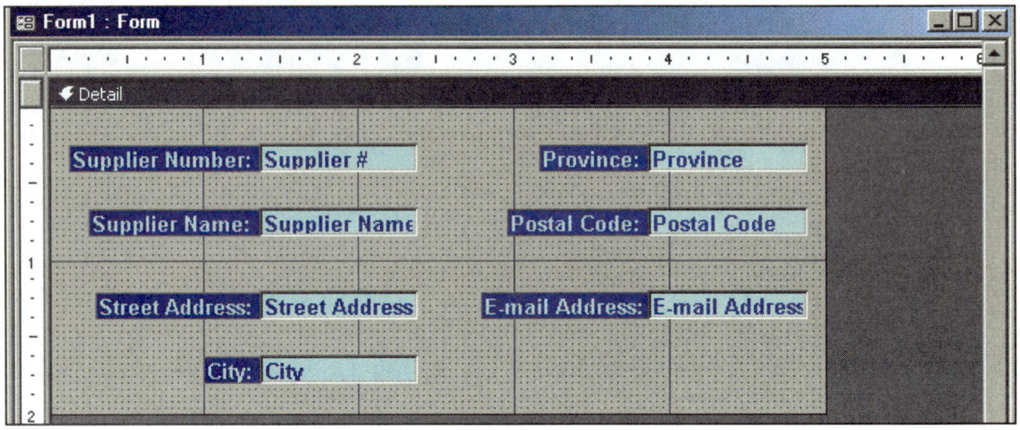

Adding Controls Using the Toolbox

The Toolbox is a palette of control object buttons that automatically appears when a form is displayed in Design view. With the buttons on this Toolbox, shown in figure 5.10, you can add and modify controls in the form. (Figure 5.10 identifies a few of the buttons on the toolbar.) If the Toolbox is not visible, click the Toolbox button on the Form Design toolbar. To add a control in Design view, click the desired button on the Toolbox. This causes the mouse pointer to change to a crosshair pointer with an icon attached. The icon that displays will vary depending on the control object button selected. Move the pointer to the position on the form where you want to place the object and then drag to create the object. Use the sizing handles that display around the control to increase or decrease the size.

FIGURE 5.10 *Toolbox Buttons*

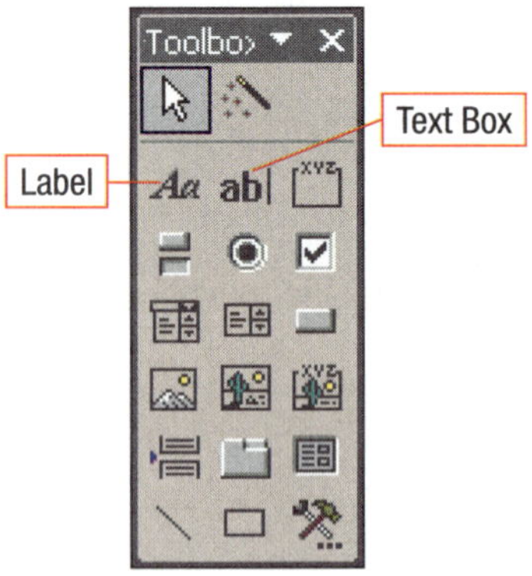

Adding a Form Header and Form Footer

A form in Design view can contain up to three sections—Detail, Form Header, and Form Footer. The Detail section is the only section that displays by default. You created a form in exercise 5 in the Detail section of the form. A Form Header displays at the top of the form in Form view and at the beginning of a printout started from the Form view screen. A Form Footer appears at the bottom of the form in Form view and at the end of a printout started from the Form view screen.

Display a Form Header and Form Footer by clicking View on the Menu bar and then clicking Form Header/Footer. Another method is to right-click on the Form 1 : Form title bar and then click Form Header/Footer at the shortcut menu.

To insert text in a Form Header or Form Footer use the Label button on the Toolbox. Click the Label button and then draw the label in the Form Header or Form Footer. Key text inside the label control object and apply the desired formatting.

Label

Apply formatting to a Form Header with options at the FormHeader properties sheet. Display this sheet by right-clicking the Form Header gray border bar and then clicking Properties at the shortcut menu. Complete similar steps to display the FormFooter properties sheet.

exercise 6

ADDING A FORM HEADER AND FORM FOOTER TO A FORM

1. Open the Outdoor Options database file.
2. If necessary, click the Forms button on the Objects bar.
3. Double-click *Suppliers Form* in the list box.
4. Add and modify a Form Header and Form Footer in Design view by completing the following steps:
   a. Change to the Design view by clicking the View button on the Form View toolbar.
   b. Add and modify a Form Header by completing the following steps:
      1) Right-click on the Suppliers Form : Form title bar and then click Form Header/Footer at the shortcut menu.

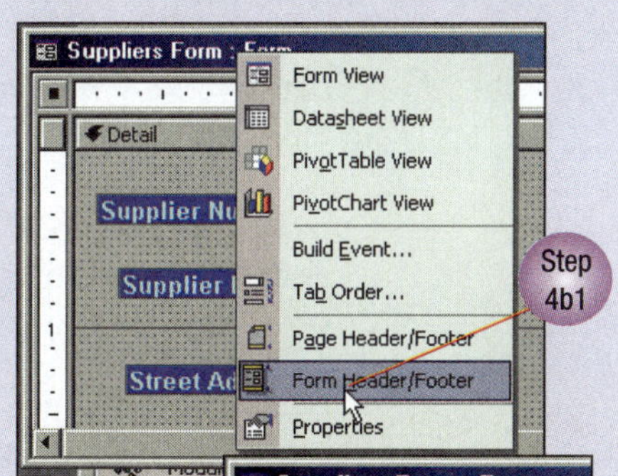

      2) Increase the height of the Form Header section by positioning the pointer at the top of the gray Detail border line until the pointer changes to a black vertical line with an up- and down-pointing arrow, and then drag the mouse down to the approximate height shown at the right.

      3) Click the Label button on the Toolbox. (If the Toolbox is not displayed, click the Toolbox button on the Form Design toolbar.)

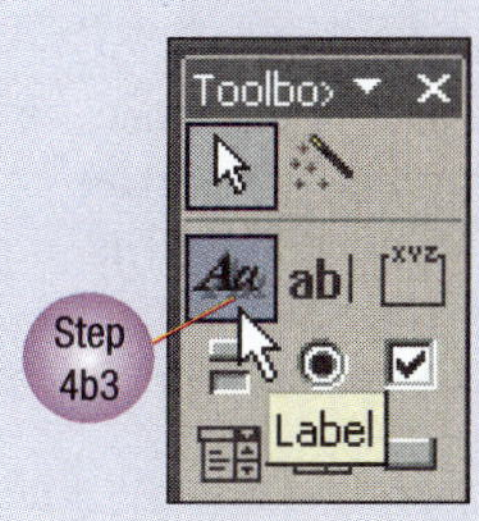

4) Position the crosshair pointer with the label icon attached to it at the top left edge of the first black gridline in the Form Header section, drag the mouse down to the approximate height and width shown at the right, and then release the mouse button.

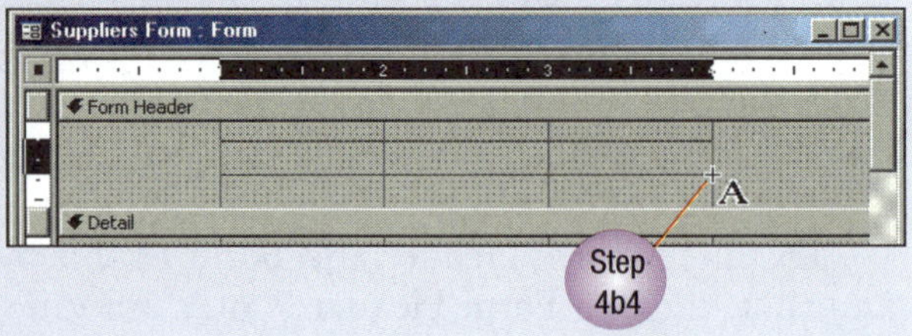

5) A label box will appear with the insertion point automatically positioned in the top left edge of the box. Key **Outdoor Options Suppliers Form** and then click outside the box.
6) Click once on the label control object to select it.
7) Right-click on the Suppliers Form : Form title bar and then click Properties at the shortcut menu.
8) Click the Format tab at the Label properties sheet.
9) Click in the Font Name text box (you will need to scroll down the Format list box to display this text box), click the down-pointing triangle at the right, and then click *Arial* at the drop-down menu. (You will need to scroll up the drop-down menu to display *Arial*.)
10) Click in the Font Size text box, click the down-pointing triangle at the right, and then click *14* at the drop-down menu.
11) Click in the Font Weight text box, click the down-pointing triangle at the right, and then click *Bold* at the drop-down menu.
12) Click outside the label control box. (Increase the height and width of the label control box so the entire title displays.)

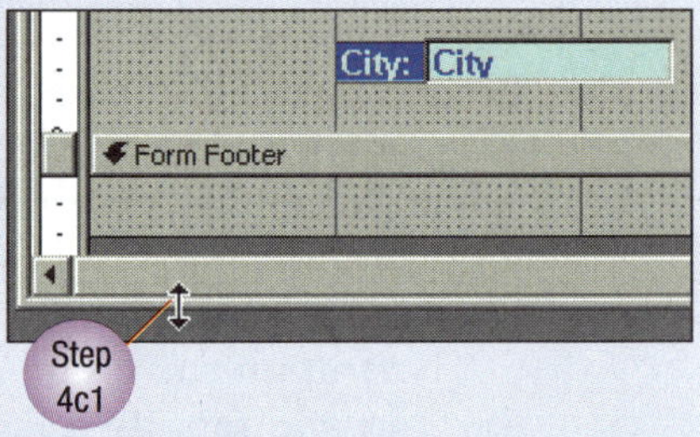

c. Add and modify a Form Footer by completing the following steps:
1) Drag down the bottom border of the form to display the Form Footer section.
2) Click the Label button on the Toolbox.
3) Position the crosshair pointer with the label icon attached to it at the top left edge of the first black gridline in the Form Footer section, drag the mouse down and to the right to the approximate height and width shown at the right, and then release the mouse button.

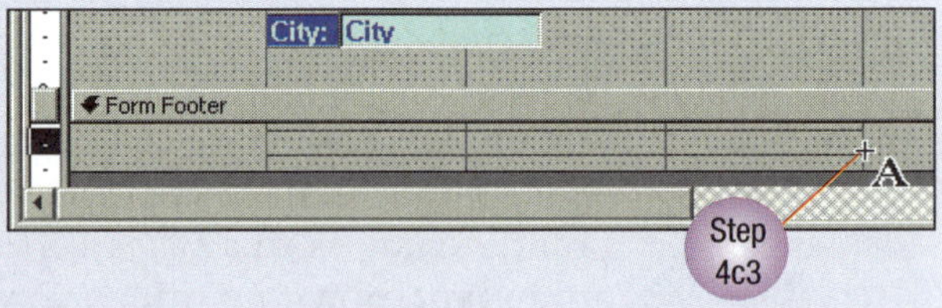

4) A label box will appear with the insertion point automatically positioned in the box. Key **Suppliers Form designed by Student Name** (key your name instead of *Student Name*) and then click outside the box.
5) Click once on the label control object to select it. (The Label properties sheet should be visible. If it is not visible, right-click on the Suppliers Form : Form title bar and then click Properties at the shortcut menu.)
6) If necessary, click the Format tab at the Label properties sheet.
7) Make the following changes:
   a) Change the font name to Arial.
   b) Change the font size to 10.

c) Change the font weight to bold.

8) Click outside the label control box.

5. Close the properties sheet. (To do this, click the Close button that displays in the upper right corner of the sheet [contains an *X*].)
6. View the form in Form view by clicking the View button on the Form Design toolbar.
7. Click the Save button to save the form.
8. Click the New Record button that displays along the bottom of the form.

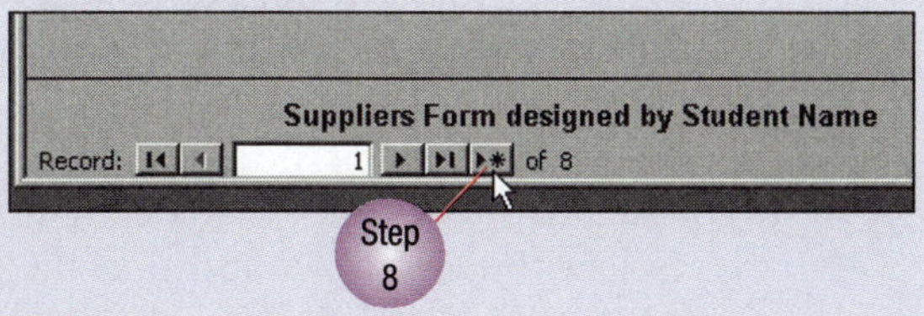

9. Add the following record:

Supplier Number	=	**44**
Supplier Name	=	**Everwear Supplies**
Street Address	=	**4500 Second Avenue**
City	=	**Vancouver**
Province	=	**BC**
Postal Code	=	**V2V 6K2**
E-mail Address	=	**everwear@emcp.com**

10. Print the currently displayed form.
11. Close the Suppliers Form.
12. Close the Outdoor Options database file.

Adding a Calculated Control

A calculated control uses a mathematical equation to determine the contents that are displayed in the control object. Insert a calculated control field in Design view by creating a text box control object and then entering the mathematical equation in the text box. A calculated field is used to perform mathematical operations on existing fields, but it does not exist in the table associated with the form. In exercise 7, you will create a calculated control in a form that divides the order amount by the number of units.

HINT

Press Ctrl + Enter to begin a new line in a text box.

Key a mathematical expression in a calculated control box. Begin the expression with the equals sign (=) and insert square brackets around field names. Use mathematical operators such as +, -, *, and / to perform calculations.

exercise 7

CREATING A FORM IN DESIGN VIEW AND ADDING A CALCULATED CONTROL

1. Open the Outdoor Options database file.
2. At the Outdoor Options : Database window, if necessary, click the Forms button on the Objects bar.
3. Create a form in Design view by completing the following steps:
   a. Double-click the *Create form in Design view* option in the list box.
   b. At the Design grid, right-click on the Form1 : Form title bar and then click Properties at the shortcut menu.
   c. At the Form properties sheet, click the All tab.

d. Click in the Record Source text box, click the down-pointing triangle at the right, and then click *Orders* at the drop-down list.

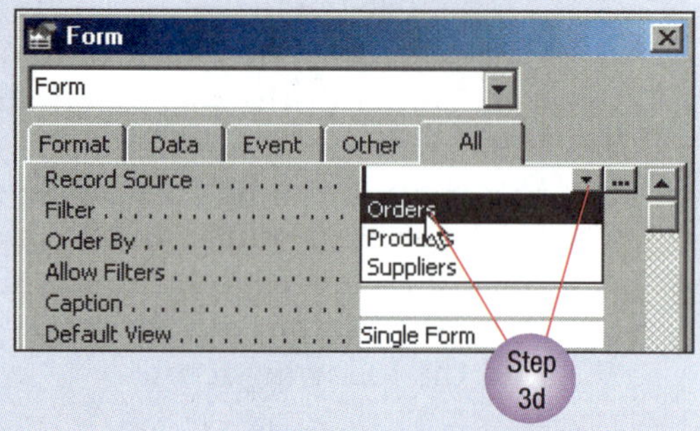

e. Drag the fields in the field list box to the Design grid to the approximate locations shown in figure 5.11.

f. Select the three label and text box control objects at the left side of the Design grid and then align them at the right.

g. Select the two label and text box control objects at the right side of the Design grid and then align them at the right.

h. Select the label and text box control objects located at the bottom of the design grid and align them at the right. (This moves the label control object next to the text box control object.)

i. Add a calculated control field by completing the following steps:
   1) Click the Text Box button on the Toolbox. (If the Toolbox is not visible, click the Toolbox button on the Form Design toolbar.)
   2) Position the crosshair pointer with the text box icon attached below the Amount text box control and then drag the outline of a box approximately the same size as the text box control above it.

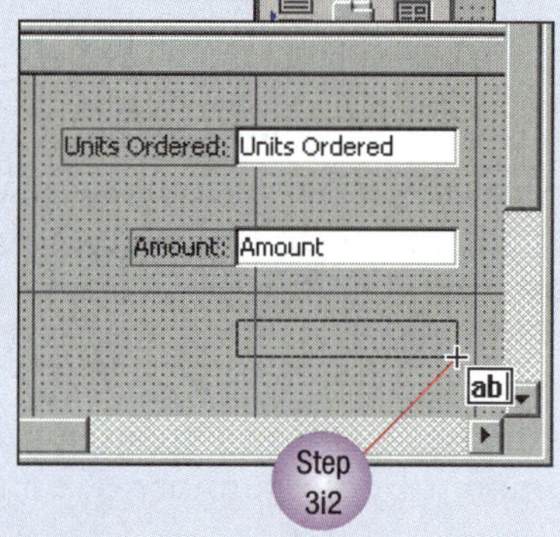

   3) Click in the text box control (which currently displays *Unbound*), key **=[Amount]/[Units Ordered]**, and then click outside the control to deselect it.
   4) Click the label control object adjacent to the text box control (which currently displays *Text6* [your number may vary]) to select it.
   5) Click the label control object again to position the insertion point inside the label box.
   6) Delete the current entry, key **Unit Price:**, and then click outside the label control to deselect it.
   7) Move and/or size the calculated control and the label control to align them with the fields displayed above.

j. Click the View button on the Form Design toolbar to display the form in Form view. Notice the Unit Price amount displays aligned at the left edge of the control. Change the format properties for the calculated control by completing the following steps:
   1) Click the View button on the Form View toolbar.
   2) Click the text box calculated control to select it.
   3) At the Text Box properties sheet, click the Format tab.
   4) Click in the Format text box (you may need to scroll up to display this text box), click the down-pointing triangle at the right, and then click *Currency* at the drop-down list.

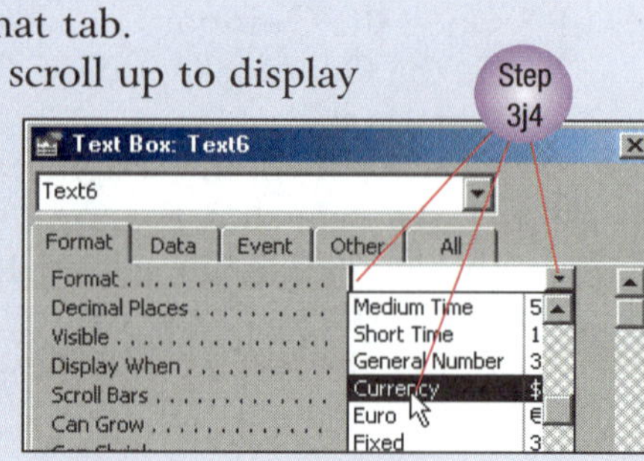

   5) Click in the Text Align text box (you will need to scroll down the list to display this text box), click the down-pointing triangle at the right, and then click *Right* at the drop-down list.

6) Close the Text Box properties sheet.

4. View the form in Form view by clicking View button on the Form Design toolbar.
5. Save the form and name it Orders Form.
6. Display and then print the first record.
7. Close the Orders Form.
8. Close the Outdoor Options database file.

FIGURE 5.11 ***Exercise 7***

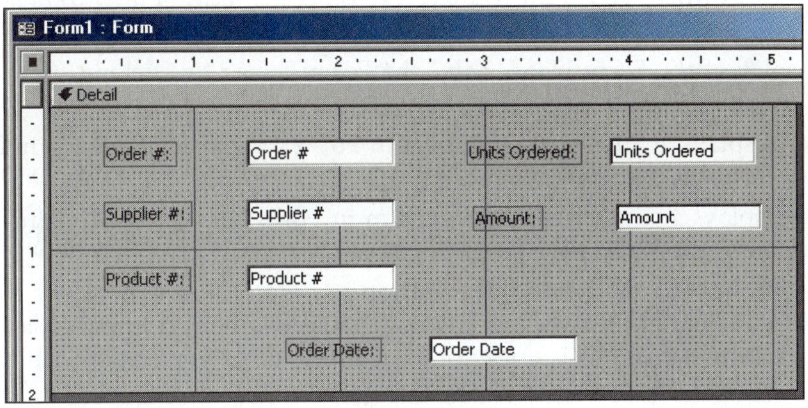

CHAPTER summary

- A form generally improves the ease with which data is entered into a table. A form can be created with the AutoForm feature and also with the Form Wizard.
- A record in a form displays with navigation buttons that are used to display various records in the form.
- Print a form in the same manner as a table. Changes can be made to the page margins and/or page orientation at the Page Setup dialog box.
- Add a new record to a form by clicking the New Record button on the Form View toolbar or by clicking the button at the bottom of the record that displays with a right-pointing triangle followed by an asterisk.
- Delete a record by displaying the record and then clicking the Delete Record button on the Form View toolbar.
- The Form Wizard walks you through the steps for creating a form and lets you specify the fields you want included in the form, a layout for the records, the desired formatting, and a name for the form.
- A form can be created with fields from tables that are connected by a one-to-many relationship.
- A form is comprised of a series of controls, which are objects that display titles or descriptions, accept data, or perform actions.

- In Design view, you can use fields from a table to create controls in the Design grid and also add controls with buttons on the Toolbox palette.
- Associate a table with the form to use fields to create controls.
- Move control objects in the Design grid. A label control and its corresponding text box control for a field can be moved individually or together.
- Use the sizing handles around a selected control object to change the size of the object.
- Customize control objects with options at the properties sheet.
- To align control objects in the Design grid, select the objects, click Format, point to Align, and then click the desired alignment at the side menu.
- To add a control using a button on the Toolbox, click the button, move the pointer to the position on the form where you want to place the object, and then drag to create the object.
- Turn on the display of the Form Header and the Form Footer by clicking View and then Form Header/Footer.
- A Form Header displays at the top of the form in Form view and at the beginning of a printout started from the Form view screen.
- A Form Footer displays at the bottom of the form in Form view and at the end of a printout started from the Form view screen.
- A calculated control uses a mathematical equation to determine the contents that are displayed in the control object. A calculated field is used to perform mathematical operations on existing fields, but it does not exist in the table associated with the form.

COMMANDS review

Command	Mouse/Keyboard
Create a form with AutoForm	Open table; click New Object button, then click AutoForm
Add a new record in a form	Display record, then click New Record button on Form View toolbar; or click button containing right-pointing triangle followed by asterisk
Delete a record in a form	Display record, click Delete Record button on Form View toolbar
Begin Form Wizard	Open database file, click New button, then double-click *Form Wizard*
Display the form Design view	Click Forms button on the Objects bar, and then double-click *Create form in design view*

CONCEPTS check

Completion: On a blank sheet of paper, indicate the correct term, symbol, or command for each item.

1. To create a form with the AutoForm feature, open the database file, click the table in the list box, and then click this button on the Database toolbar.
2. Use these buttons, which appear along the bottom of a record in a form, to display the first record in the form, the previous record, the next record, or the last record.
3. Click this button on the Form View toolbar to add a new record to the form.
4. Click this button on the Form View toolbar to delete a record from the form.
5. In the form Design view, add controls with buttons on this palette.
6. This section of the form in Design view is set up as a grid.
7. This appears at the bottom of the form in Form view and at the end of a printout started from the Form view screen.
8. This type of control uses a mathematical equation to determine the contents that are displayed in the control object.

SKILLS check

Assessment 1

1. Open the Outdoor Options database file.
2. Use the AutoForm feature to create a form with the data in the Suppliers table.
3. After creating the form, add the following records to the Suppliers form:

Supplier #	=	**12**
Supplier Name	=	**Seaside Suppliers**
Street Address	=	**4120 Shoreline Drive**
City	=	**Vancouver**
Province	=	**BC**
Postal Code	=	**V2V 8K4**
E-mail Address	=	**seaside@emcp.com**
Supplier #	=	**34**
Supplier Name	=	**Carson Company**
Street Address	=	**120 Plaza Center**
City	=	**Vancouver**
Province	=	**BC**
Postal Code	=	**V2V 1K6**
E-mail Address	=	**carson@emcp.com**

4. Delete the record containing information on Manning, Inc.
5. Save the form with the name offered by Access (Suppliers).

6. Print and then close the Suppliers form.
7. Close the Outdoor Options database file.

Assessment 2

1. Open the Outdoor Options database file.
2. At the Outdoor Options : Database window, click the Forms button on the Objects bar.
3. Delete the Suppliers form that displays in the list box. (For assistance, refer to exercise 3, step 3.)
4. Create a form for the Suppliers table using the Form Wizard. Use all of the fields in the Suppliers table to create the form. You determine the format style. Name the form Suppliers.
5. When the Form Wizard is finished, add the following record:

Supplier #	=	**50**
Supplier Name	=	**Binder Corporation**
Street Address	=	**9033 East 32nd**
City	=	**Vancouver**
Province	=	**BC**
Postal Code	=	**V2V 3K2**
E-mail Address	=	**binder@emcp.com**

6. Delete the record containing information on Langley Corporation.
7. Save the Suppliers form.
8. Print the Suppliers form and then close the form.
9. Close the Outdoor Options database file.

Assessment 3

1. Open the Outdoor Options database file.
2. Create a form from two related tables using the Form Wizard with the following specifications:
   a. At the first Form Wizard dialog box, insert the following fields in the Selected Fields list box:
      From the Products table:
         Product #
         Product
         Units on Order
      From the Suppliers table:
         Supplier #
         Supplier Name
         Street Address
         City
         Province
         Postal Code
   b. Do not make any changes at the second Form Wizard dialog box.
   c. Do not make any changes at the third Form Wizard dialog box.
   d. You determine the format style at the fourth Form Wizard dialog box.
   e. At the fifth Form Wizard dialog box, key the name **Units on Order**.
   f. When the first record displays, print the form.
   g. Close the record that displays.
3. Close the Outdoor Options database file.

Assessment 4

1. Open the Outdoor Options database file.
2. Open the Orders table and then make the following changes:
   a. Display the table in design view.
   b. Insert a row above *Order Date.*
   c. Specify the following for the new row:

Field Name	=	*Unit Price*
Data Type	=	*Currency*
Description	=	*Unit price*

   d. Save the table.
   e. Change to Datasheet view and then enter the following in the Unit Price field in the specified order number record:

Order #4	=	**72.25**
Order #5	=	**112.00**

   f. Save and then close the table.
3. Create a form by design with the following specifications:
   a. Create a form by design with all of the fields in the Orders table *except* the *Amount* field. (You determine the location of the fields in the Design grid.)
   b. Add a calculated control that multiplies the Unit Price by the Units Ordered. Change the format of the text box calculated control to *Currency*.
   c. Apply formatting of your choosing to the label and text box control objects. (Change at least the Font Name, Fore Color, and Back Color.)
   d. Add the Form Header **Outdoor Options – Orders Form**. Change the Font Name, Font Size, and Font Weight of the Form Header. (You determine the font, size, and weight.)
   e. Add the Form Footer **Order Totals**. Change the Font Name, Font Size, and Font Weight of the Form Footer. (You determine the font, size, and weight.)
   f. Save the form and name it Order Totals.
   g. Change to the Form view.
   h. Print the currently displayed record.
4. Close the Order Totals form.
5. Close the Outdoor Options database file.

Assessment 5

1. The New Form dialog box contains a number of options for creating a form. In this chapter, you have used the Form Wizard to prepare forms. Experiment with two other options available at the New Form dialog box—AutoForm: Columnar and AutoForm: Tabular.
2. After experimenting with these two wizards, open the Outdoor Options database file and then complete the following:
   a. Use the AutoForm: Columnar Wizard to create a form with all of the fields in the Suppliers table. Print the first record that displays and then close the form.
   b. Use the AutoForm: Tabular Wizard to create a form with all of the fields in the Products table. Print the first record that displays and then close the form.
3. Close the Outdoor Options database file.

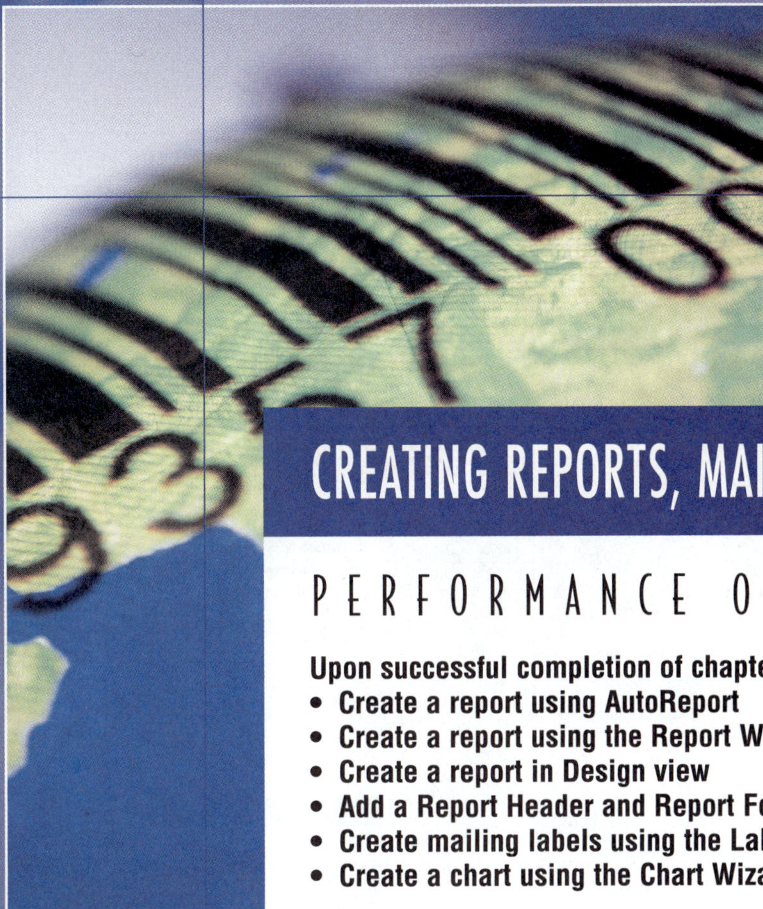

CHAPTER 6

CREATING REPORTS, MAILING LABELS, AND CHARTS

PERFORMANCE OBJECTIVES

Upon successful completion of chapter 6, you will be able to:

- **Create a report using AutoReport**
- **Create a report using the Report Wizard**
- **Create a report in Design view**
- **Add a Report Header and Report Footer**
- **Create mailing labels using the Label Wizard**
- **Create a chart using the Chart Wizard**

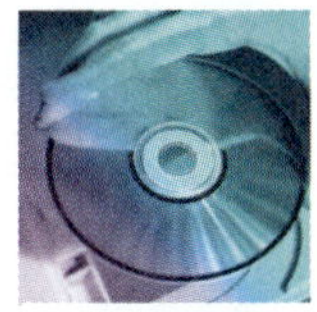

Outdoor Options • Hilltop

In this chapter, you will learn how to prepare reports from data in a table using the AutoReport feature and also the Report Wizard. A report lets you specify how data will appear when printed. You will also learn how to create mailing labels using the Label Wizard and how to create a chart with the Chart Wizard.

Creating Reports

The primary purpose for inserting data in a form is to improve the display of the data and to make data entry easier. Data can also be inserted in a report. The purpose for this is to control what data appears on the page when printed. Reports generally answer specific questions (queries). For example, a report could answer the question *"What customers have submitted claims?"* or *"What products do we currently have on order?"* Access includes the AutoReport feature that automatically creates a report based on data in a table and also the Report Wizard that walks you through the process of creating a report. Like the Form Wizard, you specify fields, format style, and the report name when creating a report.

HINT
Create a report to control what data appears on the page when printed.

Creating a Report Using AutoReport

The AutoReport feature automatically creates a plainly formatted report in a columnar arrangement. To use the AutoReport feature, select the desired table, click the down-pointing triangle at the right side of the New Object button on the Database toolbar, and then click AutoReport at the drop-down list.

exercise 1

CREATING A REPORT USING AUTOREPORT

(Note: Delete any database files from your disk.)

1. Copy the Outdoor Options database file from the CD that accompanies this textbook to your disk. Remove the read-only attribute from the Outdoor Options database file.
2. Open the Outdoor Options database file.
3. At the Outdoor Options : Database window, click the Tables button on the Objects bar.
4. Create and print a report using AutoReport by completing the following steps:
   a. Click *Suppliers* in the list box to select the Suppliers table.
   b. Click the down-pointing triangle at the right side of the New Object button on the Database toolbar.
   c. At the drop-down list that displays, click AutoReport.
   d. When the report displays in Print Preview, view the report, and then click the Print button on the Print Preview toolbar.
   e. Click the Close button at the right side of the Suppliers title bar.
   f. At the message asking if you want to save the changes to the design of the report, click the No button.
5. Close the Outdoor Options database file.

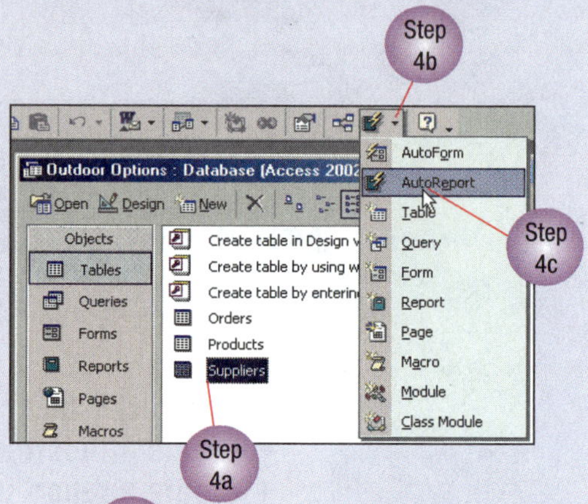

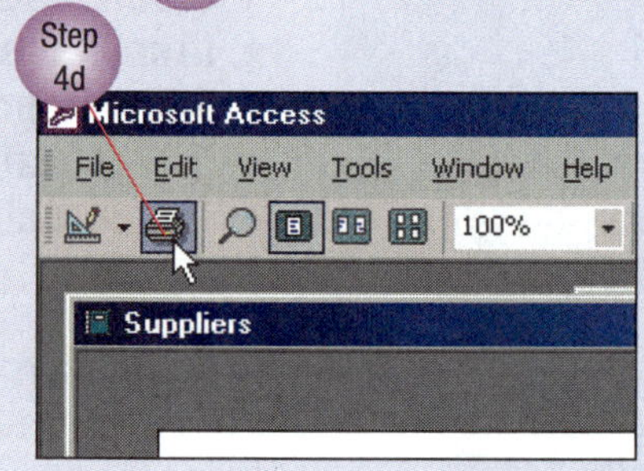

Creating a Report Using the Report Wizard

To create a report using the Report Wizard, open the database file, click the Reports button on the Objects bar, and then click the New button. At the New Report dialog box, double-click *Report Wizard* in the list box. The first Report Wizard dialog box is similar to the first Form Wizard dialog box. Choose the desired table with options from the Tables/Queries option box. Specify the fields you want included in the report by inserting them in the Selected Fields list box and then clicking the Next button.

HINT
The second Report Wizard dialog box only opens if you select fields from more than one table.

At the second Report Wizard dialog box, shown in figure 6.1, you can increase or decrease the priority level of fields in the report. To increase the priority level, click the desired field name in the list box at the left side of the dialog box, and then click the button containing the greater than symbol (>). To decrease the priority level, click the desired field, and then click the button containing the less than symbol (<). This changes the sample information displayed at the right side of the dialog box. After specifying the field levels, click the Next button.

FIGURE 6.1 *Second Report Wizard Dialog Box*

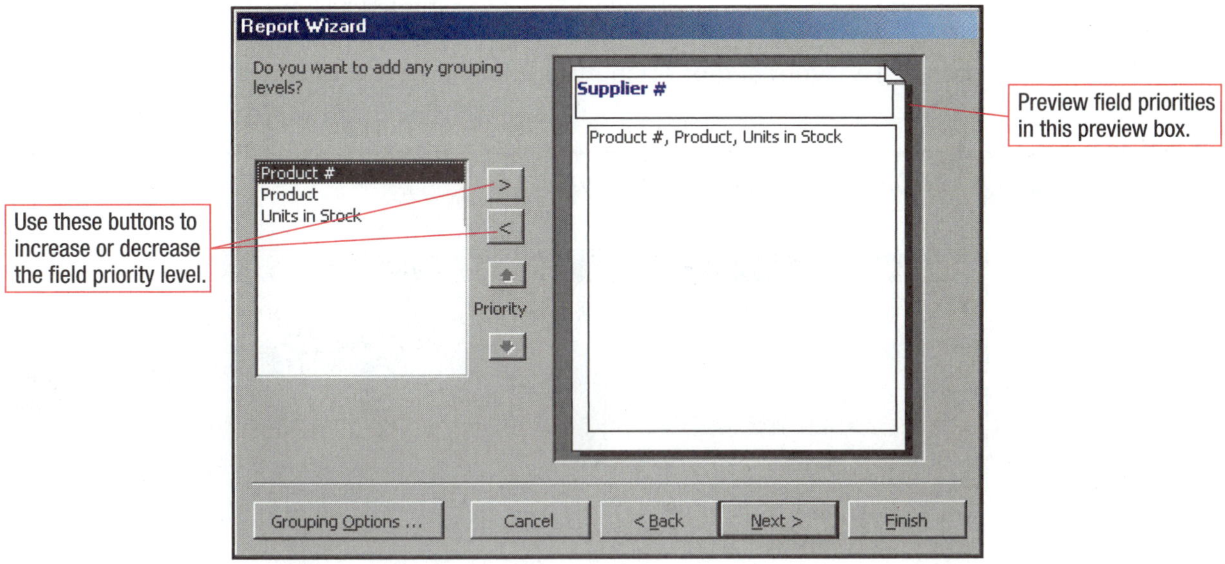

You can specify the order in which records are displayed in the report at the third Report Wizard dialog box shown in figure 6.2. To specify a sort order, click the down-pointing triangle at the right of the text box preceded by a number 1, and then click the field name. The default sort is done in ascending order. This can be changed to descending by clicking the button that displays at the right side of the text box. After identifying the sort order, click the Next button.

FIGURE 6.2 *Third Report Wizard Dialog Box*

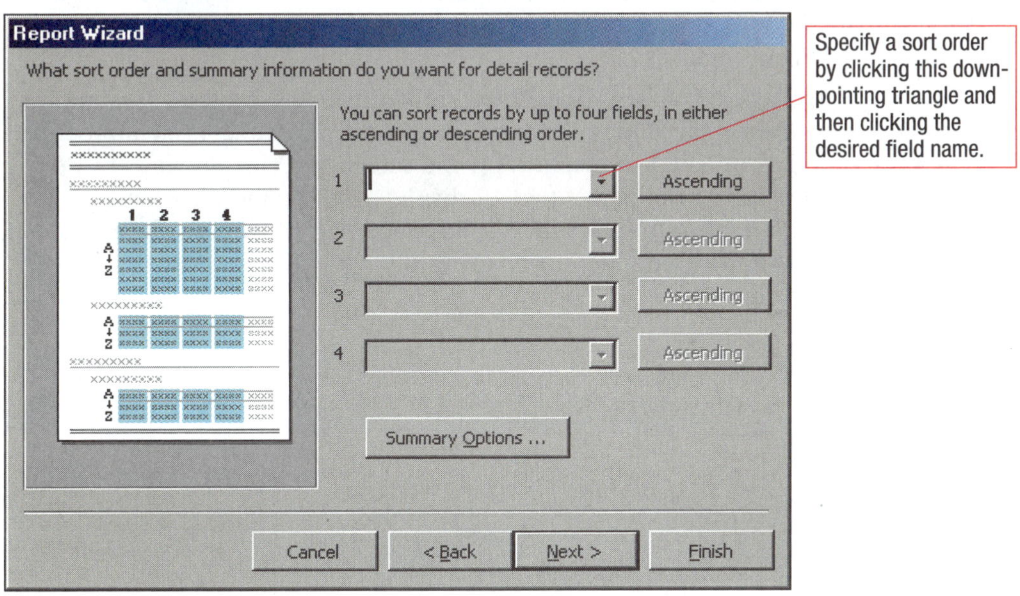

The layout of the report is determined in the fourth Report Wizard dialog box shown in figure 6.3. You can choose from a variety of layouts such as *Stepped*, *Block*, *Outline 1*, *Outline 2*, *Align Left 1*, and *Align Left 2*. Click a layout option and a sample of the layout is displayed on the sample page at the left side of the dialog box. The page orientation can also be selected at this dialog box. After choosing a layout and/or orientation, click the Next button.

FIGURE 6.3 **Fourth Report Wizard Dialog Box**

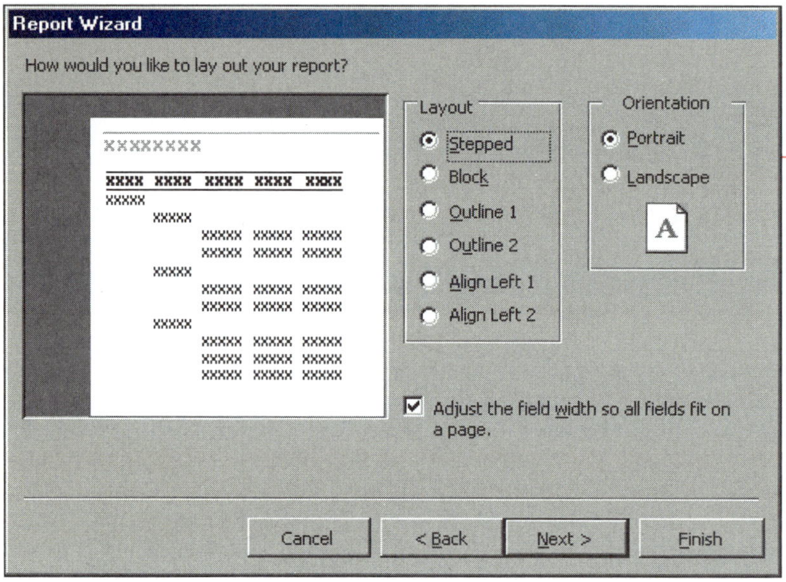

At this Report Wizard dialog box, choose a layout and orientation.

The Report Wizard offers several report styles at the fifth Report Wizard dialog box shown in figure 6.4. Click a report style and the wizard will display a sample at the left side of the dialog box. Click the Next button to display the sixth Report Wizard dialog box.

HINT

Switch to the Design view to make changes to the report design.

At the sixth Report Wizard dialog box, shown in figure 6.5, key a name for the report, and then click Finish. Creating the report may take a few moments. When the report is finished, it displays on the screen in Print Preview. In Print Preview, you can change the percentage of display of data and also send the report to the printer. To print the report, click the Print button on the Print Preview toolbar. After viewing and/or printing the report, close Print Preview by clicking the Close button.

FIGURE 6.4 *Fifth Report Wizard Dialog Box*

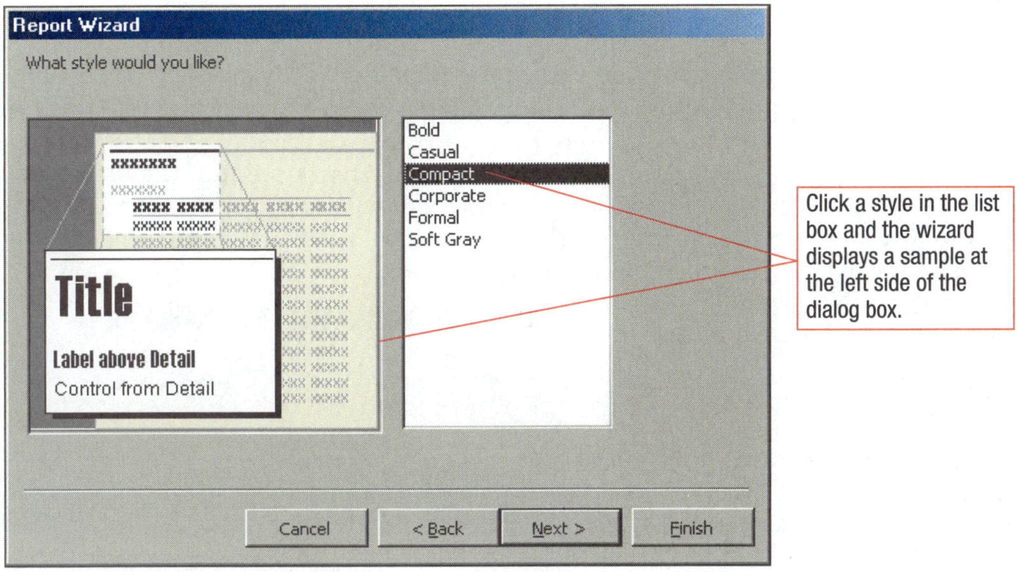

FIGURE 6.5 *Sixth Report Wizard Dialog Box*

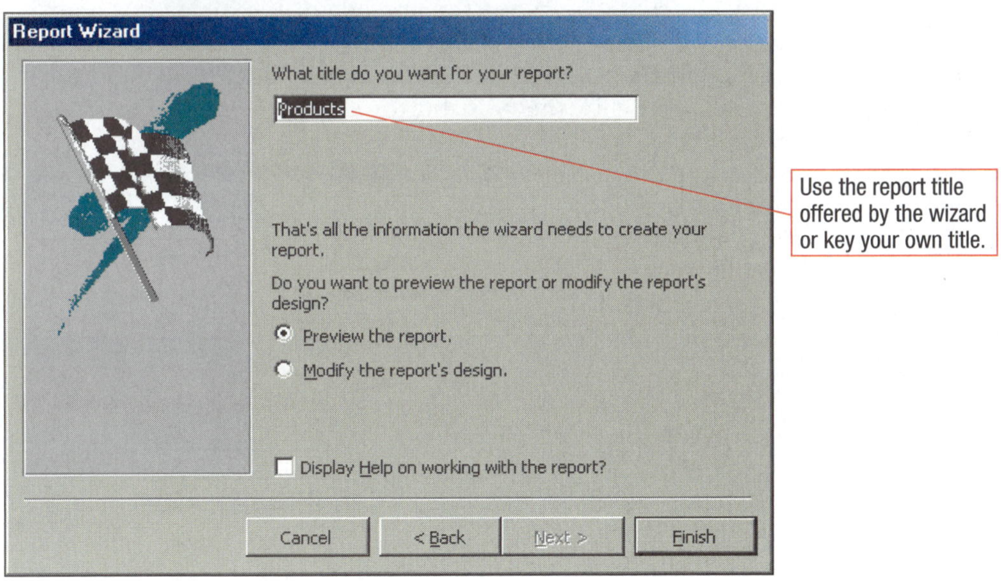

exercise 2

USING THE REPORT WIZARD TO PREPARE A REPORT

1. Open the Outdoor Options database file.
2. At the Outdoor Options : Database window, click the Reports button on the Objects bar.
3. Create a report with the Report Wizard by completing the following steps:
   a. Click the New button on the window toolbar.
   b. At the New Report dialog box, double-click the *Report Wizard* option in the list box.
   c. At the first Report Wizard dialog box, click the down-pointing triangle at the right side of the Tables/Queries option box, and then click *Table: Products* at the drop-down list.
   d. Insert the following fields in the Selected Fields list box:

      Product #
      Product
      Supplier #
      Units in Stock

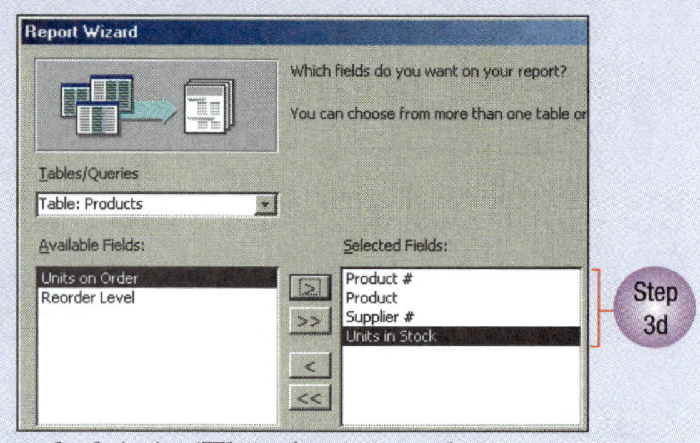

   e. After inserting the fields, click the Next button.
   f. At the second Report Wizard dialog box, decrease and increase priority levels by completing the following steps:
      1) Click the button to the right of the list box that displays with a less than symbol (<). (This decreases the priority level of the *Supplier #* field.)
      2) Click *Product* in the list box that displays at the left side of the dialog box and then click the button to the right of the list box that displays with a greater than symbol (>). (This increases the priority level of the *Product* field.)
   g. After specifying the priority levels, click the Next button.
   h. At the third Report Wizard dialog box, specify that the records are to be sorted by the Product # in ascending order by completing the following steps:
      1) Click the down-pointing triangle at the right of the text box preceded by a *1*.
      2) At the drop-down menu that displays, click *Product #*.

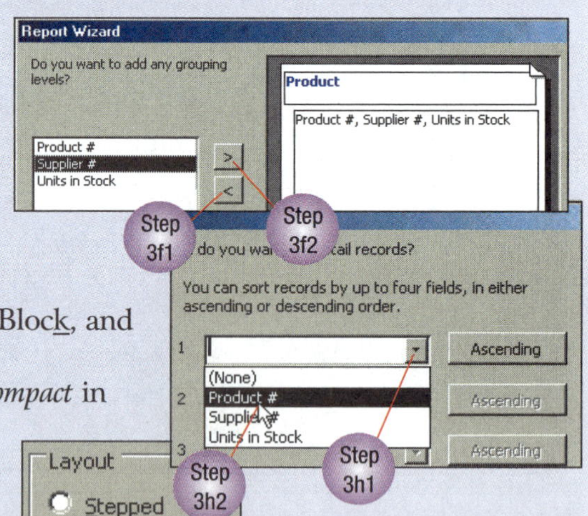

   i. Click the Next button.
   j. At the fourth Report Wizard dialog box, click Block, and then click the Next button.
   k. At the fifth Report Wizard dialog box, click *Compact* in the list box, and then click the Next button.
   l. At the sixth Report Wizard dialog box, click the Finish button.
   m. When the report displays in Print Preview, view the report, and then click the Print button that displays on the Print Preview toolbar.
   n. Click the Close button at the right side of the Products title bar.

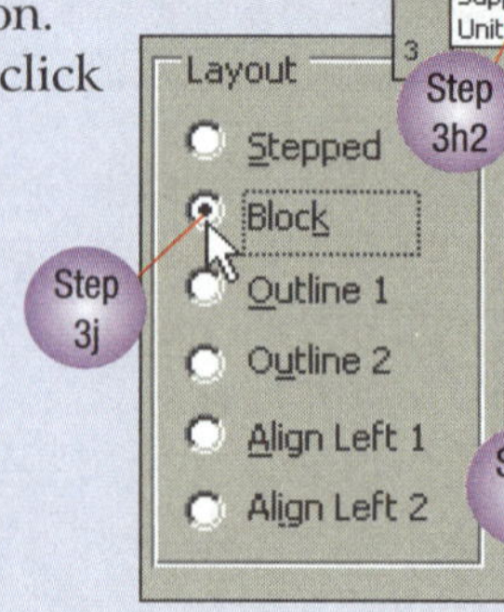

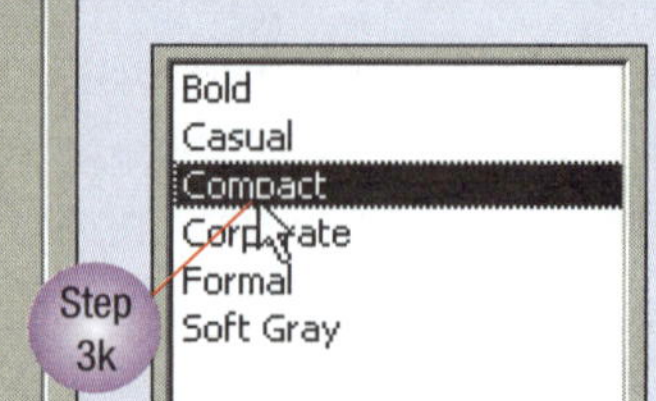

4. Close the Outdoor Options database file.

Preparing a Report Based on Two Tables

In the previous chapter on creating forms, you learned to create a form with fields from related tables. Fields from related tables can also be used to create a report. The steps to prepare a report with fields from two tables are basically the same as those you completed in exercise 2. The only difference is that an additional Report Wizard dialog box displays during the steps asking you to specify whether the fields should be grouped by the fields from the primary table or fields from the related table. In exercise 3, you will prepare a report with fields from the Products table and also the Suppliers table. These tables are joined by a one-to-many relationship.

exercise 3

PREPARING A REPORT WITH FIELDS FROM TWO TABLES

1. Open the Outdoor Options database file.
2. At the Outdoor Options : Database window, click the Reports button on the Objects bar.
3. Create a report with the Report Wizard by completing the following steps:
    a. Click the New button on the window toolbar.
    b. At the New Report dialog box, double-click *Report Wizard* in the list box.
    c. At the first Report Wizard dialog box, insert the following fields in the Selected Fields list box:
    From the Suppliers table:
    Supplier Name
    Street Address
    City
    Province
    Postal Code
    From the Products table:
    Product
    Product #
    d. After inserting the fields, click the Next button.
    e. At the second Report Wizard dialog box, make sure *by Suppliers* is selected in the list box in the upper left corner, and then click the Next button.
    f. At the third Report Wizard dialog box, increase the priority level of the *Supplier Name* field. To do this, make sure *Supplier Name* is selected in the list box, and then click the button containing the greater than symbol (>).
    g. Click the Next button.
    h. At the fourth Report Wizard dialog box, click the Next button. (Do not specify a sort order.)
    i. At the fifth Report Wizard dialog box, click Align Left 1, and then click the Next button.

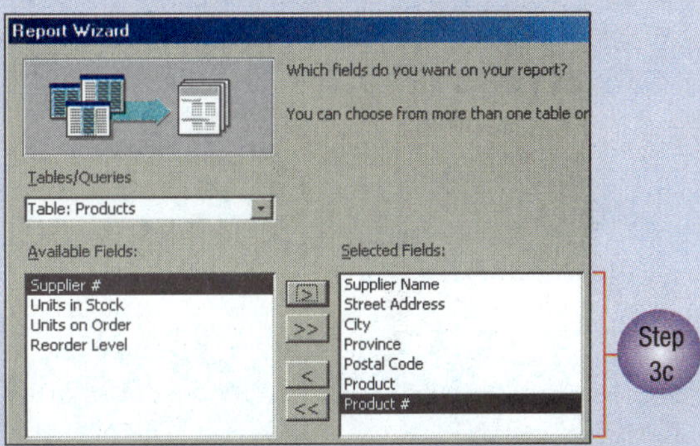

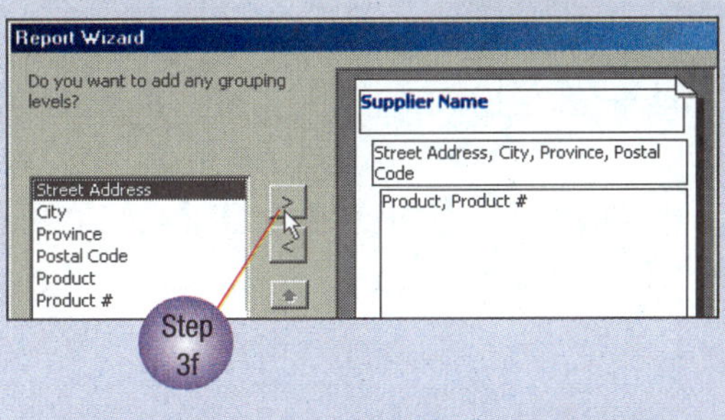

j. At the sixth Report Wizard dialog box, click *Corporate* in the list box, and then click the Next button.
k. At the seventh Report Wizard dialog box, click the Finish button.
l. When the report displays in Print Preview, view the report, and then click the Print button that displays on the Print Preview toolbar.
m. Click the Close button (displays with an *X*) that displays at the right side of the Suppliers title bar.
4. Close the Outdoor Options database file.

Creating a Report in Design View

A report, like a form, is comprised of a series of controls, which are objects that display titles or descriptions, accept data, or perform actions. In the reports you created in this chapter, Report Wizard created the controls for the report using fields from the tables. A report, like a form, can be created in Design view. To display the report Design view, click the Reports button on the Objects bar, and then double-click *Create report in Design view*.

A report can include up to five sections including Report Header, Page Header, Detail, Page Footer, and Report Footer. These five sections are identified in the sample report shown in figure 6.6.

The Report Header generally includes the title of the report and/or the company logo. The Page Header appears at the top of each page and generally includes column headings identifying the data in the report. The Detail section of the report contains the data from the table. The Page Footer appears at the bottom of each page and might include information such as the page number. The Report Footer appears on the last page of the report and might include information such as the person designing the report.

Using Fields to Add Controls

HINT
Other methods for displaying the property sheet include pressing Alt + Enter or double-clicking the control.

To add fields to a report in Design view, associate the report with the desired table. To do this, right-click the Report1 : Report title bar and then click Properties at the shortcut menu. This displays the Report properties sheet. At the Report properties sheet, click the All tab, and then click in the Record Source text box. Click the down-pointing triangle that displays at the right side of the text box and then click the desired table. This displays the table fields in a field list box. Using the mouse, drag the desired field from the field list box to the Design grid.

HINT
Display Help on a property by clicking in the property and then pressing F1.

Moving, Resizing, and Customizing Control Objects

The steps to move, resize, and/or customize control objects in report Design view are the same as the steps to remove, resize, and/or customize control objects in form Design view. Select an object and then either move the individual object or move the label control object and the text box control object together. Customize control objects with options at the properties sheet. (The name of the properties sheet will vary depending on what is selected.)

When a field is added to the report in Design view, a label control containing the field name and a text box control used to display data are placed adjacent to each other. The label control containing the field name is included for descriptive

FIGURE 6.6 *Sample Report*

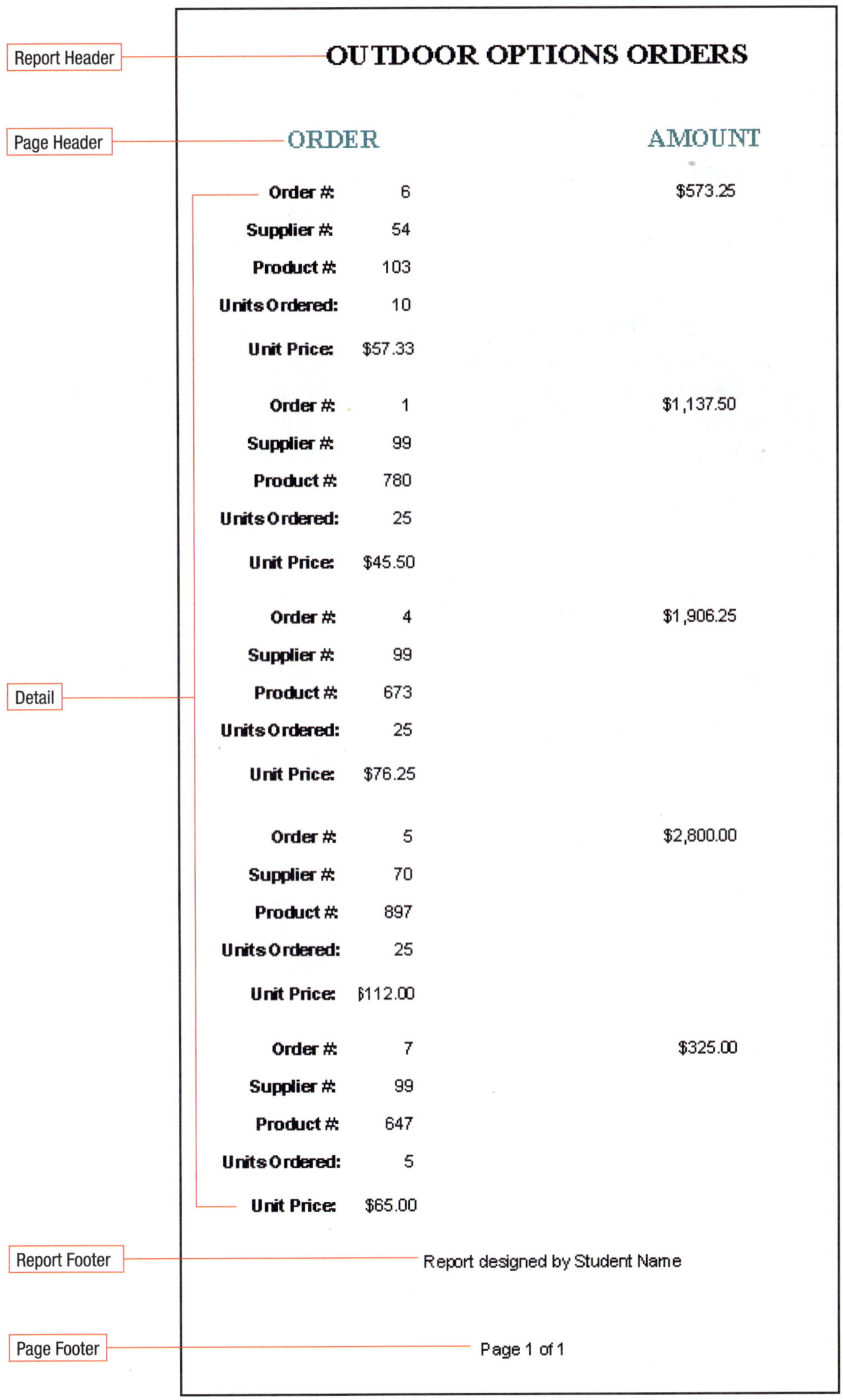

purposes so that the user knows which data to key into the corresponding text box. In a report, a column heading is generally included in the Page Header describing the data and, therefore, some label control objects may not be needed.

Adding Controls Using the Toolbox

Add controls to the report using buttons on the Toolbox. To add a control in Design view, click the desired button on the Toolbox. This causes the mouse pointer to change to a crosshair pointer with an icon attached. The icon that displays will vary depending on the control object button selected. Move the pointer to the position on the form where you want to place the object and then drag to create the object. Use the sizing handles that display around the control to increase or decrease the size.

Adding a Report Header and Report Footer

The Design view, by default, displays the Detail section and the Page Header and Page Footer. To add a Report Header and/or Report Footer to a report, click View on the Menu bar and then click Report Header/Footer. Another method is to right-click on the Report 1 : Report title bar and then click Report Header/Footer at the shortcut menu.

To insert text in a Page Header, Report Header, Page Footer, or Report Footer, use the Label button on the Toolbox. Click the Label button and then draw the label in the desired section. Key text inside the label control object and apply the desired formatting.

exercise 4 — CREATING, CUSTOMIZING, AND FORMATTING A REPORT IN DESIGN VIEW

1. Open the Outdoor Options database file.
2. At the Outdoor Options : Database window, click the Reports button on the Objects bar.
3. Create the report shown in figure 6.6 in Design view by completing the following steps:
   a. Double-click the *Create report in Design view* option in the list box.
   b. At the Design grid, right-click in the Report1 : Report title bar and then click Properties at the shortcut menu.
   c. At the Report properties sheet, click the All tab.
   d. At the Report properties sheet with the All tab selected, click in the Record Source text box, and then click the down-pointing triangle that displays at the right side of the text box.
   e. At the drop-down list that displays, click *Orders*.
   f. Drag the *Order #* field from the field list box to the Design grid to the approximate location shown at the right.
   g. Drag the other fields (*Supplier #*, *Product #*, *Units Ordered*, and *Amount*) from the field list box to the Design grid in the approximate locations shown at the right.

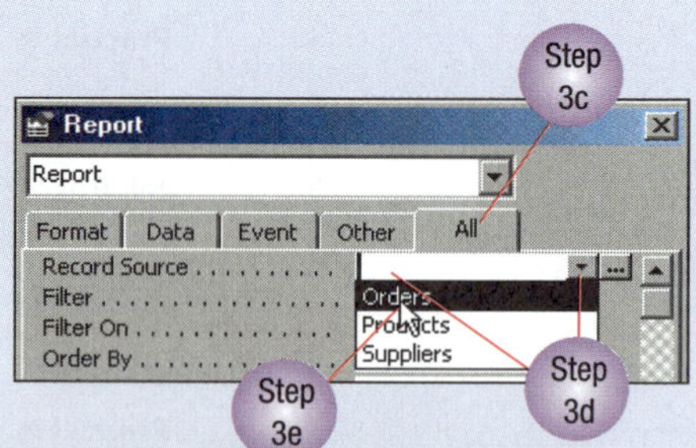

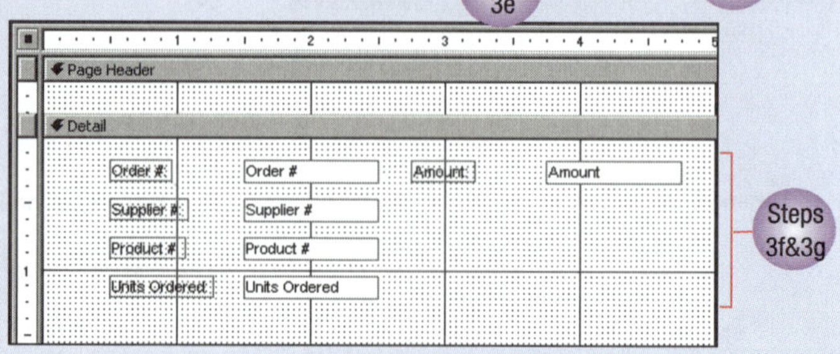

h. Delete the label control object for the Amount. (The label control object contains *Amount* with a transparent background [gray dots from the grid show through].)

i. Insert a calculated control field by completing the following steps:

1) Click the Text Box button on the Toolbox. (If the Toolbox is not visible, click the Toolbox button on the Form Design toolbar.)

2) Position the crosshair pointer with the text box icon attached below the Units Ordered text box control and then drag to create a box approximately the same size as the text box control above.

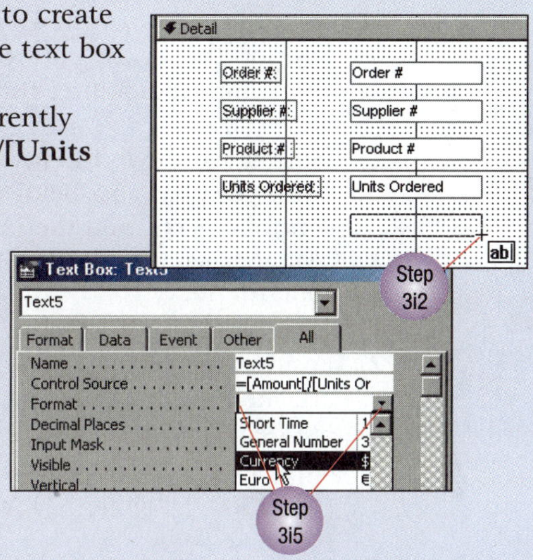

3) Click in the text box control (which currently displays *Unbound*) and key **=[Amount]/[Units Ordered]**.

4) Click outside the box and then click the text box control to select it.

5) With the text box control selected, click in the Format text box in the Text Box properties sheet (you may need to scroll up to display the Format text box), click the down-pointing triangle, and then click *Currency* at the drop-down menu.

6) Click outside the text box control to deselect it.

j. Change the caption in the new label control box by completing the following steps:

1) Click the label control box to select it (contains *Text 5* [your number may vary]).

2) Click in the Caption text box located in the Label properties sheet. (You may need to scroll up to display the Caption text box.)

3) Delete the text currently displayed in the Caption text box and then key **Unit Price:**.

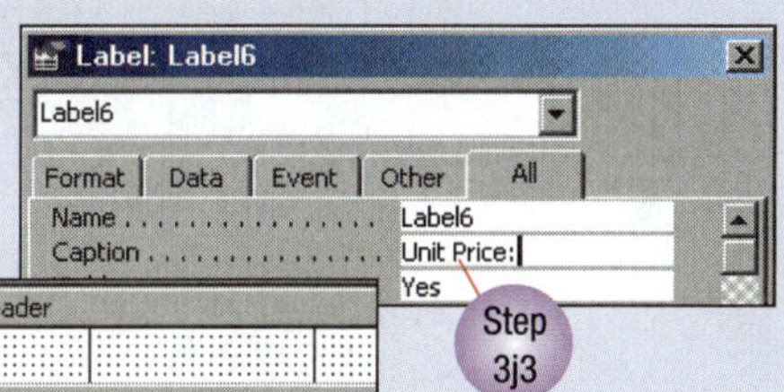

k. Decrease the size of the text box controls as shown at the right.

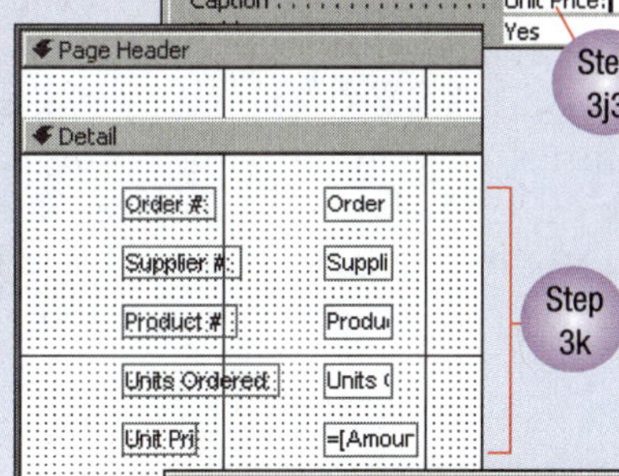

l. Select the label control objects at the left side of the Design grid (just the label control objects—not the text box control objects) and then align them at the right.

m. With the label object control boxes still selected, change the Font Weight to bold.

n. With the label object control boxes still selected, change the text alignment to right. To do this, click in the Text Align text box in the Multiple selection properties sheet (you may need to scroll down the list to display this text box), click the down-pointing triangle, and then click *Right* at the drop-down menu.

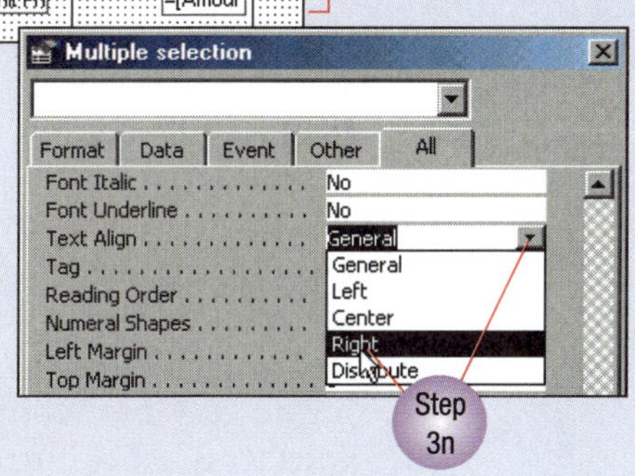

o. With the label object control boxes still selected, position the mouse pointer on one of the selected boxes and then click the right mouse button. At the shortcut menu that displays, point to Size, and then click To Fit at the side menu.

p. Select all of the text box control objects (contain a white background) and then click in the Text Align text box in the Multiple selection properties sheet. Click the down-pointing triangle at the right side of the text box and then click *Right* at the drop-down menu.

q. Decrease the height of the Detail section by completing the following steps:
   1) Position the mouse pointer on the top of the gray bar containing the text *Page Footer* until the pointer turns into an up- and down-pointing arrow with a line between.
   2) Hold down the left mouse button, drag up until the border displays just below the bottom label and text box control objects, and then release the mouse button.

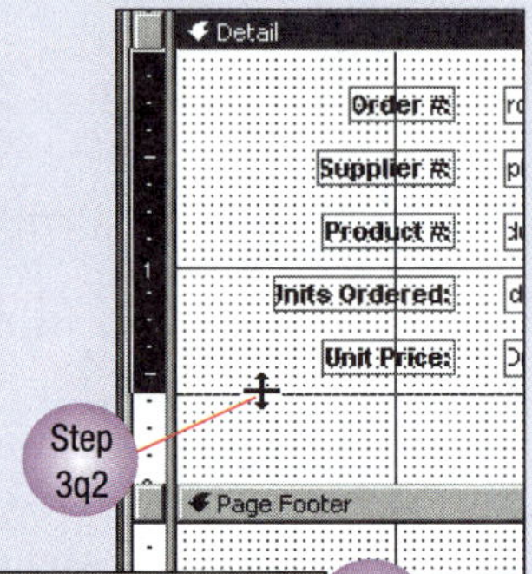

r. Add column headings in the Page Header by completing the following steps:
   1) Click the Label button on the Toolbar.
   2) Position the crosshair pointer with the label icon attached to it near the first black gridline in the Page Header section, drag the mouse down to the approximate height and width shown at the right (and in figure 6.7), and then release the mouse button.
   3) Key **ORDER** in the label control box and then click outside the box.
   4) Use the Label button on the Toolbox to create the AMOUNT label shown in figure 6.7.

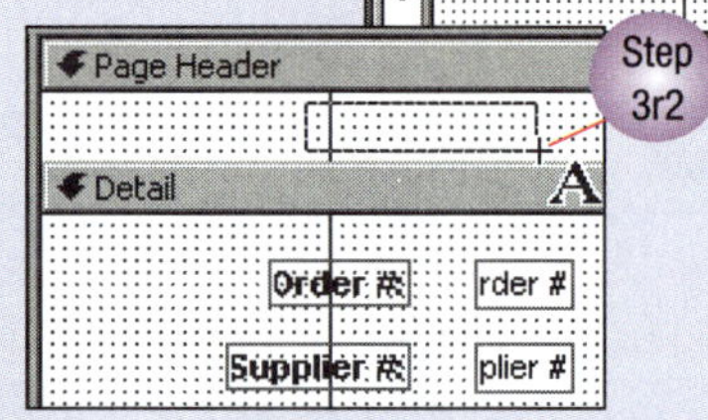

   5) Select the two labels and then apply the following formatting:
      a) Change the Font Name to Times New Roman.
      b) Change the Font Size to 12.
      c) Change the Font Weight to bold.
      d) Change the Fore Color to dark teal (fourth color from the left in the third row from the top in the color palette).
   6) Increase the size of the label control boxes so the entire text displays in each label.

s. Insert page numbering in the Page Footer by completing the following steps:
   1) Click Insert and then Page Numbers.
   2) At the Page Numbers dialog box, make the following changes:
      a) Click *Page N of M* in the Format section.
      b) Click *Bottom of Page [Footer]* in the Position section.
      c) Click OK to close the dialog box.

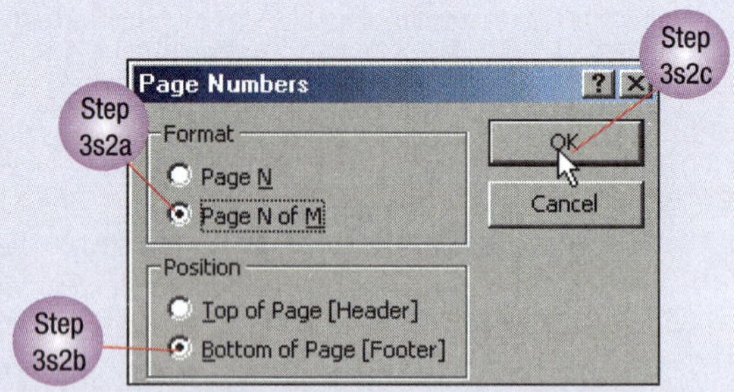

t. Add a Report Header by completing the following steps:
   1) Display the Report Header and Report Footer by clicking View on the Menu bar and then clicking Report Header/Footer.
   2) Increase the Report Header section by about 0.5 inch by dragging down the top of the gray bar (contains the words *Page Header*).
   3) Click the Label button on the Toolbox.

4) Drag to create a label box inside the Report Header that is large enough to hold the title shown in figure 6.7.
5) Key the text **OUTDOOR OPTIONS ORDERS** inside the label and then click outside the box.
6) Click the label control box and then apply the following formatting:
 a) Change the Font Name to Times New Roman.
 b) Change the Font Size to 14.
 c) Change the Font Weight to bold.
 d) Change the Fore Color to dark teal (the fourth color from the left in the third row from the top).
7) Click outside the label box to deselect it.

u. Add a Report Footer by completing the following steps:
 1) Increase the height of the Report Footer section by about 0.5 inch. (To do this, drag down the bottom edge of the Report Footer section.)
 2) Click the Label button on the Toolbox and then draw a label box inside the Report Footer large enough to hold the text shown in figure 6.7.
 3) Key the text **Report designed by Student Name** (insert your name instead of *Student Name*).

4. Close the properties sheet. (To do this, click the Close button that displays in the upper right corner of the sheet [contains an *X*].)
5. View the report in Print Preview by clicking the View button on the Report Design toolbar.
6. Check the headings *ORDER* and *AMOUNT* and make sure the headings display approximately centered over the information in columns. (If they do not, change to Design view, move the heading or headings to the desired location, and then change back to Print Preview.)
7. Print the report by clicking the Print button on the Print Preview toolbar.
8. Click the View button to return to the Design view.
9. In Design view, save the report and name it Orders Report.
10. Close Orders Report.
11. Close the Outdoor Options database file.

FIGURE 6.7 ***Exercise 4***

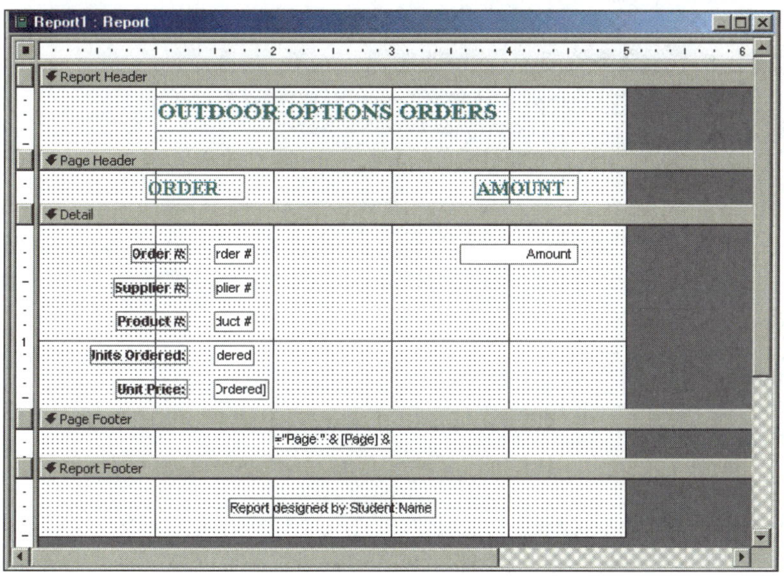

Preparing Mailing Labels

HINT
Use the Label Wizard to easily create mailing labels.

Access includes a mailing label wizard that walks you through the steps for creating mailing labels with fields in a table. To create mailing labels, open the database file, click the Reports button on the Objects bar, and then click the New button. This displays the New Report dialog box. At this dialog box, specify the table where the information for creating the mailing labels is located, and then double-click *Label Wizard* in the list box.

At the first Label Wizard dialog box shown in figure 6.8, specify the label size, units of measure, and the label type, and then click the Next button.

FIGURE 6.8 ***First Label Wizard Dialog Box***

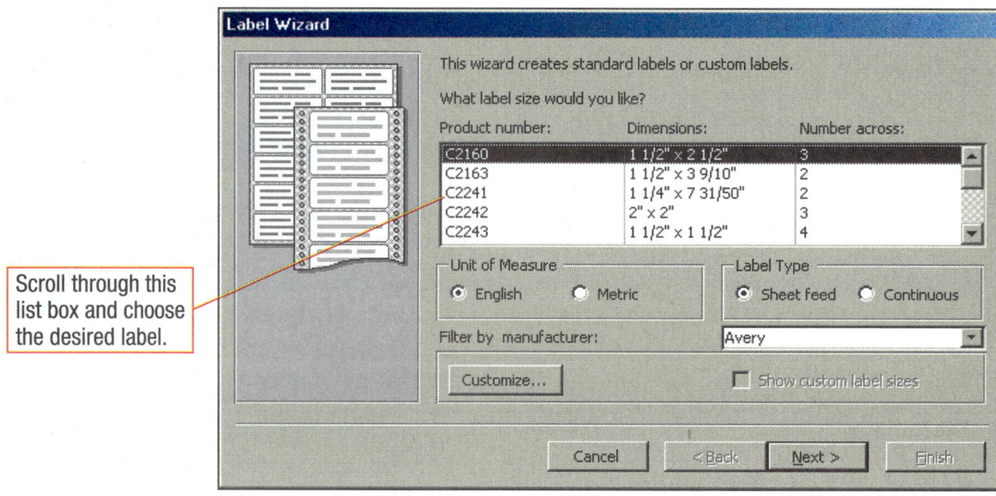

At the second Label Wizard dialog box shown in figure 6.9, specify the font name, size, weight, and color, and then click the Next button.

FIGURE 6.9 ***Second Label Wizard Dialog Box***

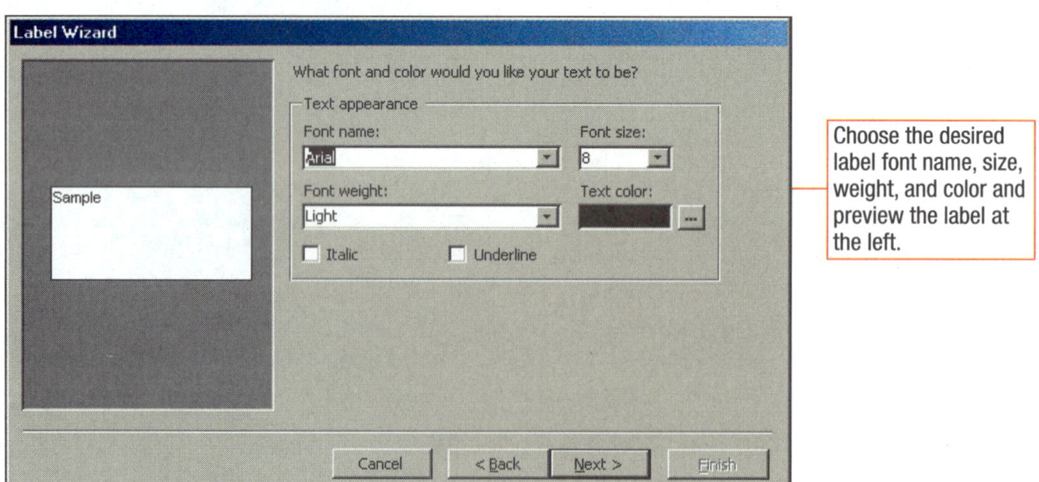

Specify the fields you want included in the mailing labels at the third Label Wizard dialog box shown in figure 6.10. To do this, select the field in the Available fields list box, and then click the button containing the greater than symbol (>). This moves the field to the Prototype label. Insert the fields in the Prototype label as you want the text to display on the label. After inserting the fields in the Prototype label, click the Next button.

FIGURE 6.10 ***Third Label Wizard Dialog Box***

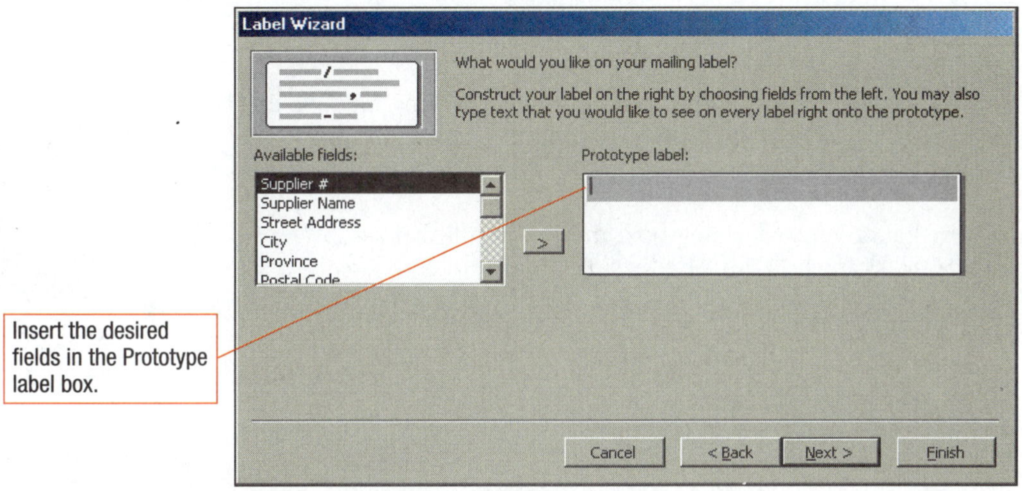

At the fourth Label Wizard dialog box, shown in figure 6.11, you can specify a field from the database file by which the labels are sorted. If you want the labels sorted (for example, by last name, postal code, etc.), insert the field by which you want the fields sorted in the Sort by list box, and then click the Next button.

FIGURE 6.11 ***Fourth Label Wizard Dialog Box***

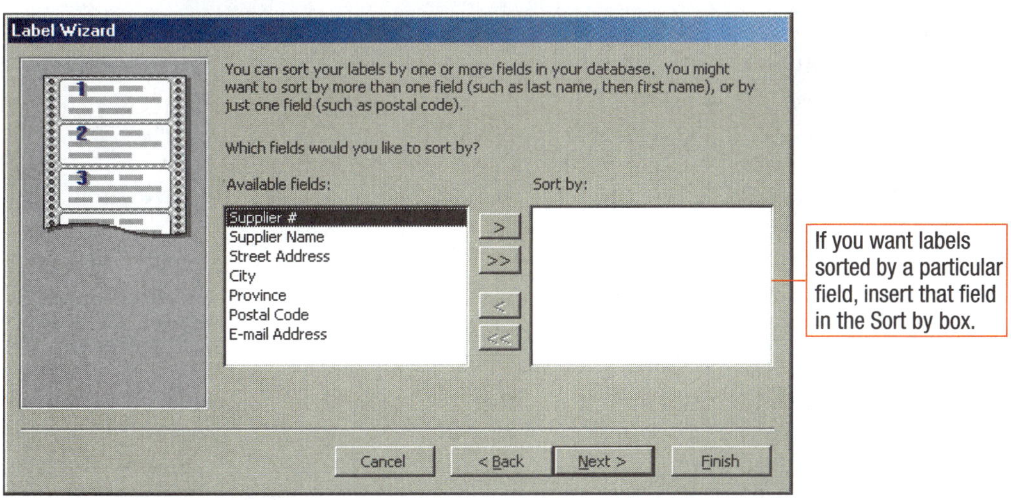

At the last Label Wizard dialog box, key a name for the label file, and then click the Finish button. After a few moments, the labels display on the screen in Print Preview. Print the labels and/or close Print Preview.

exercise 5

PREPARING MAILING LABELS

1. Open the Outdoor Options database file.
2. At the Outdoor Options : Database window, prepare mailing labels with supplier names and addresses by completing the following steps:
   a. Click the Reports button on the Objects bar.
   b. Click the New button on the window toolbar.
   c. At the New Report dialog box, click the down-pointing triangle at the right of the *Choose the table or query where the object's data comes from* option box, and then click *Suppliers* at the drop-down menu.
   d. Double-click *Label Wizard* in the list box.
   e. At the first Label Wizard dialog box, make the following changes:
      1) Click *English* in the Unit of Measure section. (Skip this step if *English* is already selected.)
      2) Click the down-pointing triangle at the right side of the Filter by manufacturer option and then click *Avery* at the drop-down list. (Skip this step if *Avery* is already selected.)
      3) Make sure *C2160* is selected in the Product number list box.
      4) Click the Next button.

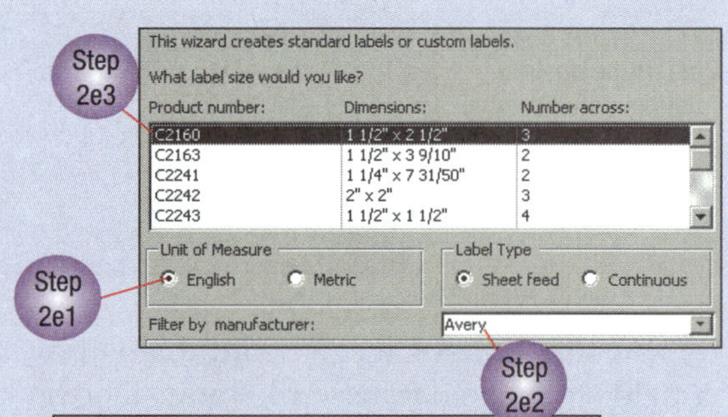

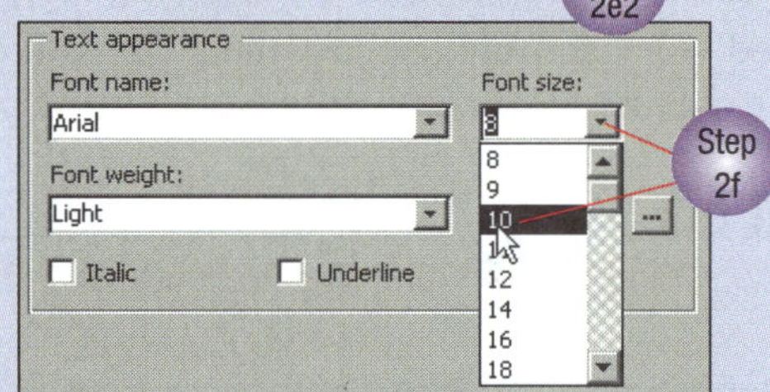

   f. At the second Label Wizard dialog box (see figure 6.9), change the font size to 10, and then click the Next button.
   g. At the third Label Wizard dialog box, complete the following steps to insert the fields in the Prototype label:
      1) Click *Supplier Name* in the Available fields list box and then click the button containing the greater than symbol (>).
      2) Press the Enter key (this moves the insertion point down to the next line in the Prototype label).
      3) With *Street Address* selected in the Available fields list box, click the button containing the greater than symbol (>).
      4) Press the Enter key.
      5) With *City* selected in the Available fields list box, click the button containing the greater than symbol (>).
      6) Key a comma (,) and then press the spacebar.
      7) With *Province* selected in the Available fields list box, click the button containing the greater than symbol (>).
      8) Press the Enter key.
      9) With *Postal Code* selected in the Available fields list box, click the button containing the greater than symbol (>).

10) Click the Next button.

h. At the fourth Label Wizard dialog box, sort by postal code. To do this, click *Postal Code* in the Available fields list box and then click the button containing the greater than symbol (>).

i. Click the Next button.

j. At the last Label Wizard dialog box, click the Finish button. (The Label Wizard automatically names the label file Labels Suppliers.)

3. Print the labels by clicking the Print button on the Print Preview toolbar.
4. Close the labels file. (To do this, click the Close button that displays at the right side of the Labels Suppliers Report title bar.)
5. Close the Outdoor Options database file.

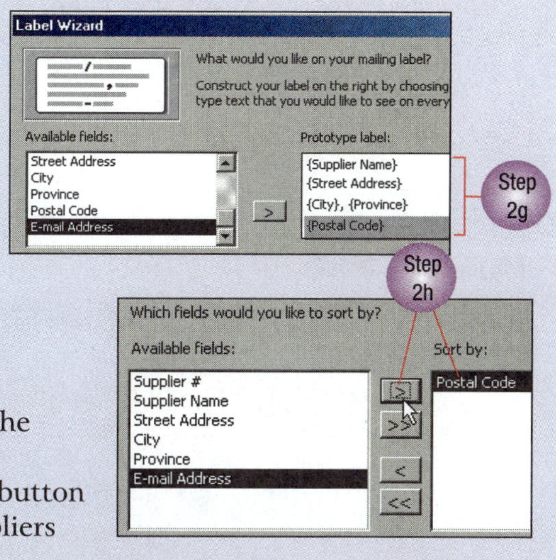

Creating a Chart

HINT

Create a chart with data from a table to provide a visual display of data.

Access includes a Chart Wizard you can use to display data more visually than a table, form, or report. Use the Chart Wizard to create a chart with data from a table. To create a chart with the Chart Wizard, open the database file, click either the Forms button or the Reports button on the Objects bar, and then click the New button. Specify the table containing the fields to be included in the chart and then double-click the *Chart Wizard* option in the list box. This displays the first Chart Wizard dialog box, shown in figure 6.12.

HINT

The Chart Wizard is shared by Microsoft Office programs.

FIGURE 6.12 **First Chart Wizard Dialog Box**

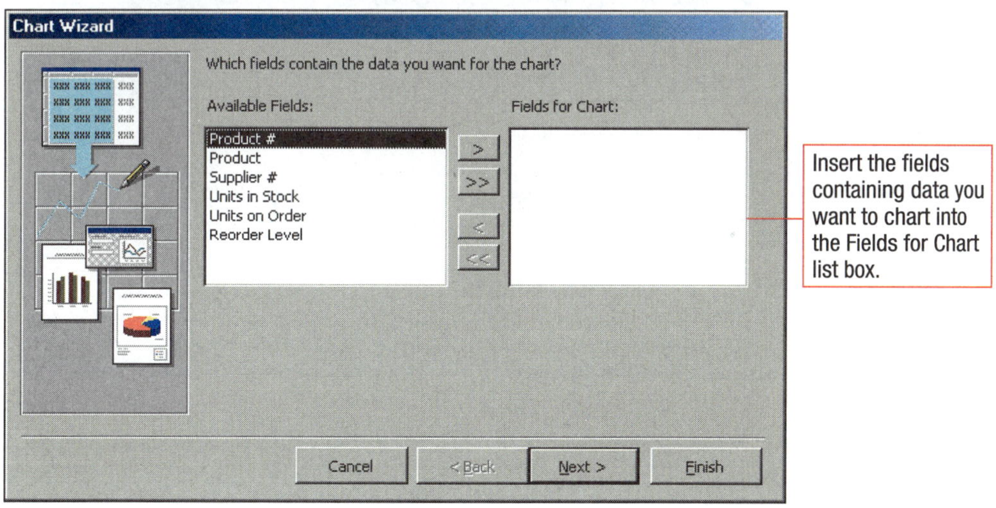

At the first Chart Wizard dialog box, insert the fields you want included in the chart in the Fields for Chart list box. The first field inserted in the Fields for Chart list box will be used by the Chart Wizard as the x-axis in the chart. After inserting the fields, click the Next button. This displays the second Chart Wizard dialog box, shown in figure 6.13.

FIGURE 6.13 ***Second Chart Wizard Dialog Box***

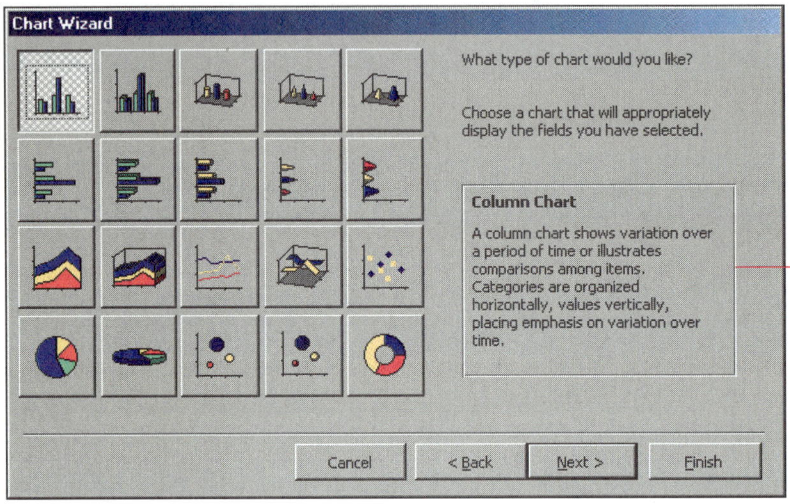

Click the desired chart, and information about the chart displays in this section.

Choose the chart type at the second Chart Wizard dialog box. To do this, click the icon representing the desired chart, and then click the Next button. This displays the third Chart Wizard dialog box, shown in figure 6.14.

FIGURE 6.14 ***Third Chart Wizard Dialog Box***

Customize the chart by dragging and dropping field buttons to the sample chart.

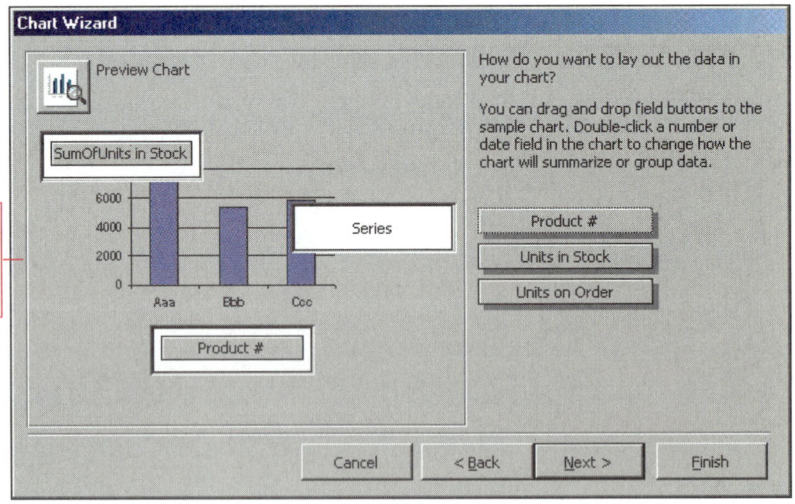

At the third Chart Wizard dialog box, specify how you want labels to appear in the chart. To do this, double-click a label in the preview chart. At the drop-down menu that displays, click the desired label option. At this Chart Wizard dialog box, you can also add another field to the chart. For example, in exercise 6, you will be charting Units on Order as well as Units in Stock. To do this, you will drag the desired field from the right side of the dialog box to the appropriate location in the preview chart. When all changes have been made, click the Next button. At the fourth, and last, Chart Wizard dialog box, key a name for the chart, and then click the Finish button.

exercise 6

CREATING A CHART

1. Open the Outdoor Options database file.
2. Click the Tables button on the Objects bar.
3. Open the Products table by double-clicking *Products* in the list box.
4. Delete the records of those products where zero *(0)* displays in the *Units on Order* field (at the warning message, click Yes). After deleting the records, click the Save button on the Table Datasheet toolbar, and then close the Products table.
5. At the Outdoor Options : Database window, click the Reports button on the Objects bar.
6. Create a chart with fields from the Products table by completing the following steps:
   a. Click the New button on the window toolbar.
   b. At the New Report window, click the down-pointing triangle at the right of the *Choose the table or query where the object's data comes from* option, and then click *Products*.
   c. Double-click *Chart Wizard* in the list box.
   d. At the first Chart Wizard dialog box, complete the followings steps:
      1) With *Product #* selected in the Available Fields list box, click the button containing the greater than symbol (>).
      2) Click *Units in Stock* in the Available Fields list box and then click the button containing the greater than symbol (>).
      3) With *Units on Order* selected in the Available Fields list box, click the button containing the greater than symbol (>).
      4) Click the Next button.
   e. At the second Chart Wizard dialog box, click the Next button.
   f. At the third Chart Wizard dialog box, complete the following steps:
      1) Position the arrow pointer on the Units on Order button at the right side of the dialog box, hold down the left mouse button, drag the outline of the button to the bottom of the *SumOfUnits in Stock* field that displays in the preview chart, and then release the left mouse button.

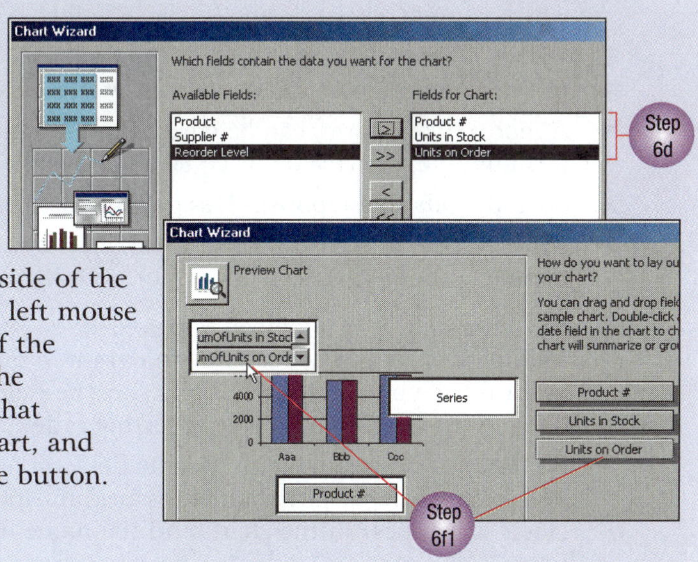

2) Double-click the *SumOfUnits in Stock* field that displays in the preview chart.
3) At the Summarize dialog box, double-click *None* in the list box. (This changes *SumOfUnits in Stock* to *Units in Stock*. By default, the Chart Wizard will sum the number of units in stock. Changing the field to *Units in Stock* tells the Chart Wizard to simply display the number of units in stock and not the sum.)
4) Double-click the *SumOfUnits on Order* field that displays in the preview chart.
5) At the Summarize dialog box, double-click *None* in the list box. (This changes *SumOfUnits on Order* to *Units on Order*.)
6) Click the Next button.

g. At the fourth Chart Wizard dialog box, key **Product Units**, and then click the Finish button.

7. With the chart displayed in Print Preview, print the chart by clicking the Print button on the Print Preview toolbar.

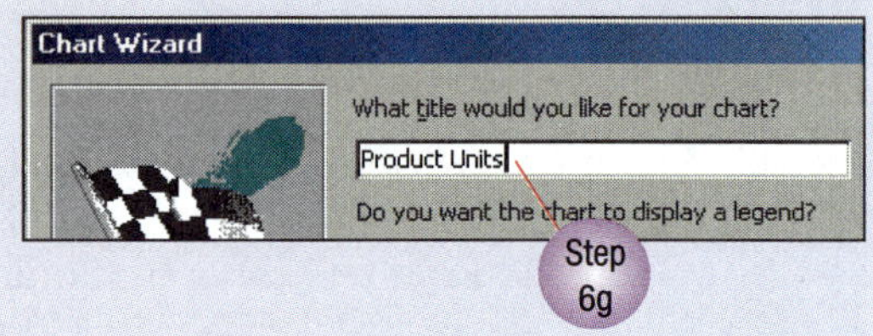

8. After the chart is printed, click the Close button that displays at the right side of the Report1 : Report title bar. At the message asking if you want to save the changes to the design of the report, click No.
9. Close the Outdoor Options database file.

CHAPTER summary

- Data in a table can be inserted in a report, which lets you control how the data appears on the page when printed.
- Use the AutoReport feature to automatically create a plainly formatted report in a columnar arrangement.
- The Report Wizard walks you through the steps for creating a report and lets you specify the fields you want included in the report, the level of fields in the report, the order in which records display in the report, the layout of the report, the report style, and a name for the report.
- Like a form, a report can be created with fields from related tables.
- A report, like a form, can be created in Design view. A report includes up to five sections including Report Header, Page Header, Detail, Page Footer, and Report Footer.
- To add fields to a report in Design view, associate the report with the desired table.
- Move, resize, and customize control objects in the report Design view in the same manner as control objects in the form Design view.
- Use buttons on the Toolbox to add controls to a report in Design view.
- Mailing labels can be created with data in a table using the Label Wizard. The Label Wizard lets you specify the label type; the fields you want included in the labels; the font name, size, weight, and color; a sorting order; and a name for the mailing label file.
- A chart can be created with specific fields in a table using the Chart Wizard. The Chart Wizard lets you specify the fields you want included in the chart, the chart type, how labels will appear in the chart, and the name for the chart file.

COMMANDS review

Command	Mouse/Keyboard
Create report using AutoReport	Open database file, click desired table, click down-pointing triangle at right side of New Object button on Database toolbar, then click AutoReport
Begin Report Wizard	Open database file, click New button, then double-click *Report Wizard*
Display the report Design view	Click Reports button on the Objects bar, and then double-click *Create report in Design view*
Begin Label Wizard	Open database file, click New button, specify table, then double-click *Label Wizard*
Begin Chart Wizard	Open database file, click New button, specify table, then double-click *Chart Wizard*

CONCEPTS check

Completion: On a blank sheet of paper, indicate the correct term, symbol, or command for each item.

1. Click the down-pointing triangle at the right side of this button to display the AutoReport option.
2. Use this to guide you through the steps for creating a report.
3. When all of the steps in the Report Wizard are completed, the report displays in this view.
4. This appears at the top of each page of a report and generally includes information such as column headings identifying the data in the report.
5. Use these to increase or decrease the size of a selected control object.
6. To create a chart with the Chart Wizard, open the database file, and then click either the Forms button or this button on the Objects bar.
7. When creating a chart with the Chart Wizard, the first field inserted in the Fields for Chart list box will be used as this axis in the chart.
8. Suppose you are using the Report Wizard with the Outdoor Options database file to show information on what products are currently on order, from what company, and the e-mail address of each company. At the first Report Wizard step, what fields would you insert from the Products table and what fields would you insert from the Suppliers table?
9. When using the Chart Wizard, specify the fields in the Products table (in the Outdoor Options database file) you would use to create a chart that shows the reorder level for products.

SKILLS check

(Note: Copy the Hilltop database file from the CD that accompanies this textbook to your disk and then remove the read-only attribute from the database file. Before completing the following assessments, consider deleting the Outdoor Options database file from your disk.)

Assessment 1

1. Open the Hilltop database file.
2. Click the Tables button on the Objects bar.
3. Use AutoReport to create a report with the Inventory table.
4. When the report displays in Print Preview, print the report.
5. Close the report without saving it.
6. Close the Hilltop database file.

Assessment 2

1. Open the Hilltop database file.
2. Create a report using the Report Wizard with the following specifications:
   a. At the first Report Wizard dialog box, insert the following fields in the Selected Fields list box:
      From the Equipment table:
         Equipment
      From the Inventory table:
         Purchase Date
         Purchase Price
         Available Hours
   b. At the second Report Wizard dialog box, make sure *Equipment* is selected, and then click the button containing the greater than symbol (>).
   c. Do not make any changes at the third Report Wizard dialog box.
   d. At the fourth Report Wizard dialog box, choose the Align Left 1 option.
   e. At the fifth Report Wizard dialog box, choose the *Soft Gray* option.
   f. At the last Report Wizard dialog box, click the Finish button. (This accepts the default report name of Equipment.)
   g. When the report displays in Print Preview, print the report.
   h. Close the report.
3. Close the Hilltop database file.

Assessment 3

1. Open the Hilltop database file.
2. Create a report using the Report Wizard with the following specifications:
   a. At the first Report Wizard dialog box, insert the following fields in the Selected Fields list box:
      From the Customers table:
         Customer
      From the Invoices table:
         Date
         Hours

From the Equipment table:

Equipment

From the Rates table:

Rate

b. At the second Report Wizard dialog box, make sure *by Customers* is selected.
c. Do not make any changes at the third Report Wizard dialog box.
d. Do not make any changes at the fourth Report Wizard dialog box.
e. At the fifth Report Wizard dialog box, choose the Block option.
f. At the sixth Report Wizard dialog box, choose the *Casual* option.
g. At the last Report Wizard dialog box, name the report Rentals.
h. When the report displays in Print Preview, print the report.
i. Close the report.

3. Close the Hilltop database file.

Assessment 4

1. Open the Hilltop database file.
2. Use the Label Wizard to create mailing labels (you determine the label type) with the customer names and addresses and sorted by customer names. Name the mailing label file Customer Mailing Labels.
3. Print the mailing labels.
4. Close the mailing labels file and then close the Hilltop database file.

Assessment 5

1. Open the Hilltop database file.
2. Click the Reports button on the Objects bar and then click the New button.
3. At the New Report dialog box, specify that you want to choose fields from the Inventory table, and then double-click the *Chart Wizard*.
4. Create a chart with fields in the Inventory table with the following specifications:
   a. At the first Chart Wizard dialog box, insert **Equipment #**, **Available Hours**, **Service Hours**, and **Repair Hours** in the Fields for Chart list box.
   b. Do not make any changes at the second Chart Wizard dialog box.
   c. At the third Chart Wizard dialog box, make the following changes:
      1) Drag the Service Hours button to the bottom of the *SumOfAvailableHours* field that displays in the preview chart.
      2) Drag the Repair Hours button to the bottom of the *SumOfServiceHours* field that displays in the preview chart.
      3) Double-click *SumOfAvailableHours* that displays in the preview chart (you will need to scroll up the list to display this option), click *None* at the Summarize dialog box, and then click OK.
      4) Double-click *SumOfServiceHours* that displays in the preview chart, click *None* at the Summarize dialog box, and then click OK.
      5) Double-click *SumOfRepairHours* that displays in the preview chart, click *None* at the Summarize dialog box, and then click OK.
   d. At the fourth Chart Wizard dialog box, key **Available Hours**, and then click Finish.
5. Print the chart and then close it without saving the changes.
6. Close the Hilltop database file.

Assessment 6

1. The New Report dialog box contains options for creating a report. In this chapter, you have used the Report Wizard to prepare reports. Experiment with two other options available at the New Report dialog box—AutoReport: Columnar and AutoReport: Tabular.
2. After experimenting with these two wizards, open the Hilltop database file and then complete the following:
   a. Use the AutoReport: Columnar Wizard to create a report with all of the fields in the Inventory table. Print the report that displays and then close the report.
   b. Use the AutoForm: Tabular Wizard to create a report with all of the fields in the Customers table. Print the report that displays and then close the report.
3. Close the Hilltop database file.

CHAPTER 7

IMPORTING AND EXPORTING DATA

PERFORMANCE OBJECTIVES

Upon successful completion of chapter 7, you will be able to:

- **Export Access data to Excel**
- **Export Access data to Word**
- **Merge Access data with a Word document**
- **Import data to a new table**
- **Link data to a new table**
- **Use the Office Clipboard**

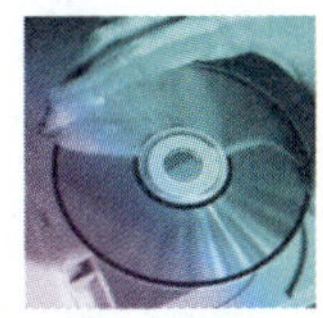

Access Chapter 07C

Microsoft Office XP is a suite of programs that allows easy data exchange between programs. In this chapter you will learn how to export data from Access to Excel and Word, merge Access data with a Word document, import and link data to a new table, and copy and paste data between programs.

Using OfficeLinks

One of the advantages of a suite of programs like Microsoft Office is the ability to exchange data from one program to another. Access, like the other programs in the suite, offers a feature to export data from Access into Word and/or Excel. Exporting data can be easily accomplished with the OfficeLinks button on the Database toolbar.

OfficeLinks

HINT
Data exported from Access to Excel is automatically saved as an Excel workbook with the *.xls* extension.

Exporting Data to Excel

Access data saved in a table, form, or report can be exported to Excel. Use an option from the OfficeLinks drop-down menu to export data from Access to Excel. The data is saved as an Excel file in the folder where the Access file is located. Excel is automatically started when the file is opened.

To export data to Excel, open the database file, and then click the name of the table, form, or report you want saved in Excel. With the object selected, click the down-pointing triangle at the right side of the OfficeLinks button on the Database toolbar, and then click Analyze It with Microsoft Excel at the drop-down menu. The data is converted to an Excel

HINT
You can export a datasheet as unformatted data to Excel or other spreadsheet programs.

worksheet, Excel is opened, and the data is displayed in a worksheet. The worksheet is automatically saved with the same name as the name in the database file, except the Excel extension of *.xls* is added to the name.

exercise 1

SAVING A TABLE AS AN EXCEL WORKSHEET

(Note: Before completing computer exercises, delete any database files from your disk. Next, copy to your disk the Access Chapter 07C *subfolder from the* Access 2002 Core *folder on the CD that accompanies this textbook and make* Access Chapter 07C *the active folder.)*

1. Copy the Hilltop database file from the CD that accompanies this textbook to the Access Chapter 07C folder on your disk and then remove the read-only attribute from Hilltop.
2. Open the Hilltop database file and then click the Tables button on the Objects bar.
3. Save the Invoices table as an Excel worksheet and format the worksheet by completing the following steps:
   a. Click once on *Invoices* in the list box. (This selects the table.)
   b. Click the down-pointing triangle at the right side of the OfficeLinks button on the Database toolbar.
   c. At the drop-down menu that displays, click Analyze It with Microsoft Excel.
   d. When the data displays on the screen in Excel as a worksheet, make the following changes:
      1) Select cells A1 through F15.
      2) Click Format on the Menu bar and then click AutoFormat.
      3) At the AutoFormat dialog box, double-click the Classic 2 autoformat.
      4) With cells A1 through F15 still selected, click the Center button on the Formatting toolbar.
   e. Click the Save button on the Standard toolbar.
   f. Click the Print button on the Standard toolbar.
   g. Close the worksheet and then exit Excel.
4. Close the Hilltop database file.

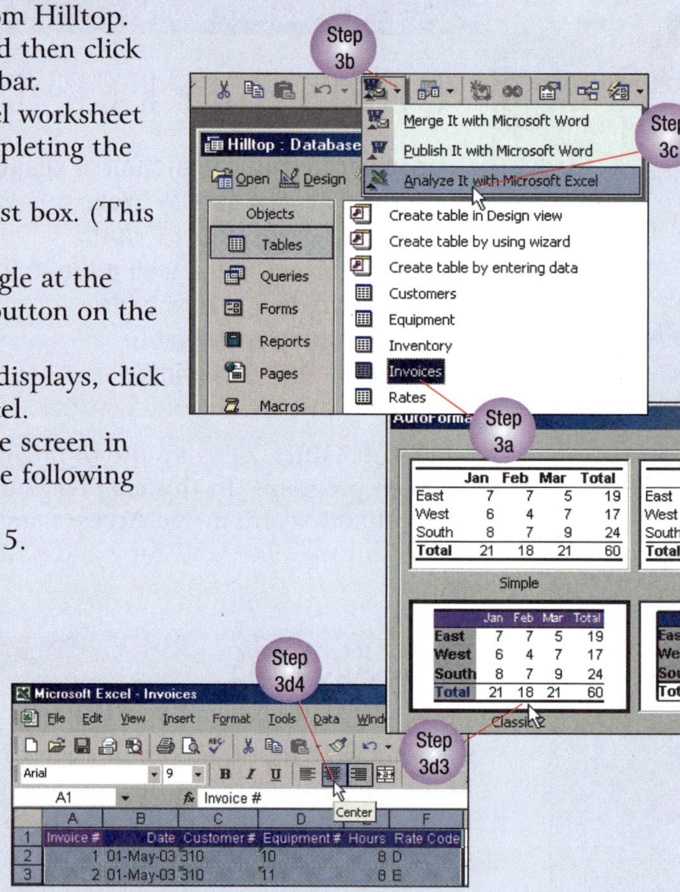

When you use the Analyze It with Microsoft Excel option from the OfficeLinks drop-down menu, the table becomes an Excel worksheet. All Excel editing capabilities are available for changing or modifying the worksheet. A form can also be converted to a worksheet with the Analyze It with Microsoft Excel option.

exercise 2

SAVING A FORM AS AN EXCEL WORKSHEET

1. Open the Hilltop database file.
2. Create a form with fields in the Inventory table by completing the following steps:
   a. At the Hilltop : Database dialog box, click the Forms button on the Objects bar.
   b. Double-click *Create form by using wizard*.
   c. At the first Form Wizard dialog box, click the down-pointing triangle at the right of the Tables/Queries option box, and then click *Table: Inventory* at the drop-down list. Click the button containing the two greater than symbols (>>) to insert all of the *Inventory* fields in the Selected Fields list box.
   d. After entering the fields, click the Next button.
   e. At the second Form Wizard dialog box, click the Next button.
   f. At the third Form Wizard dialog box, click *Blueprint* in the format style list box, and then click the Next button.
   g. At the fourth Form Wizard dialog box, key **Equipment Inventory**, and then click the Finish button.
   h. When the first record displays, click the Close button.

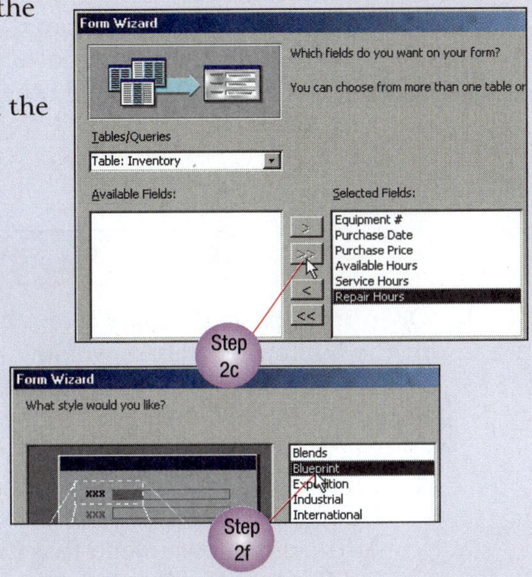

3. Save the Equipment Inventory form as an Excel worksheet and format the worksheet by completing the following steps:
   a. Click once on *Equipment Inventory* in the list box. (This selects the form.)
   b. Click the down-pointing triangle at the right side of the OfficeLinks button on the Database toolbar.
   c. At the drop-down menu that displays, click Analyze It with Microsoft Excel.
   d. When the data displays on the screen in Excel as a worksheet, make the following changes:
      1) Select cells A1 through F11.
      2) Click Format on the Menu bar and then click AutoFormat.
      3) At the AutoFormat dialog box, double-click the Colorful 1 autoformat. (You will need to scroll down the list box to display Colorful 1.)
      4) Select cells A2 through B11 and then click the Center button on the Formatting toolbar.
      5) Select cells D2 through F11 and then click the Center button on the Formatting toolbar.
   e. Click the Save button on the Standard toolbar.
   f. Print and then close the worksheet.
   g. Exit Excel.
4. Close the Hilltop database file.

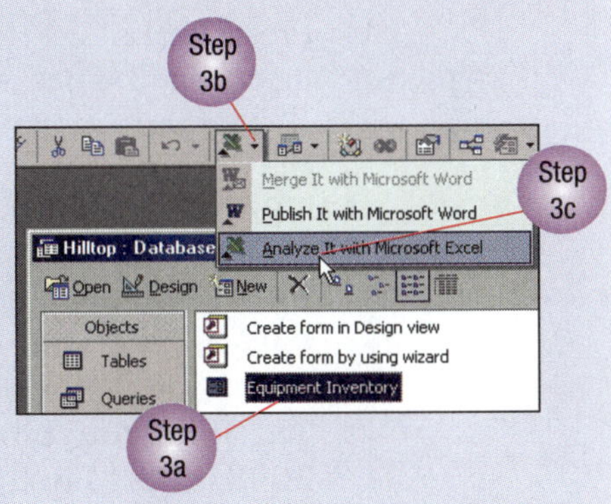

HINT

Data exported from Access to Word is automatically saved in the rtf (rich-text format) file format.

Exporting Data to Word

Export data from Access to Word in the same manner as exporting to Excel. To export data to Word, open the database file, select the table, form, or report you want to export to Word, and then click the OfficeLinks button on the Database toolbar. At the drop-down menu that displays, click Publish It with Microsoft Word. Word is automatically opened and the data is inserted in a Word document. The Word document is automatically saved with the same name as the table, form, or report you selected, except the file extension *.rtf* is added to the name. An *rtf* file is saved in "rich-text format," which preserves formatting such as fonts and styles. A document saved with the *.rtf* extension can be opened with Microsoft Word and other Windows word processing or desktop publishing programs.

exercise 3

SAVING A TABLE AS A WORD TABLE

1. Open the Hilltop database file.
2. At the Hilltop : Database window, click the Tables button on the Objects bar.
3. Save the Invoices table as a Word table and then add additional text to the Word document by completing the following steps:
   a. Click once on *Invoices* in the list box. (This selects the table.)
   b. Click the down-pointing triangle at the right side of the OfficeLinks button on the Database toolbar.
   c. At the drop-down menu that displays, click Publish It with Microsoft Word.
   d. When the data displays on the screen in Word as a table, add text to the document (not the table) by completing the following steps:
      1) Press the Enter key three times. (This will insert blank lines above the table.)
      2) Move the insertion point to the beginning of the document, turn on bold, and then key **TRANSACTIONS: 05/01/2003 - 05/03/2003**.
      3) Press the Enter key twice and then key the following text (the text is displayed in bold here for easier reading—do not key the text in bold):
      The following table displays the rentals that occurred between May 1, 2003, and May 3, 2003.
   e. Click the Save button on the Standard toolbar.
   f. Print the document.
   g. Close the document and then exit Word.
4. Close the Hilltop database file.

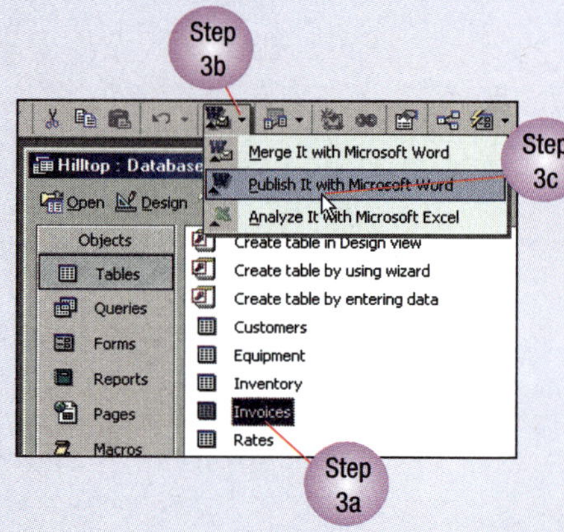

exercise 4

SAVING A REPORT AS A WORD DOCUMENT

1. Open the Hilltop database file.
2. At the Hilltop : Database window, click the Reports button on the Objects bar.
3. Create a report with the Report Wizard by completing the following steps:
   a. Click the New button on the toolbar.
   b. At the New Report dialog box, double-click *Report Wizard* in the list box.
   c. At the first Report Wizard dialog box, insert the following fields in the Selected Fields list box:
      From the Customers table:
         Customer
      From the Equipment table:
         Equipment
      From the Invoices table:
         Date
         Hours

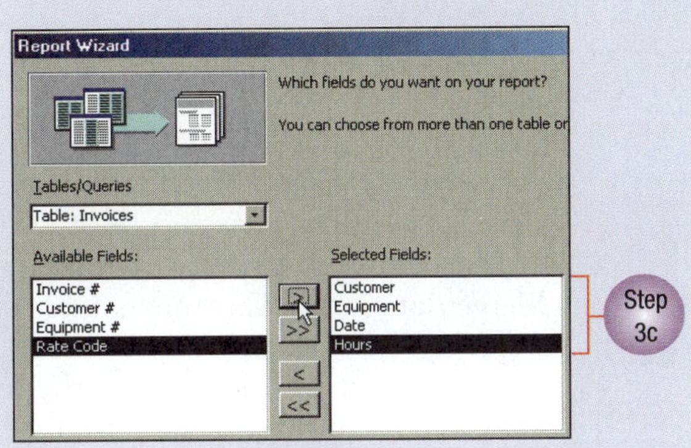

   d. After inserting the fields, click the Next button.
   e. At the second Report Wizard dialog box, make sure *by Customers* is selected in the list box in the upper left corner, and then click the Next button.
   f. At the third Report Wizard dialog box, click the Next button.
   g. At the fourth Report Wizard dialog box, click the Next button.
   h. At the fifth Report Wizard dialog box, click Align Left 1, and then click the Next button.
   i. At the sixth Report Wizard dialog box, click *Corporate* in the list box, and then click the Next button.
   j. At the seventh Report Wizard dialog box, key **Customer Report**, and then click the Finish button.
   k. When the report displays in Print Preview, view the report, and then click the Print button that displays on the Print Preview toolbar.
   l. Click the Close button (displays with an *X*) that displays at the right side of the Customer Report title bar.
4. Save the Customer Report as a Word document by completing the following steps:
   a. Click once on *Customer Report* in the list box.
   b. Click the down-pointing triangle at the right side of the OfficeLinks button on the Database toolbar.
   c. At the drop-down menu that displays, click Publish It with Microsoft Word.

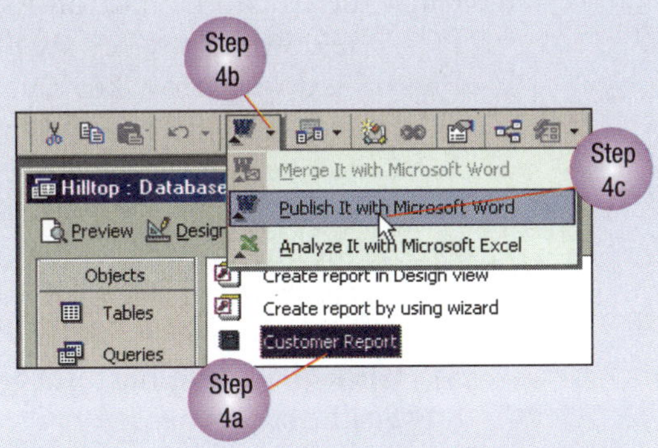

   d. When the data displays on the screen in Word, print the report by clicking the Print button on the Standard toolbar.
   e. Click the Save button (to save the document with the default name of Customer Report).
   f. Close the document and then exit Word.
5. Close the Hilltop database file.

HINT

You can use the Word Mail Merge Wizard to create a mail merge document in Word 2002 that links to Access 2002 data.

Merging Access Data with a Word Document

Data from an Access table can be merged with a Word document. When merging data in an Access table with a Word document, the data in the Access table is considered the data source and the Word document is considered the main document. When the merge is completed, the merged documents display in Word.

When merging Access data, you can either key the text in the main document or merge Access data with an existing Word document. In exercise 5, you will merge Access data with an existing Word document and in exercise 6, you will key the main document.

exercise 5 — MERGING ACCESS DATA WITH A WORD DOCUMENT

1. Open the Hilltop database file.
2. At the Hilltop : Database window, click the Tables button on the Objects bar.
3. Merge data in the Customers table with a Word document by completing the following steps:
   a. Click once on *Customers* in the list box.
   b. Click the down-pointing triangle at the right side of the OfficeLinks button on the Database toolbar.
   c. At the drop-down menu that displays, click Merge It with Microsoft Word.
   d. At the Microsoft Word Mail Merge Wizard dialog box, make sure *Link your data to an existing Microsoft Word document* is selected, and then click OK.
   e. At the Select Microsoft Word Document dialog box, make sure the *Access Chapter 07C* folder on your disk is the active folder, and then double-click the document named *Hilltop Letter*.

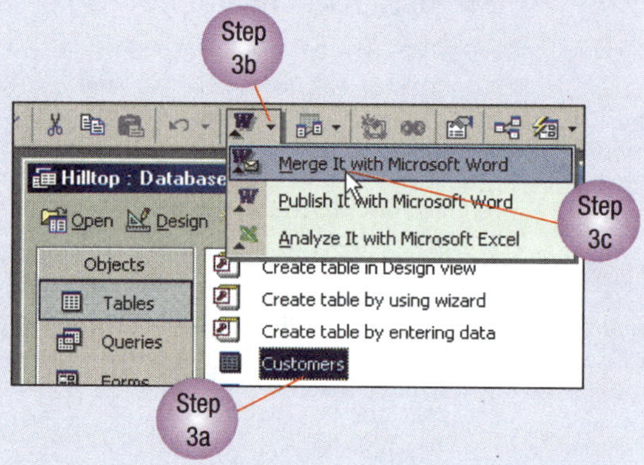

   f. Click the Maximize button located at the right side of the Hilltop Letter title bar.
   g. Press the down arrow key six times (not the Enter key) and then key the current date.
   h. Press the down arrow key five times and then insert fields for merging from the Customers table by completing the following steps:
      1) Click the Insert Merge Fields button located towards the left side of the Merge toolbar.
      2) At the Insert Merge Field dialog box, double-click *Customer* in the Fields list box. (This inserts the *«Customer»* field in the document.)
      3) Click the Close button to close the Insert Merge Field dialog box.
      4) Press Enter, click the Insert Merge Fields button, and then double-click *Street Address* in the Fields list box of the Insert Merge Field dialog box.
      5) Click the Close button to close the dialog box.
      6) Press Enter, click the Insert Merge Fields button, and then double-click *City* in the Fields list box.

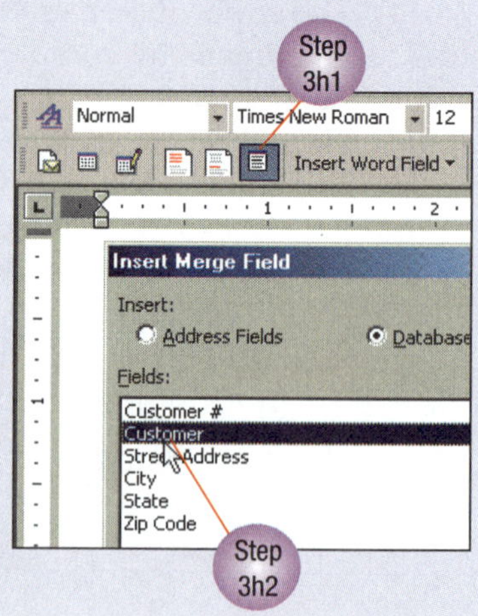

7) Click the Close button to close the dialog box.
8) Key a comma (,) and then press the spacebar.
9) Click the Insert Merge Fields button and then double-click *State* in the Fields list box.
10) Click the Close button to close the dialog box.
11) Press the spacebar, click the Insert Merge Fields button, and then double-click *Zip Code* in the Fields list box.
12) Click the Close button to close the dialog box.
13) Replace the letters *XX* that display toward the bottom of the letter with your initials.

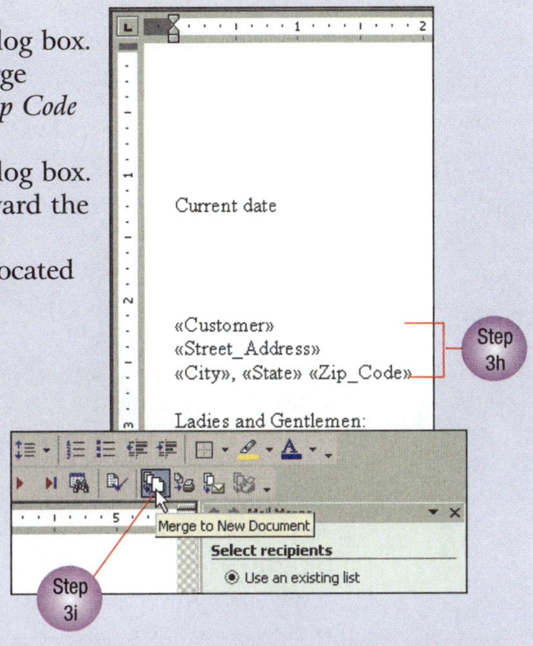

i. Click the Merge to New Document button located towards the right side of the Merge toolbar.
j. At the Merge to New Document dialog box, make sure All is selected, and then click OK.
k. When the merge is completed, save the new document as Word C07 Ex05 in the *Access Chapter 07C* folder on your disk.
l. Print the first two letters of Word C07 Ex05. (To do this, select the first two letters in the document, display the Print dialog box, click the Selection option, and then click OK. Letters are separated by a section break rather than a page break so you cannot print the first two pages by identifying page numbers.)
m. Close Word C07 Ex05 and then close Hilltop Letter, without saving the changes.
n. Exit Word.
4. Close the Hilltop database file.

exercise 6

MERGING ACCESS DATA WITH A NEW WORD DOCUMENT

1. Open the Hilltop database file.
2. At the Hilltop : Database window, click the Tables button on the Objects bar.
3. Merge data in the Customers table to a new Word document by completing the following steps:
   a. Click once on *Customers* in the list box.
   b. Click the down-pointing triangle at the right side of the OfficeLinks button on the Database toolbar.
   c. At the drop-down menu that displays, click Merge It with Microsoft Word.
   d. At the Microsoft Word Mail Merge Wizard dialog box, click the *Create a new document and then link the data to it* option, and then click OK.
   e. Click the Maximize button located at the right side of the Document1 title bar.

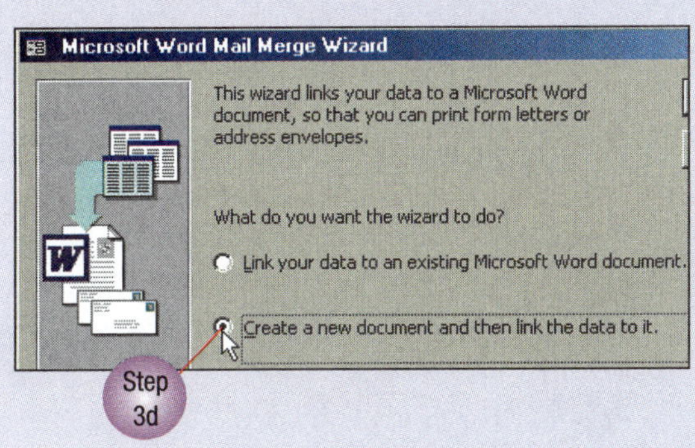

f. Complete the following steps to key text and insert fields in the blank Word document:
   1) Press Enter six times.
   2) Key the current date.
   3) Press Enter five times.
   4) Insert the following fields at the left margin in the order shown below (start by clicking the Insert Merge Fields button located towards the left side of the Mail Merge toolbar).

      «Customer»
      «Street_Address»
      «City», «State» «Zip_Code»

   5) Press Enter twice and then key the salutation **Ladies and Gentlemen:**.
   6) Press Enter twice and then key the following paragraph of text. (The paragraph is displayed here in bold for easier reading—do not key the paragraph in bold. After keying the Hilltop e-mail address, Word will convert it to a hyperlink. Immediately click the Undo button to remove the hyperlink and then continue keying the remainder of the paragraph.)

      We have installed a new computer system for receiving rental equipment requests electronically. If you are interested in requesting equipment online, you may contact us at hilltop@emcp.com or visit our Web site at www.emcp.net/hilltop. If you need assistance with an online request, please contact us at (303) 555-9066.

   7) Press Enter twice and then key the following complimentary close (at the left margin):

      Sincerely,

      Lou Galloway
      Manager

      XX:Word C07 Ex06

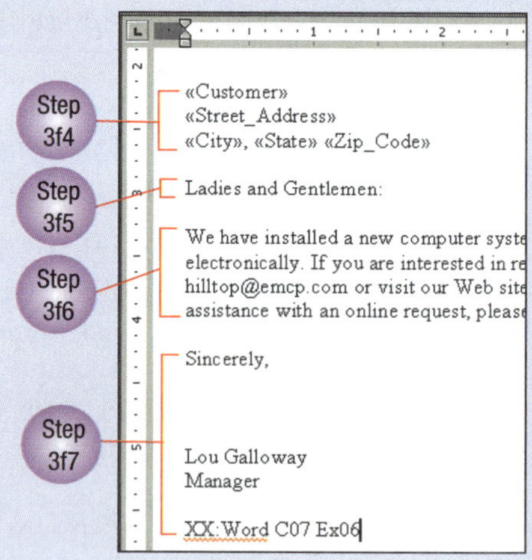

g. Click the Merge to New Document button located towards the right side of the Merge toolbar.
h. At the Merge to New Document dialog box, make sure All is selected, and then click OK.
i. When the merge is completed, save the new document as Word C07 Ex06 in the *Access Chapter 07C* folder on your disk.
j. Select and then print the first two letters of Word C07 Ex06. (See exercise 5, step 31.)
k. Close Word C07 Ex06.
l. Save the main document as Word Hilltop Letter in the *Access Chapter 07C* folder on your disk and then close Word Hilltop Letter.
m. Exit Word.

4. Close the Hilltop database file.

Merging Query Data with a Word Document

A query performed in Access can be saved, and then data from that query can be merged with a Word document. To do this, you would open the database file, complete the query, and then save the query. With the query name selected in the database file, you would click the OfficeLinks button on the Database toolbar and then click the Merge It with Microsoft Word option. You would specify whether you want to merge with an existing Word document or create a new document and then insert the appropriate fields.

exercise 7 — PERFORMING A QUERY AND THEN MERGING WITH A WORD DOCUMENT

1. Open the Hilltop database file.
2. Perform a query with the Simple Query Wizard and modify the query by completing the following steps:
   a. Click the Queries button on the Objects bar.
   b. Double-click *Create query by using wizard* in the list box.
   c. At the first Simple Query Wizard dialog box, click the down-pointing triangle at the right of the Tables/Queries option box, and then click *Table: Customers*.
   d. Click the button containing the two greater than symbols (>>) to insert all of the fields in the Selected Fields list box.

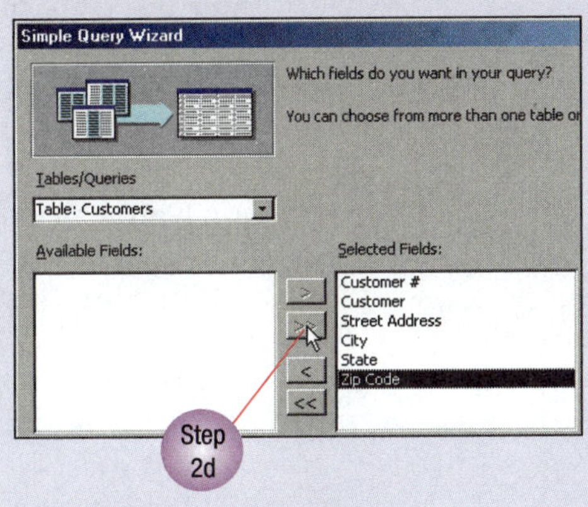

   e. Click the Next button.
   f. At the second Simple Query Wizard dialog box, click the *Modify the query design* option, and then click the Finish button.
   g. At the Customers Query : Select Query window, insert the query criterion by completing the following steps:
      1) Click in the Criteria: text box in the *City* column.
      2) Key **Denver** and then press Enter.

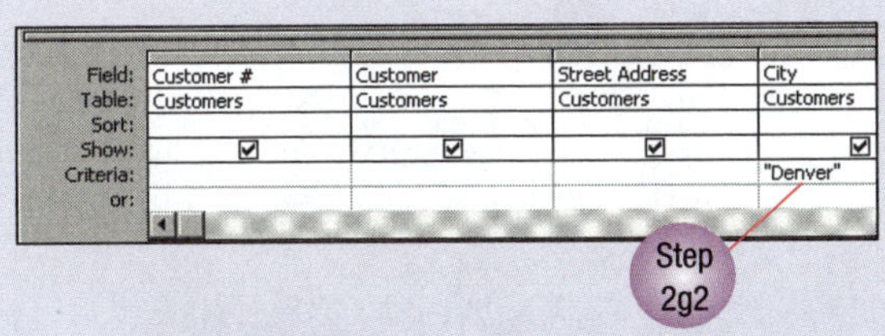

   h. Click the Run button on the Query Design toolbar. (Those customers located in Denver will display.)
   i. Save the query as Denver Query by completing the following steps:
      1) Click File and then Save As.
      2) At the Save As dialog box, key **Denver Query**, and then press Enter or click OK.

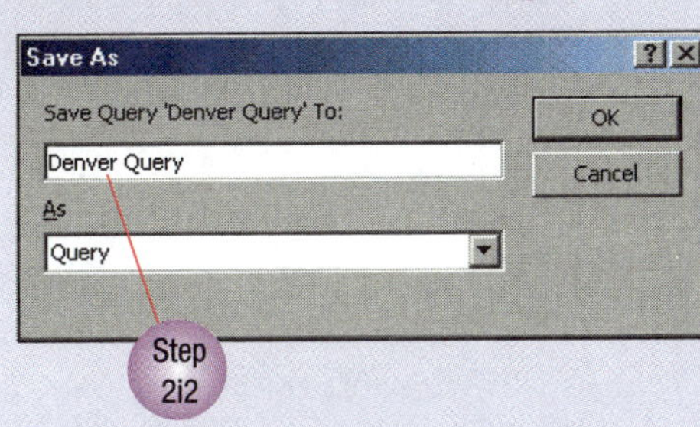

   j. Close the Denver Query by clicking the Close button at the right side of the query title bar.
3. Merge the Denver Query to a new Word document by completing the following steps:
   a. Click *Denver Query* in the Hilltop : Database window list box.

b. Click the down-pointing triangle at the right side of the OfficeLinks button on the Database toolbar.
c. At the drop-down menu that displays, click Merge It with Microsoft Word.
d. At the Microsoft Word Mail Merge Wizard dialog box, click the *Create a new document and then link the data to it* option, and then click OK.
e. Click the Maximize button located at the right side of the Document1 title bar.
f. Complete the following steps to key text and insert fields in the blank Word document:
   1) Press Enter six times.
   2) Key the current date.
   3) Press Enter five times.
   4) Insert the following fields at the left margin in the order shown below (start by clicking the Insert Merge Fields button at the left side of the Mail Merge toolbar).

      «Customer»
      «Street_Address»
      «City», «State» «Zip_Code»

   5) Press Enter twice and then key the salutation **Ladies and Gentlemen:**.
   6) Press Enter twice and then key the following paragraphs of text. (The paragraphs are displayed here in bold for easier reading—do not bold the paragraphs.)

      We have just opened a new branch office in downtown Denver to better serve our Denver customers. The branch office hours are 7:30 a.m. to 7:00 p.m. Monday through Friday, 8:00 a.m. to 5:00 p.m. Saturday, and 9:00 a.m. to 3:30 p.m. Sunday.

      Our new branch is located at 7500 Alameda Avenue. Stop by during the next two weeks and receive a 10% discount on your next equipment rental.

   7) Press Enter twice and then key the following complimentary close (at the left margin):

      Sincerely,

      Lou Galloway
      Manager

      XX:Word C07 Ex07

g. Click the Merge to New Document button located toward the right side of the Mail Merge toolbar.
h. At the Merge to New Document dialog box, make sure All is selected, and then click OK.
i. When the merge is completed, save the new document as Word C07 Ex07 in the *Access Chapter 07C* folder on your disk
j. Print and then close Word C07 Ex07.
k. Save the main document and name it Word Branch Letter.
l. Close Word Branch Letter and then exit Word.

4. Close the Hilltop database file.

Importing and Linking Data to a New Table

In this chapter, you learned how to export Access data to Excel and Word. Data from other programs, such as Excel and Word, can also be imported into an Access table. For example, you can import data from an Excel worksheet and create a new table in a database file. Data in the original program is not connected to the data imported into an Access table. If you make changes to the data in the original program, those changes are not reflected in the Access table. If you want the imported data connected to the original program, link the data.

Importing Data to a New Table

To import data, open the database file, click File, point to Get External Data, and then click Import. At the Import dialog box that displays, double-click the desired document name. This activates the Import Wizard and displays the first Wizard dialog box. The appearance of the dialog box varies depending on the document selected. Complete the steps of the Import Wizard specifying information such as the range of data, whether or not the first row contains column headings, whether you want to store the data in a new table or store it in an existing table, the primary key, and the name of the table.

exercise 8

IMPORTING AN EXCEL WORKSHEET INTO AN ACCESS TABLE

(Note: Before completing this exercise, open Excel and then open Excel Worksheet 01 [located in your Access Chapter 07C *folder]. Save the worksheet with Save As and name it Excel C07. Close Excel C07 and then exit Excel.)*

1. Copy the Southwest Insurance database file from the CD that accompanies this textbook to your disk and then remove the read-only attribute.
2. Open the Southwest Insurance database file and click the Tables button on the Objects bar.
3. Import an Excel worksheet into a new table in the Southwest Insurance database file by completing the following steps:
   a. Click File, point to Get External Data, and then click Import.
   b. At the Import dialog box, make the *Access Chapter 07C* folder on your disk the active folder.
   c. Change the Files of type option to *Microsoft Excel.*
   d. Double-click *Excel C07* in the list box.
   e. At the first Import Spreadsheet Wizard dialog box, click the Next button.
   f. At the second Import Spreadsheet Wizard dialog box, make sure there is a check mark in the First Row Contains Column Headings option, and then click the Next button.

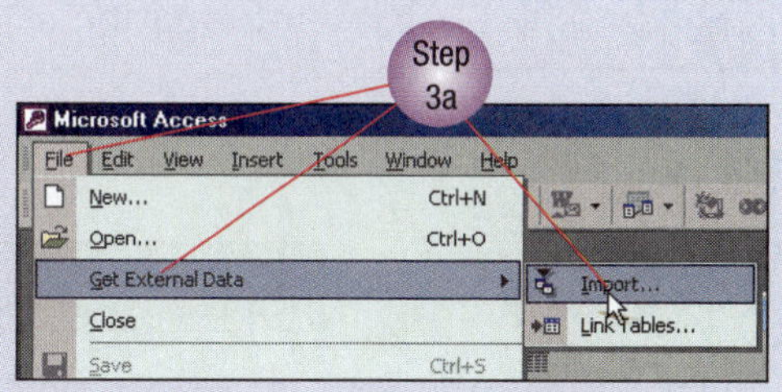

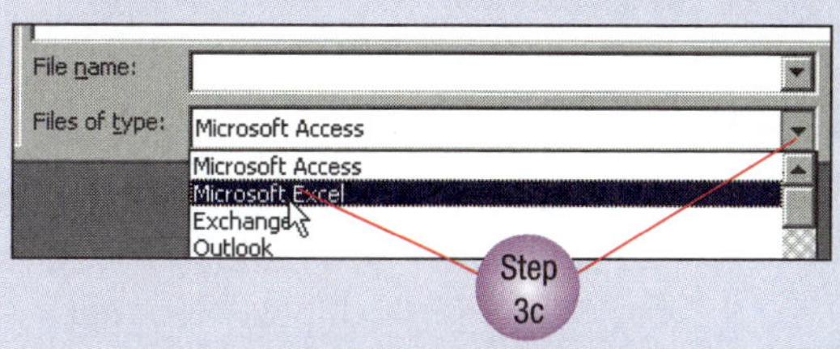

g. At the third Import Spreadsheet Wizard dialog box, make sure the In a New Table option is selected, and then click the Next button.
h. At the fourth Import Spreadsheet Wizard dialog box, click the Next button.
i. At the fifth Import Spreadsheet Wizard dialog box, click the Choose my own primary key option (this inserts *Policy #* in the text box located to the right of the option), and then click the Next button.
j. At the sixth Import Spreadsheet Wizard dialog box, key **Policies** in the Import to Table text box, and then click the Finish button.
k. At the message saying the data was imported, click OK.

4. Open the new Policies table in Datasheet view.
5. Print and then close the Policies table.
6. Close the Southwest Insurance database file.

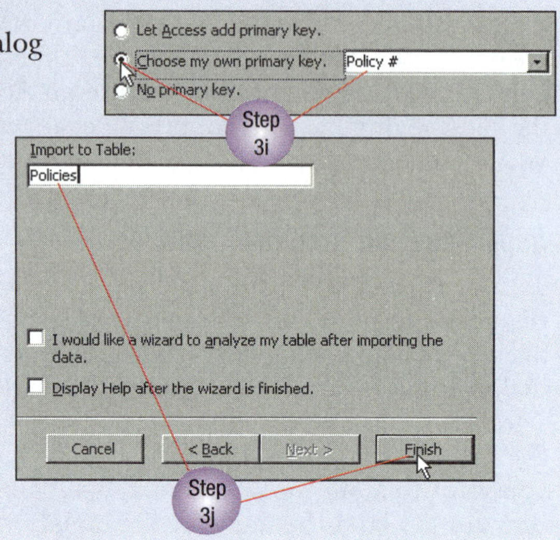

Linking Data to a New Table

Imported data is not connected to the source program. If you want the data to be connected, link the data. When the data is linked, changes made to the data in the source program are reflected in the data in the destination program and changes made in the destination program are reflected in the source program.

To link data to a new table, open the database file, click File, point to Get External Data, and then click Link Tables. At the Link dialog box, double-click the desired file name. This activates the Link Wizard and displays the first Wizard dialog box. Complete the steps of the Link Wizard specifying the same basic information as the Import Wizard.

HINT
Linked data is not copied into a new table but remains within the original database file.

exercise 9

LINKING AN EXCEL WORKSHEET WITH AN ACCESS TABLE

1. Open the Southwest Insurance database file and then click the Tables button on the Objects bar.
2. Link an Excel worksheet with a new table in the Southwest Insurance database file by completing the following steps:
   a. Click File, point to Get External Data, and then click Link Tables.
   b. At the Link dialog box, make sure the *Access Chapter 07C* folder on your disk is the active folder, and then change the Files of type option to *Microsoft Excel*.
   c. Double-click *Excel C07*.

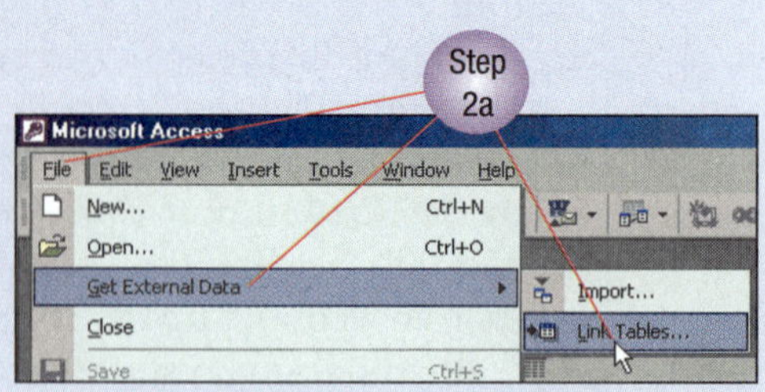

d. At the first Link Spreadsheet Wizard dialog box, make sure *Show Worksheets* is selected, and that *Sheet1* is selected in the list box, and then click the Next button.

e. At the second Link Spreadsheet Wizard dialog box, make sure there is a check mark in the First Row Contains Column Headings option, and then click the Next button.

f. At the third Link Spreadsheet Wizard dialog box, key **Linked Policies** (in the Linked Table Name text box), and then click the Finish button.

g. At the message stating the linking is finished, click OK.

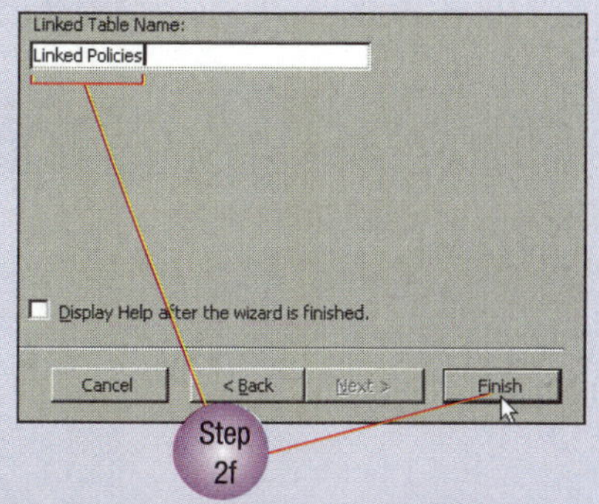

3. Open the new Linked Policies table in Datasheet view.
4. Change the number *745* in the *Premium* column to *850*.
5. Add the following new record in the specified fields:

Policy #	=	**227-C-28**
Client #	=	**2130**
Premium	=	**685**

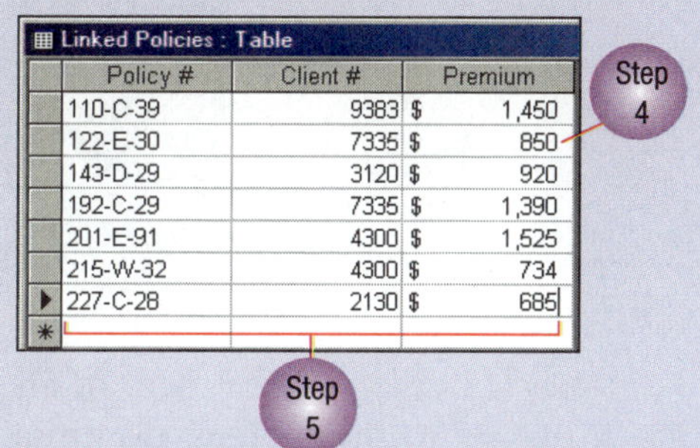

6. Save, print, and then close the Linked Policies table.
7. Open Excel and then open Excel C07. Notice that the information in this table contains the changes made to the Linked Policies table in Access.
8. Close Excel C07 and then exit Excel.
9. In Access, close the Southwest Insurance database file.

Using the Office Clipboard

Use the Office Clipboard to collect and paste multiple items. You can collect up to 24 different items in Access or other programs in the Office suite and then paste the items in various locations. To copy and paste multiple items, display the Clipboard Task Pane shown in figure 7.1 by clicking Edit and then Office Clipboard.

FIGURE

7.1 *Office Clipboard Task Pane*

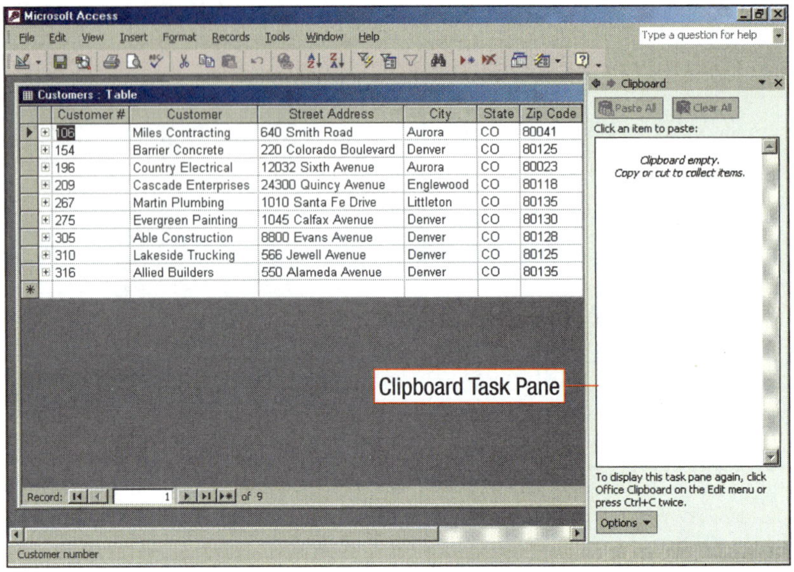

Select data or an object you want to copy and then click the Copy button on the toolbar. Continue selecting text or items and clicking the Copy button. To insert an item from the Clipboard Task Pane to a field in an Access table, make the desired field active, and then click the button in the Clipboard Task Pane representing the item. If the copied item is text, the first 50 characters display. When all desired items are inserted, click the Clear All button to remove any remaining items from the Clipboard Task Pane.

You can copy data from one table to another in an Access database file or from a file in another program to an Access database file. In exercise 10, you will copy data from a Word document and paste it into a table. Data can also be collected from documents in other programs such as PowerPoint and Excel.

exercise 10

COLLECTING DATA IN WORD AND PASTING IT IN AN ACCESS TABLE

1. In Access, open the Hilltop database file.
2. Open the Customers table in Datasheet view.
3. Copy data from Word and paste it into the Customers table by completing the following steps:
   a. Open Word, make the *Access Chapter 07C* folder on your disk the active folder, and then open Hilltop Customers.
   b. Display the Clipboard Task Pane by clicking Edit and then Office Clipboard.
   c. Select the first company name *Stone Construction* and then click the Copy button on the Standard toolbar.
   d. Select the street address, *9905 Broadway*, and then click the Copy button.

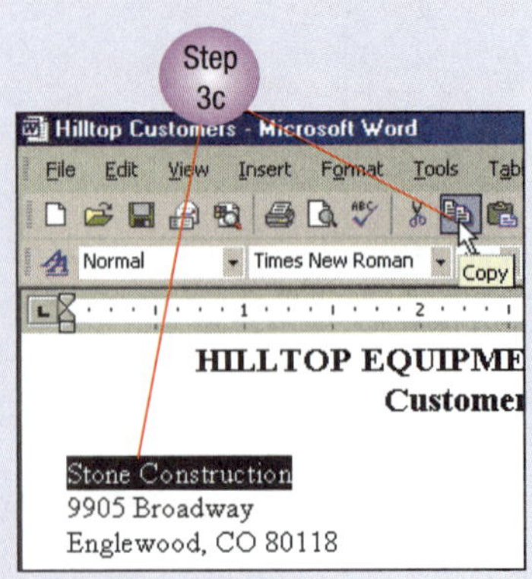

e. Select the city, *Englewood,* and then click the Copy button.
f. Select the state, *CO,* and then click the Copy button.
g. Select the Zip Code, *80118,* and then click the Copy button.
h. Click the button on the Taskbar representing the Access Customers table. (Make sure you are in Datasheet view.)
i. Click in the first empty cell in the *Customer #* field and then key **178**.
j. Display the Clipboard Task Pane by clicking Edit and then Office Clipboard.
k. Click in the first empty cell in the *Customer* field and then click *Stone Construction* in the Clipboard Task Pane.
l. Click in the *Street Address* field and then click *9905 Broadway* in the Clipboard Task Pane.
m. Click in the *City* field and then click *Denver* in the Clipboard Task Pane.
n. Click in the *State* field and then click *CO* in the Clipboard Task Pane.
o. Click in the *Zip Code* field and then click *80118* in the Clipboard Task Pane.
p. Click the Clear All button on the Clipboard Task Pane.

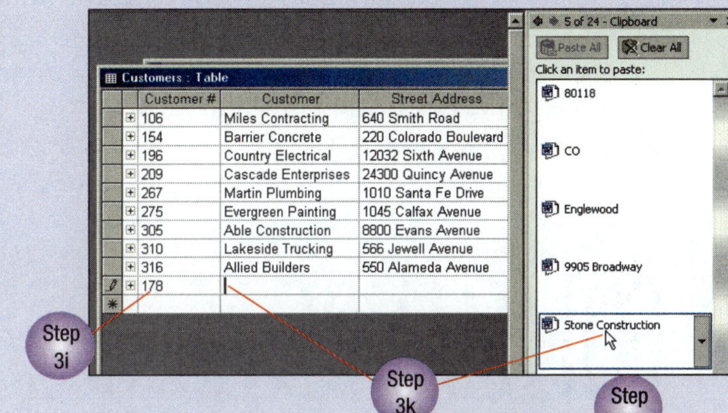

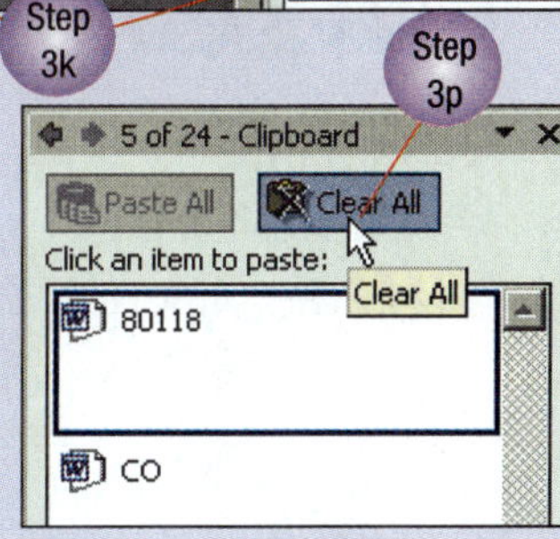

4. Complete steps similar to those in 3c through 3p to copy the information for Laughlin Products and paste it into the Customers table. (The Customer # is 225.)
5. Close the Clipboard Task Pane by clicking the Close button (contains an *X*) located in the upper right corner of the task pane.
6. Save and then print the Customers table.
7. Close the Customers table and then close the Hilltop database file.
8. Make Word the active program, close Hilltop Customers, and then exit Word.

CHAPTER summary

- A table, form, or report can be exported to Excel with the Analyze It with Microsoft Excel option at the OfficeLinks drop-down menu.
- When data is exported to Excel, the data becomes an Excel worksheet with all Excel editing capabilities available.
- A table, form, or report can be exported to Word with the Publish It with Microsoft Word option from the OfficeLinks drop-down menu.
- An Excel worksheet or a Word document created from Access data is automatically saved with the same name as the table, form, or report selected. A different file extension, however, is added to the document name.

- Access data can be used to merge with a Word document. Access uses the data from the table as the data source and merges the data with a Word document called the main document.
- Access data can be merged with an existing Word document or merged with a new document.
- A query performed in Access can be saved, and then data from that query can be merged with a Word document.
- Data from another program can be imported into an Access table. Access contains an Import Wizard that guides you through the importing data steps.
- Data from another program can be linked to an Access table. Changes made to the data in the source program are reflected in the data in the destination program and changes made in the destination program are reflected in the source program.
- Use the Clipboard Task Pane to collect up to 24 different items in Access or other programs and paste them in various locations.

COMMANDS review

Command	Mouse/Keyboard
Display OfficeLinks drop-down menu	Click OfficeLinks button on Database toolbar
Begin the Import Wizard	Open Access database file, click File, point to Get External Data, and then click Import
Begin the Link Wizard	Open Access database file, click File, point to Get External Data, and then click Link Tables
Display the Clipboard Task Pane	Click Edit, Office Clipboard

CONCEPTS check

Completion: On a blank sheet of paper, indicate the correct term, symbol, or command for each item.

1. Click this option from the OfficeLinks drop-down menu to export the selected table, form, or report to Excel.
2. Click this option from the OfficeLinks drop-down menu to export the selected table, form, or report to Word.
3. Click this option from the OfficeLinks drop-down menu to Merge Access data with a Word document.
4. Access data exported to Excel is saved with this file extension.
5. Access data exported to Word is saved with this file extension.
6. If you want imported data connected to the original program, do this to the data.
7. Display this task pane to collect up to 24 different items in Access or other programs and then paste them in various locations.

SKILLS check

Assessment 1

1. Copy the database file named Legal Services from the CD that accompanies this textbook to the Access Chapter 07C folder on your disk. Remove the read-only attribute from the Legal Services database file.
2. Open the Legal Services database file.
3. Create a form named Billing using the Form Wizard with the following fields:

   From the Billing table:
   Billing #
   Client ID
   Date
   Hours

   From the Rates table:
   Rate

4. When the form displays, close it.
5. At the Legal Services : Database window, create an Excel worksheet with the Billing form.
6. Make the following changes to the Excel Billing worksheet:
   a. Select cells A1 through E12 and then apply the Classic 2 autoformat.
   b. Select cells A1 through E1 and then click the Center button on the Formatting toolbar.
   c. Select cells A2 through B12 and then click the Center button on the Formatting toolbar.
   d. Save the Billing worksheet.
   e. Print and then close the Billing worksheet.
   f. Exit Excel.
7. Close the Legal Services database file.

Assessment 2

1. Open the Legal Services database file.
2. Create a report named Client Billing using the Report Wizard with the following fields:

   From the Clients table:
   First Name
   Last Name

   From the Billing table:
   Date
   Hours

   From the Rates table:
   Rate

3. When the report displays, print and then close the report.

4. At the Legal Services : Database window, create a Word document with the Client Billing report. In the Word document, add the following text *above* the report data:

   LEGAL SERVICES
   330 Jackson Street
   Kent, WA 98043
   (253) 555-3490

   CLIENT BILLING INFORMATION

5. Select the text you just keyed and then apply a typeface, type size, and font color that closely matches the existing text in the report.
6. Save the Word document with Save As and name it Word C07 Report.
7. Print Word C07 Report, close it, and then exit Word.
8. Close the Legal Services database file.

Assessment 3

1. Open the Legal Services database file.
2. Merge data in the Clients table to a new Word document using the Merge It with Microsoft Word option from the OfficeLinks drop-down menu.
3. Click the Maximize button located at the right side of the Document1 title bar.
4. Compose a letter with the following elements:
   a. Press Enter six times, key the current date, and then press Enter five times.
   b. Insert the proper field names for the inside address. *(Hint: Use the Insert Merge Fields button on the Mail Merge toolbar.)*
   c. Insert a proper salutation.
   d. Compose a letter to clients that includes the following information:

      The last time you visited our offices, you may have noticed how crowded we were. To alleviate the overcrowding we are leasing new offices in the Meridian Building and will be moving in at the beginning of next month.

      Stop by and see our new offices at our open house planned for the second Friday of next month. Drop by any time between 2:00 and 5:00 p.m. We look forward to seeing you.

   e. Include an appropriate complimentary close for the letter. Use the name and title *Marjorie Shaw, Senior Partner* for the signature and add your reference initials and the document name (Word C07 SA03).
5. Merge to a new document and then save the document with the name Word C07 SA03 in the Access Chapter 07C folder on your disk.
6. Select and then print the first two letters in the document and then close Word C07 SA03.
7. Close the main document without saving it and then exit Word.
8. Close the Legal Services database file.

Assessment 4

1. Open the Legal Services database file.
2. Extract records from the Clients table of those clients located in Kent and then name the query Kent Query.
3. Merge the Kent Query to a new Word document using the Merge It with Microsoft Word option from the OfficeLinks drop-down menu.

4. Click the Maximize button located at the right side of the Document1 title bar.
5. Compose a letter with the following elements:
   a. Press Enter six times, key the current date, and then press Enter five times.
   b. Insert the proper field names for the inside address.
   c. Insert a proper salutation.
   d. Compose a letter to clients that includes the following information:

      The City of Kent Municipal Court has moved from 1024 Meeker Street to a new building located at 3201 James Avenue. All court hearings after the end of this month will be held at the new address. If you need directions to the new building, please call our office.

   e. Include an appropriate complimentary close for the letter. Use the name *Thomas Zeiger* and the title *Attorney* in the complimentary close and add your reference initials and the document name (Word C07 SA04).
6. Merge to a new document and then save the document with the name Word C07 SA04 in the Access Chapter 07C folder on your disk.
7. Select and then print the first two letters in the document and then close Word C07 SA04.
8. Close the main document without saving it and then exit Word.
9. Close the Legal Services database file.

Assessment 5

1. Open the Legal Services database file and click the Tables button on the Objects bar.
2. Import Excel Worksheet 02 (located in the Access Chapter 07C folder on your disk) into a new table named Cases. (Use the Import Spreadsheet Wizard to do this.)
3. Open the Cases table in Datasheet view.
4. Print and then close the Cases table.
5. Close the Legal Services database file.

Assessment 6

1. Use the Access Help feature to learn how to compact and repair a database file.
2. In Microsoft Word, prepare a memo to your instructor explaining what compacting and repairing does to a database file, the reason for doing it, and the steps required. Save the memo as Word C07 SA06. Print and then close Word C07 SA06.
3. In Access, open the Legal Services database file and then compact and repair the file.
4. Close the Legal Services database file.

CHAPTER 8

CREATING WEB PAGES AND USING DATABASE WIZARDS

PERFORMANCE OBJECTIVES

Upon successful completion of chapter 8, you will be able to:

- **Save a table as a Web page**
- **Apply a theme to a Web page**
- **Create hyperlinks in a Web page**
- **Create a database with sample data using a Database Wizard**
- **Manipulate data within the database file**

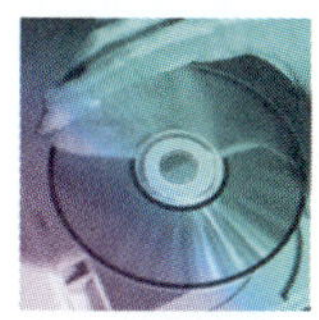

Outdoor Options • Hilltop

In previous chapters, you learned to use wizards to organize fields in a variety of formats including queries, forms, reports, mailing labels, and charts. Access also includes a wizard that walks you through the steps for creating a data access page along with a number of Database Wizards you can use to create an entire database file. In this chapter, you will use the Page Wizard to create a data access page from data in a table and you will also create a database file using a Database Wizard.

Creating a Data Access Page

Make Access data available for viewing on the Internet or on a company's intranet by saving the data as a data access page. A data access page is a special type of Web page designed for viewing and working with data from the Internet or intranet. Data saved as a Web page can be viewed in the default browser, formatting can be applied to the Web page, and hyperlinks can be inserted in the Web page.

HINT
A data access page is stored in a separate file in HTML format.

HINT
Other users on the Internet or on a company intranet can work with a data access page.

Saving a Table as a Web Page

Access contains a wizard that walks you through the steps for creating a data access page. To use this wizard, open the desired database file, click the Pages button on the Objects bar, and then double-click *Create data access page by using wizard* in the list box. Complete the Page Wizard steps to create the data access page. The Page Wizard steps are similar to the wizard steps for creating a form or report.

When you create a data access page, the Page Wizard specifies a folder and subfolders for Web page files. This is because a Web page generally consists of a variety of items that are inserted in individual files. For example, each bullet image and clip art image or picture in a Web page is saved in a separate image file. Inserting all of these files into folders makes it easier for you to take this information to another location. For example, you can copy the contents of a Web page folder and all of its subfolders to another computer or onto a disk.

HINT
Modify a data access page in Design view.

Another method for creating a data access page is to create the page in Design view. To do this, open the desired database file, click the Pages button on the Objects bar, and then double-click *Create data access page in Design view*. This displays the Design grid where you can create the form with the desired objects. Use the Toolbox to add control objects to the grid. With buttons on the Toolbox, you can also add Web page features such as hyperlinks and scrolling text.

Applying a Theme to a Web Page

Some interesting and colorful formatting can be applied to a Web page with options at the Theme dialog box shown in figure 8.1. To display this dialog box, click Format and then click Theme. Click a theme in the Choose a Theme list box and a preview displays at the right side. Click OK to close the dialog box and apply the theme to the page. (You can also double-click a theme at the Theme dialog box.)

FIGURE 8.1 **Theme Dialog Box**

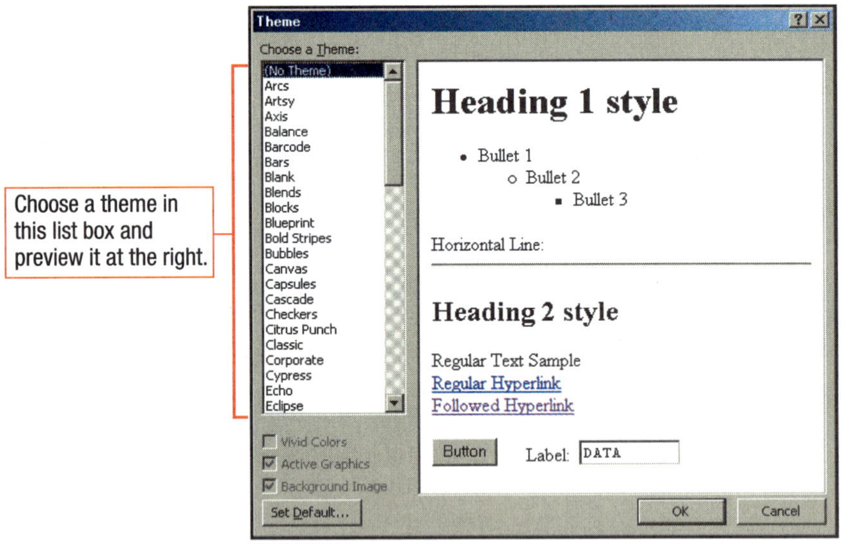

Previewing a Web Page in Web Page Preview

When creating a Web page, you may want to preview it in your default Web browser. Depending on the browser you are using, some of the formatting may not display in the browser. To preview a Web page in your default Web browser, click File and then Web Page Preview.

exercise 1

SAVING A TABLE AS A WEB PAGE

(Note: Delete the Access Chapter 07C folder from your disk.)

1. Copy the Outdoor Options database file from the CD that accompanies this textbook to your disk and then remove the read-only attribute from Outdoor Options.
2. Create a Web page by completing the following steps:
   a. At the Outdoor Options : Database window, click the Pages button on the Objects bar.
   b. Double-click *Create data access page by using wizard* in the list box.
   c. At the first Page Wizard dialog box, click the down-pointing triangle at the right side of the Tables/Queries option box, and then click *Table: Products* in the drop-down list.
   d. Click the button containing the greater than symbols (>>) (this inserts all of the fields in the Selected Fields list box.
   e. Click the Next button.
   f. At the second Page Wizard dialog box, click the button containing the less than symbol (<) to reduce the priority of *Supplier #*.
   g. Click the Next button.
   h. At the third Page Wizard dialog box, click the Next button.
   i. At the fourth Page Wizard dialog box, make sure the Modify the page's design option is selected, and then click the Finish button. (The completed data access page displays on the screen in Design view.)

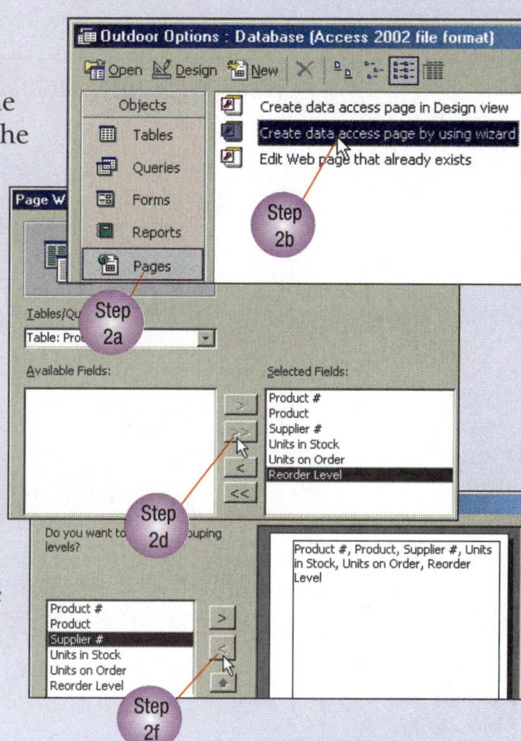

3. Click the text *Click here and type title text* and then key **Outdoor Options - Products**.
4. Apply a theme to the page by completing the following steps:
   a. Click Format and then Theme.
   b. At the Theme dialog box, click *Blends* in the Choose a Theme list box, and then click OK.

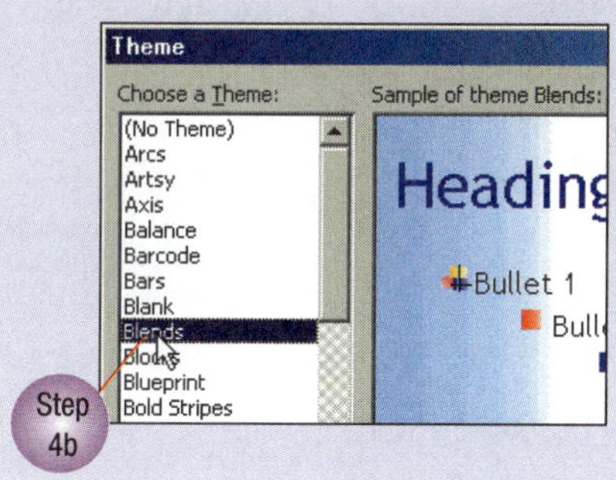

5. Click the View button to change to the Page view.
6. Save the access data page and name it **Products Web Page**.
7. Make sure you are connected to the Internet and then view the page in the default Web browser by clicking File and then Web Page Preview. (If you are not connected to the Internet, a message may display telling you that the page might not be able to connect to data. At this message, click OK.)
8. In Web Page Preview, use the navigation buttons along the bottom of the form to display various records.
9. Close the browser by clicking File and then Close.
10. Close the data access page and then close the Outdoor Options database file.

Creating Hyperlinks

Toolbox

Hyperlink

You can create a hyperlink in your Web page. To do this, display the Web page in Design view and then display the Toolbox by clicking the Toolbox button on the Page Design toolbar. Click the Hyperlink button on the Toolbox and then, using the mouse, drag in the Design view window to create a box. When you release the mouse button, the Insert Hyperlink dialog box displays as shown in figure 8.2. At this dialog box, key the text in the Text to display text box that you want to display in the Design view. Click in the Address text box, key the Web site URL, and then click OK.

FIGURE 8.2 ***Insert Hyperlink Dialog Box***

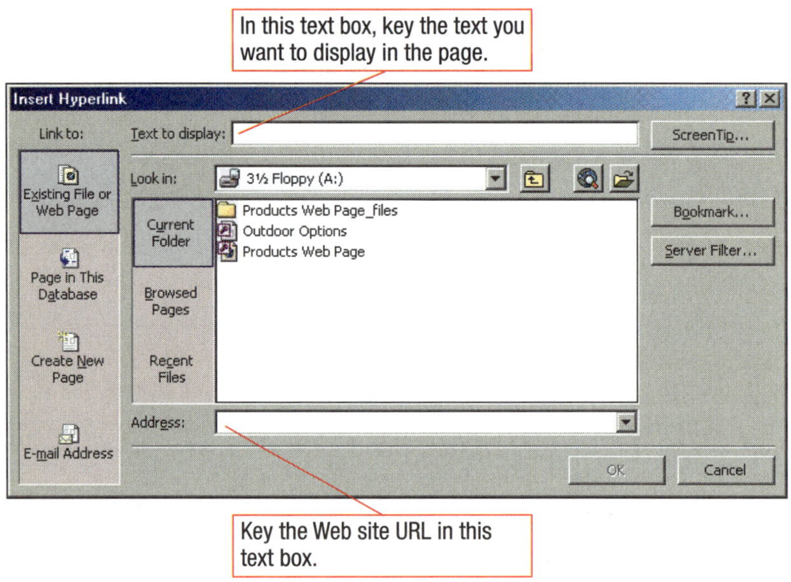

HINT

A hyperlink is a pointer from one object to another. A hyperlink generally points to a Web page but it can also point to a file, a program, a picture, or an e-mail address.

Another method for creating a hyperlink is to key the URL in a label in the Design view. When you key the complete URL, Access automatically converts the URL to a hyperlink and changes the color of the URL.

exercise 2

SAVING A TABLE AS A WEB PAGE AND INSERTING HYPERLINKS

1. Open the Outdoor Options database file.
2. Create a Web page by completing the following steps:
   a. At the Outdoor Options : Database window, click the Pages button on the Objects bar.
   b. Double-click *Create data access page by using wizard* in the list box.
   c. At the first Page Wizard dialog box, click the down-pointing triangle at the right side of the Tables/Queries option box, and then click *Table: Suppliers* at the drop-down list.
   d. Click the button containing the two greater than symbols (>>). (This inserts all of the fields in the Selected Fields list box.)
   e. Click the Next button.

f. At the second Page Wizard dialog box, click the Next button.
g. At the third Page Wizard dialog box, click the Next button.
h. At the fourth Page Wizard dialog box, make sure the Modify the page's design option is selected, and then click the Finish button. (The completed data access page displays on the screen in design view.)

3. Click the text *Click here and type title text* and then key **OUTDOOR OPTIONS**. (You may need to scroll to the top of the data access page window to see this text.)
4. Apply a theme to the page by completing the following steps:
   a. Click Format and then Theme.
   b. At the Theme dialog box, click *Capsules* in the Choose a Theme list box, and then click OK.
5. Add two hyperlinks to the page that will allow the user to jump to the Parks Canada site and the United States National Park Service site by completing the following steps:
   a. Increase the size of the page window by dragging down the bottom border of the window. (This gives you space to create the hyperlinks.)
   b. Click the Toolbox button on the Page Design toolbar to turn on the display of the Toolbox. (Skip this step if the Toolbox is already displayed.)
   c. Click the Hyperlink button on the Toolbox.
   d. Position the crosshair pointer with the hyperlink icon attached to it towards the bottom of the window. Drag the mouse down to the approximate height and width shown at the right and then release the mouse button.
   e. At the Insert Hyperlink dialog box, make the following changes:
      1) Click in the Text to display text box and then key **Parks Canada**.
      2) Click in the Address text box and then key **http://parkscanada.pch.gc.ca**.
      3) Click OK.
   f. Click the Hyperlink button on the Toolbox.
   g. Position the crosshair pointer with the hyperlink icon attached to it to the right of the *Parks Canada* hyperlink, and then drag to create a box.
   h. At the Insert Hyperlink dialog box, make the following changes:
      1) Click in the Text to display text box and then key **National Parks Service**.
      2) Click in the Address text box and then key **http://www.nps.gov**.
      3) Click OK.

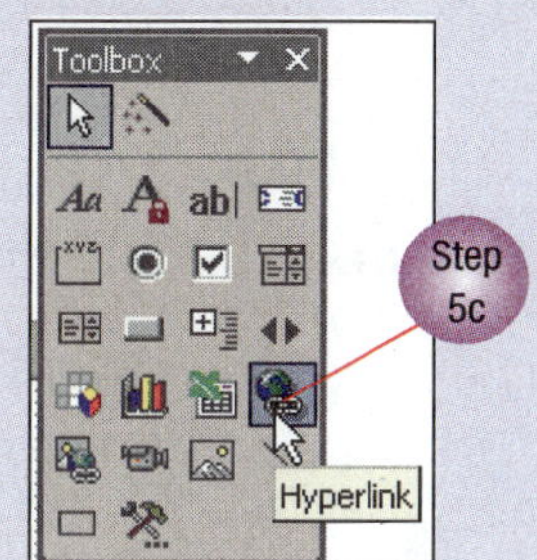

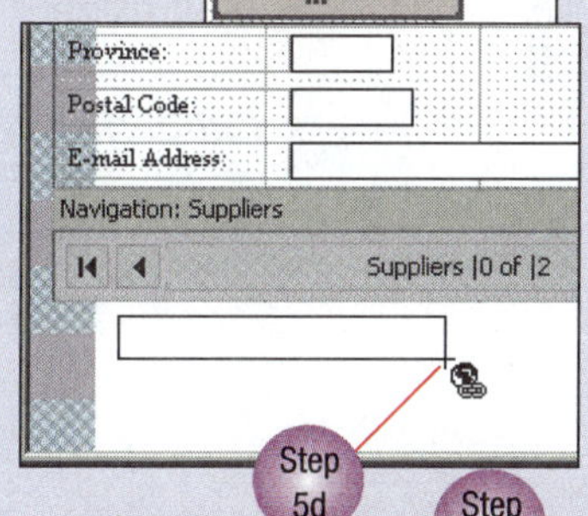

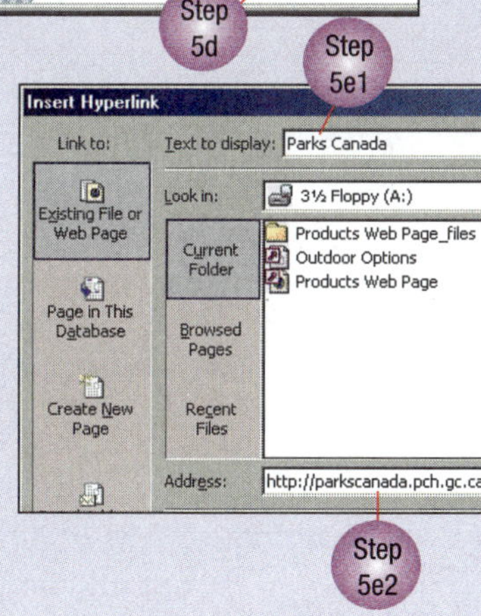

6. Click the View button to change to the Page view.
7. Save the access data page and name it Suppliers Web Page.
8. View the page in the default Web browser by clicking File and then Web Page Preview.
9. In Web Page Preview, complete the following steps:
   a. Click the *Parks Canada* hyperlink.
   b. At the Parks Canada home page, navigate to a particular page that interests you.
   c. Close the page by clicking File and then Close.

d. At the Suppliers Web Page, click the *National Parks Service* hyperlink.
e. At the National Parks Service home page, navigate to a particular page that interests you.
f. Close the page by clicking File and then Close.

10. Close the browser by clicking File and then Close.
11. Close the data access page and then close the Outdoor Options database file.

Creating a Database with a Wizard

New

Access provides numerous Database Wizards you can use to create database files. These wizards include all of the fields, formatting, tables, and reports needed to manage data. Most of the work of creating the database file is done for you by the wizard. In exercise 3, you will be using the Contact Management Database Wizard to create a contact management database file. To see a list of available Database Wizards, click the New button on the Database toolbar (first button from the left). This displays the New File Task Pane. Click the *General Templates* hyperlink in the New File Task Pane and the Templates dialog box displays. Click the Databases tab and the dialog box displays as shown in figure 8.3.

FIGURE 8.3 ***Templates Dialog Box with Databases Tab Selected***

Database Wizards available for creating database files.

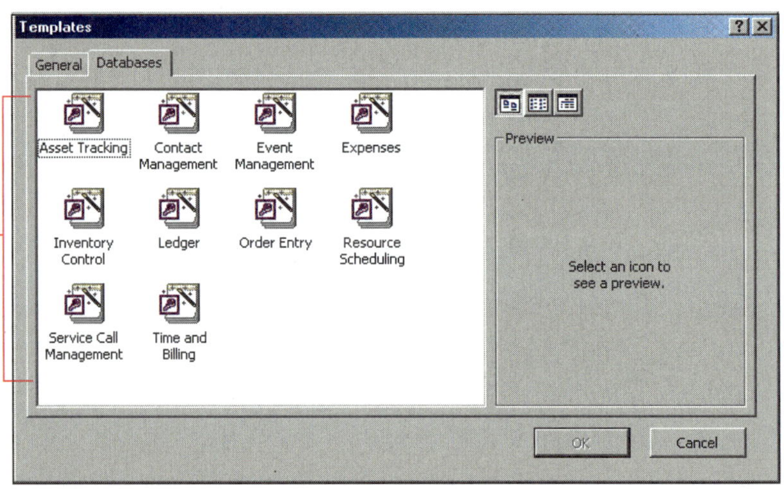

HINT Choose the wizard that creates the database that meets your needs most closely.

If your dialog box displays with fewer wizards than what you see in figure 8.3, not all components of the Access program were installed. You may need to run the Microsoft Installation process again to include the Database Wizards.

At the Templates dialog box with the Databases tab selected, double-click the desired wizard. This displays the File New Database dialog box. At this dialog box, key a new name for the database or accept the default name provided by Access, and then press Enter or click Create.

After a few moments, the first Database Wizard dialog box displays as shown in figure 8.4. This dialog box shows information about the Contact Management database you will create in exercise 3. Depending on the database you choose, this information will vary. After reading the information in the dialog box, click the Next button.

FIGURE

8.4 *First Database Wizard Dialog Box (for Contact Management)*

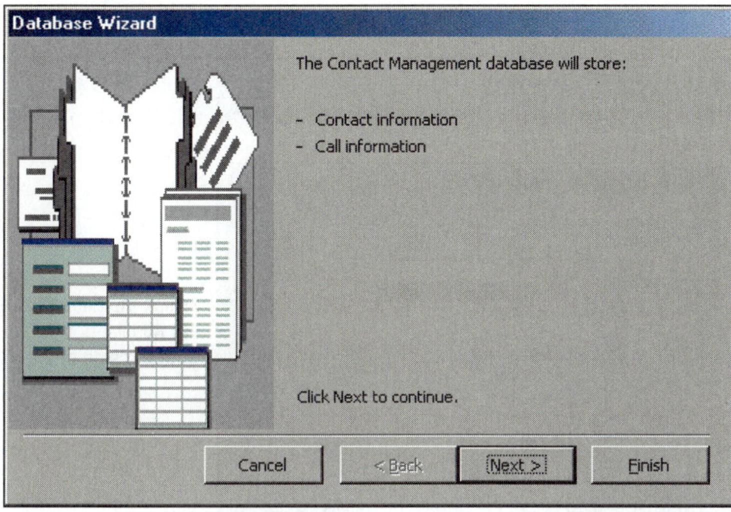

This dialog box displays information on what the database will store.

At the second Database Wizard dialog box, shown in figure 8.5, notice how the wizard provides predesigned tables displayed in the Tables in the database list box and also fields displayed in the Fields in the table list box. Most field names in the Fields in the table list box are preceded by a check mark. Some tables may include fields in the Fields in the table list box that display in italics with no check mark in the check box. These are additional fields that are not included as part of the table. If you want one of these extra fields included in a table, click the check box to insert a check mark. When all changes are made to this dialog box, click the Next button.

HINT

Optional fields display in italics.

FIGURE

8.5 *Second Database Wizard Dialog Box*

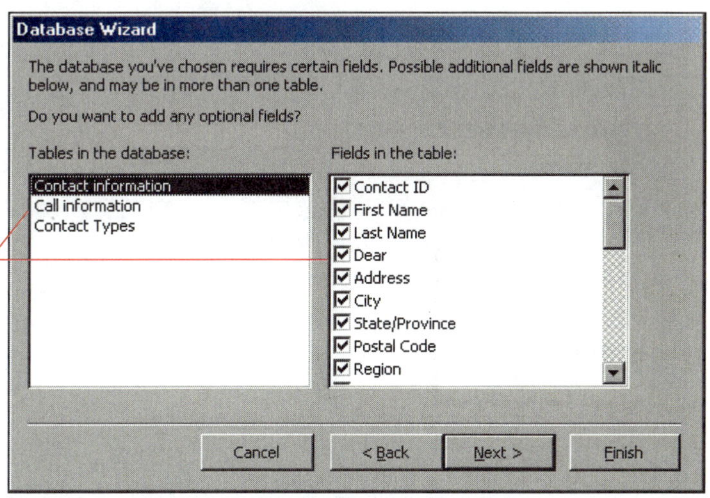

The database wizard provides predesigned tables and fields.

Choose a screen display at the third Database Wizard dialog box, shown in figure 8.6. A sample displays at the left side of the dialog box. After choosing the screen display, click the Next button.

FIGURE 8.6 ***Third Database Wizard Dialog Box***

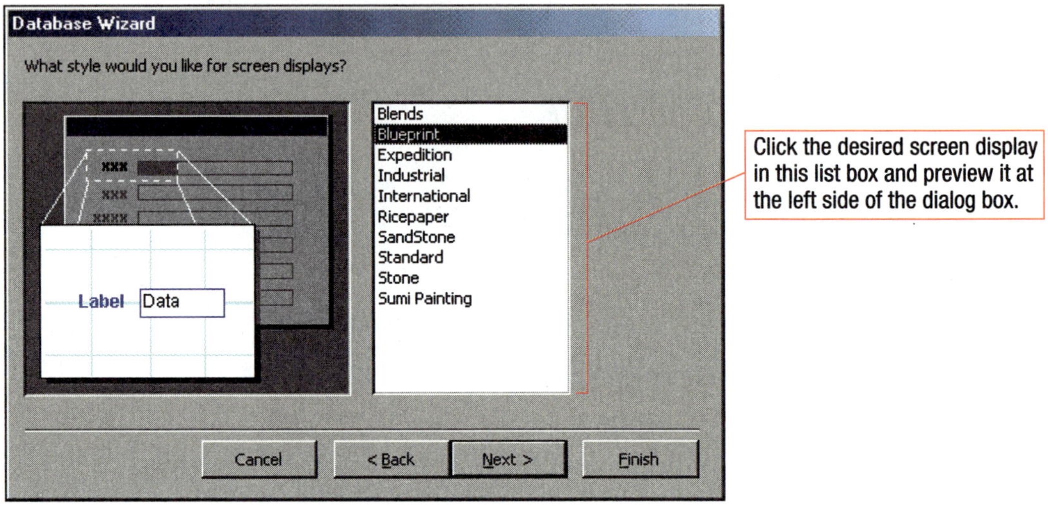

The fourth Database Wizard dialog box, shown in figure 8.7, asks you to choose a style for printed reports. Like the previous dialog box, a sample displays at the left side of the dialog box. After choosing the style, click the Next button.

FIGURE 8.7 ***Fourth Database Wizard Dialog Box***

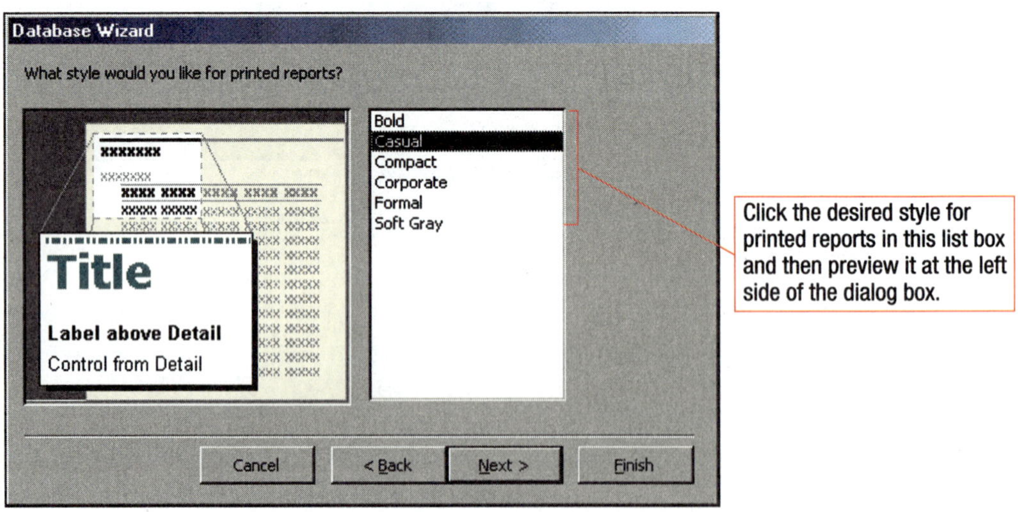

Key a name for the database or accept the default at the fifth Database Wizard dialog box shown in figure 8.8. At this dialog box, you can also choose to include a picture in all reports. After making these decisions, click the Next button.

FIGURE 8.8 ***Fifth Database Wizard Dialog Box***

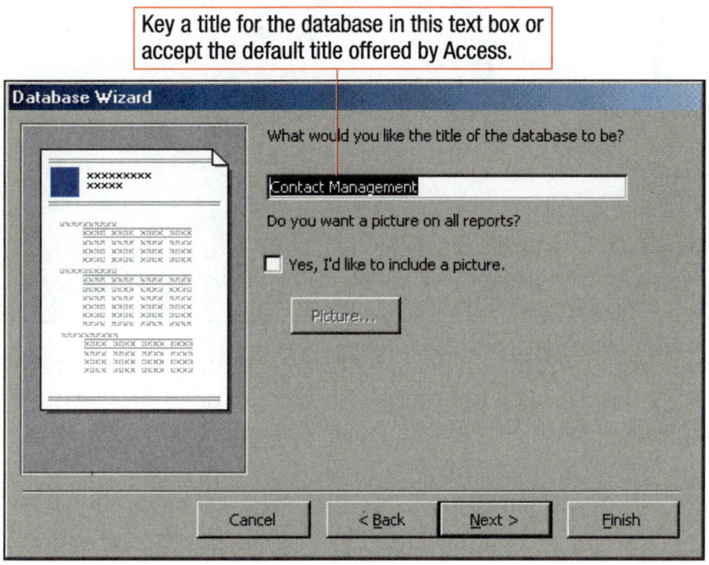

The sixth (and last) Database Wizard dialog box tells you that the wizard has all of the information it needs to build the database. By default, the database will start when the database is completed. Remove the check mark from this option if you do not want the database to start when completed. Click the Finish button and the wizard builds the database. This process can take several minutes.

When the database is completed, a Main Switchboard displays as shown in figure 8.9 and the Database window is minimized and displays in the bottom left corner of the Access window. With options on the Switchboard, you can choose to enter or view products, enter or view other information in the database, preview reports, change the switchboard items, or exit the database. The Switchboard is intended for people who use the database rather than work on the design of the database. To bypass the Switchboard, click the Minimize button located in the upper right corner of the Switchboard title bar. Display the Database window by clicking the Maximize button located on the Database title bar.

Minimize

Maximize

FIGURE

8.9 *Main Switchboard*

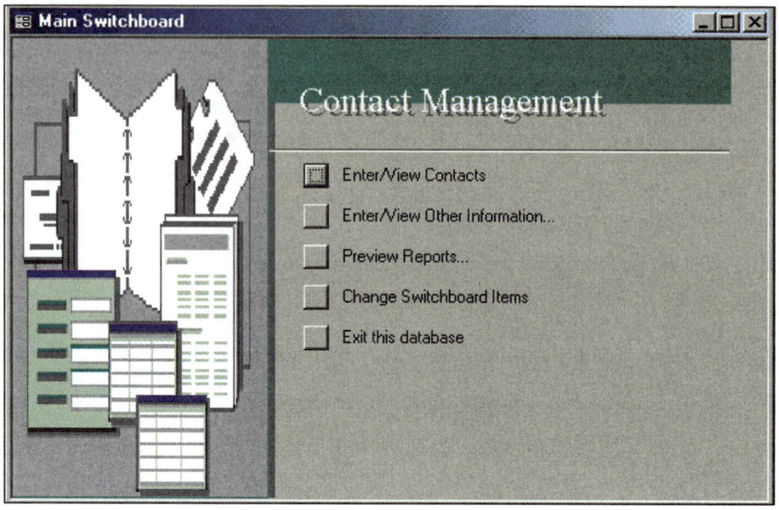

In exercise 3, you will be creating a contact management database. When the database is completed, you will enter two records and then view some of the different tables and forms contained in the database.

exercise 3

CREATING A CONTACT MANAGEMENT DATABASE WITH A WIZARD

(Before completing exercise 3, delete all files from your disk.)

1. Create a contact management database by completing the following steps:
   a. At the blank Access screen, click the New button on the Database toolbar.
   b. Click the *General Templates* hyperlink in the New File Task Pane.
   c. At the Templates dialog box, click the Databases tab.
   d. Double-click *Contact Management* in the list box.
   e. At the File New Database dialog box, key **Contacts** and then press Enter or click the Create button.
   f. At the first Database Wizard dialog box (see figure 8.4), read the information, and then click the Next button.
   g. At the second Database Wizard dialog box (see figure 8.5), click the Next button. (This tells the wizard to use all default tables and fields.)
   h. At the third Database Wizard dialog box (see figure 8.6), click *Blueprint* in the list box, and then click the Next button.
   i. At the fourth Database Wizard dialog box (see figure 8.7), click *Casual* in the list box, and then click the Next button.
   j. At the fifth Database Wizard dialog box (see figure 8.8), click Next.
   k. At the sixth Database Wizard dialog box, click the Finish button.
   l. After a few minutes, the Main Switchboard displays.
2. At the Main Switchboard, complete the following steps:

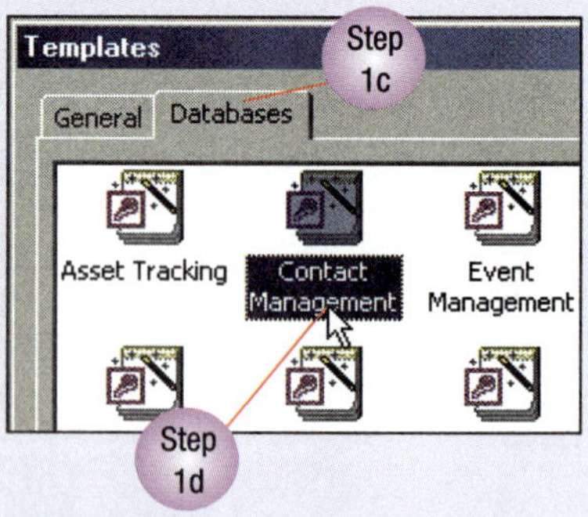

a. Click the Enter/View Contacts button and then enter the following information in the specified fields:

First Name	=	**Robin**	*Contact ID*	=	(AutoNumber)
Last Name	=	**Osborn**	*Title*	=	**Manager**
Company	=	**Westside Storage**	*Work Phone*	=	**(612) 555-4550**
Dear	=	**Ms. Osborn**	*Work Extension*	=	**245**
Address	=	**403 West 22nd**	*Mobile Phone*	=	**(612) 555-1209**
City	=	**St. Cloud**	*Fax Number*	=	**(612) 555-4590**
State/Province	=	**MN**			
Postal Code	=	**55200**			
Country	=	**U.S.A.**			

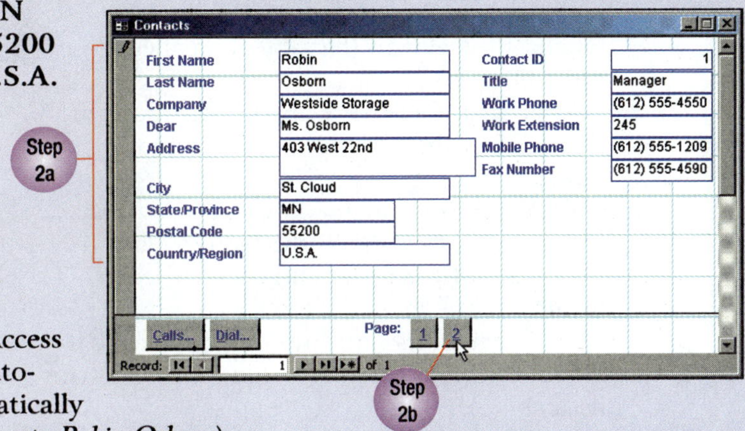

b. Click the 2 button that displays towards the bottom of the record. (This displays page 2 of the record.) Enter the following information in the specified fields:

Contact Name	=	(Access automatically inserts *Robin Osborn*)
Contact Type	=	(skip this field)
Email Name	=	**rosborn@emcp.com**
Referred By	=	**Samuel Eldred**
Notes	=	(skip this field)

c. Click the New Record button, click the *1* button, ,and then key the following information in the specified fields:

First Name	=	**Carol**	*Contact ID*	=	(AutoNumber)
Last Name	=	**Hoyt**	*Title*	=	**Owner**
Company	=	**Hoyt Construction**	*Work Phone*	=	**(612) 555-4322**
Dear	=	**Ms. Hoyt**	*Work Extension*	=	**10**
Address	=	**900 North 21st**	*Mobile Phone*	=	**(612) 555-4100**
City	=	**St. Cloud**	*Fax Number*	=	**(612) 555-4201**
State/Province	=	**MN**			
Postal Code	=	**55200**			
Country	=	**U.S.A.**			

d. Click the 2 button that displays towards the bottom of the record. (This displays page 2 of the record.) Enter the following information in the specified fields:

Contact Name	=	(Access automatically inserts *Carol Hoyt*)
Contact Type	=	(skip this field)
Email Name	=	**choyt@emcp.com**
Referred By	=	**Jared Snyder**
Notes	=	(skip this field)

3. Click the Save button on the toolbar to save the records.
4. Close the Contacts form.
5. Close the Main Switchboard and display the Contacts : Database window by completing the following steps:
   a. With the Main Switchboard displayed, click the Close button that displays at the right side of the title bar. (This closes the Main Switchboard and displays the minimized Contacts.)

b. Click the Restore button on the minimized Contacts title bar. (This displays the Contacts : Database window with the Forms button selected.)

6. View various tables, forms, and reports in the database file by completing the following steps:
   a. Click the Tables button on the Objects bar.
   b. Double-click *Calls* in the list box, (this opens the Calls table), look at the fields in the table, and then close the table.
   c. Double-click *Contact Types* in the list box, look at the fields in the table, and then close the table.
   d. Double-click *Contacts* in the list box, look at the fields in the table, and then close the table.
   e. Click the Forms button on the Objects bar.
   f. Double-click *Contacts* in the list box, look at the layout of the form, and then close the form.
   g. Click the Reports button on the Objects bar.
   h. Double-click *Alphabetical Contact Listing* in the list box.
   i. When the report displays, print it by clicking the Print button.
   j. Close the report.

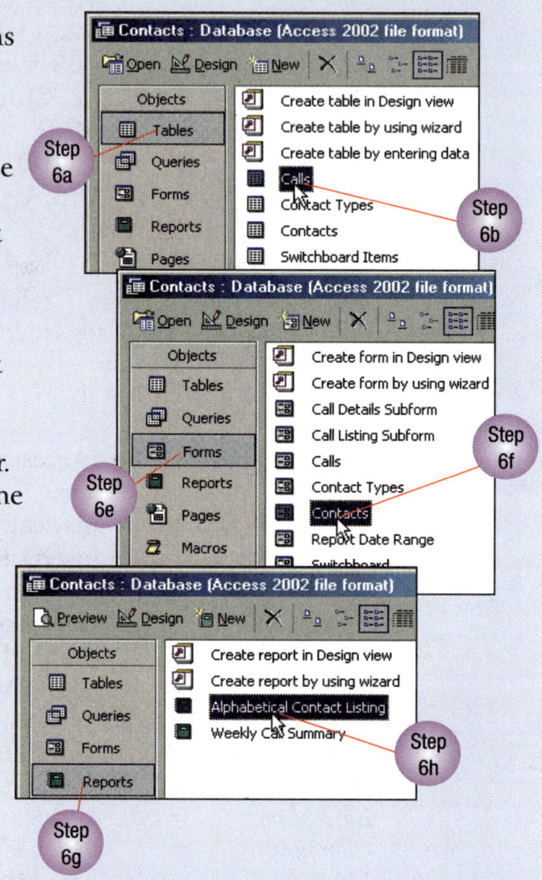

7. Investigate the relationship between tables created by the wizard by completing the following steps:
   a. With the Contacts : Database window displayed, click the Relationships button on the Database toolbar.
   b. At the Relationships window, notice the one-to-many relationship created by the wizard. View information about the relationship by completing the following steps:
      1) Position the arrow pointer on the black line connecting *ContactID* in the Contacts table with *ContactID* in the Calls table and then click the *right* mouse button.
      2) At the shortcut menu that displays, click Edit Relationship. This displays the Edit Relationships dialog box, which displays information on the type of relationship created between the tables.

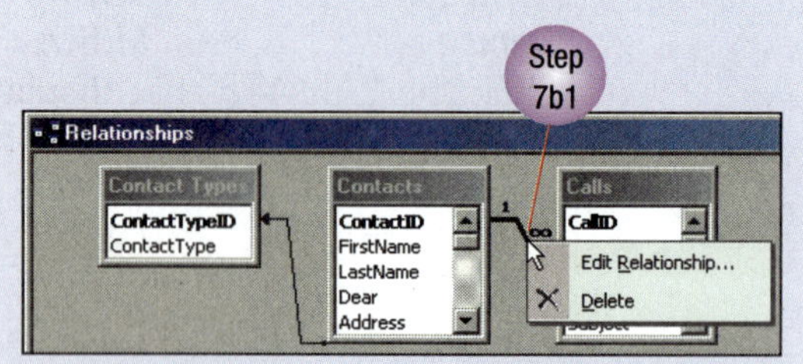

      3) After viewing the information in the Edit Relationships dialog box, click the Cancel button.
   c. Click the Close button at the right side of the Relationships window title bar.

8. Close the Contacts database file.

Viewing a database file created by the Database Wizard provides you with an example of what can be included in a database file. Consider using some of the other wizards displayed in the Templates dialog box with the Databases tab selected. Each database is set up differently with different tables, forms, and reports. The sample Contacts database you created in exercise 3 is fairly large—it will probably occupy over 1,000 kilobytes of space on your disk. For this reason, you will delete the Contacts table.

exercise 4

DELETING THE CONTACTS DATABASE FILE

1. At the blank Access screen, click the Open button on the Database toolbar.
2. At the Open dialog box, click *Contacts* in the list box, and then click the Delete button on the dialog box toolbar.
3. At the message asking if you are sure you want to delete the database file, click Yes.
4. Click Cancel to close the Open dialog box.

CHAPTER summary

- Make Access data available for viewing on the Internet or on a company's intranet by saving the data as a data access page.
- Data saved as a Web page can be viewed in the default browser, formatting can be applied to a data access page, and hyperlinks can be inserted.
- Apply theme formatting to a Web page with options at the Theme dialog box.
- Preview a Web page in the default browser by clicking File and then Web Page Preview.
- One method for displaying the Insert Hyperlink dialog box is to click the Hyperlink button on the Toolbox and then drag to create a box.
- Access provides numerous Database Wizards that will create a variety of database files including all of the fields, formatting, tables, and reports needed to manage the data.
- Database Wizards are displayed in the Templates dialog box with the Databases tab selected.
- A database file created with a wizard can be modified.

COMMANDS review

Command	Mouse/Keyboard
Display New File Task Pane	File, New; or click New button on Database toolbar
Display Templates dialog box	Click *General Templates* hyperlink in New File Task Pane
Begin data access Page Wizard	Open database file, click Pages button on the Objects bar, then double-click *Create data access page by using wizard*
Display Theme dialog box	Format, Theme
Preview Web page in default browser	File, Web Page Preview
Display Hyperlink dialog box	Click Hyperlink button on Toolbox and then drag to create a box

CONCEPTS check

Completion: On a blank sheet of paper, indicate the correct term, symbol, or command for each item.

1. Make Access data available for viewing on the Internet or on a company's intranet by saving the data as this.
2. Review a Web page in the default browser by clicking File and then this.
3. Display a list of Database Wizards by displaying the Templates dialog box with this tab selected.
4. To display the New File Task Pane, click this button on the Database toolbar.
5. When a Database Wizard is done creating a database, this displays giving you options for entering or viewing information in the database, previewing reports, changing items, or exiting the database.
6. Delete a database file at this dialog box.
7. List the steps you would complete to create a sample database with the Ledger Database Wizard.

SKILLS check

Assessment 1

1. Copy the Hilltop database file from the CD that accompanies this textbook to your disk and then remove the read-only attribute from Hilltop.
2. Create a Web page using the data access Page Wizard with the fields from the Inventory table. (You determine the title of the page.)
3. Apply a theme of your choosing to the page.
4. Change to the Page view.
5. Save the data access page and name it **Inventory Web Page**.
6. View the page in the default Web browser, use navigation buttons along the bottom of the window to display various records, and then close the browser.
7. Close the data access page and then close the Hilltop database file.

Assessment 2

1. Open the Hilltop database file.
2. Create a Web page using the data access Page Wizard with the fields from the Customers table. (You determine the title of the page.)
3. Apply a theme of your choosing to the page.
4. Add a hyperlink to the page that will allow the user to jump to the City of Denver Web site at www.denvergov.org. (You determine the location of the hyperlink.)
5. Add a hyperlink to the page that will allow the user to jump to the State of Colorado Web site at www.state.co.us. (You determine the location of the hyperlink.)
6. Change to the Page view.
7. Save the access data page and name it **Customers Web Page**.
8. View the page in the default Web browser, use navigation buttons along the bottom of the window to display various records, and then click each hyperlink to jump to the specified Web site.
9. Close the browser, close the data access page, and then close the Hilltop database file.

Assessment 3

1. Use the Expenses Database Wizard to create a database with the following specifications:
   a. At the File New Database dialog box, key **Expenses** as the database file name.
   b. At the third Database Wizard dialog box, you determine the type of screen display.
   c. At the fourth Database Wizard dialog box, you determine the style for reports.
2. When the database file is completed and the Main Switchboard displays, enter information on expenses for one employee by completing the following steps:
   a. Click the Enter/View Expense Reports by Employee button that displays in the Main Switchboard.
   b. At the Expense Reports by Employee window, key the following in the specified fields (you will be skipping many of the fields):

      First Name = **Nina**
      Last Name = **Schueller**

Title	=	**Manager**
Employee #	=	**210**

c. Click the Expense Report Form button that displays in the lower left corner of the dialog box.

d. At the Expense Reports window, key the following in the specified fields (you will be skipping fields):

Exp Rpt Name	=	**Marketing Seminar**
Exp Rpt Descr	=	**Two-day Marketing Seminar**
Dept Charged	=	**Marketing Department**
Date Submitted	=	**5/14/03**

e. Create three expense categories by completing the following steps:

1) Double-click in the first box below the *Expense Category* heading (located towards the bottom of the window). (This displays the Expense Categories window.)

2) At the Expense Categories dialog box, enter the following three records:

Expense Category	=	**Airfare**
Expense Account#	=	**10**
Expense Category	=	**Meals**
Expense Account#	=	**20**
Expense Category	=	**Lodging**
Expense Account#	=	**30**

f. After entering the third record, click the Close button to close the Expense Categories window.

g. At the Expense Reports window, enter the following in the specified fields (located towards the bottom of the window):

Expense Date	=	**5/10/03**
Expense Category	=	**Airfare**
Description	=	**Airline ticket**
Amount	=	**$850**
Expense Date	=	**5/11/03**
Expense Category	=	**Meals**
Description	=	**Daily meals**
Amount	=	**$52.00**
Expense Date	=	**5/12/03**
Expense Category	=	**Meals**
Description	=	**Daily meals**
Amount	=	**$48**
Expense Date	=	**5/12/03**
Expense Category	=	**Lodging**
Description	=	**Hotel**
Amount	=	**$220**

h. Click the Preview Report button located in the lower left corner of the window.
i. When the report displays, print the report by clicking the Print button on the Print Preview toolbar.
j. Close the Expense Report.
k. Close the Expense Reports form.
l. Close the Expense Reports by Employee form.

3. View the relationships between tables by completing the following steps:
   a. Close the Main Switchboard.
   b. Click the Restore button on the minimized Expenses database file.
   c. With the Expenses : Database window displayed, click the Relationships button on the Database toolbar.
   d. After viewing the relationships between tables, click the Close button to close the Relationships window.
   e. Display a few tables and forms to see the how data is organized.
4. Close the Expenses database file.
5. Delete the Expenses database file.

Assessment 4

1. You can get help for Microsoft Office XP programs, such as Access, using the Help feature. Assistance is also available from resources on the Web. Use the Access Help feature to learn about the Help resources available on the Web.
2. After reading the information on Web resources, make sure you are connected to the Internet and then visit at least one Web site that provides information on Microsoft Office XP. Print at least one page from a site you visit.
3. Create a Word document explaining the resources available. Save the document and name it Web Resources. Print and then close Web Resources.

WORKPLACE Ready

Creating Forms and Reports

ASSESSING proficiency

In this unit, you have learned to create forms and reports in Access. You also learned how to use Access wizards, export Access data to Word and Excel, import and link data, and create data access pages and insert hyperlinks.

(Note: Before completing unit assessments, delete any database files from your disk. Next, copy to your disk the Access Unit 02C *subfolder from the* Access 2002 Core *folder on the CD that accompanies this textbook.)*

Assessment 1

1. Use Access to create a database for clients of a mental health clinic. Name the database file Lancaster Clinic. Create a table named Clients that includes the following fields (you determine the data type, field size, and description):

   Client # (primary key)
   Client Name
   Street Address
   City
   State
   Zip Code
   Telephone Number
   Date of Birth
   Diagnosis ID

2. After creating the table, save it and name it Clients. Switch to Datasheet view and then enter the following data in the appropriate fields:

   Client #: **1831**
   George Charoni
   3980 Broad Street
   Philadelphia, PA 19149
   (215) 555-3482
   Date of Birth: **04/12/1958**
   Diagnosis ID: **S**

   Client #: **3219**
   Marian Wilke
   12032 South 39th
   Jenkintown, PA 19209
   (215) 555-9083
   Date of Birth: **10/23/1981**
   Diagnosis ID: **OCD**

   Client #: **2874**
   Arthur Shroeder
   3618 Fourth Avenue
   Philadelphia, PA 19176
   (215) 555-8311

   Client #: **5831**
   Roshawn Collins
   12110 52nd Court East
   Cheltenham, PA 19210
   (215) 555-4779

Date of Birth: **03/23/1953**
Diagnosis ID: **OCD**
Client #: **4419**
Lorena Hearron
3112 96th Street East
Philadelphia, PA 19132
(215) 555-3281
Date of Birth: **07/02/1984**
Diagnosis ID: **AD**

Date of Birth: **11/03/1963**
Diagnosis ID: **S**
Client #: **1103**
Raymond Mandato
631 Garden Boulevard
Jenkintown, PA 19209
(215) 555-0957
Date of Birth: **09/20/1974**
Diagnosis ID: **MDD**

3. Save, print, and then close the Clients table.
4. Create a database table named Diagnoses that includes the following fields:
   Diagnosis ID (primary key)
   Diagnosis
5. After creating the table, save it and name it Diagnoses. Switch to Datasheet view and then enter the following data in the appropriate fields:
   Diagnosis ID = **AD**
   Diagnosis = **Adjustment Disorder**

   Diagnosis ID = **MDD**
   Diagnosis = **Manic-Depressive Disorder**

   Diagnosis ID = **OCD**
   Diagnosis = **Obsessive-Compulsive Disorder**

   Diagnosis ID = **S**
   Diagnosis = **Schizophrenia**

6. Create a table named Employees that includes the following fields (you determine the data type, field size, and description):
   Provider # (primary key)
   Provider Name
   Title
   Extension
7. After creating the table, save it and name it Employees. Switch to Datasheet view and then enter the following data in the appropriate fields:
   Provider #: **29**
   Provider Name: **James Schouten**
   Title: **Psychologist**
   Extension: **399**

   Provider #: **15**
   Provider Name: **Lynn Yee**
   Title: **Child Psychologist**
   Extension: **102**

   Provider #: **33**
   Provider Name: **Janice Grisham**
   Title: **Psychiatrist**
   Extension: **11**

   Provider #: **18**
   Provider Name: **Craig Chilton**
   Title: **Psychologist**
   Extension: **20**

8. Save, print, and then close the Employees table.
9. Create a table named Billing that includes the following fields (you determine the data type, field size, and description):

Billing # (primary key; Set Data Type as AutoNumber)
Client #
Date of Service
Insurer
Provider #
Hourly Fee

10. After creating the table, save it and name it Billing. Switch to Datasheet view and then enter the following data in the appropriate fields:

Client #: **4419**
Date of Service: **03/01/2003**
Insurer: **Health Plus**
Provider #: **15**
Hourly Fee: **$95.00**

Client #: **1831**
Date of Service: **03/01/2003**
Insurer: **Self**
Provider #: **33**
Hourly Fee: **$85.00**

Client #: **3219**
Date of Service: **03/02/2003**
Insurer: **Health Plus**
Provider #: **15**
Hourly Fee: **$95.00**

Client #: **5831**
Date of Service: **03/02/2003**
Insurer: **Penn-State Health**
Provider #: **18**
Hourly Fee: **$90.00**

Client #: **4419**
Date of Service: **03/03/2003**
Insurer: **Health Plus**
Provider #: **15**
Hourly Fee: **$75.00**

Client #: **1103**
Date of Service: **03/04/2003**
Insurer: **Penn-State Health**
Provider #: **18**
Hourly Fee: **$95.00**

Client #: **1831**
Date of Service: **03/04/2003**
Insurer: **Self**
Provider #: **33**
Hourly Fee: **$85.00**

Client #: **5831**
Date of Service: **03/04/2003**
Insurer: **Penn-State Health**
Provider #: **18**
Hourly Fee: **$90.00**

11. Save, print, and then close the Billing database table.
12. Close the Lancaster Clinic database file.

Assessment 2

1. Open the Lancaster Clinic database file and then create the following one-to-many relationships:
   a. *Client #* in the Clients table is the "one" and *Client #* in the Billing table is the "many."
   b. *Diagnosis ID* in the Diagnoses table is the "one" and *Diagnosis ID* in the Clients table is the "many."
   c. *Provider #* in the Employees table is the "one" and *Provider #* in the Billing table is the "many."
2. Use the AutoForm feature to create a form with the data in the Clients database table.
3. After creating the form, add the following record to the Clients form:

Client #: **1179**
Timothy Fierro
1133 Tenth Southwest

Philadelphia, PA 19178
(215) 555-5594
Date of Birth: **12/07/1987**
Diagnosis ID: **AD**

4. Save the form as Clients, print the form, and then close the form.
5. Add the following records to the Billing table:

Client #: **1179**	*Client #:* **1831**
Date of Service: **03/08/2003**	*Date of Service:* **03/09/2003**
Insurer: **Health Plus**	*Insurer:* **Self**
Provider #: **15**	*Provider #:* **33**
Hourly Fee: **$95.00**	*Hourly Fee:* **$85.00**

6. Save and then print the Billing table.
7. Close the Billing table and then close the Lancaster Clinic database file.

Assessment 3

1. Open the Lancaster Clinic database file.
2. Create a form with fields from related tables using the Form Wizard with the following specifications:
   a. At the first Form Wizard dialog box, insert the following fields in the Selected Fields list box:
      From the Clients table:
         Client #
         Date of Birth
         Diagnosis ID
      From the Billing table:
         Insurer
         Provider #
   b. Do not make any changes at the second Form Wizard dialog box.
   c. Do not make any changes at the third Form Wizard dialog box.
   d. You determine the format style at the fourth Form Wizard dialog box.
   e. At the fifth Form Wizard dialog box, key the name **Provider Information**.
   f. When the first record displays, print the form.
   g. Close the record that displays.
3. Close the Lancaster Clinic database file.

Assessment 4

1. Open the Lancaster Clinic database file.
2. Use the Label Wizard to create mailing labels (you determine the label type) with the client names and addresses and sorted by Zip Code. Name the mailing labels report Client Mailing Labels.
3. Print the mailing labels.
4. Close the mailing labels report and then close the Lancaster Clinic database file.

Assessment 5

1. Open the Lancaster Clinic database file.
2. Create an Excel worksheet with the Billing table, with the following specifications:
   a. In Excel, select the cells in the worksheet containing data and then apply an autoformat of your choosing.
   b. Save the worksheet. (Excel will automatically name it Billing.)
   c. Print the worksheet.
3. Exit Excel.
4. Close the Lancaster Clinic database file.

Assessment 6

1. Open the Lancaster Clinic database file.
2. Merge data in the Clients table to a blank Word screen. *(Hint: Use the Merge It with Microsoft Word option from the OfficeLinks drop-down menu.)* You determine the fields to use in the inside address and an appropriate salutation. Key **March 10, 2003**, as the date of the letter and key the following text in the body of the document:

   The building of a new wing for the Lancaster Clinic will begin April 1, 2003. We are excited about this new addition to our clinic. With the new facilities, we will be able to offer additional community and group services along with enhanced child-play therapy treatment.

   During the construction, the main entrance will be moved to the north end of the building. Please use this entrance until the construction of the wing is completed. We apologize in advance for any inconvenience this causes you.

   Include an appropriate complimentary close for the letter. Use the name and title *Marianne Lambert, Clinic Director* for the signature and add your reference initials and the document name (Word U02 PA06).
3. Merge to a new document and then save the document with the name Word U02 PA06.
4. Select and then print the first two letters of the document and then close Word U02 PA06.
5. Save the main document as Construction Letter and then close Construction Letter.
6. Exit Word and then close the Lancaster Clinic database file.

Assessment 7

1. Open the Lancaster Clinic database file
2. Click the Tables button on the Objects bar.
3. Import Excel Worksheet 03 from the Access Unit 02C folder on your disk into a new table named Staff Hours. (Use the Import Spreadsheet Wizard to do this.)
4. Open the Staff Hours table in Datasheet view.

5. Print and then close the Staff Hours table.
6. Use the Form Wizard to create a form with the following specifications:
   a. Use all of the fields from the Staff Hours table.
   b. You determine the layout and the style of the form.
   c. Name the form Staff Wages.
   d. When the form is completed, change to Design view and add the following:
      1) Add a calculated control that multiplies the Hours by the Rate. (Name this calculated control Wages.)
      2) Format the calculated control text box so that the format is changed to *Currency* and the decimal places option is set to 2.
      3) Insert the company name, **Lancaster Clinic,** in the Form Header and increase the size of the company name (you determine the size.).
      4) Make any other changes you feel are necessary to create an attractive form.
   e. Change to the Form view.
   f. Print only the first record in the form.
   g. Close the Staff Wages form.
7. Close the Lancaster Clinic database file.

Assessment 8

1. Open the Lancaster Clinic database file.
2. Create a Web page using the data access Page Wizard with the fields from the Billing table. (You determine the title of the page.)
3. Apply a theme of your choosing to the page.
4. Change to the Page view.
5. Save the data access page and name it Billing Web Page.
6. View the page in the default Web browser, use navigation buttons along the bottom of the window to display various records, and then close the browser.
7. Close the data access page and then close the Lancaster Clinic database file.

WRITING activities

The following activities give you the opportunity to practice your writing skills along with demonstrating an understanding of some of the important Access features you have mastered in this unit. Use correct grammar, appropriate word choices, and clear sentence constructions.

Activity 1

The director at Lancaster Clinic has asked you to add information to the Lancaster Clinic database file on insurance companies contracted by the clinic. You need to create another table that will contain information on insurance companies. The director wants the table to include the insurance company name, address, city, state, and Zip Code along with a telephone number and a name of a representative. You determine the field names, data types, field sizes, and description for the table and then include the following information (in the appropriate fields):

Health Plus
4102 22nd Street
Philadelphia, PA 19166
(212) 555-0990
Representative: Byron Tolleson

Penn-State Health
5933 Lehigh Avenue
Philadelphia, PA 19148
(212) 555-3477
Representative: Tracey Pavone

Quality Medical
51 Cecil B. Moore Avenue
Philadelphia, PA 19168
(212) 555-4600
Representative: Lee Stafford

Delaware Health
4418 Front Street
Philadelphia, PA 19132
(212) 555-6770
Representative: Melanie Chon

Print the insurance company table. Create a form with the insurance company table and then print the form.

Open Word and then write a report to the clinic director detailing how you created the table. Include a title for the report, steps on how the table was created, and any other pertinent information. Save the completed report and name it U02 Act01. Print and then close U02 Act01.

Activity 2

Merge data in the insurance company table to a blank Word screen. You determine the fields to use in the inside address and an appropriate salutation. Compose a letter to the insurance companies informing them that Lancaster Clinic is providing mental health counseling services to people with health insurance through their company. You are sending an informational brochure about Lancaster Clinic and are requesting information from the insurance companies on services and service limitations. Include an appropriate complimentary close for the letter. Use the name and title *Marianne Lambert, Clinic Director* for the signature and add your reference initials. When the merge is completed, name the document containing the merged letters U02 Act02. Print the first two letters in the merged document and then close U02 Act02. Close the main document without saving it and then exit Word. Close the insurance company table and then close the Lancaster Clinic database file.

INTERNET project

Health Information Search

In this activity, you will search the Internet for information on a health concern or disease that interests you. You will be looking for specific organizations, interest groups, or individuals who are somehow connected to the topic you have chosen. It may be an organization that raises money to support research, it may be a support group that posts information or answers questions, or you may find information about clinics or doctors who specialize in your topic. Try to find at least ten different groups that support the health concern you are researching.

Record information about the organizations you found in your database. Create a database file in Access and create a table in that file to store the results of your search. Design the table so that you can store the name, address, phone number, and web site URL of the organizations you find. You will also want to identify the connection the group has to your topic (supports research, interest group, treats patients, etc). Create a report to summarize your findings. In Microsoft Word, create a letter that could be used to write for further information about the organization. Then use the names and addresses in your database to merge with the letter. Select and then print the first two letters that result from the merge. Finally, write a paragraph describing information you found out about the health concern while searching the Web that you previously did not know.

JOB study

City Improvement Projects

In this activity you are working with the city council in your area to keep the public informed of the progress being made on improvement projects throughout the city. These projects are paid for through tax dollars voted on by the public, and the city council feels that an informed public leads to a good voter turnout when it is time to make more improvements.

Your job is to create a database file and a table in the database that will store the following information for each project: a project ID number, a description of the project, the budgeted dollar amount to be spent, the amount spent so far, the amount of time allocated to the project, and the amount of time spent so far. Enter five city improvement projects into the table (sample data created by you). Create a query based on the table that calculates the percent of budgeted dollars spent so far and the percent of budgeted time spent so far. Generate a report that will include a chart showing the percentages of dollars and time spent so far for each project. Finally, save the report as a Web page to be viewed by the public. Include an attractive theme and a link to your city's home Web site (or a city of your choice).

INDEX

A

B

C

D

E

F

G

H

I

J

K

L

M

S

T

U

V

W

Y